chronicle

CONTENTS AT A GLANCE

chris crawford
on game design

New Riders

201 West 103rd Street, Indianapolis, Indiana 46290
An Imprint of Pearson Education
Boston · Indianapolis · London · Munich · New York · San Francisco

chris crawford
on game design

International Standard Book Number: 0-13-146099-4

Library of Congress Catalog Card Number: 2003107022

Printed in the United States of America

First printing: June 2003

07 06 05 04 03   7 6 5 4 3 2 1

Interpretation of the printing code: The rightmost double-digit number is the year of the book's printing; the rightmost single-digit number is the number of the book's printing. For example, the printing code 03-1 shows that the first printing of the book occurred in 2003.

TRADEMARKS

WARNING AND DISCLAIMER

CREDITS

Publisher

Stephanie Wall

Production Manager

Gina Kanouse

Senior Product Marketing Manager

Tammy Detrich

Publicity Manager

Susan Nixon

Executive Development Editor

Lisa Thibault

Project Editor

Jake McFarland

Copy Editor

Jill Batistick

Indexer

Lisa Stumpf

Composition

Gloria Schurick

Manufacturing Coordinator

Dan Uhrig

Interior Designer

Alan Clements

Cover Designer

Aren Howell

TABLE OF CONTENTS

CONTENTS

CONTENTS

CONTENTS

CONTENTS

CONTENTS

ABOUT THE AUTHOR

 **Chris Crawford** is the "grand old man" of computing game design. He sold his first computer game in 1978, joined Atari in 1979, and led Games Research there. During his time at Atari, he wrote the first edition of *The Art of Computer Game Design* (Osborne, 1984), which has now become a classic in the field. After Atari collapsed in 1984, Chris became a freelance computer game designer. All in all, Chris has 14 published computer games to his credit—all of which he designed and programmed himself. He founded, edited, and wrote most of *The Journal of Computer Game Design*, the first periodical devoted to game design. He founded and led the Computer Game Developers' Conference (now the Game Developers' Conference) in its early years. Chris has lectured on game design at conferences and universities all over the world. For the last ten years, he has been developing technology for interactive storytelling.

ABOUT THE TECHNICAL REVIEWERS

These reviewers contributed their considerable hands-on expertise to the entire development process for *Chris Crawford on Game Design*. As the book was being written, these dedicated professionals reviewed all the material for technical content, organization, and flow. Their feedback was critical to ensuring that *Chris Crawford on Game Design* fits our reader's need for the highest-quality technical information.

Dustin Clingman began programming at the age of 13 on the Apple IIe computer. A storyteller at heart, Dustin began making pen and paper expansions for the wildly popular **Dungeons & Dragons**. His efforts blossomed into a true love affair for games and game development when he learned to combine his imagination with the technical requirements of programming. At age 14, Dustin wrote his first game, **Seeker**, on the Apple IIe. Today, Dustin is a professor of Game Design and Development at Full Sail Real World Education in Winter Park, Florida and President of the game studio Zeitgeist Games, Inc. (www.zeitgeistgames.com). Dustin frequently speaks at IGDA events and conferences around the country. His current and recent projects include Game Designer on the Zeitgeist title, **Blackmoor**; serving as a contributing author on *Get in the Game!* (New Riders, 2002); and programming credits on **Java Gran Prix**, an F1 simulator for Sun Microsystems.

Greg Costikyan has designed more than 30 commercially released board, role-playing, computer, online, and wireless games. He is a five-time winner of the Origins Award and has been inducted into the Adventure Gaming Hall of Fame for a lifetime of accomplishment as a game designer. His games have been selected on more than a dozen occasions for inclusion in the Games 100, *Games* magazine's annual round-up of the best 100 games in print. He co-founded Unplugged Games, one of the first North American wireless game start-ups. He writes about games, game design, and game industry business associations for publications including *Salon*, the *New York Times*, *Wall Street Journal Interactive*, *Game Developer* magazine, and his blog. He is the author of multiple industry reports on the games industry. He has also written four published science fiction novels.

TELL US WHAT YOU THINK

As the reader of this book, you are the most important critic and commentator. We value your opinion and want to know what we're doing right, what we could do better, what areas you'd like to see us publish in, and any other words of wisdom you're willing to pass our way.

As the Publisher for New Riders Publishing, I welcome your comments. You can fax, email, or write me directly to let me know what you did or didn't like about this book—as well as what we can do to make our books stronger. When you write, please be sure to include this book's title, ISBN, and author, as well as your name and phone or fax number. I will carefully review your comments and share them with the author and editors who worked on the book.

Please note that I cannot help you with technical problems related to the topic of this book, and that due to the high volume of email I receive, I might not be able to reply to every message.

Fax: 317-581-4663

Email: **stephanie.wall@newriders.com**

Mail: Stephanie Wall
            Publisher
            New Riders Publishing
            201 West 103rd Street
            Indianapolis, IN 46290 USA

introduction

Twenty years have passed since I wrote my first book, *The Art of Computer Game Design*. Much has transpired during that time: Games have grown up. Twenty years ago, one programmer working for less than a year could produce a top-quality game. Nowadays, a team of a dozen specialists labors for several years to give birth to a commercial product. A dozen narrow specialties have sprung up: game designer, level designer, sound effects designer, 3D programmer, AI programmer, music designer, writer, and more. Budgets for games have risen from about $25K in 1980 to several million dollars today—a hundredfold increase! And the hardware on which we work has improved by at least a thousandfold.

Yet games haven't become a thousandfold or even a hundredfold better. Today's games are unquestionably more impressive than the games of 1982, but the advances we have seen aren't commensurate with the progress of the hardware or the budgets. Indeed, some people who nostalgically play the old-time games aver that modern games are no more fun. Games are bigger, splashier, more impressive, but not much more fun, they claim.

1

LESSON

Game design is not at all the same as game programming.

De gustibus non est disputandem—you can't argue about taste. We'll never agree on just how much more fun the new games are. But we can agree that the games have not improved commensurately with the technology. Clearly, technological progress does not automatically make games more fun. There's something else at work here, something that can't be nailed down in program code. It's often called the *fun factor*, but I don't like the term—it suggests that fun is a standard component that can be stuffed into a game somewhere between the mouse input code and the 3D graphics engine. I prefer to think of it as simply good game design: a soft, fuzzy concept involving a great deal of expertise, some rules of thumb, and strong intuition.

Game design shares nothing with game programming; they are completely separate fields of endeavor. True, a game designer must understand programming just as a game programmer must know something of game design. Yet as these two fields have progressed, they have diverged; master game designers focus their energies on mental challenges utterly different from those that bedevil master game programmers. This book is about the problems of game design; it has no truck with technical problems, for which a plethora of books await the reader.

Since game design is so soft and fuzzy, this book cannot offer simple answers with the directness and clarity that a technical work could provide. Alas, we must struggle with vague theories instead of precise formulations; rough guidelines instead of polished specifications; abstract concepts instead of direct rules. In many cases we must accept mutually incompatible concepts, uncertain where the dividing line between them lies. It comes with the job.

Fortunately, we have a vast array of experience on which to draw. In the last twenty years, some twenty thousand games have been published. Most of these were pretty lousy; some were good; and a handful were excellent. We can learn from all of these games. Indeed, the turkeys are the most instructive, because often a turkey fails for a single, easily identified reason. A thousand factors make a great game; it's impossible to evaluate them separately when they all sing together in perfect harmony. But when just one factor sings off-key, it stands out with terrible clarity.

My first book, *The Art of Computer Game Design*, was still being read and recommended twenty years after its publication; I intend for this book to be similarly long-lived. Therefore, I shall not be citing the current popular games. I shall limit my commentary to the great classics, milestones that should be available to any prospective designer. Occasionally, I will pick out some special turkey that beautifully illustrates a design blunder, but when I do so, I shall attempt to describe the game adequately.

2

LESSON

It's easier to learn from turkeys than from masterworks.

definitions, definitions

The world of game design has been swamped in a madcap array of terminology. We've got *videogames*, *computer games*, and just plain old *games.* We've got *sims*, *shooters,* and *RPGs.* Even the basic terminology is difficult to make sense of. My dictionary uses 6.5 column inches to define *game* and 12 column inches to define *play*. Meanwhile, it takes only 3 column inches to define such a common verb as *eat* and only 1 column inch to define *food*. Our concepts of games and play are spread out all over the intellectual world; they're almost as blandly overgeneralized as the all-purpose, one-size-fits-all verbs *get* and *go* (14 column inches each). With this anarchic mob of terms jabbering at us, it's easy for confusion to arise. I must therefore prepare you by defining what I mean by various terms. I don't claim that my definitions are, well, definitive; I'm sure that other people put different spins on some of these terms. I can only explain how I shall use the terms in this book.

Figure 1.1 puts a variety of terms into perspective.

Art ←— beauty —— Creative Expression

money ↓

Movies, Books, etc. ←— non-interactive —— Entertainment

interactive ↓

Toys ←— no goals —— Playthings

goals ↓

Puzzles ←— no competitor —— Challenges

competitor ↓

Competitions ←— no attacks —— Conflicts

attacks allowed ↓

Games

1.1 *Taxonomy of creative expressions.*

Let's step through this diagram item by item. The top entry, *creative expression*, is certainly broad enough to include all works that could possibly be of interest to us. It is broken down by the question, "What is the primary motivation of the creator?" If the creator's primary goal is to make money, then I call the result *entertainment*. If the creator's primary goal is to make something that is beautiful, then I call it *art*. My distinction is crude, I confess, but it works for me. There are lots of other, better definitions of art, but the simple-mindedness of this definition appeals to my simple mind.

We turn away from art to examine entertainment. I break this down based on the question, "Is it interactive?" If not, then our entertainment belongs in the same class with movies, books, plays, and all that crowd. There are plenty of people who can do that stuff brilliantly; let's keep moving.

I use the loosey-goosey term *plaything* to refer to interactive entertainments of any kind. Okay, it's not an impressive term, but it'll have to do. With playthings, the dividing question is, "Is there a defined goal associated with the use of this item?" If not, then I call it a *toy*. A player uses a toy in an unstructured fashion, without pursuing an explicit goal. This does not mean that the player's actions are arbitrary, for the player can still be engaged in exploratory play, determining in some fashion the behavior of the toy. The player's exploration may indeed show some structure, but this structure is not directed toward the satisfaction of any goal other than the determination of the behavior of a system. For example, a child may play with a crawling insect as a toy by attempting to determine the insect's response to various obstacles that the child places before the insect. The child may follow a methodology of his own devising and still be said to be using the insect as a toy. However, if the child sets himself the goal of confining the insect to a defined region, then the insect is no longer a toy. Examples of software toys are **SimCity** and **The Sims**.

But if you are pursuing some defined goal, then I call the activity in question a *challenge*. You are pitting yourself against some problem. I break down challenges with the discriminating question, "Is there an active agent against whom you compete?" Now, this gets us into some tricky matters of perception. Just what constitutes an active agent? We normally think of humans as our active agents, but computers have blurred the issue. When you play against a computer, you're not playing against a human being, but the algorithms against which you compete sure do seem human—especially when they outwit you!

We can solve this problem by reducing it to simpler levels. Consider a child playing with a ball. The ball's behavior is unusual from the child's point of view. According to "child physics," things fly away when you throw them, but a ball bounces back! This violates "child physics"; therefore, it cannot belong to the class of objects that obey the laws of "child physics." Since it cannot belong to the class of inanimate objects, it must instead belong to the only other class of object the child knows: the class of animated objects such as people and animals. The ball appears to the child to possess a limited kind of free will and is therefore perceived as an active agent. Thus, the issue turns on the perception of the user, and the critical question becomes, "Does there *appear* to be an active agent against whom you compete?" If the answer is no, then I call the activity in question a *puzzle*; otherwise, it's a *conflict*. The difference between a puzzle and a conflict is purely subjective. Most of the simpler videogames appear initially to be games, but after some amount of use, the player recognizes the algorithms at work and the activity becomes a puzzle rather than a game. It's all in the perception of the player.

Conflicts are challenges with purposeful opponents. There are two subclasses of this class: *competitions* and *games*. They are differentiated by the ability of the opponents to impede each other's performance by some form of attack, which could be quite indirect or abstract. If the opponents are constrained from impeding each other and instead devote the entirety of their attentions to optimizing their own performance, then the conflict is a *competition*, such as a race. It is against the rules of a race for the racers to take direct action against each other (such as tripping, stabbing, and mudslinging). If such actions are permitted, then the activity is no longer a pure race, but has been transmogrified to a game.

This leaves *games* as conflicts in which the players directly interact in such a way as to foil each other's goals. In other words, if you can shoot back at the other guy, and he shoots at you in a manner that convinces you that he's out to get you, then it's a game. Of course, the shooting need not be with bullets; a game could have two players engaged in subtle political maneuvering against each other.

There are plenty of other definitions of the term "game." Kevin Maroney defines it as "A form of play with goals and structure," which comports nicely with my diagram.

Greg Costikyan offers this definition:

> "A game is a form of art in which participants, termed players, make decisions in order to manage resources through game tokens in the pursuit of a goal."

This conflicts with my definition in that it unreservedly defines games to be an art form, while I maintain that games are a form of entertainment. However, definitions of art fall outside the pale of reasoned discussion; each of us has our definition of art and I will not attempt to force my own simplistic definition onto the reader. Fortunately, the clarity of my overall definition of terms is not diminished by simply lopping the top line from the diagram.

Greg's reference to a goal for the game certainly comports well with my definition. The reference to game tokens strikes me as a throwback to the days of boardgames, although if taken metaphorically to mean "any old game elements," then I suppose it doesn't hurt—but it doesn't seem to add much, either. Similarly, the reference to managing resources sounds like a strategy gamer's approach to the problem, but when taken with a strong dose of terminological indulgence, it can be applied to most game activities. And explaining that participants are players reminds me of Johnson's definition of "net."

Eric Zimmerman defines "game" this way:

> "An activity with some rules engaged in for an outcome."

This definition would make the act of driving a car into a game, which might not be far from the truth for some drivers.

some milestone games

some milestone games

If you want to write novels, you've got to read lots of novels. If you want to make movies, you've got to watch lots of movies. And if you want to design games, you've got to play lots of games. Every game designer must try out a wide and exotic array of games. With about a thousand computer games released every year, it's impossible for any individual to be familiar with everything.

Indeed, any competent game designer is too busy making games to have the time to play many. Nevertheless, it is important to try out a variety of games, and I list here some games that I think would provide a broad education to any budding game designer. My list is far from complete, and it excludes many excellent games. My criterion for selecting a game for inclusion in this list was not the quality or success of the game, but the extent to which it explores interesting design concepts or defines a genre.

For the most part, I have concentrated on older games, not because they are better, but because they are simpler. Most modern games are huge conflations of many different ideas, and so it's difficult to learn the component concepts from these games. Most of the older games had one clear conceptual leap.

Unfortunately, many of these older games are difficult or impossible to find these days. You can find many of the computer games on the Web at retrogame sites, but in many cases, you'll need to obtain emulation software that permits your PC to act like an old computer. The old boardgames, on the other hand, can be found only at auction sites like eBay.

Old-Style Games

These are the golden oldies, the games that have become classics and are part of the culture.

Monopoly

Monopoly is the most successful boardgame of all time. Designed in the 1930s, it concerns real estate transactions. Players acquire property; charge rent; assemble monopolies; buy, sell, and trade land; develop that land; and attempt to become the richest player by impoverishing the other players. The game offers an excellent balance between resource management and predatory play. It is, however, saddled with the old cliché of a path of steps along which one moves by rolling dice. That concept had already been overused when **Monopoly** was introduced during the Depression.

Traditional Card Games

There are plenty of such games, and although their place in our culture is ebbing, they remain instructive. Certainly poker is an important game for the game designer to experience. As played by nonprofessionals, it is a game of great depth, requiring more expertise with psychology than probability.

Board Wargames

This medium flourished in the 1960s and 70s, and unleashed a tidal wave of creativity. There were, of course, a preponderance of dull, predictable designs, but several designers, especially Jim Dunnigan and Redmond Simonsen of Simulations Publications, Inc. (SPI), produced dazzling designs. Herewith are a few of the more noteworthy games of that period.

Napoleon at Waterloo

Designed by Jim Dunnigan and published by SPI around 1973. A marvelously clean, simple design; it was wargaming reduced to its essence. It is simple to learn, easy to play, and yet captures all the elements of good wargame design.

StarForce Alpha Centauri

Designed by Redmond Simonsen, published by SPI around 1971. A truly weird space combat game centered on psionic powers. Movement is made in great leaps from solar system to solar system, and combat is executed by mentally wrestling with opponents, with the loser being hurled out of the area, leaving the winner in possession of the prize. The tactics of the game are very strange indeed! For sheer creative genius, this game is unsurpassed.

War in the East

Designed by Jim Dunnigan, published by SPI around 1974. This was the first "monster" game, requiring four mapboards and hundreds of pieces to represent the Eastern Front during World War II. It took me four months to play the game. I don't recommend that you play it, but it is edifying to contemplate the vast scale of the game, the meticulously written rules, and the determination of players who tackled it.

Battle for Germany

Designed by Jim Dunnigan, published by SPI around 1975. Simulates the invasion and conquest of Germany in 1945. A brilliant design splitting each player into two personalities. One player controls the western Allies, Britain and USA, and also the East German armies defending against the Russians. The other player controls the Soviets and the West German armies defending against the Allies. The winner is the one who makes most progress in his front. A brilliant exercise in simultaneous attack and defense.

Russian Civil War

Designed by Jim Dunnigan, published by SPI around 1975. This is the most brilliant wargame ever designed. To capture the fluid, chaotic nature of the Russian Civil War (1918–1922), Dunnigan stripped away any identity from the players. There are two opposing sides, the Reds and the Whites, but each player controls armies belonging to both sides. The armies operate independently across the vast reaches of the Russian Empire, attacking each other in isolated battles. Each time a battle is fought, the player controlling the winners takes possession of the loser's dead units, putting them into a pile at the side of the board. While the Reds have the advantage, their victory is by no means assured. At the end of the game, one of the two sides has been wiped out and the other side is declared the winning side. The winning player, however, is he who has accumulated more dead bodies of the losing side, and fewer dead bodies from the winning side. The result is a crazy contest of shifting goals and sudden reverses.

Breitenfeld

Designed by Jim Dunnigan, published by SPI around 1974. This was the best of the Thirty Years' War Quadrigames, which featured a combat system guaranteed to produce desperate battles. When two units fought, the loser was usually "disrupted," meaning that the defeated unit was turned over, couldn't move very far, and was especially vulnerable to destruction. Unfortunately, the winner would sometimes be disrupted as well. Thus, as the battle heated up, players found their armies disintegrating into disruption. The best tactic was always to attack your enemy's disrupted units in an effort to kill them before they could rally and return to normal combat readiness. The battles always ended with each general desperately looking for one last undisrupted regiment to throw into the fight and turn the tide. The resolution of the game was always in doubt up until the last turn, and the ending was always dramatic.

Battles of General MacArthur

A truly obscure game with a very clever combat system. Units moved from point to point on the map, limited not by intrinsic capabilities but rather by total fuel supply. The player threw the dice, and the result determined the total number of movement steps the player's armies could take. The result was an elegant game of maneuver, in which victory did not always go to the bigger army.

Diplomacy

One of the great classics of gaming; an absolute must-play for all game designers. Designed in the 1960s, this game is unlike anything you've ever played. Each player has a small number of armies and fleets; each turn, the player writes down orders for each of his armies and fleets. These orders are simple: move into an adjacent region or hold the current position. The unit density is so low that such moves would normally yield standoffs as single armies push against single armies to no effect. However, if two players coordinate their moves against a third player, they can usually obtain numerical superiority and win the battle. Of course, such cooperative relationships are transitory; yesterday's ally is today's opponent. The web of alliances and betrayals shifts every turn, making an endlessly fascinating game. Forty years after its creation, **Diplomacy** retains a strong fan base. **Space Invaders**, half its age, is utterly obsolete.

Other Non-Computer Games

Most games before computer games were boardgames, but there were some other games that were so creative, so utterly different, that they just don't belong in the same category. Herewith are a few.

Cosmic Encounter

Originally designed in 1972, this 30-year-old game is still one of the greatest around. It inspired two later games on this list, **Illuminati** and **Magic the Gathering**. The game's greatness lies in its self-modifying nature; players can modify the rules of game during the game. It's a little confusing, but it is definitely an enormously enjoyable game; there are still fan clubs that get together to play. How many other games can make that boast?

Dungeons & Dragons

Created by Dave Arneson and E. Gary Gygax, this was the game that launched an entire industry. The original concept, now encrusted with many layers, was clean, simple, and great fun. One person, called the *Dungeon Master (DM)*, designs and maps out a dungeon populated with dragons, monsters, treasures, special armor and weapons, money, and so on. A group of players then gathers around a table and the DM assigns each player a character endowed with varying degrees of such traits as strength, health, agility, charisma, and so on. All interactions are carried out around the table, as the DM describes the situation in which the players find themselves and the players describe their actions to the DM, who in turn calculates the results of these actions. For example, the players might find themselves confronted with an ice monster. Some of them might run to the rear of the group seeking protection; others will charge forward to fight the monster. The wizard of the group might attempt to use a fireball spell to melt the ice monster, while the strongman might hack away with sword or axe.

The rulebook provides the background that the players use to make decisions about fighting or running away; the imagination of the DM weaves the game into a story. There have been many attempts to get **D&D** working on a computer, but none have approached what a good DM can do with players sitting around a table.

Illuminati

Designed and published by Steve Jackson in 1983. A brilliant card game based on conspiracy theories. Players are dealt cards representing a variety of groups, such as the American Nazi Party, the Boy Sprouts, the CIA, and so on. Each group has special abilities and assets. Players lay down their cards in an effort to take control of groups already on the table. In the process, they build, right on the table, an intricate network of secret control. Did you know that the Republican Party is actually controlled by Goldfish Fanciers, who in turn are commanded by The Gnomes of Zurich? The strategies used in this game are subtle and devious, and the results can be hilarious. The game also includes my all-time favorite game element: a card for "Orbital Mind Control Lasers."

Magic the Gathering

Designed and published by Wizards of the Coast. This game generated quite a sensation when it was launched in the early 1990s. Vaguely like a fantasy role-playing game in its feel, this game used cards to mediate conflicts. What made the game a huge success was a design element that was really a brilliant bit of marketing: There were a huge number of special cards that could be used to implement unique strategies. However, to obtain those special cards, one had to purchase additional decks of cards, each of which contained mostly the conventional cards, but might contain one of the special cards. Addicted players therefore purchased huge numbers of decks, seeking out the surprise cards. The game was well designed, but the marketing trick is what made it a huge commercial success.

Whack-A-Mole

This is a mechanical arcade game. The horizontal playing surface is about four feet wide by two feet deep, and is pockmarked with holes. When the machinery begins running, little wooden moles pop out of the holes for a second, and then pop back down. The player must whack the moles with the supplied soft bat to score points. Simple, dumb, even brutal it may sound, but in fact the game is frigorific. Its appeal comes from the kinesthetic power of the game. Actually whacking them with a bat is fun! This game is hard to find, but definitely worth the search; it will teach you the power of kinesthetic factors.

Videogames

Videogames certainly changed the face of gaming, and surely most readers of this book were brought up on videogames, so there's no point in defining them. I offer here a list of the old classics that got the industry started. There are plenty of great newer games, but these games staked out the territory.

Space Invaders

Surely the first huge videogame hit, this game is a must-play for all game designers. As far as I know, the game had no obvious predecessors; it was an original creation. The army of little monsters in the sky, marching steadily downward, raining destruction on the hapless player, made a compelling image, and the extremely simple gameplay (slide sideways while shooting) made this game accessible to everybody. Interestingly, the vertical screen structure of the game arose more from technical considerations than game design considerations; the game is a magnificent example of a designer capturing the essential nature of the technology and exploiting it to the fullest.

Pac-Man

Such an important classic that every game designer should play it. **Pac-Man** wasn't particularly innovative; it represented the culmination of a long series of maze games. For example, an earlier game by Atari, **Dodge 'Em**, had the same system of dots that the player passed over to remove. It also had the opponent who attempted to crash into the player. **Pac-Man** added more opponents and made the dots edible. The difference between the two games is dramatic; it demonstrates just how critical the role of fine-tuning is.

Space Panic

This is the grandaddy of all platform games. The gameplay was simple. The screen had some four floors and a variety of bad guys chasing the player. The player could climb ladders up and down between the floors and could dig holes in a floor. When anybody stepped into a hole, they would fall through and be destroyed upon hitting the next floor. Thus, the player maneuvered about, trying to sucker the bad guys into the holes he had dug. Later games added the ability to jump over holes.

Donkey Kong

Donkey Kong changed the concept somewhat by making the floors tilted so that they connected with each other like a long ramp. The bad guys became rolling barrels that the player could leap over, and additional special-case obstacles were added. From there, development of the genre consisted of little more than adding more doo-dads and gew-gaws.

Dragon's Lair

This turkey is important as an object lesson in technological opportunism. This was the first significant laserdisc game to enter the market. It boasted beautiful imagery by the Don Bluth team. For the first time in history, the images on the screen weren't jaggy blocks, but smoothly animated cartoon characters. It was a sensation! Everybody rushed to create laserdisc games to compete with it.

The problem was, the gameplay was terrible. The player, as a bold knight, sought to enter a dragon's lair and rescue the princess. As the cartoon played, various dangers or challenges would present themselves, and the player had to respond with the correct button-press within a tight time interval. If he failed, a wonderfully animated display of the knight being burned up, falling into a deep pit, being crushed, etc., would end the game. If he succeeded, he proceeded to the next challenge. The game was basically a series of these binary challenges. If you passed Challenge #1, Challenge #2, Challenge #3...Challenge #N, then you rescued the princess and won the game.

I take some pride in being the only person in the universe to dismiss the game as a technological flash in the pan. Everybody else laughed at me, rushed to build their own laserdisc games, and lost their shirts. A version for personal computers was produced during the late 80s.

Computer Games

In the earliest days, computer games were easily distinguished from videogames; videogames played on consoles didn't have much computer power and tended to appeal to younger kids, while computer games were played on more expensive personal computers and so tended to appeal to older boys. With the passage of time, the distinctions have shifted and blurred somewhat. Videogames are still played on televisions and so lack the graphic resolution of the much bigger computer monitors. Videogames remain the province of younger players, but we are seeing greater overlap between videogames and computer games.

Star Raiders

This game single-handedly launched the Atari personal computers. It was the first 3D space combat game, and it blew everybody's socks off. The game was designed by Doug Neubauer, one of the engineers who designed the hardware for the Atari computers. Realizing just how powerful the hardware was, he set to work creating a game that would take full advantage of that power. As it happened, **Star Raiders** tapped less than half of the display power of the Atari hardware, but even that was so far ahead of everything else that the game dazzled all who saw it. These old Atari games can be experienced by obtaining an Atari emulator for modern Windows machines; a variety of sites on the Web offer such emulators.

Eastern Front (1941)

I confess that this is my own design, published in 1981, but I believe that the game deserves attention for a number of breakthroughs. It was the first game to use a smooth-scrolling map; it had top-notch AI for the time; and it sported a clean user interface, something uncommon in wargames of the time.

Wizardry

A straight copy of **Moria**, **Wizardry** was a game designed for the Plato networked computer system of the late 1970s and early 1980s. **Moria** was the first successful copy of **Dungeons & Dragons** to appear on a computer; however, since it is impossible to play **Moria**, you'll have to settle for **Wizardry**.

Dandy

Designed by John Palevich and published by the Atari Program Exchange in 1983, this game presented a grossly simplified version of **Dungeons & Dragons** ("D and D"—get it?). In the process, John created something entirely new. Although the game could be played by a single player, it really took off when two or more players cooperated. This was the first game to really exploit the cooperative element in an entertaining way. Although it wasn't a big commercial success, Atari paid homage to the idea by ripping it off with **Gauntlet**, an arcade game.

Deadline

A text adventure game that blew open the doors of a staid and stagnant genre. Text adventures had been around since the original version, **Adventure**, showed up at mainframe computer centers in the mid-70s. They were easy to program and quickly showed up on personal computers. In 1979, when I joined Atari, there was already a text adventure editing program written in BASIC for the Atari Home Computer. The genre piddled along fitfully until 1984, when **Deadline** came along. It was a whodunnit with the player as a gumshoe, trying to assemble the clues into a presentable case. The publisher went on to produce a series of imaginative text adventures, including **Planetfall**, **Trinity**, **A Mind Forever Traveling**, and **The Hitchhiker's Guide to the Galaxy**. Because these games were text only, it is not difficult to find versions that run on modern machines.

M. U. L. E.

Designed by Dan Bunten, published by Electronic Arts in 1983. In my mind, this is the finest computer game ever designed. By this I mean that nobody has ever so brilliantly exploited the strengths of the platform on which the game was delivered. The players are colonists of a distant planet who must develop land using a M.U.L.E. device, then sell the product of their land and buy the commodities they need to operate. The marketplace phase is pure genius, transforming buying and selling into a crazy competition that's loads of fun. The game boasts delightfully whimsical graphics and a funky musical accompaniment; the elements all combine to produce the greatest game design of all time.

Balance of Power

The second Crawford game in this list. It presented cold war geopolitics. The game is notable for its unique mechanics, which involved such things as treaties, financial aid, military aid, and direct military intervention. Yet there were no battles or direct combat; everything was presented in terms of political decisions. What made the game exciting was the diplomatic confrontation that could lead to nuclear war. Such confrontations were high-stakes games of bluff; misjudging your opponent could lead to mutual annihilation. The game was realistic enough to be taken seriously; it garnered severe criticism from zealots on both ends of the political spectrum.

King's Quest

An early graphic adventure. All the gameplay of a traditional adventure game, with pretty pictures to boot. Not much more.

Trust & Betrayal (a.k.a. Siboot)

Yet another Crawford design, this game was not a commercial success, but it was one of my most innovative efforts. The player engaged in a series of nightly "dream battles" involving something rather like a rock-scissors-paper game. The trick to the game, however, lay in the player's activities during the day. Meeting with other characters, the player attempted to garner information from them by flattery, alliance, intimidation, or any other technique that might seem appropriate. The central action was the making of a deal in which the player swapped information in his possession for information from the other character. This act constituted a betrayal of the person whose information he revealed; should that character find out that the player had betrayed him, he would be angry and take his revenge. Additional layers of betrayal were possible by revealing the deals other people had agreed to. All of this was carried out using an iconic language that permitted a broad range of expressions.

SimCity

By Will Wright. This was the game that everybody, myself included, thought would never get anywhere. But there was something addictive about trying to get your city working better and better all the time. The player starts the game with a plot of land, some people, and some money. He starts building a city, establishing residential areas, retail areas, industrial areas, and so forth. He must build roads and mass transit systems to permit residents to reach their jobs, police stations to suppress crime, and fire stations to fight fires. Tax revenues are generated by the retail and industrial areas; those tax revenues are used to fund the various public services. All the various factors in the game must be juggled against each other; should the population grow too rapidly for the transportation infrastructure, the citizens will become discontented with the traffic delays. Not enough police stations allows crime to run rampant, again causing dissatisfaction. More adventurous players are invited to unleash a variety of disasters on their cities, such as fires, earthquakes, and of course the gigantic monster who likes to stomp on buildings.

The 7ᵗʰ Guest

This was the personal computer's answer to **Dragon's Lair**. The programmer, Graeme Devine, was brilliant with video technology, creating an engine capable of playing video from the slow CD's of the time. The designer, Rob Landeros, had a cinematist's feel for imagery and emotion. Together, they built a smashingly beautiful product with truly haunting, genuinely frightening imagery. Unfortunately, like **Dragon's Lair**, the gameplay was insufficient to carry the product—it was nothing more than obscure puzzle-solving. Once again, everybody rushed to do video-based CD games. The continuing advances in video technology on personal computers kept the patient technically alive long after brain death had occurred. The sequel, **The 11ᵗʰ Hour**, sold reasonably well, but that was the end of the series.

Myst

The 3D rendering analogue of **The 7ᵗʰ Guest**. The designers had produced a number of games with exactly the same gameplay; these games had sold moderate amounts, but they were basically just graphic adventure games like **King's Quest** and so generated little excitement. But these guys were the first kids on the block to use 3D rendering engines to produce splendiferous imagery to tack onto their graphic adventure games. Whoosh—glorious success! Just like **The 7ᵗʰ Guest**, the sequel sold reasonably well, and that was the end of the series.

Doom

The first big hit 3D first-person shooter. It was preceded by **Castle Wolfenstein**, but that game was shareware and didn't penetrate the public consciousness as deeply. Moreover, **Doom** made some significant advances that blew open the doors on this kind of game. The history of game design in the 90s is mostly a story of people trying to outdo **Doom**.

Civilization

Sid Meier's great classic strategy wargame was based on the equally classic game **Empire**. However, Sid went far beyond the original in creating this masterpiece. The basic "conquer the world" design was there, complete with cities as generators of military units, but Sid took it much further: Cities could grow and develop their own economic and industrial potential, supplement their defenses, or build great projects that benefited all the cities owned by the player. This made for a less militaristic game. The most important element for all game designers to learn from this game is the fine-tuning.

Civilization is without doubt one of the most carefully tuned games ever created. The interplay between military, scientific, economic, and industrial factors is complex and intricately balanced.

3

Those who would build the future must understand the past.

Warcraft

This game kicked off a major revival in real-time strategy games. Normally resource management is associated with turn-sequencing, but **Warcraft** showed a way to handle the problem in real-time play. It certainly wasn't the first real-time strategy game, nor the best, but it stands as something of a milestone in the genre.

Secret Weapons of the Luftwaffe

Flight simulators have been around since the very beginning of personal computers, and there have been many important ones, but I will single out this game as the best overall example of the genre. It lacks the mind-numbing complexity of **Falcon** and the magnificent graphics of the modern games, but its combination of simple play and great fun made a big impression on the industry.

Populous

The first "god game," **Populous** is important for the more indirect style of gameplay that it introduced. Instead of directly commanding your effective units, you indirectly affected the growth and development of an autonomous community. Although such ideas had been explored much earlier in Jim Dunnigan's designs, Peter Molyneaux translated these ideas into computer format with excellent results. Sadly, few other designs have developed these concepts; Peter has single-handedly developed them.

play

You can't design games if you don't understand play—and play is a complex and tricky human behavior. We dismiss it too readily as child's activity, and therefore something devoid of depth and richness, but in fact play extends far beyond the realm of the child and touches a wide range of human life. Appreciating the many facets of play is a vital first step in understanding game design.

The finest definition of play (and the most complete discussion of the subject) is to be found in Johan Huizinga's *Homo Ludens: A Study of the Play Element in Culture* (Beacon Press, 1986). Huizinga defines play as follows:

> **"A voluntary activity or occupation executed within certain fixed limits of time and place, according to rules freely accepted but absolutely binding, having its aim in itself and accompanied by a feeling of tension, joy, and the consciousness that it is 'different' from 'ordinary life.'"**

History of Play

Play certainly started out simply enough. Early mammals learned to play as a way of polishing the complex neural circuitry that they were born with. A young colt has most of the circuitry in place to walk and to run, but getting everything coordinated with the sense of balance, the visual field, and internal neural inputs takes a certain amount of practice, which is accomplished through a form of play known as gamboling.

Jumping, dancing, darting, and running in young herbivores are immediately recognizable as play, yet they serve the deadly serious purpose of learning the fine points of maneuvering in a world full of predators.

The hunting mammals took the process even further, using play as a means of honing their hunting skills. The stalking, pouncing, wrestling games that felines play are all exercises meant to learn the skills of the hunt.

But humans took the concept of play the furthest. Lord knows they had to—with infants popping out of the womb several years before they were truly ready to take on the world, they needed every opportunity to learn the complex skills necessary to survive.

Play's role in our childhood is so dominating that we cannot let go of it when we grow up; we continue to insinuate the concepts of play into everything we do. And these play-concepts have been integrated into our culture. Our culture is stocked with a great many behavior patterns or templates that we use to guide our actions. I still recall the nervousness with which I endured my first formal meal: a lunch with a prospective employer. I fretted over my table manners, worrying at each step what the proper behavior was. Should I place my napkin on my lap as soon as I sit down, or wait until food is served? I knew that there was a specific program of behaviors expected of me, but I was unsure of many of its details. We could just as easily refer to such behaviors as rituals, but the difference between a ritual and a game is trifling.

Consider, for example, the elaborate mating games played by teenagers in an earlier, simpler time. One form of game-ritual was the school dance, where each person was expected to wear a special costume and dance with members of the opposite sex. The dances themselves were specified by the music that was played and the fashion of the time. After they were old enough to obtain a driver's license, the games changed. The rules required the boy to pick up the girl, where he would pass inspection by the girl's father. Then the boy took the girl to dinner, often at a restaurant frequented by others from the same social group. Later, the boy might take the girl to a movie. Afterwards, with the girl's consent, the boy might take her to a private location to "make out." Finally, the boy took the girl home before the deadline set by her father, where the girl was expected to provide a goodbye kiss.

Play Is Metaphorical

All play in some sense represents something from the non-play universe. We often confuse this metaphorical aspect of play as simulation. Play is not necessarily a simulation of anything in particular, but it does generate mental associations with real-world issues. In many cases, those associations are in fact generated by means of simulation. For example, a flight simulation allows us to play at flying, and it does so by presenting us with a careful simulation of the experience of piloting an aircraft. But simulation is a small part of a larger picture; metaphor is the broader term that more completely expresses this aspect of the nature of play.

A good example of this is provided by the series of combat flight simulators designed by Larry Holland for LucasArts Games in the early 1990s (**BattleHawks**, **Battle of Britain**, and **Secret Weapons of the Luftwaffe**). These games deliberately magnified combat results to heighten the emotional intensity of the game. You could shoot down half a dozen enemy aircraft in a single mission. These results were, of course, wildly unrealistic; many fighter pilots went through the entire war without shooting down a single aircraft. But an accurate simulation of World War II fighter combat would have been dreadfully boring. You'd take off, fly for several hours to the combat zone, hear all sorts of excitement over the radio, fly around looking for enemy aircraft, and when you found some, there would either be too many (in which case you dared not approach) or too few (in which case they would run as you approached). Very rarely would you chance upon an encounter with even enough odds to entice both sides to accept battle, and even then the chances of actually making a hit, much less a kill, were low. After many hours sweating in the freezing cold, you'd return home empty-handed. That's what a simulation would show. But a game is another matter; it must model the emotional realities of air combat, and from that point of view, all the missed opportunities and eventless hours are non-entities. The only thing that matters is shooting and being shot at; therefore, a good air combat game will twist reality around to emphasize the emotionally significant parts.

Consider, for another example, the old classic game **Space Invaders**. This game cannot be said to simulate anything from our experience. There have never been arrays of little space monsters marching back and forth across the sky, slowly closing in on us. Nor is such a situation even plausible. **Space Invaders** simulates nothing. I see in this game not a simulation but an excellent metaphor for the frustrations of the individual in our society. All the social rules and institutions are arrayed against us; they march in lockstep as they threaten to suffocate us. They rain their nasty poop onto our heads; we can only dodge them. But we do have one gun with which to shoot back, and if we dodge quickly, we can defeat them. It's a compelling metaphor for the predicament with which we all struggle; that's why it was such a huge success. Even more interesting is the fact that there were many, many variations and improvements upon the basic design, and none of them caught on like the original. The designers of these imitations tweaked the components of the design, but they lost the power of the metaphor.

A similar case can be made for another old classic: **Pac-Man**. There had been plenty of maze-chase games before **Pac-Man**, and many afterward, but none seemed to have the emotional power of that particular combination of design characteristics. It can't be due to any success or failure in simulation—**Pac-Man** doesn't simulate anything! What **Pac-Man** captures so well is the frantic nature of our working lives. We rush about, collecting some meaningless dots (carrying out our daily tasks), while bad guys chase us, just waiting to trip us up on some minor mistake. It's frantic, it's mechanical, it's relentless—it's just like our daily lives. There were plenty of variations on the **Pac-Man** design, but none of them got the metaphor to hit home so closely.

Sadly, the current mania for photo-realistic graphic detail has distracted us from the power of metaphor. Games are now designed with acute attention to every graphic detail, and our continuing successes in this direction have only encouraged this misdirected attention. There remains a huge opportunity here for games that operate in a metaphorical sense, rather than the overly explicit works now in vogue. A game should not be a mere stripped-down version of a simulation; it can reach far into the weird world of human emotional associations to find its truth.

> Good games do not simulate physical reality; they mirror emotional reality.

Play Must Be Safe

Every now and then I read some young whippersnapper designer suggesting some sort of feedback device that pro-vides negative feedback to the player. Most often it takes the form of a device that provides an electrical shock if the player transgresses the expectations of the game. At other times people have suggested unpleasant noises or forcing the player to start all over.

All of these ideas violate one of the fundamental elements of play: It's safe. The whole idea of play is to give the player an experience without the danger that might nor-mally accompany that experience.

A revealing manifestation of this problem lies in the matter of frequent game saving, especially in role-playing games. Most players take the precaution of saving their game before attempting anything risky. If something does go wrong, they simply restore the game to its previous state and avoid the mistake that led them into trouble. Some game designers, on the other hand, resent this ploy; they seem to believe that the elation of victory is made sweeter by the humiliation of defeat. Such designers fail to appreciate this fundamental law of play. Some games involve a considerable investment of time to play; players naturally want to feel that their investment is safe. Without the assurance of safety, players will resort to conservative, careful, plodding strategies—which aren't much fun.

Good games permit the player to undo his last move, or play it over, instantly. The quicker and more easily the player can correct a mistake, the safer he will feel and the more exploratory and playful his play will be. Losing should be a rare event, just frequent enough to maintain the illusion of risk, but not frequent enough to intimidate the player.

The player must not merely *be* safe; he must *feel* safe. Some games foist myriad unpleasant surprises on the player. When such surprises provide nothing more than momentary excitement, they enhance the play of the game. But when they threaten to set the player back substantially, they harm the play of the game out of proportion to the setback actually inflicted. If the player fears mines lurking underneath every step he takes, he won't take many steps.

The fascinating paradox of play is that it provides the player with dangerous experiences that are absolutely safe. This is best exemplified by roller coasters. The rider is assured of the safety of the roller coaster before consigning his personal safety to it. He knows that it was built to careful standards and inspected by outsiders. More to the point, he knows that thousands of people have ridden the roller coaster before him, without any accidents. He is therefore assured of his safety. Yet the whole point of the roller coaster is to convince his senses that he is about to die. The wild gyrations, high speeds, and great heights all suggest imminent destruction. It is the perception of danger coupled with the certainty of safety that makes the experience so much fun. Roller coaster designers know that even one accident in a million rides would destroy the pleasure for all riders. They push the experience as far as possible in the direction of perceived danger while maintaining complete safety. A problem as simple as a squeaking wheel or a scraping sound can shatter the rider's perception of safety and ruin the experience, even if it does not actually compromise his safety.

We see exactly the same phenomenon in many movies. Consider, for example, the old classic **Raiders of the Lost Ark**. In the first five minutes of this movie, the hero faces ten deadly threats—and escapes every one. Each appears to offer little chance of survival, yet somehow Indiana Jones cheats death each time. The sense of underlying safety amid horrific dangers is an irresistible allure in a movie; we love it. Games should do the same.

Play Need Not Be Exotic

Some game designers believe that play must have an exotic, escapist aspect to be successful. Put the player in the shoes of some barbarian prince, they say, or a laser-pistol-packing space swashbuckler, and the player can escape the dull tedium of his meaningless life. These designers have missed the underlying truth at work. Players don't need to be spirited away to an exotic world; they want to face and overcome interesting challenges, and the pragmatic world in which they live goes to great lengths to minimize all risk.

Skateboarding games allow players the chance to skateboard in environments forbidden to real skateboarders—but these environments need not be alien wastelands with

Keep the player on the razor edge of failure, but don't let him fall.

The whole world is fun; you don't need to look under rocks or in caves for it.

menacing tendrils and hidden caves. They can just as easily be freeways, factories, or fishing ships—places that are not so much exotic as challenging. One need merely look to the vast success of **The Sims**, which one wag has dubbed "a housekeeping simulator," to realize just how unimportant an exotic setting can be. There's still plenty of challenge in getting the characters functioning smoothly and happily.

The Fun Factor

The English word "fun" has no cognate in any other language. Every other language has words for happiness, enjoyment, pleasure, and so forth, but it seems that no other language has a word that expresses the special kind of playful happiness that is encompassed in the word "fun." Indeed, most people place the words "game," "play," and "fun" in a straightforward relationship:

- "Game" is the formal activity that you perform.
- "Play" is the actual behavior that you engage in.
- "Fun" is the experience or emotion that you derive from that behavior.

This relationship leads to a simple conclusion: Games and play must lead to fun. If a game isn't fun, it's a bad game. It sounds perfectly logical, and it is flatly wrong.

The problem with this reasoning lies in the fact that the words "game," "play," and "fun" are in flux. They have historically been associated with the behavior of children, yet in the last century, with the creation of significant amounts of leisure time, adults have taken up play as well. This new, adult kind of play is still play by any definition, but the word "fun" doesn't quite fit the adult's experience. When two friends play a hard-fought game of tennis, are they having fun? Do bird watchers brave the elements to have fun? How about the lady who putters around in the garden trying to raise the perfect rose? A truly broad definition of "fun" would of course cover all these activities, but most of the time we use "fun" in a much narrower sense. Some game designers seem to want it both ways: They claim that play covers a universe of entertainment activities, but then apply much narrower criteria to the evaluation of the merits of a game. The same people who argued yesterday that gardening is a form of play will tomorrow deride a gardening game as utterly devoid of fun.

"Fun" is a misleading word to be using just yet. It is a semantic chameleon, changing its meaning in each new context. I continue to use the word informally and loosely, but I never use that word in serious design analysis. Games don't have to be fun to provide entertainment, rewarding play, or just nice feelings. Condemning a game as "not fun" is about as useful as calling it "crummy"; it expresses an emotional reaction but offers absolutely nothing that you can get your hands on. Let's banish this term from our serious game design discussions.

Use the word "fun" as you would any other approbatory term, such as "cool," "far out," "groovy," or "neat-o."

challenge

challenge

We measure ourselves by the challenges we face. In the universe of possibilities that encompasses what we could be, it is the challenges we face up to that delineate who we actually are. We therefore go through life seeking new challenges that permit us to expand our identities. Once a challenge has been overcome, it is no longer a challenge, and we move on to a new challenge. We seek our challenges in all spheres of our lives: social, work, romantic, and artistic. Sometimes we fail and adjust our challenges accordingly. Sometimes we succeed and raise the notch a level. But no matter the outcome, we continue our quest for challenges that expand our identities.

Challenge Necessitates Rules

All challenges take place in some sort of defined context, setting the conditions under which the challenge is presented. Sometimes that context is financial, in which case a contract specifies the conditions. Sometimes the challenge takes the form of a job; a great variety of factors specify what is and is not permitted, expected, and required. Some challenges are physical in nature, in which case the laws of physics define the nature of the challenge.

Most challenges are at heart voluntary efforts on our part. We don't sign a contract unless we believe ourselves able to meet its conditions. We don't accept a job offer unless we accept the challenges it offers us. And of course, all sports, in which we accept a physical challenge, are voluntary.

The conditions under which a challenge is presented are its rules. Some rules are imposed upon the player by forces outside his control. The water skier cannot change the nature of water, nor can the rock climber defy gravity. Other rules are administrative in nature, such as the rules that organize the pyramid of games in a tournament. But the important rules are those that define the nature of the challenge and that make it a truly interesting challenge.

For example, mountain climbing would be so much easier with a helicopter—but that would remove all the challenge. Plenty of other technological aids could assist the mountain climber, but most climbers have a set of self-imposed rules that limit their utilization of such aids. After all, the point of mountain climbing is not to get to the top of the mountain, but rather to challenge oneself.

The Point Is the Challenge, Not the Goal

I once designed a little exercise game for myself. I hung a motorcycle tire from a rope tied to the ceiling of a high garage. Halfway up the rope I also attached a heavy weight. This created a *compound pendulum*, whose mechanical properties are quite complicated. When the tire is placed in motion, the intermediate weight is dragged along with it, and starts oscillating in its own fashion, dragging the tire in its turn. From ground level, the tire appears to gyrate in wild and unpredictable ways. Then I drew a circle one meter in diameter on the floor directly underneath the pivot point of the rope. This was the field of play.

The goal of the game was to hit the tire with my sword as many times as possible, without stepping outside the circle or being touched by the tire. This required me to weave, duck, twist, and turn to evade the tire when I couldn't hit it. Of course, hitting the tire sent it off in new and more complicated gyrations. It was an excellent game and provided me with much all-body exercise.

Quite proud of my design, I showed it off to another designer. I explained the rules to him and handed him the sword. He stepped inside the circle and began lightly tapping the tire with the sword. When I asked him what he was doing, he replied, "Winning the game."

My game designer friend's clever trick demonstrates a crucial factor in the enjoyment of challenge: It's easy to ruin a good challenge by exploiting loopholes in the rules. No matter how carefully you set up the challenge, somebody will think of a way to subvert your system. One solution to this problem is to write reams of rules to prevent every imaginable form of cheating. For example, I wonder if baseball has a rule that makes it illegal for a runner to shoot opposing players to prevent them from tagging him out. Probably not. But in what we call "friendly games," players rely on simple rules and reject clever tricks that subvert the challenge of the game. "No fair!" is a cry that makes up for a lot of complicated rule-mongering.

A variation on this problem is called the "lock on victory." This is a strategy or technique that guarantees success. For example, in the classic game **MazeWar**, one of the earliest multiplayer games, the players move around through a maze shooting at each other. Sometimes a player would back up into a dead end, facing the only entrance. The moment somebody passed by, the dirty rat would shoot them. Since nobody could ever get into position to shoot the rat quickly enough, he was guaranteed never to lose. This behavior was perfectly legal within the framework of the rules, but everybody knew that it was "no fair."

This is a key element of challenge that is often misunderstood. The player's formal goal is to beat the system enclosing the challenge, but the player's ultimate goal is to overcome the challenge. Thus, even the cheater who finds a way to beat the rules without beating the challenge feels unsatisfied with the result. Of course, with computers, it's much easier to enforce rules— you simply make undesired behavior impossible to execute. Nevertheless, you should always be aware of this potential problem.

8

LESSON

Eliminate
loopholes
that allow
the player to
evade the
challenge of
the game.

I well remember a big wargame that I played many years ago with a friend. There was an unfortunate ambiguity in the rules; we both perceived the problem and, after some discussion, agreed on a patch to the rules that fixed the problem. Unfortunately, the patch itself had an unintended ambiguity, and the two of us interpreted that ambiguity in opposite fashions. We played the game for many hours and then, as the game came to its climax, my opponent pounced with a move that I thought was illegal. Only then did we discover our misunderstanding. All our hours of careful play had been a complete waste of time; the game was ruined. We abandoned the game and parted in foul moods; each of us felt that the other had somehow been stupid to misunderstand our agreement.

The primary purpose of rules is to prevent strategies that subvert the challenge. In most sports games, there is some sort of boundary and any play that goes "out of bounds" is forbidden by the rules. That's because, if players could run around outside the boundary, then they'd come up with all sorts of creative ways to circumvent the real challenge of the game.

There are a myriad ways to play a game, but a good design ensures that only the challenging ways are possible. This raises an interesting design problem: What constitutes a challenging strategy? There is no objective answer to that question. Tic-tac-toe is challenging for some people and devoid of challenge for others. Your job as a designer is to define the challenge in the game and then make that challenge as clear and precise as possible.

Dimensions of Challenge

Every challenge forces us to bring to bear some combination of skills. In many recreational challenges, that combination tends to zero in on particular skills. The primary challenge for a competitor in a ski race is a matter of physical strength and coordination, but other skills such as reading snow, judging distances, and gauging speeds are also vital.

Most recreational challenges are centered on particular mental skills. It is true that physical sports require superb musculature, but in very few sports—running and weightlifting, for example—is musculature the primary factor in success. In most sports, the precise control of that musculature is more important to success. Thus, we can characterize most challenges by the nature of the mental challenge they offer us. Here are some categories.

Cerebellar Challenges

The cerebellum sits at the base of the brain; the spinal cord enters it. In engineering terms, you could call the cerebellum the control module for motor functions. High-level brain decisions are passed to the cerebellum, which breaks each command down into smaller, precisely timed commands to trigger particular muscle bundles. These commands go down the brain stem to the spinal cord and thence to the muscles in the body (see Figure 4.1).

There are only a few sports that are exclusively cerebellar in nature; the discus, shot-put, and javelin are three. Such

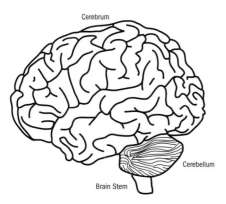

4.1 *The brain.*

sports don't involve much sensory input; they don't require accuracy of aim. The goal is to throw the projectile as far as possible. The thrower can do the job almost with his eyes closed; it's a pure motor-control challenge.

Sensorimotor Challenges

Most cerebellar challenges include a sensory element. You don't just trigger muscles in some predetermined sequence; you must use your senses (most often vision) to direct and control the muscular activity. A simple example of this is throwing a projectile to hit a target. As it happens, the task of accurately throwing an object is not easily handled by neurons. Consider, for example, the mechanics of throwing a balled-up sheet of paper into a wastebasket. The timing of muscle activity, and especially the release of the ball, must be accurate to within about a millisecond. Unfortunately, a single neuron takes a few milliseconds to fire. It's like timing an eyeblink with a stopwatch—the event being timed is faster than the timer. So how do we do it? The trick is achieved by applying large numbers of neurons and using their average value. Statistically, the average time of firing of a hundred neurons is ten times more precise than the timing of a single neuron. Throw enough neurons at the problem, and you can get as much precision as you desire.

And that's what the human brain does. It applies huge numbers of neurons to the task and thereby attains high precision in throwing. In fact, the ability to accurately throw a projectile is the one area of physical action in which human capability bests any other creature on the planet. So the next time somebody tries to humble you with tales of a hawk's visual acuity, a cat's reflexes, a bat's echolocation, or a cheetah's speed, retort by asking, "Yeah, but can they shoot baskets?"

I can't think of any sensorimotor challenges that are explicitly aural; as far as I can recall, all sensorimotor challenges require the integration of visual information with motor response. At its simplest form, we can call this "hand-eye coordination," but in many such challenges, it's not just the hands that are responding. Indeed, here we arrive at one of the most striking distinctions between sports and videogames. In all sensorimotor-challenging sports, even those relying primarily on manual activity, the entire body is involved in the task. Even the trivial task of tossing the paper ball into the wastebasket requires the player to rotate his chair, lean his body, twist his neck, and position his arms. Yet the videogame player seems to work best with most of his body immobile; even the upper arms move but little. It's all in the thumbs.

Pushing the Pathways Down

The neural pathways utilized in such sensorimotor challenges are complex. Preprocessed visual data passes from the retina to the visual cortex at the back of the brain, where it is further processed into visually meaningful components such as walls, floor, targets, and so forth. From there it travels to the cerebral cortex, where it undergoes high-level processing. In other words, the cerebral cortex recalls the rules of the game and its goals, integrates the information from the visual cortex, decides what to do about the situation, and passes those decisions down to the cerebellum, which translates them into muscle action (see Figure 4.2).

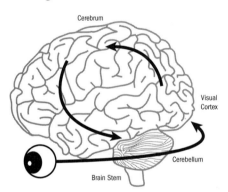

As you might imagine, all this processing is quite time-consuming and so the beginning player can be slow and clumsy. The difference between a beginner and a skilled player is that the skilled player has learned to build shorter, faster neural pathways from the visual cortex to the cerebellum (see Figure 4.3).

4.2 *Information flow in the brain when first learning a videogame.*

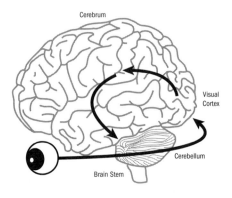

Cerebrum

Visual Cortex

Cerebellum

Brain Stem

4.3 *Shortened pathways for information flow yield faster responses and more successful play.*

By moving the pathways lower into the brain, the player reduces the amount of processing required to react to events in the game or sport. Decision-making is no longer conscious or deliberate. It is often described as "instinctive." The player sees, and the player acts without conscious thought. There's still plenty of mental processing going on, but it's faster because it is no longer part of the elaborate (shall I say bureaucratic?) structure of conscious thought.

It is one of the wonders of the human brain that we can learn so readily. Any process that we concentrate on repetitively can develop its own custom neural pathways that render its operation faster and smoother, requiring less mental effort. In effect, whenever we learn a task, we reduce the amount of conscious effort required to carry it out. When I first began to use a keyboard, I had to concentrate on the locations of the keys. After literally millions of keystrokes, my brain has burned that information into its neural pathways. I think of a word, my fingers move, and the word appears on the screen. All the mental computations go on in a deeper, lower level of mental processing beneath my conscious awareness.

Even more striking is the ability of the brain to learn different tasks with different degrees of facility. Typing on a keyboard is now a subconscious process for me, while the particulars of my word processor are a little less familiar; some of the commands take a fraction of a second of thought to recall. Commands that I use rarely demand my full attention to recall. My brain's organization of its knowledge is an elegantly proportioned and optimized system; the more often I perform a task, the more deeply it is driven into my subconscious and the faster my execution of the task is.

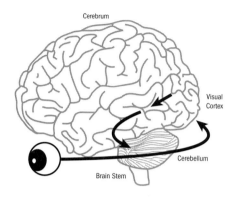

4.4 *Information flow in the brain of an expert player.*

This ability to drive task execution deeper and deeper can be taken to dramatic extremes. There's no reason why a player cannot learn a task this well (see Figure 4.4).

In such a case, the player is able to attain extremely high levels of performance because the neural pathways are much shorter and lower in the processing hierarchy of the brain.

This extreme degree of proficiency is most difficult to attain in sports, because the exercise of these pathways necessarily entails lots of exhausting muscle activity. You can only practice your sport so many hours a day before your aching muscles put a stop to your exercise.

But what if we could invent a sport that didn't involve so much exhausting muscular activity? What if all that mental activity could still be going on, but it used only muscles that didn't require lots of strength, muscles that are used for lots and lots of low-power activity? These muscles wouldn't tire, and so the player could go for hours and hours, attaining previously unheard-of levels of proficiency. This, it would seem, would be the ultimate exercise of this learning capability, and it would surely be an exciting sport, wouldn't it?

Technology has in fact provided us with just such a sport: the videogame. A kid can sit in front of a videogame for hours, working his fingers frantically but never tiring. In the process, he can push those neural pathways down so deep in his brain that his game-reflexes become inhumanly quick. The parent watching a kid playing such a videogame has difficulty keeping up with the action on the screen, so fast are the kid's reflexes. It's truly mind-boggling.

Of course, no videogame is ever mastered; no matter how good the kid is, there's always something new to learn, some reflex that can be made sharper and quicker. So the kid never relaxes.

Oftentimes when I am engaged in a friendly telephone conversation, I will perform light housework: putting things away, sorting socks, that kind of thing. I hate housework because it's so mindless; telephone-time is the ideal time to do this work because I can carry out these almost subconscious tasks while engaging my conscious effort on my conversation with my friend. That's the real value of learning something so well that it takes little mental effort; we can carry out the dumb task while also performing some other more mentally challenging work.

But this is not how kids play videogames. There's always a new skill to master, so the kid devotes his entire mental resource to the learning process. All his mentation is concentrated in that low-level processing. And this causes something most curious to happen: conscious processing shuts down. Parents can readily attest to this phenomenon; calling the kid to dinner yields a muttered acknowledgement and no action. A kid can start playing a videogame at eight in the evening and still be there at midnight, unaware of the passage of time. "Johnny, there's a lion loose in the room" will elicit an "Okay, Mom" and nothing more. Some parents report that only physically interposing themselves between player and screen can break the kid's trance.

Altered States of Consciousness

It's not quite correct to refer to this phenomenon as a *loss of consciousness*; it's really an altered state of consciousness. And just as the hippies of the 60s were entranced (literally) by drug-induced altered states of consciousness, so too are kids today entranced (literally) by videogame-induced altered states of consciousness.

This alarming analogy gains strength with deeper consideration. There are several particulars in which the analogy between videogame and drugs rings true.

First is the element of pleasure. We are programmed to learn, and successful learning is intrinsically pleasurable. Just as the "runner's high"
is triggered by endorphins released by a certain level of exercise, there
seems to be some kind of "videogamer's high" attained at a certain level
of proficiency. Videogames are carefully designed to provide the player
with a steady stream of learning successes; it's called the *learning
curve* of the game. At each point in the game, the player has only to
make a small improvement in his performance to earn an explicit and
often dramatic reward. It's like eating popcorn; each piece is small but
tastes so good that you readily move on to the next piece, until you suddenly realize that you have consumed a gallon of popcorn.

Videogamers have difficulty describing the precise nature of their pleasurable experience, although they will readily confirm just how much they
enjoy the game. Perhaps this is due to the inarticulateness intrinsic to
kids; perhaps it is because the experience has no parallel in the real
world. They describe their state of consciousness in terms frighteningly
similar to those used by drug addicts. They are "in tune with the game" or
"in the groove of the game." They feel that they are united with the game;
they anticipate its behavior so intimately that they almost identify with it.

Second, videogamers report the same sense of power and invulnerability
that drug users experience. Drug users report the feeling that they are
smarter, more creative, and able to see more deeply into the mysteries
of their souls. Videogamers report similar experiences of power and
invulnerability. When they are playing in a videogame high, dangers rush
at them, but they flow along with the game, unwounded, untouched, and
incapable of being injured.

Third is the loss of awareness of the dull, depressing world in which they
live. Just as some people drink to forget, some videogamers slip out of a
world of overbearing parents, demanding teachers, and dismal failure, to
enter a world of simple challenges and frequent glorious success. Their
loss of awareness of the world around them is no happenstance; it's an
important part of the appeal of the experience.

Lastly, there is the addictive nature of videogames. As with drugs, addiction is not an inevitable outcome of use; some personalities seem more resistant to addiction, others less so. But there is no question that some kids become addicted to videogames. They partake of videogame pleasures to the detriment of other activities in their lives. Their sense of priorities is distorted in favor of the games. They are unable to stop. Let's face it: This is addiction.

There are, of course, many differences between the videogame experience and the drug experience: the absence of any outright chemical influence the large number of videogamers who do not fall victim to addiction and the greater subtlety of videogame mental effects. I am not claiming that all videogamers are no different from drug users; rather, I'm claiming that *some* of the more extreme videogamers share *some* symptoms with drug users.

It is only a matter of time before some researcher carries out a detailed study of brain activity in videogamers and compares it with brain activity in drug users. When that study is published, you do NOT want to be holding stock in any videogame company!

Spatial Reasoning

There really isn't any such thing as a pure sensorimotor challenge; a certain amount of spatial reasoning is necessarily involved. In other words, when the player sees a bad guy pop up, the player must perform a certain amount of spatial reasoning to estimate the amount of danger posed by the bad guy, the likelihood of successfully shooting him, and so forth. Some spatial reasoning is performed directly in the visual cortex in the back of the brain; some is so everyday in nature as to be easily performed in other areas; some is so specific to a game that it must be performed in the most general (and therefore slowest) manner. Much of the learning process of a fast game is a matter of moving the spatial reasoning process into lower regions of the brain.

However, some games don't rely so much on fast hand-eye coordination, and so they are able to present the player with more complex spatial problems requiring more subtle exercise of spatial reasoning. Strategy wargames, for example, require the player to analyze spatial patterns of military units, looking for weaknesses in the front lines, potential lines of advance and retreat, and so forth.

Pattern Recognition

Jim Dunion of Atari Research first demonstrated the possibilities with a delightful real-time puzzle in which the player was presented with a random pattern of colored dots that slowly dissolved into a recognizable image, such as a famous face. The player had only to recognize the image and type in its name; his score was the amount of time left before the image was fully revealed. This game had pattern recognition as its sole challenge, but pattern recognition often shows up as a secondary challenge in many games. Some shooters encourage the player to recognize particular monsters when they are far away, the better to ready an appropriate early response.

Many boardgames make strong use of pattern recognition. Chess, checkers, and Go all require lots of pattern recognition, although there's plenty of sequential reasoning mixed in as well. The board wargames also push pattern recognition hard; the player must analyze a front line to identify weak spots and strong points.

Computers have always been weaker than nervous systems at pattern recognition; the only way computers manage it now is to painstakingly convert a pattern recognition problem into a sequential reasoning problem, which can then be solved with computer power.

A pattern need not be strictly visual; it can take a more abstruse form. Upon entering a new room, a player in an RPG must quickly evaluate the tactical situation and the pattern of positions and capabilities of the hostile inhabitants of the room. If that pattern looks particularly dangerous, the player might want to retreat, but a less threatening pattern would require a completely different approach. The most abstruse expression of such pattern recognition comes in strategy wargames, where the player must evaluate the enemy's deployments to determine the best area in which to aim an attack or the most vulnerable area to defend.

Sequential Reasoning

When we string together long sequences of steps, we are engaging in sequential reasoning. Examples of such activities are mathematical calculations, writing a computer program, or planning a travel route. Most games require some sort of sequential reasoning, but chess is the exemplar of complex sequential reasoning. The typical chess player must examine many possible sequences of moves. Since this is something that computers excel in, it should come as no surprise that computers can beat people at this task.

Many computer games are designed by people who are programmers at heart, and they tend to overemphasize sequential reasoning because it comes so easily to them. Be on guard against this tendency; keep a lid on the sequential reasoning (unless, of course, your use of sequential reasoning is deliberately intrinsic to the design). Most people find highly sequential tasks, such as long calculations or memorizing complex sequences of actions, to be a tedious challenge.

Numerical Reasoning

We all have to juggle numbers in our heads. Should I buy the small jar of peanut butter or is the large jar a better buy? If Fresno is 180 miles away, can I get there before dinnertime? This kind of arithmetic or numerical reasoning is a special form of sequential reasoning, and most people find it particularly odious. Computers shine at numerical calculations, so you should never challenge your player in this dimension. Let the computer crunch the numbers for the player.

Resource Management

In many games, especially strategy games, the player must carefully marshal a limited supply of scarce resources to handle the various problems he faces. In shooters, resource management might cover only ammunition and health, but in more complex games, the player might have to juggle dozens of resources. Some degree of resource management comes easily to most people. However, as with sequential reasoning (but to a lesser degree), some games tend to overdo it. In particular, some game designers seem to design by grabbing an existing game and adding some more resource management.

Some of the best designers argue that resource management is central to game design, and if we grant them broad indulgence in the meaning of the term "resource," they're right. For example, consider a social interaction in which you must convince another player to carry out some action. You could beg and plead, promising that you'll be very appreciative if that player relents to your importunations. I suppose that you could call this the expenditure of some sort of social relationship resource, like "friendship brownie points." Indeed, the Indonesians have a word for this concept: *tanagadalang*. However, I find this approach to social relationships too cold for my taste; I think it's more effective, in the long run, to design social interactions in somewhat more humanistic terms than "resources."

Social Reasoning

Now here's an underdeveloped source of challenge for computer games! There's no mystery why social reasoning is so weak in computer games: Most game designers are socially incompetent geeks whose social reasoning skills are microscopic. It's pretty hard to design a game about a challenge you don't understand. Indeed, a number of game designers have angrily rejected my claims on this matter by denying that such a thing as social reasoning even exists.

Although I phrase my put-down of game designers in kinder, gentler terms, the problem at work here is quite serious: autism. Psychologists are now realizing that autism is not some single-valued disease that strikes a few unlucky souls; it is instead a broad-spectrum malady that affects millions of people to greater or lesser degrees. In its most benign form, autism expresses itself as a general reluctance to interact with others, a shyness or social clumsiness. Sound like anybody you know? How about programmers? Although most programmers are perfectly healthy, the field attracts people with social skill deficits. This explains why so much of the output of programmers is so user-intolerant. With most software, such personality traits do no more damage than to make software difficult to use, costing us billions of dollars in lost productivity and accidents. But with games, the results are really serious: It's pretty hard to entertain people when you simply can't relate to them!

The cluelessness of the game design community with regard to social reasoning is truly breathtaking. One of the perennial questions among game designers is this: "How can we entice more female players into our fold?" Answers to this question have ranged from "Put a bow on Pac-Man's head and call him Ms. Pac-Man" (seriously! Midway actually did this!) to "Give them *pink* BFGs (Big Guns)" (not so seriously). Game designers can't seem to come to grips with the fact that social reasoning fascinates most women. You can see it most easily in the difference between the typical "guy movie" and the typical "chick flick." The guy movie sports a hero with a huge torso, bulging arms, a big gun in one hand, and a girl whose breast measurements exceed her IQ in the other arm. The chick flick is about social relationships. Chicks go to guy movies as an act of social cooperation with their guy; guys refuse to go to chick flicks because such movies bore them out of their skulls.

Clearly, if we want to appeal to more women, we want to build games that challenge their social reasoning skills. At the moment, this looks rather difficult to do; it's so much easier to calculate the trajectory of a bullet than to figure out why Jane left John. However, I suspect that, when we do produce games with strong social challenge, we will use simplified systems of interpersonal relations that will be iconically represented; when this happens, we will likely think that it looked obvious all along.

Challenge and Identity

Work on social reasoning designs.

The challenges we pursue most eagerly are those that best exercise what is especially human about us. Consider how many sports involve some sort of throwing or projectile-controlling activity. No other species can control projectiles as accurately as we can, and many of our sports challenge us in this especially human skill. We define ourselves by the limits we can push through. Each person has their own unique sense of those limits and the challenges that best define them; for this reason, good game design should cover a broad range of challenges. Individual games cannot cover everything, but games as a medium should be able to provide a cornucopia of challenges. Right now, the cupboard is heavily stocked with a few standard challenges; much work remains.

conflict

Conflict makes challenge personal. It's one thing to be challenged by a cliff waiting to be climbed, or a puzzle waiting to be solved, but it's entirely another thing to go up against a real live opponent. A simple challenge just sits there waiting for you to come; you can ignore it or tackle it at your leisure. But a challenge coming from a human being is of entirely another order—you can't just sit there thinking about it. You accept the challenge or you slink away.

Conflict is the stressor that reveals character and ability. Challenge without conflict is entirely predictable; when you go mano a mano with a crossword puzzle, you know exactly what you're getting into. But when you enter into a conflict with an active agent, you no longer enjoy the initiative; that other person could come at you from any direction, challenging you in ways that you might not have anticipated. Conflict enlivens and animates challenge; without conflict, challenge is limp and passive. Narrative operates under the same constraint; conflict puts the protagonist under stress, forcing choices that reveal character.

Games,
like stories,
require
conflict to
have any
life.

Mars, Venus, and Conflict

Some game designers, laden with more testosterone than
experience, maintain that women can't handle conflict or
are afraid of it. Female conflict over issues that are vital to
female interests can be just as ferocious as male conflicts,
but they differ in two respects. First, women don't go
around with a chip on their shoulders, seeking out conflict
as men are wont to do. Second, women don't play out their
conflicts in the same dimensions that men do. Where men
rely heavily on physical forms of conflict, women tend
toward social conflict.

The two sex's attitudes toward each other in this respect
are illuminating. In matters of conflict, men regard women
as sneaky and deceitful. Men wonder why women can't just
come out in the open, look you in the eye, and punch you
in the nose. They conveniently overlook the fact that a
woman using such an approach is almost certain to be
worsted in a fistfight. Women, by contrast, view men as
primitive louts when it comes to conflict. They wonder why
men hit first and ask questions later. The fact that hierar-
chies are central to male identity is lost on most women.
Understanding these differences is crucial to designing
games that appeal to women.

Dimensions of Conflict

We humans have evolved a myriad of dimensions of conflict. After all, if you can't beat your opponent in an existing
dimension, why not make up a new dimension in which you
can beat him? Thus human creativity has been bent toward
the development of all kinds of conflict, and designers now
have only to pick over this feast to find one dimension
capable of providing interesting possibilities.

Physical

This is the oldest and most fundamental dimension of conflict. Bash the other guy on the head, kick him in the butt, or punch him in the nose. People have been resolving their disputes in this fashion since, well, before they were human. Early on, we humans applied our tool-making skills to the problem and invented "the weapon"—a big stick or a rock—and we've been improving it ever since.

We should differentiate between physical conflict as a means of establishing dominance and physical conflict as a means of eliminating others. Sometimes the use of physical force is only a means of intimidating a rival, and so can take more symbolic means. A gorilla pounding his chest makes a deep resonant sound indicating the volume of his torso, and by implication, the magnitude of his upper body strength. An animal's growl serves a similar function. Baring the teeth is another example of demonstrating physical prowess prior to actual physical conflict. Humans pound the table with their fists, shout, or grind their teeth as demonstrations of physical strength. And if simple demonstrations are insufficient to intimidate a rival, the actual application of physical force tends to concentrate on the area that combines the greatest emotional impact with the least actual injury: the face.

Physical conflict "to the death" is another matter entirely. In animal behavior, deadly conflict is rarely mixed with dominance conflict; typically, dominance conflict is applied to members of one's own species, where deadly conflict is applied to other species. The only exceptions I can think of are wolves and humans.

Verbal

Language is another of our uniquely human inventions, and we can only guess how early in linguistic history the first insult appeared—but there's little doubt that it preceded, say, the first love poem. Linguistic conflict normally takes several different forms. The first is the "insult battle," in which two rivals compete to see who can produce the most humiliating insult. Another verbal conflict is the "boasting battle," in which the two combatants attempt to outdo each other in exaggerated tales of physical prowess.

While such battles are usually executed with some jocularity, serious insults play a large and varied role in human conflict. We have a colorful menu of simple one-shot imprecations. Then there are the escalatory sequences: "You talking to ME?" "Smile when you say that, pardner!" "You wanna make something of it?" More interesting are the more sophisticated forms of insult, such as the left-handed compliment: "Dear, you are *so* daring to show up wearing last year's fashions!" Or the crypto-insult, using terminology that the victim cannot fathom: "You look charmingly coprophilous today, my dear!"

A particularly effective form of verbal conflict is narrative assault, in which the attacker tells a fascinating story to a spellbound audience— but the story contains elements inimical to the interests of the story-teller's opponent. A perfect example of such verbal conflict is provided by the famous Apple Macintosh "1984" commercial, in which a youthful female athlete smashes a symbol of oppression and dehumanization. Apple's target was the IBM PC, which had established dominance in the market. The beauty of the approach is that it permits no effective response. What was IBM to do, broadcast a commercial with a dictator hunting down and capturing the Macintosh woman?

The insulting joke is perhaps the most cruelly effective form of verbal assault. There is nothing more humiliating than to be laughed at, and the fury this kindles in the victim paralyzes his ability to prepare a riposte in kind.

Political

In this form of conflict, the combatants seek to recruit allies and under-mine their opponent's social alliances. The most common term for such behavior is "back-stabbing," but in truth a great many behaviors are encompassed herein. Something so simple as a friendly conversation with a third party can be carried out with malevolent political intent, even if the conversation itself is friendly and pleasant. Once again, humans have developed an impressive array of such behaviors: bad-mouthing, insinuation, questioning another's credentials, framing the victim for some crime he did not commit, falsely informing the victim's allies that he has betrayed them, and so on.

Economic

A rarer medium of conflict is the economic arena. If you can't punch your adversary, insult him, or discredit him, perhaps you can financially ruin him. This is of course the primary form of conflict in business environments, but it can also be extended to other arenas. Smuggle some rotten meat into your enemy's food products, and you can ruin him financially.

Directness of Conflict

Conflict can be prosecuted with varying degrees of directness. The most direct conflict places the two combatants face to face at arm's length; whether they are punching each other or insulting each other, their conflict is about as direct as it can get. But conflict need not be so simple; recourse to indirection can often yield more interesting possibilities.

The simplest step here is to increase the physical distance between the two combatants. Guns do this admirably well; but there are plenty of so-called "indirect weapons" that project an explosive to a distant location. I still recall the great satisfaction I felt while playing **Doom**, sending a rocket into a distant target. The bad guys were just a few moving pixels. The rocket approached, exploded, and the pixels were motionless. Ah, success...no muss, no fuss.

Even more indirection is achieved when the combatants cannot see each other. The attacker tosses a grenade through a window and then imagines the consternation of his victims as they realize what is about to happen. But why stop there? What if the attacker sets a time bomb and then escapes to a distant location, checking his watch to confirm the bomb's detonation? Such conflict may be less direct than watching your victim's blood splatter all over you, but it can be equally satisfying to pursue. An even greater degree of indirection can be attained with a booby trap; as the attacker, you don't know when or whom you'll nail with your evil device, but you are still applying lethal force.

Another form of indirection can be implemented through agents. Instead of shooting the bad guy yourself, the player provides strategic control of an agent who makes the tactical decisions about whom to shoot and when. In effect, the player commands an army of robots who fight under his generalship.

The highest degree of this form of indirectness arises when the player's identity is distributed among several agents. The best example of this kind of indirection is Jim Dunnigan's brilliant design, **Russian Civil War**, which was described in Chapter 2, "Some Milestone Games."

There is also indirectness of approach to consider. Sure, you can directly kill the enemy, but what if you shoot the rope holding the big weight under which he is standing? Frederick the Great of Prussia executed such indirectness of approach better than any general in history. In one campaign, he maneuvered his army down one road, which threatened his enemy's supply lines, so the enemy repositioned himself to a safer location. Frederick again marched to the side, again placing his enemy in a vulnerable location. This process continued for several months until the enemy found himself trapped in an impossible situation, at which point the enemy surrendered. Frederick had won a campaign without firing a shot.

Indirectness of approach need not be confined to spatial dimensions. The German submarine campaign during World War II was an indirect approach to defeating England's armies by starving them of supplies. The USA has done much the same thing to Iraq since 1990 by establishing a trade embargo that strangles Iraq's economy, thereby crippling its military potential while also, in what is known as "collateral damage," starving its population. Since around the year 2000, the USA has gone on the financial offensive against terrorists, freezing their bank accounts and thereby incapacitating them; the USA's ability to intercept their telecommunications has enervated them. These are all supremely indirect approaches in a vicious war.

Note that, in general, indirect approaches tend to be less violent. They are also more subtle and often take longer to achieve their goals. Those hotheads who wanted to "nuke Osama" in the fall of 2001 would certainly have been gratified by the immediate demonstration of power and the big explosions, and they would have succeeded in rearranging the rocks on various Afghan mountainsides, but in practice, pulling the teeth of the Al-Qaeda network has required years of slow, patient effort and is still not completed.

Intensity of Conflict

Conflict is carried out with varying degrees of intensity. It's easiest to think of conflict resolution as a process that requires a given amount of conflict. That conflict can be concentrated into a short time, in which case the conflict is intense, or it can be spread out over a longer time, in which case it is less intense. This distinction directly bears on the design of your game. Intense conflict necessitates a short game; a longer game requires less intensity. Many designers fail to grasp this simple concept; they create games of long-duration intensity. The monsters just keep coming, the killing is non-stop, and the player is exhausted when the game finally ends. While less experienced players revel in such intensity, it is in general not a good idea, as I will explain in the next section. A well-paced game design will rely on more indirect, less intense forms of conflict if it is to last a long time.

Violence

We are now in a position to address one of the most vexing problems facing the computer games industry: violence in games. The industry's response to the accusations leveled against it (that computer games are too violent) has disappointed me. For the most part, people in the industry circle the wagons and deny the problem. They denigrate their accusers, wrap themselves in the First Amendment, and close their minds to all arguments. This saddens me because all this ruckus is so avoidable. Game designers cling to violence only because they cannot imagine other forms of conflict.

Consider violence in terms of the three elements I have just presented: dimension, directness, and intensity. Violence is the most intense, direct, physical form of conflict. What strikes me is the industry's obsession with the most extreme manifestations of these elements. Conflict in many games is about as physical as it can get; recall **Mortal Kombat's** crowning moment, when the player has overcome his opponent, and the words "Finish him!" appear on the screen, at which point the player rips out his opponent's head and spine. Directness is another overdone element; why do so many games put the player in close proximity to his opponents? Why do violent games so rarely place the violent act outside the view of the player? And of course, the kill-or-be-killed approach of many games is far and away the most intense expression of conflict. As the character Quark once said on the television show *Star Trek: Deep Space Nine*, "Why do we have to kill so many? Couldn't we just wound some?" Not in many games, apparently.

Thus, violence in games represents the most extreme form of conflict: gorily physical, utterly direct, and maximally intense. My objection to this is not so much moral as aesthetic: Do we have do use a bludgeon when we design? Violence in games is like Wagner played for 18 hours with the bass turned up. It's like chocolate cereal in chocolate milk with chocolate sprinkles and chocolate fudge on top. It's like a newsgroup correspondent whose vocabulary is dominated by "fuck," "shit," and "crap." It's overdone. It's so much of the same thing that it's distasteful.

Intensity and the Evolution of Taste

There is a good reason for all this intensity: It's a kid thing. The world that children inhabit bubbles with the most amazing things, and kids snarf up all that excitement with gusto. They want to experience life to its fullest, and so they push everything to its limit.

Consider candy, for example. Candy is fun food. What makes candy so special among foods? I think that it's because candy is intensely pleasurable. Have you ever noticed just how intense an experience candy provides? It doesn't taste merely good; candy makes your tongue jump up and shout with joy. Now, there are other intense gustatory experiences—chili peppers, for example. But they are not intensely pleasurable. A chili pepper makes your tongue scream, not laugh. Of course, because it's such an intense experience, candy must be taken in small doses. You don't eat an entire meal of candy, just a small piece.

When I was a child, I loved candy. It was my favorite food. But as I grew older, I became bored with the taste of candy. I wanted more subtlety and more variety in my eating experiences. By the time I was a teenager, my tastes had matured to favor such sophisticated foods as hamburgers, pizza, and hot dogs. As I grew older, my quest for subtlety and variety led me to try Chinese food, different breads, barbecue sauces, Italian food, cheeses, salads—all manner of foods.

The aggregate efforts of millions of people pursuing similar courses has spawned a huge gustatory universe populated with a staggering variety of culinary delights: Thai food, peanut butter, wines, T-bone steaks, Béarnaise sauce, blackened foods, caviar, dill bread, and on and on. And one small subset of this universe is the world of candy, characterized by several traits: It is fun, intensely pleasurable food, best taken in small doses, and primarily appreciated by children.

Cartoons

Now consider cartoons. Cartoons are the most fun form of video. Sure, I enjoy many forms of video, but cartoons make me laugh more. What makes cartoons so much fun? I think that it has to do with the fact that they are so intensely pleasurable. Look at the colors in a cartoon: all bright, loud colors—no soft pastels or delicate shades here. Or consider the pace of a cartoon. Everything happens at breakneck speed. Characters dash about frenetically, never giving the viewer a second to catch his breath. And there's nothing subtle about danger in cartoons. Characters are assailed by falling safes, flocks of flying knives, sizzling sticks of dynamite, and falls from cosmic heights.

Herein lies some of the pleasurable aspect of cartoons, for the characters are never seriously hurt by all this mayhem. Explosions merely blacken their faces. Falls from great heights produce body-shaped craters from which the character emerges, to wobble away unhurt. The impact of a falling safe flattens the character, who peels himself up from the ground to reinflate his body as if it were a balloon. This disjunction between terrible danger and lack of serious harm is a pleasurable release; it is fun.

The intensity of cartoons requires them to be short, only a few minutes' duration. This point is exemplified by the movie *Who Framed Roger Rabbit?*, which started with a magnificent cartoon lasting all of three and a half minutes. Then the cartoon transformed into a movie: The bright colors softened, the pace slowed down to that of real life, and the intensity dropped down to a level that could be sustained for two hours.

When I was a kid, cartoons were my favorite form of video. I'd watch them all day long, if I could. But as I grew older, I became bored with the sameness of cartoons. I longed for characters who were more than cute little animals. I wanted some conflict that was resolved with more subtlety than a mallet-blow to the head. I wanted more variety and more subtlety in my video. So I began to watch more sophisticated programs,

programs like *Gilligan's Island* and *Lost in Space*. And later still, I started watching even more serious video, so that now my viewing habits include movies like *When Harry Met Sally*, *Out of Africa*, and *Koyaanisqatsi*.

Most of us followed an analogous path, and now our combined tastes have created a huge universe of video pleasures, including comedies, how-to shows, mysteries, game shows, pornographic movies, talk shows, action-adventure movies, soap operas, kiddie shows, and many more forms of video. Cartoons comprise a small subset of this gigantic universe, distinguishable by the fact that they are fun, intensely pleasurable, best taken in small doses, and primarily appreciated by children.

Comics

Consider comics. (For the purposes of this discussion, I shall exclude from consideration the serious comics of recent years, such as *Maus*. Instead, I shall consider only the mainstream comics.) Comics are fun; I get a kick out of reading them. Comics are fun because they are intensely pleasurable. Look at the drawing style in the comics: bold, clean lines, with no hint of subtlety. The colors are bright and pure. The characters, conflicts, and events in the comics are always intense. Good guys are as good as they come; bad guys are ugly, deformed, and truly evil. The good guys always win; that's one of the things that makes comics fun.

Comics always come in small doses, largely because their intensity cannot be maintained over a long time. Their first audience is children. When I was a kid, I used to read comics all the time. After a while, though, I grew bored with the sameness of comics. I wanted more variety, more subtlety in my reading. So I began to read more mature fare: Jules Verne and Mark Twain. Later I graduated to Thoreau, Hemingway, and Shakespeare. Now I read Toynbee, Braudel, and von Clausewitz.

Each of us has pursued a similar evolution, starting with comics and proceeding to more subtle literature. Jointly, our courses have spawned a gigantic universe of literature, with newsmagazines and science books, cookbooks and sci-fi novels, the *National Enquirer* and *Playboy*, dictionaries, car repair books, economics textbooks, devotional literature, and even this book. And way over in one corner of this universe is a tiny subset of literature known as comics, unique in that they are fun, intensely pleasurable, best taken in small doses, and especially appreciated by children.

Videogames

These considerations explain the obsession with violence that saturates videogames. Violence is the most intense, direct, and physical form of conflict available; therefore, kids want to experience it. And it's intensely pleasurable, because the kid expects to kill off all the bad guys and win the game. Videogames are in the same league with candy, cartoons, and comic books...and they appeal to precisely the same audience.

What's different is that they are not part of a vast universe of computational delights, teeming with diversions appealing to a wide array of tastes. Our player is an astronaut floating alone in a vast, dark universe with no stars, no galaxies, nothing. Where are the games to appeal to his more mature tastes? Where are the games that are analogous to Caesar salads, nightly news, or bodice-ripper novels? Where are the bagel-and-cream-cheese games, the Archie Bunker games, the Jacquiline Susanne games? Where are the games about a boy and his dog or the prostitute with a heart of gold?

The reason for this emptiness, I think, has to do with the nativity of computer games. The other three pleasures all existed in forms quite separate from the kiddie-forms; indeed, the kiddie-corners of their universes were not explored until well after the main areas of the universe had been developed. We were eating nuts and berries long before we invented jellybeans; the first cartoons appeared more than a decade after the first silent movies; and literature got started thousands of years before the first entertainment-oriented comic books were created.

But computer games were the very first form of entertainment on the computer. The very first computer game, **SpaceWar**, featured two space-ships floating around in space shooting at each other. We didn't know the first thing about designing games when we got started, so we slapped together the simplest possible designs—designs with intense, violent conflict. It is the tragedy of computer games that they were too successful too early. It's as if Homo erectus had been so successful that he spread all over the world, occupied every possible ecological niche, and thereby blocked the evolution of larger-brained hominids.

Don't dismiss too quickly my pessimistic assessment of the state of computer games; the free market is not as free as many designers realize. Economists have a concept called "barriers to entry"; it refers to the difficulties that some new product or service encounters in trying to make its way in the marketplace. Suppose, for example, that you were to wake up tomorrow morning with a brilliant new idea for an operating system. Suppose this operating system was clean, foolproof, perfectly secure...all the things that we want from an ideal operating system. Suppose that you coded up this operating system over the next few months, and that when you tested it, it outperformed every other operat-ing system on the market by large margins. In this hypothetical universe, your operating system would enter the marketplace, demonstrate its superiority to customers, and replace all existing operating systems, making you richer than Bill Gates. Sounds great, doesn't it? Well, dream on, friend, because it ain't gonna happen. No matter how much better your operating system is, Windows will crush it because Windows is the established leader and Microsoft has erected cosmically high barriers to entry for any competitor.

The situation is even worse with games. With operating systems, Microsoft is motivated to continually improve its product and will introduce major innovations if it feels that they are warranted. In the world of games, there is no Microsoft, just a collection of competitors. And remember that the "games community" comprises much more than just the publishers. There are distributors, retailers, and customers, too. This entire community has developed in the last twenty years or so, and it has learned what works and what doesn't. This entrenched community knowledge ensures that computer games remain trapped in the kiddie corner.

Let's try the superior-product fantasy I used a few paragraphs back. Let's suppose that you come up with a brilliant new idea for a game. It's not a candy-game, to be sure; it's more subtle, more mature, less violent, and so on. You're sure that millions of 36-year-old housewives will love it. So you design and produce the game on your own dime (let's assume that you're rich and have lots of dimes). You take your game to a publisher and show it off. No matter how good your game is, the publisher will not take it. He knows the marketing numbers inside and out, and he knows that 36-year-old housewives don't spend much money on games. Sure, this game would sell to 36-year-old housewives—if they were buying. But they're not, so your game is dead meat.

But let's assume that you get lucky and find a publisher who's altruistic enough to publish your game. He's violating his business sense, but is willing to take a flyer for a good cause. Good for you!

It's not over yet. Now the publisher has to convince the distributors to stock the game. Distributors all run on razor-thin margins, so they're some of the most conservative businessmen in the world. They will not stock a game unless they *know* that it will sell. You have to prove the certainty of success by comparing it to other games that have sold well. They'll all turn your publisher down, and your game will never be distributed.

But wait! Let's suppose that you get lucky and find a crazy distributor willing to stock your game. What a stroke of luck! Now all you have to do is convince the retailers to carry it.

Good luck. Retailers zealously guard their precious shelf space. They won't let anything onto that shelf space unless they know that it will move. And how can you prove that your product will sell? It's never been tried before!

But let's be idiotically optimistic here and assume that you find some retailers with shelf space to burn. They agree to carry your product. Success is at last within your grasp, right?

Wrong! The 13-year-olds who patronize the games store aren't interested in your adult game. "Bor-ring!" they'll exclaim, and walk away. And what about those 36-year-old housewives for whom the game is designed? Well, they certainly won't be going into a games store. They know perfectly well that games are for kids. Why should they go into a store like that?

Of course, the Internet changes things; with the Internet, you cut out those obstructionist distributors and retailers. But you still have to find a way to reach those 36-year-old housewives, and you still have to find a publisher, and each of these is a killer problem all by itself.

Thus, the games industry is trapped in a hole of its own making. Like comic books, even the most brilliant of unconventional works will not be sufficient to batter down the walls of expectations placed on us by the market. So perhaps reading this book is a complete waste of time. But I have never been one to shrink from hopeless quests, and I hope that you are similarly inclined. Recruit a Sancho Panza; the more Don Quixotes there are attacking this windmill, the better the chance we have of killing it.

interactivity

Every language has its own special words, words that express an idea better than any other word in any other language. There really isn't any other word in the world that quite expresses the idea of the English word "fun." There are plenty of words for "humorous" or "enjoyable" or "playful," but nothing that quite catches the combination of informality, enjoyment, and near-vulgarity that our word "fun" connotes. We have shamelessly stolen such words from other languages. "Taboo," for example, is stolen from a Polynesian word; can you think of any other word that really captures the idea of that word? There are gobs of words we have stolen from European languages: entrepreneur, manana, schadenfreude, presto. But there's one word, a German word, that we haven't yet stolen that should be high on our list of targets: schwerpunkt. It means "focal point" or "concentration of effort point" or "central point of attack." It's a beautiful word because it expresses an idea that we just don't have in English: the notion that, in any effort, you have many necessary tasks, but there is one central task that must take first place in your considerations.

Consider, for example, what an army does. An army fights, right? And who does the fighting? Soldiers, right? But wait a minute: The soldier can't fight unless there's a cook who keeps him fed. No cook, no fighting. Ergo, cooks are just as necessary as soldiers. We therefore deduce that the cook is just as important as the soldier, because he's just as necessary. Same thing goes for truck drivers who bring the ammunition to the front, and the clerks who keep track of the food and ammunition, and the guys who dig the latrines, and so on. All of these people are necessary, and so they are just as important as the soldier. But if you are the soldier, the guy who has to charge through fire and death to face the enemy, would you agree that these other people are every bit as worthy as you are? They may be necessary, and they may be important, but they're not central to the task. The soldier is the whole point and purpose of the effort. He's the schwerpunkt. And the soldier's fundamental task is to fight. So the schwerpunkt object in an army is the soldier and the schwerpunkt action is fighting.

Or consider a computer system. What goes into a working computer system? Well, there's a power supply—you can't have a working computer without a power supply. There's also a plastic box, a motherboard, lots of solder, plenty of wires and cables—all these things are absolutely necessary to a working computer, and I suppose you could argue that they are therefore important. But they're really not the heart of the computer. If you want to get down to the absolute core, it's got to be the CPU. That's the real essence of any computer. When you describe your new computer to someone, do you say, "It's a beige tower system with a 200-watt power supply and an 8 inch by 10 inch motherboard?" No, the very first thing you specify is the CPU and its clock speed: It's a 900MHz G4. That's the real schwerpunkt of the computer: its CPU. And what does a CPU do? It *processes*; after all, it is the Central *Processing* Unit. Thus, the schwerpunkt object in a computer is the CPU and the schwerpunkt action in a computer is processing.

So let us now determine the schwerpunkt of games. What is it that is absolutely central to games, the one element that is more than important, more than necessary, but indeed the entire point and purpose of games? The answer we immediately pounce upon is "play"; after all, what else do you do with a game than play it? Unfortunately, although that answer is certainly correct, it's not very useful; like the infamous term *fun factor*, we can never really pin down what elements of game design are useful to support good play. Can we snuffle about and develop a more useful answer?

History

At this point, let's consider an important historical observation: Computers gave gaming a big boost. Sure, there were plenty of games before computers came along, but with the advent of computers, games suddenly seized a much larger portion of our consciousness. Before computers, gaming was a petty industry, employing a few thousand people at most. In the twenty years since personal computers burst upon the scene, gaming has suddenly exploded into a major industry, rivaling Hollywood in sales and employees. Something about computers made a big, big difference in games. What was that magic element?

If you answered "video," you get twenty lashes with a wet noodle. Video entertainment has been around since 1910! And the same thing goes for sound, music, or even text; all those media have been around for long before the computer made its appearance.

The magic element that computers brought to the party was their processing power, their ability to crunch numbers. That processing power made games so much more compelling. But processing power is an internal trait of computers—the user never directly experiences processing power. Instead, the user experiences processing power through the interactivity that the computer offers.

Consider the most common use of personal computers: word processing. What is it about word processing that is so damned useful? It's not the ability to print out text that's clean and neat—we've had typewriters that could do that for nearly a century before word processing became available. Moreover, word processing made typewriters obsolete in a matter of a few years. Clearly, the ability to get clean, mechanically generated text is not the primary appeal of word processing.

The real power of word processing lies in its interactivity. You type something on your screen, and if you make a mistake, it takes only a second to hit the Delete key and correct the typo. If you misspell a word, your spell checker will flag the error for you and you can fix it. If you don't like the way a sentence reads, you can rewrite it. If you don't like the order of paragraphs, you can rearrange them with a simple cut and paste. It's the interactivity between user and computer that makes word processing so powerful. Take the interactivity out of a word processor, and all you've got left is a typewriter. Take the interactivity out of a spreadsheet, and all you've got left is a calculator.

Just as the schwerpunkt of computers is processing, so too the schwerpunkt of all software is interactivity—and this goes double for games. The turbo-charged interactivity that computers brought to gaming transformed the medium from wimp to superhero. Graphics, animation, sound, and music are all necessary to gaming, and they're all important, but they're not the schwerpunkt. Interactivity (sometimes called "gameplay") is the real schwerpunkt of games.

Other Attributes of the Computer

There exists within the game design community a school of thought that holds interactivity to be nothing more than a useful component in the design of entertainment software. According to this school, the computer is a wondrous tool offering a variety of capabilities, such as graphics, animation, music, and sound. Interactivity is seen as just another capability to be used or neglected according to the tastes and intentions of the designer.

The one thing that computers can unquestionably do better than anything else is interactivity. And they do it much, *much* better than any other medium. They internalize the rules, carry out calculations, permit immensely more complicated behaviors, and present the results far better than any other medium. Many years ago, before computers were available, somebody published a board air combat game. That's right, a flight sim done on paper. The game was technically successful in that it did, after all, present air combat in a functional manner. But it was a failure in terms of gameplay; it didn't feel at all like flying an airplane.

Let me present the argument in the language of business. Interactivity is the "basis of competitive advantage" of the computer. Sure, the computer can do a lot of things, but the one thing that it does better than any of the competing media is interactivity. And the wise businessman always throws his resources behind his basis of competitive advantage.

Interactivity is the essence of what you are selling.

You aren't convinced? Okay, how about a military maxim: "Fight on the ground of your own choosing." The wise general offers battle only on the terrain best suited to the strengths of his forces and takes maximum advantage of the weaknesses of his opponent. If his biggest advantage is in cavalry, he will choose to fight on flat open ground where the cavalry can do its job best. Sure, he'll fight with his infantry and artillery, too, but the tactical primacy will go to the cavalry.

So too it must be with interactivity. Yes, the computer can do graphics and animation and sound, but these capabilities are not the primary strength of the computer. Interactivity is the real strength of the computer, and it must be given primacy in our designs.

None of this suggests that graphics, animation, and sound should be eliminated from our designs. These are necessary supporting elements in the overall design. The better we are able to marshal them to heighten interactivity, the more successful our designs will be. But necessity does not convey equality. The ability to use a keyboard is absolutely necessary to a programmer, but typing skill is nowhere near as important to good programming as clear thinking.

So What Is Interactivity?

I have written an entire book on the subject of interactivity (*The Art of Interactive Design*, No Starch Press, 2002), and I suggest that you consult that book for more material on interactivity. However, I will present here a quickie synopsis of the core concepts.

There is one common experience we all share that is truly, fundamentally, interactive: a conversation. If you take some time to consider carefully the nature of conversations, you'll come to a clearer understanding of interactivity. A conversation, in its simplest form, starts out with two people. I'll call them Joe and Fred. The conversation begins when Joe expresses something to Fred. At this point, the ball is in Fred's corner. He performs three steps in order to hold up his end of the conversation:

1. Fred listens to what Joe has to say. He expends the energy to pay attention to Joe's words. He gathers in all of Joe's words and assembles them into a coherent whole.

2. Fred thinks about what Joe said. He considers, contemplates, and cogitates. The wheels turn as Fred develops his response to Joe's statement.

3. Fred expresses his response back to Joe. He formulates the words and speaks them.

Now the tables are turned; the ball is in Joe's court. Joe must listen to what Fred says; Joe must think about it and develop a reaction; then Joe must express his reaction back to Fred. This process goes back and forth until the participants terminate it. Thus, a conversation is a cyclic process in which each participant in turn listens, thinks, and speaks.

We can generalize the example of the conversation to get a definition of interactivity:

> A cyclic process in which two active agents alternately (and metaphorically) listen, think, and speak.

Of course, the task of the game designer is to automate interactivity, to replace one of the participants in the conversation with a machine. We can therefore rephrase the problem of designing interactive entertainment as follows: "How can we program the computer to be an entertaining conversational (metaphorically speaking) partner?"

The overall answer is simple: In order to be a good conversational partner, the computer must perform all three steps in the conversational sequence—and it must perform them all well. It must listen well, giving the player the opportunity to say anything relevant to the situation. It must think well, coming up with interesting and relevant reactions to the player's input. And finally, it must speak well, expressing its reaction clearly. It's not good enough for the computer to perform one or two of the steps well, as compensation for performing a third step poorly. All three steps must be performed well in order for the computer to achieve entertaining interaction.

To substantiate this, I need only refer you to your own experience with conversations. How many times have you had a conversation with somebody who could not perform one of the three steps well? For example, have you ever had a conversation in which the other party did not listen to what you were saying? Perhaps this person could think very well, and was quite articulate in expressing his reactions, but if he didn't listen to what you were saying, was the conversation not a waste of time? And how many times have you had a conversation with a person who listened well, but just couldn't think well—in other words, a dummy? Don't you find conversations with dolts to be a waste of your time? Or how about the conversations with people who just can't express themselves? They stammer and struggle to articulate their ideas, but they do such a poor job of it that the entire conversation isn't worth the effort.

Thus, in order to have a good conversation, both parties must be able to perform all three steps well. This rule can be generalized to all forms of interaction. Thus, if the computer is going to engage in something like a conversation, then it must perform all three steps. It must listen to the user, think about what he has said, develop an interesting and entertaining reaction to the user's input, and then it must express that reaction back to the user. And it must perform all three steps well.

Is More Interactivity Better?

Now I turn to a more difficult question: If interactivity is accorded primacy in entertainment software design, then is not more interactivity better than less interactivity? Put more baldly, is a more interactive product better than a less interactive product? I think so.

My first argument in favor of greater interactivity relies on the primacy of interactivity. Since interactivity is the basis of competitive advantage of the computer, it is only fit and proper that we should emphasize it. The more we emphasize interactivity in our designs, the more fully we utilize the true strength of the computer as an artistic medium.

Consider the cinema by way of example. Very roughly speaking, and all other factors being equal, the more cinematic a movie is, the better the movie. We can argue long and hard over the precise definition of "cinematic," but surely we can agree that it involves the special capabilities of the camera to capture motion, to pan, zoom, and move, to cut between scenes, and so forth. Surely a movie that fails to use these techniques will be inferior to a movie that does, other factors being equal. Thus, we can say that a more cinematic movie is superior to a less cinematic movie. Of course, there are many exceptions to the general rule: a poorly executed more cinematic movie is not superior, and a movie whose artistic intent requires a less cinematic style could still be a superior work. There are other exceptions as well, but I think that the general rule holds true.

An additional argument arises from the fact that the interactive arts are still in their infancy. We have just scratched the surface of this medium; we do not fully understand interactivity. Our ignorance is reflected in the body of work we have created. In the vast universe of potential computer games, the set of actual games that we have created lies crowded down in a small corner, huddled together in common low interactivity. Taking all of our computer games and entertainments as a group, the amount of interactivity that we offer is a faint and clumsy whisper of what should be possible.

Perhaps a mathematical approach might better illuminate my point. Imagine a scale of interactivity, running from 0 to 100 units of interactivity, with 100 representing interactivity so intense that it lies beyond human comprehension. Imagine all the games in the universe placed on this scale. Now, in an ideal world, these games would yield a bell curve, with a few high-interactivity games, a few low-interactivity games, and a great many games in the middle of the bell curve. But we have not attained this ideal bell curve. Our ignorance denies us the middle and upper portions of the bell curve, constraining us to the lower end of the curve. All of our work lies crowded down there.

This is my second reason why more interactivity is better than less interactivity. We need to move up that bell curve, to explore areas of interactivity that previously have been inaccessible. The low end of the scale is already heavily populated with designs; the middle and upper reaches of the scale are empty. This is why I hold a more interactive game in higher esteem than a less interactive one. This is why I honor a designer who goes where no designer has gone before more than one who hews to more familiar territory.

Of course, when we have populated the bell curve more fully, the day will come when some genius creates a game that is too interactive. But that day is far distant.

How Do We Measure Interactivity?

What, precisely, do we mean when we talk about "high" interactivity and "low" interactivity? Is an intense, fast-paced action game more interactive than a complex, slow-moving strategy game? I don't think so. We need merely hearken back to my standard example of interactivity: a conversation. What makes a conversation more or less interactive? Certainly it's not the speed with which the interlocutors speak. To achieve high conversational interactivity, each person must perform high-quality listening, high-quality thinking, and high-quality speaking. For an intense conversation, you must *really* listen to the other person, really hear what they're saying. You must think carefully about what they said, gauging their true meaning. And finally, you must choose your words carefully to state your thoughts with perfect clarity. When all these goals are met smoothly, the conversation is intense.

Thus, a highly interactive game would listen very well to its player, think well about the player's inputs, and produce clear, expressive outputs. We have done a good job with the third step in this process, but what about the first two? Do you really believe that players can say everything that they might want to say during a game? Does the input structure permit them to make the full range of reasonable moves? And does the thinking structure of the game permit the computer to challenge the player as an equal?

So there is our way of measuring interactivity. You can estimate the interactivity level of any game by asking three questions:

- How much of what the player might desire to say does the game permit the player to actually say?
- How well does the game think about the player's inputs?
- How well does the game express its reactions?

Let's apply this metric to some games. We'll start with the generic fast-paced action game. This game permits the player to say only a limited range of words: move up, down, left, right, and so forth. It does permit the player to say them quickly. It's processing of the player's input is rather simplistic: All it does is move the player around on a map. Its expressiveness is quite complete, within the limited purview of the game. We can conclude that such a game supports a small amount of interaction at a very fast pace; the end result is certainly highly interactive, but the bulk of its interactivity is derived from its speed rather than the brilliance of its design.

So let's jump to the other end of the scale with a ponderous strategy game like **Civilization**. The pace is much slower, but the player has a much wider range of things to say, and the game executes a much more complex set of algorithms. In other words, the listening and thinking are much deeper in this game. Of course, the expressiveness of the game is certainly up to snuff. We conclude that **Civilization** is also a highly interactive game, even though it operates at a slower pace. The slow pace of the game is compensated for by the richer listening and thinking.

Thus, you can achieve a high interactivity game in a variety of ways. A fast pace can certainly help, although it is no guarantee of high interactivity. The important thing is to keep the players active. They can either do a few things rapidly or a great many things slowly—but they must be mentally active at every step.

Low-Interactivity Entertainment Designs

Let me now turn to low-interactivity products. They have a dismal history. Low-interactivity entertainment is not a new idea. In the first big boom of computer games, from 1981 to 1984, a number of low-interactivity games were attempted. One of these was **Alien Gardens**, published by Epyx. You were a kind of alien bee flitting through a garden of alien flowers, trying to pollenize them. It was a very low-key game, definitely low in the interactivity department. All you could do was buzz around and, every now and then, try to touch a flower, which might kill you or reward you. Unfortunately, the difference between flowers was arbitrary. The game made no sense and ranks as one of the great turkeys of computer game history.

1985 saw another low-interactivity product: **Little Computer People**, from Activision. This odd product created a small family on your screen, moving around their dollhouse in the course of their daily activities. You the player watched them. The product attracted much attention from the press, but it was not, I believe, much of a commercial success, largely because the player didn't do very much. Much later, Will Wright came up with a much better implementation of the concept with **The Sims**. **The Sims** offered the player more interactivity than **Little Computer People**, and was accordingly a great success.

Epyx roared back in 1988 with more low-interactivity products: its line of VCR games, released with much hype and excitement. Realizing the clumsiness inherent in the serial format of a videotape, the designers rightly limited interaction to the bare minimum, focusing most of their attention on providing interesting footage for the player, who would occasionally fast forward or rewind. Here was the ultimate couch potato game. You didn't need a computer to play it and you didn't have to do much work. All you did was sit back and watch the tape and occasionally push a button on your remote control. Sounds great, right? It sounded great to a number of publishers, who frantically put together their own VCR products. Yet, despite some expensive marketing campaigns, VCR games bombed. They were a total disaster. Mindscape shipped one product and cancelled the second one, even though it was ready to ship, because the first game had failed so completely.

Another experiment in this direction was the CinemaWare line of games. These games were strong on spectacle and weak on interaction. The marketing thrust of the CinemaWare line was that these games were just like movies, except that you could play with them. Most of the design effort was put into making lots of pretty pictures and animated sequences. The gameplay itself was weak. The first line in the series, **Defender of the Crown**, by Kellyn Beeck, created quite a sensation and sold very well. But after that, it seemed to be all downhill. CinemaWare went bust a few years later.

Another good example is the experience of Cyan, a game developer. Cyan's first game, **The Manhole**, was a low-interactivity adventure game for children. It sold enough copies to keep Cyan alive, but little more. Then they came up with **Cosmic Osmo**, sporting the same low interactivity but better cosmetics. Again, they made enough money to stay alive, but not much more. The big hit came with **Myst**, another adventure game. This time, however, the interactivity was more involved and the cosmetics were sensational. **Myst** sold like hotcakes, Cyan got filthy rich, and all seemed bright. Then they released a sequel to **Myst**, entitled **Riven**. It sold moderately well. A third game in the series, **Exile**, also did reasonably well, but again did not approach **Myst** in sales. Cyan continued in business by developing and licensing the **Myst** brand.

The same pattern shows up over and over. Laserdisc games made a huge sensation, but then faded away almost as quickly as they burst upon the scene. They were low-interactivity games. **The 7ᵗʰ Guest,** by Rob Landeros and Graeme Devine, was a huge hit in the early 1990s, sporting low-interactivity puzzles mated with glorious animations. Their sequel, **The 11ᵗʰ Hour**, sold reasonably well, but not sensationally well. And there were no further games in that series. Cliff Johnson made a minor splash with a brilliant collection of puzzles, followed it up with a sequel that didn't sell well, and then disappeared.

Low-interactivity games sound like a great idea, such a great idea that people keep going back and doing them over and over. And, in pure Darwinian fashion, the companies that have cast their lot with low-interactivity games have suffered extinction. Epyx, CinemaWare, and

Mindscape were all reduced to ashes; only Cyan broke the curse. But the survivors seem unable to learn from their competitors' failures; low-interactivity games keep popping up like some time-hopping Sisyphusian dodo bird bent on repeating its extinction in as many eras as possible.

Why have low-interactivity games been such a dismal failure? One would think that there should be some small fragment of a market for them. Why is the historical experience so decisively negative in defiance of common sense?

There are two answers, I think. The first is that the available hardware is not up to the task. We have not yet hit the right combination of ingredients to build good low-interactivity games. The VCR gives lots of imagery, but its access times are so slow that even low-interactivity games suffer. The computer itself simply cannot generate or maintain images of enough variety and quality to entertain the player by themselves. The DVD should solve both problems. It offers faster access times than videotape, yet much greater image capacity than the computer. Whether the combination will be fast enough and visually rich enough to overcome the inherent weakness of low interactivity, I cannot say.

The second answer is more pessimistic. I have long maintained that interactivity is the essence of the gaming experience, and that the quality of the interaction determines the quality of the game. If this be true, then the very notion of low-interactivity games is intrinsically wrong-headed, and such products will inevitably fail.

An Interesting Exception

There is a small group of low-interactivity games that have been somewhat successful. These are the games produced by Cyan (**Manhole** and **Cosmic Osmo**) and Amanda Goodenough (**Inigo Gets Out**, **Your Faithful Camel**, et al), and a number of products from Broderbund. They are low-interactivity games, really more like vaguely linear stories with some buttons to press. They have been moderately successful. What is striking is that all of these products are designed for young children. It appears that our industry's Darwinian methods have at last found a suitable habitat for this otherwise less-than-fittest species of game.

Why is it that low-interactivity products are successful with young children when they don't seem to work with older players? I think that the answer can be found by asking another: Why don't high-interactivity products work with young children? Try foisting **SimCity**, **Robotron**, or **Half-Life** on a five-year-old, if you're willing to risk accusations of child abuse. The poor kid will be overwhelmed by such games. He just doesn't have the perspicacity to handle such a game. What's left for him but the low-interactivity games?

Workload Versus Payoff

Some thinkers have observed that many of the highly interactive games impose a large workload on the player. To master a fast-paced action game, you've got to practice, practice, practice. To make sense of a big strategy game like **Civilization**, you've got to study a heavy manual. Lower interactivity games, they note, impose less work on the player. Taking full advantage of this property of low-interactivity games should yield viable products—or so they argue.

To evaluate this line of reasoning, I suggest that we start with high-interactivity games and then move toward lower interactivity. What do we gain and lose as we move in this direction? As we lose interactivity, we reduce the total quantity of decision-making that the player must perform. This reduces his workload. It also reduces his ability to creatively influence the outcome of the game. In other words, as we reduce the interactivity of the game (its gameplay), the player's degree of participation in the outcome is diminished and he therefore becomes less involved in the outcome, which becomes more predetermined.

But there's a catch: The player's workload is not proportional to the quantity of decision-making. Decision-making consists of two parts: a laborious process of learning the basic parameters for making the decision, and a faster process of applying those parameters. The player must go through the first process whether he makes one decision or a hundred. Thus, his workload is equal to a fixed quantity (learning the rules) plus a variable quantity (playing the game).

An example might help here. Suppose I present you with two games. The first is a truly minimal-interactivity game. You will be asked to make one decision during the entire game. It is a murder mystery game, the climax of which places you in a room with the six main suspects and a gun. You must decide whom to shoot. That's exactly one decision—about as little interactivity as you can get. Yet you will likely ask a great many questions before making your decision. Can I shoot more than once? Can somebody else shoot me? May I choose not to shoot anybody? (True gamesters will note that the problems are trivially solved by playing the game several times, experimenting with each of these options in turn. While entirely possible, this flies in the face of the stated intent of the low-interactivity game.) Note that these questions are really questions about the rules of the game. You will have a considerable workload just learning the context for your single decision, and inasmuch as the outcome of the game rides on your single decision, you had damn well better learn the rules thoroughly.

The second game is a more conventional game with many decisions. Once again you will have the workload of learning the rules of the game, and in addition to that you will have the workload of making all those decisions. Yet the workload of learning the rules is most likely the more substantial of the two. In other words, if you end up making a hundred decisions during the course of this game, your total workload will not be 100 times greater than your workload with the minimal-interactivity game. It might not even be twice as great.

Thus, as we move from the higher-interactivity game to the minimal-interactivity game, two factors are reduced: the player's workload and his ability to influence the outcome of the game. But—and this is the key point—the latter falls faster than the former. Reducing interactivity gains us only small benefits in terms of reducing workload but costs us heavily in terms of the player's ability to creatively influence the outcome of the game.

This, I think, is the real reason why low-interactivity games have been such failures. Diminishing the interactivity just makes the game less fun faster than it makes the game easier. What we gain in terms of reduced workload we more than make up for in terms of diminished fun.

Weird Ideas

Lastly, there are the blue-sky concepts for low-interactivity games. Most of these center on some form of storytelling. In one approach, the computer tells the player a story, with the player somehow providing cues that the computer uses to adjust the story to suit the player's interests. For example, if the computer mentions an encounter with a beautiful girl, and the player so indicates, the computer could proceed to describe a sexual liaison. If the player is female, it might tell of a friendship developing between the two.

The problem with this lies in the nature of the cues provided by the players. Exactly how do the players communicate their desires to the computer? If we use a series of predetermined branchpoints (a *branchpoint* is a point reached during the play of a game, at which the player must make a decision that will take him down one of several paths), the game has reverted to a conventional adventure game, and the players still must learn the language of expression for the adventure. Proponents of such schemes often fall back on deliberately vague formulations. The computer will "sense" the player's mood, they claim. I find it difficult to imagine just how this sensing will take place, and how the computer will interpret whatever it senses.

A variation on this scheme makes reference to the manner in which performing artists sense the mood of their audiences and adjust their performance accordingly. This, it is asserted, constitutes an advanced form of low interactivity that could be harnessed for new types of games. The problem lies in the input and processing required to accomplish this. The performing artist is analyzing fine shades of voice intonation and subtle nuance of facial expressions. This type of processing is way beyond anything we can process on a personal computer, even assuming that we could equip our games with microphones and television cameras to provide the input.

There is a second and more powerful argument against such schemes. Even if we could implement them, they would still be inappropriate. The performing artist who makes adjustments in response to the audience's feedback does so on a very gross average of the audience feedback. Some people will be screaming "Faster!" as others are yelling "Slower!" The artist can't do both, and so responds to the majority. What's more important is the fact that the audience understands this. We can't all have our way, so we accept the situation. But when I am the only user of a computer game, I am completely justified in expecting that I can have my way. I expect the computer to respond to my wishes. If the computer fails to understand my wishes or is incapable of executing my desires, I will be dissatisfied. So if I grunt or laugh or scowl or drum my fingers and the computer fails to get my message, the product will have failed.

Conclusions on Low-Interactivity Designs

The concept of low-interactivity entertainment is a ghost that we will never exorcise from this industry. The concept just keeps popping up like an annual flu bug. Some naïve fool will come forward with "this great new idea that nobody has ever thought of before." As I discussed, the concept seems sound on first examination, so people will probably give it credence. Who knows, some credulous publisher might be persuaded to part with development dollars to explore the idea.

Process Intensity Versus Data Intensity

Closely tied to the concept of interactivity is a concept that I describe with the phrase *process intensity versus data intensity*. *Process intensity* is the degree to which a program emphasizes processes instead of data. All programs use a mix of process and data. Process is reflected in algorithms, equations, and branches. Data is reflected in data tables, images, sounds, and text. A process-intensive program spends most of its time crunching numbers; a data-intensive program spends most of its time moving bytes around.

The difference between data and process constitutes a central construct around which the universe is built, and it shows up in every field of human intellectual inquiry. In language, it shows up as nouns and verbs. In economics, it's goods and services. In physics, it's particles and waves. In military science, it's assets and operations. And in computer science, it's bits and cycles. Process is abstract where data is tangible. Data is direct, where process is indirect. The difference between data and process is the difference between numbers and equations, between facts and principles, between events and forces, between knowledge and ideas.

Processing data is the very essence of what a computer does. There are many technologies that can store data: magnetic tape, punched cards, punched tape, paper and ink, microfilm, microfiche, and optical disk, to name just a few. But there is only one technology that can process data: the computer. This is its single source of superiority over the other technologies. Using the computer in a data-intensive mode wastes its greatest strength.

Because process intensity is so close to the essence of "computeriness," it provides us with a useful criterion for evaluating the value of any piece of software. That criterion is a vague quantification of the desirability of process intensity. It uses the ratio of operations per datum, which I call the *crunch per bit ratio*. I intend here that an operation is any process applied to a datum, such as an arithmetic operation, logical operation, or a simple Boolean inclusion or exclusion. A datum in this scheme can be a bit, a byte, a character, or a floating-point number—it is a small piece of information.

The "process intensity principle" is grand in implications and global in sweep. Like any such all-encompassing notion, it is subject to a variety of minor-league objections and compromising truths.

Objection 1: Substitutability

Experienced programmers know that data can often be substituted for process. Many algorithms can be replaced by tables of data. This is a common trick for expending RAM to speed up processing. Because of this, many programmers see process and data as interchangeable. This misconception arises from applying low-level considerations to the higher levels of software design. Sure, you can cook up a table of sine values with little trouble—but can you imagine a table specifying every possible behavioral result in a complex game such as **Balance of Power**?

Objection 2: Greater Data Capacity

A more serious challenge comes from the evolution of personal computing technology. In twenty years, we have moved from an 8-bit 6502 running at 1MHz to 64-bit CPUs running at 1GHz. This represents about a 10,000-fold increase in processing power. At the same time, though, RAM sizes have increased from a typical 4 kilobytes of RAM to perhaps 256 megabytes of RAM—a 64,000-fold increase. Mass storage has increased from cassettes holding, say, 4 kilobytes, to hard disks holding 20 gigabytes—a 5,000,000-fold increase. Thus, data storage capacity is increasing faster than processing capacity. Under these circumstances, we would be foolish *not* to shift some of our emphasis to data intensity. But this consideration, while perfectly valid, is secondary in nature; it is a matter of adjustment rather than fundamental stance.

Objection 3: "Balance"

Then there is the argument that process and data are both necessary to good computing. Proponents of this school note that an algorithm without data to crunch is useless; they therefore claim that a good program establishes a balance between process and data. While the argument is fundamentally sound, it does not suggest anything about the proper mix between process and data. It merely establishes that some small amount of data is necessary. It does not in any way suggest that data deserves emphasis equal to that accorded to process.

The importance of process intensity does not mean that data has no intrinsic value. Data endows a game with useful color and texture. An excessively process-intensive game will be so devoid of data that it will take on an almost mathematical feel. Consider, for example, this sequence of games: **checkers–chess–Diplomacy–Balance of Power**. As we move along this sequence, the amount of data about the world integrated into the game increases. **Checkers** is very pure, very clean; **chess** adds a little more data in the different capabilities of the pieces. **Diplomacy** brings in more data about the nature of military power and the geographical relationships in Europe. **Balance of Power** throws in a mountain of data about the world. Even though the absolute amount of data increases, the crunch per bit ratio remains high (perhaps it even increases) across this sequence. My point here is that data is not intrinsically evil; the amount of data can be increased if the amount of process is concomitantly raised.

A Hidden Reason: Difficulty of Abstraction

The most powerful resistance to process intensity, though, is unstated. It is a mental laziness that afflicts all of us. Process intensity is so very hard to implement. Data intensity is easy to put into a program. Just get that artwork into a file and read it onto the screen; store that sound

12

LESSON

Eschew
data-
intensive
designs;
aspire to
process-
intensity.

effect on the disk and pump it out to the speaker. There's instant gratification in these data-intensive approaches. It looks and sounds great immediately. Process intensity requires all those hours mucking around with equations. Because it's so indirect, you're never certain how it will behave. The results always look so primitive next to the data-intensive stuff. So we follow the path of least resistance right down to data intensity.

Process intensity is a powerful theoretical concept for designing all kinds of software, not just games. It is highly theoretical, and so it is difficult to understand and implement, and there are numerous exceptions and compromising considerations that arise when applying the notion. Nevertheless, it remains a useful theoretical tool in game design.

creativity: the missing ingredient

During the 1990s, the games industry managed to stomp out much of the effervescent creativity its designers had demonstrated during the 1980s. Nowadays, game design itself is a coldly mechanical process requiring little in the way of creativity. This is not to say that game designers aren't creative people; on the contrary, the best game designers are some of the most creative people I know. The problem is that in the long grind from inspiration to product, the most creative aspects of the design are ground away until the final result is little more than yesterday's big hit with a few minor embellishments.

How Serious Is the Problem?

Opinions vary on the seriousness of this problem. Two wholly subjective matters control the debate: How creative is the industry, and how creative should it be? The industry's own terminology demonstrates its dearth of creativity: We all know that a "first-person shooter" requires the player to blast bad guys as he navigates a complex 3D environment, collects weapons and ammunition, and solves puzzles. In the same fashion, we have other tightly defined genres: side scrollers, adventures, role-playing games, wargames, simulators, and so on. There are also some standard variations on these games: The addition of an external story makes a "story side scroller" or a "story puzzle game." There are also

crosses between genres, yielding role-playing wargames, strategy shooters, and so on. These techniques have been with us for years. Back in
1983, my game **Excalibur** was an unconventional strategy game with a
real-time wargame built into it.

Oddly, the terminology has shown more variability than the actual content itself. "Hand-eye coordination" games became "skill and action"
games, which later were termed "twitch" games. Through all these
changes in aliases, the gameplay has remained unchanged: Such
games require fast reactions from the player.

Younger readers may have difficulty appreciating just how little things
have changed over the decades; the latest crop of games always seems
so new and fresh. Let me frog-march you on a walk down memory lane
as we fondly recall a single genre of game: the side scroller. It all started
in 1981 with an arcade game called **Space Panic**. The player, pursued
by nasty little space aliens, ran up and down ladders, digging holes in
the floor into which the aliens fell. This was quickly followed by **Apple
Panic**, which was a straightforward copy of the original, and **Donkey
Kong**, which added sloping platforms, the ability to jump over the
oncoming barrels, and some other ways to die. The success of **Donkey
Kong** led to a sequel featuring the hero, Mario. There then followed a
whole series of "Mario" games. Throughout it all, the basic gameplay
remained unchanged. There were, of course, plenty of embellishments on
the basic concept: more dangers to overcome, more complex challenges,
and more levels. The biggest improvement came with the addition of
side scrolling, extending the playfield over a much larger area. As I write
this in 2003, Mario is still in business, still making money, and his
games are still recognizable as a direct descendent of the original
Space Panic game of 20 years ago.

Or consider the venerable old role-playing game. It all started with the
paper game **Dungeons & Dragons** in the mid-1970s. A computer version called **Moria** quickly appeared on the networked educational computer system Plato; a few years later, a direct copy of **Moria** appeared

for Apple II under the title **Wizardry**. At about the same time, a slightly different version of **Dungeons & Dragons** appeared for the Apple II with the title **Ultima**. Both **Wizardry** and **Ultima** were big successes. The marketing people for **Ultima**, undiscouraged by trivial semantic considerations, followed up the game with **Ultima II**, **III**, **IV**, and so on; I don't know what the final count of "ultimate" games will be. Throughout this endless parade of games, there were few substantial changes in the design; for the most part, each game added a few new complications and substantial cosmetic improvements. There were plenty of competitors, too, but they all slavishly toed the basic **D&D** line: Build the strength of your character; accumulate wealth, weapons, armor, spells, and other goodies; kill flocks of mindless monsters; wander varied terrains; etc., etc., etc.

The more insecure members of the games industry defend themselves by pointing to the movies. After all, they argue, Hollywood has its own time-worn genres, too. Why blame the games biz for a problem that besets all entertainment?

Hollywood's use of the term "genre," however, is considerably more elastic. Sure, we have "action," "drama," "horror," "sci-fi," "comedy," and "family," but within these broad categories lies far more diversity than anything in the games biz. Is *Men In Black* a sci-fi movie or a comedy? Does *M.A.S.H.* fall into the war category, the drama category, or the comedy category? And into what categories do we place such works as *Koyaanisqatsi*?

How did the games industry get itself into this pickle? Some industry observers claim that this is the sad but inevitable result of the maturation of the games industry. When we were younger, and budgets were smaller, publishers could afford to take a big chance on a product. Nowadays, however, with budgets running into the millions of dollars, a producer cannot take a big chance on an unconventional design. Look at Hollywood, they say; Hollywood grinds out an endless stream of me-too movies because that's the only way to make money.

To which I say: balderdash and folderol! The games industry is wise to look to Hollywood for guidance in the difficult task of managing an industry; we just haven't paid attention to how Hollywood really works. The first lesson we can learn is to have some guts. Hollywood producers have long known that sometimes you just have to take a chance. And when they do take a chance, they don't stint; where the games industry blanches at the thought of risking $3 million on a game, Hollywood girds its loins and spends $100 million. And it's not as if the risks they take are safe bets—look at *Heaven's Gate* or *Waterworld*, two big-budget flops. These guys know how to play for high stakes. These games guys just can't match the nerves of steel common in their Hollywood counterparts.

Some people will claim that Hollywood bets on talent, not scripts, and a big star can make any movie a success. Therefore, the story goes, Hollywood isn't really that gutsy; they just place their bets using a different logic. But superstars don't guarantee success: *Waterworld* and *Heaven's Gate* boasted two of the biggest stars of their day. The backers of these movies knew perfectly well the risks that they were taking. Moreover, the games industry still hasn't learned to bet on talent: Will Wright's **The Sims** had a difficult time making it through Electronic Arts; even though it was the work of a man who is arguably the best game designer in the world, EA just didn't have confidence in it and was shocked when the game was such a success. So I have been told by several EA insiders.

Where Does Creativity Come From?

While I'm pontificating on the subject of creativity, I might as well explain how one goes about being creative. Some people confuse creativity with intellectual anarchy; they figure that, in the world of creative thought, one idea is just as good as another. Not so; creativity is serious business and you don't attain high levels of creativity by random daydreaming.

Our minds are associative; new ideas are generated by combining old ideas in novel ways. This combinatorial process is not a simple additive one; you don't jam two ideas together any old way to create a new idea. Instead, they go together in pattern fashion. Consider this highly schematic representation of the concepts in your head (see Figure 7.1).

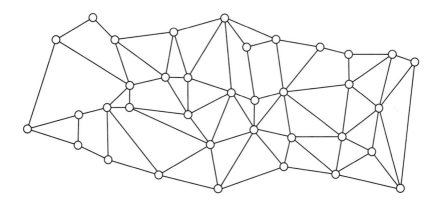

7.1 *Mental organization.*

Now, any substantial idea is really a collection of closely related concepts, like what is shown in Figure 7.2.

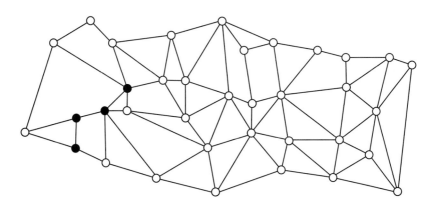

7.2 *A single extended idea.*

The trick in creativity is to notice that there's another idea in the pattern, an idea that closely resembles the first idea (see Figure 7.3).

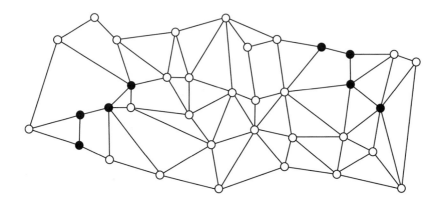

7.3 *Two analogous ideas.*

A new idea can be created by comparing the outer connections of idea #1 with the outer connections of idea #2 (see Figure 7.4).

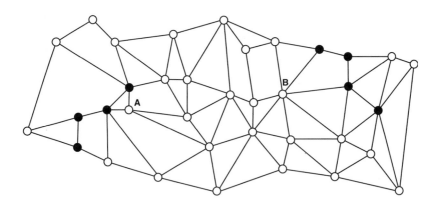

7.4 *Comparing the outer connections of the two different ideas.*

This comparison permits us to make logical connections by noting similarities. In this example, we might say, "Concept A is to the Idea #1 as Concept B is to Idea #2, so perhaps I can think about Concept B as if it were Concept A."

How to "Get Creative"

You can facilitate this process in a number of ways. The best strategy is to stuff your head full of concepts and all their associations. After all, the bigger the web of associations at your disposal, the greater the chance that you'll find some odd parallel between two ideas. Wouldn't it be great if you noticed a creatively useful connection between, say, dinosaur paleontology and Polynesian language structures? Of course, if you don't know much about dinosaur paleontology or Polynesian language structures, you'll never notice the connection, will you? You want to populate your mind with a wondrous and colorful diversity of ideas, a grand carnival of conceptual heterogeneity.

And how might you go about this task? Simple: You read. Herein lies the greatest failure of the younger game designers: They don't much believe in reading. "Hey, we're the video generation," they tell me. "We were brought up on a steady diet of video. We won't put up with all those boring books. We need some sensory stimulation." Some also claim that they can find anything they need to know on the Internet, so there's no need for books, they smugly assert.

Brace yourself: I'm putting on my "Crotchedy Old Fart" hat and I'm going to give you a lecture.

Now see here! If you think that you can learn enough about the world to design games without doing a substantial amount of reading, you're never going to amount to anything! Video is designed for the lowest-common-denominator audience—people who couldn't stumble their way through a multi-clause sentence if their lives depended on it. And the Internet contains very little of intellectual substance. The grand total of all the information that I can find on the Internet about any given topic of real intellectual interest is less that what I can get in a single good book. You try looking up Erasmus on the Internet—I guarantee you won't find anything matching what you'll get in a single good biography. Or dinosaur paleontology, or Polynesian language structures, for that

13

LESSON

Read more.

matter. Sure, maybe someday you'll find some of this stuff on the Net. But do you ever think you'll find anything like *Fiscal Accounts of Catalonia Under the Early Count-Kings (1151-1213)*, or *Conjunction, Contiguity, Contingency: On Relationships Between Events in the Egyptian and Coptic Verbal Systems*? The latter book, believe it or not, actually contributed to some of the thinking that went into writing this book. Don't kid yourself—if you want to compete with Da Big Boys, you gonna have to do some serious reading. Harrumph!

Reading is a lifelong process. I remember reading Shirer's *The Rise and Fall of the Third Reich* in sixth grade, primarily because it was the biggest book I'd ever seen in my life. And I've been at it ever since. You don't need to be as maniacal as I've been, but if your bookshelf contains little more than science fiction novels and technical manuals, you probably better reconsider your intention of becoming a game designer.

And if you think that this is just Chris Crawford's personal hobby horse, think again. Will Wright is always recommending to me these weird, strange books; I try them out and wonder what the hell is going on in his head. Sid Meier will floor you with his reading background. Dan Bunten read voraciously. Same thing goes for Brian Moriarty, Gordon Walton, Greg Costikyan, and Eric Goldberg. All the great game designers are reading addicts—and so am I. So there!

Another useful strategy is to wonder. Wonder about anything and everything. Have you figured out why the sky is blue? If not, shame on you! It's the most common wondering question anybody could ask. And for that matter, why aren't cows green? They spend their days outside in the sun eating green grass; wouldn't it make sense for them to do a little photosynthesis of their own? Why do catchy tunes, especially commercial jingles, go round and round inside our heads until we could scream? Why do young adolescent girls go bonkers at rock concerts? Why are there tiny serrations around the edges of some coins? Why do dogs bark while cats meow? All these questions have answers, and if you had wondered about them, you'd have found the answers by now.

Wonder
more.

Wondering is important because it is an exercise in tightening up the web of associations in your mind. When you eventually figure out why the sky is blue, the answer will also explain why the sunset is red—and two previously unconnected ideas will become connected in your mind. More connections make possible more comparisons, and therefore greater creativity.

Reading and wondering comprise the strategy of creative endeavor; they help build your overall creative strength. But when it comes time to tackle a particular creative challenge, you're into the world of tactics, and again I have some specific advice for you.

The first step is to translate the creative challenge into the terminology of your mind: emotion. Reason and intellectualism are not part of the fundamental architecture of the human mind. They are artifices added in the last few thousand years, part of our veneer of civilization. Scratch a modern human and you'll find a hunter-gatherer, full of fears, quick to anger, driven by lust and hunger. These are the basic driving forces of the human mind, and if you want to engage the full creative potential of that mind, you've got to express your problem in its native language of emotion. You've got to feel the problem in your heart. You've got to ache over it, agonize over it, make it hurt. You've got to perceive the problem in direct sensory terms. What does it look like? What does it smell like? If it made a sound, what would that sound be? Most important is the kinesthetic sense: What does the problem feel like in your skin?

A digression on the power of kinesthetic perception: Many times I have used a joke that Alan Kay told me to make an important point about software design. The joke goes like this:

> There was this fellow who decided he needed a new suit. So he went to a tailor and got measured for the suit. Two weeks later he showed up at the tailor's shop to try on his new suit. But when he put it on, the fit was terrible. "Look at this left sleeve!" he exclaimed. "It's way too long!" "No, no, no!" the tailor answered. "You just don't know how to wear an elegant suit. Here, all you have to do is hitch your left shoulder up high like this; see how the sleeve lines up perfectly with your wrist now?" The man tried it out, and sure enough, if he scrunched his body up and stretched the left shoulder up high, the sleeve did seem to fit well. "But what about this right leg?" he protested, "It's too short!" Again the tailor contradicted him: "You're not standing properly. If you keep the right leg straight with the knee locked, the leg looks perfect!" Again the skeptical customer tried out the tailor's suggestion, and again the correction seemed to work. Abashed, the man paid the tailor and, with hunched shoulder and locked knee, left the shop, and staggered painfully down the street. A block away, he was accosted by a passerby. "Where did you get that magnificent suit?" the stranger asked. The man lifted his contorted arm to point towards the tailor's shop. "I've got to get myself a suit from him!" the passerby exclaimed. "If he can make a suit to fit a crippled hunchback like you so well, he must be an excellent tailor!"

The moral of this story, in regards to software, is that we accommodate ourselves so willingly to poorly designed software that we start to think that the software itself is good and that we are cripples. Now, when I tell this joke to students, I embellish it by contorting myself and comedically staggering about as the hapless customer. This kinesthetic embellishment makes a deep impression on the students; later in the course I am able to instantly demolish the old "once you get used to this software, it makes perfect sense" argument by hunching myself up and staggering a few steps. Everybody laughs and the point is driven home. Once I even saw an argument at a distance, with one student hunching and staggering, and the other student making concessionary gestures. Ideas expressed kinesthetically really hit home. So *feel* the problem in your body!

It could take days, weeks, or even months to drive the problem deep into your subconscious. But once you have driven it deep enough, you'll know. You'll feel an emotional fatigue, a sense of exhausted futility. That's when it's time to stop. Take a break, perhaps even a vacation. Desist all conscious efforts at the problem and let it simmer in your subconscious. Get plenty of sleep and dreams so that it can have the time to sink its teeth into the problem. If you've done your job well, you may notice that your dreams are, in an emotionally abstract fashion, indirectly addressing the problem. As the subconscious hones in on the problem, your dreams may well become more specific about it. And one day, when your mind is distracted by some trivial task, the solution will leap out at you, whole and complete. In one blinding flash, you'll see everything and the answer will seem so simple that you'll wonder why you didn't see it before.

This is called a brainstorm, and it has been much studied and much has been learned about it. Great geniuses who have experienced brainstorms have described their experience in detail, and the common elements are widely reported. First, there's a phase of intense emotional involvement with the problem. The creator struggles mightily, but fails. Then follows a quiescent period where the creator is distracted by some extended but mindless busywork. Finally comes the brainstorm itself, and the subjects always report that the entire solution leaps upon them with suddenness.

I have used the technique with reasonable success. I can't force brainstorms to happen—sometimes I strain and strain but my mind is hopelessly constipated. But the tactic works often enough that I have made it a

permanent part of my intellectual lifestyle. If you have built up the abs
and pecs for heavy creative work, and apply this technique with the intensity it requires, odds are that you will have some creative success with it.

A Tyrannosaurus Rex for Ideas

Creative productivity is still only half the job—once you have all those
great ideas, your next task is to murder most of them. The sad truth
is that most creative ideas are bad ideas. In my career as a game
designer, I have come up with hundreds of original ideas that I ultimately abandoned. The chapters on specific games later in this book
will present only the most cogent of those ideas.

What you need is a Tyrannosaurus Rex stalking through your mind,
viciously attacking every idea you create. It should pounce instantly and
sink its teeth into the soft flesh of your idea. It should rip and tear with
bloodthirsty abandon. Most of your ideas will be torn to shreds by your
inner Tyrannosaurus. That's good—better that they be prey to your own
monster than shredded by others or, worse still, fail in the marketplace
after you've invested time, money, and reputation on them.

Thus, the ideal game designer is a prolific nursery of creative ideas,
spawning hundreds of clever new schemes, feeding these innocent new-
borns to the hungry idea-destructors. Amid all this creativity and car-
nage, a few truly great ideas will emerge.

But the balance between fecundity and predation must be perfect for
the system to work. Some people just don't generate many ideas to start
with, so they tend to cherish what few ideas they generate; it's pathetic.
When they foist their miserable little ideas on me, my inner
Tyrannosaurus jumps up and down gleefully, eager to masticate the
plump little baby ideas. In younger years, I unleashed my Tyrannosaurus
too readily, and its ferocity hurt and angered many people. Nowadays I
keep it on a short leash; if an idea is truly bad, it will probably die of
natural causes. I unleash my monster only if the baby idea actually
poses a threat of turning into something real.

Then there are the creative fonts with no inner Tyrannosaurus. They gush with ideas, a few good, most flawed. These people don't identify too closely with their intellectual children; murder one and they happily move on to the next. In general, such people can be useful and productive members of creative teams as long as they are balanced with a good Tyrannosaurus host; however, expect some tension to develop between two such people.

Get creative! Get tyrano-saurical!

The saddest group is the people whose Tyrannosaurus has taken over. Possibly because they lack self-confidence, these people never manage to get anything out of the nursery. They kill off all their ideas prematurely. Such people need to be encouraged to think out loud, to lay their ideas out even though they know the ideas to be flawed. Sometimes another member of the group can see a way around the supposedly fatal flaw, snatching the idea from the jaws of the Tyrannosaurus.

The Politics of Innovation

If your creative idea survives the attack of your Tyrannosaurus, it must face an even more terrifying monster: Executivasaurus! This is actually an entire genus of related species: Executivasaurus Marketensis, Executivasaurus Financialis, and, biggest of all, Executivasaurus Presidentens. Each has its own stalking methods, and each is a remorseless, highly efficient predator.

E. Marketensis seizes your hapless idea with one clawed hand and demands that the game be "just like last year's big hit..." then grabs it with the other and rips it apart, crying "...only different!"

E. Financialis pins your idea down to the ground under its huge foot, saying, "It must not cost more than this..." and then seizes your idea in its jaws and tears its head off, saying, "...but it must have state-of-the-art technology!"

E. Presidentens has the most insidious predatory technique. It implants its egg under the skin of its victim, then waits and watches for the egg to suck away all the life force of its unfortunate host. If the egg is successful, it takes over the body of the host; if not, E. Presidentens devours the failed host.

Shepherding a truly creative idea through an organization is much more difficult than germinating, nurturing, and developing the idea. Indeed, I consider it impossible for a creative person to push an idea through an organization; the skills required for creativity conflict with the skills required for politicking; such skills never fit inside one mind without eventually driving that mind into madness. The creative individual's best option is to team up with another person graced with the political skills to survive in the domain of Executivasaurus. The alternative is to leave the organization and start up a new company—if you can get the funding. Either way, it's a long shot. It's probably best to keep your head down and work on a sequel.

common
mistakes

Beginning game designers fall prey to a number of standard mistakes. This chapter will present and explain those mistakes, and show you how to avoid them.

Obsession with Cosmetics

This is by far the most common beginner's mistake, and even experienced designers often stumble over it. I use the term *cosmetics* to describe those elements of the game that are meant primarily to look or sound good rather than to further the gameplay itself. Another term for the same concept is *eye candy*.

There are five common motivations to equip a game with good graphics and sound:

1. To further the gameplay
2. To permit the player to show off the superior cosmetic capabilities of his new computer
3. To show off the superior technical prowess of the programmer
4. To keep up with the competition
5. To provide the player with images and sounds that are intrinsically pleasing

Reason #1: To further the gameplay by making the player's situation and options as clear as possible. This is the *only* good reason for pursuing cosmetics.

Remember, this is a game, not a movie, not a musical, not a book. Everything that you put into the game should support the gameplay. If it doesn't support the gameplay, it doesn't belong in the game.

Many game designers have difficulty understanding what is meant by "supporting the gameplay." They confuse relevance with support, and so figure that any image, animation, or sound that is relevant to the topic of the game belongs. If the game is a dungeon crawl, they figure a picture of a castle or a dragon just naturally belongs in there somewhere. This is fuzzy, sloppy thinking. In order to support the gameplay, the cosmetic feature must in some way provide the player with information that is relevant to the choices that the player must make.

An example of a useful graphic is the addition of shadows to a 3D combat game. If the player notices the shadow of an enemy just around the corner, that information is useful and will affect the player's decisions. Hence, the addition of shadows to a 3D engine is beneficial to the game design.

Many game designers erroneously believe that graphic realism necessarily enhances the entertainment experience. Figure 8.1 clears up the misconception.

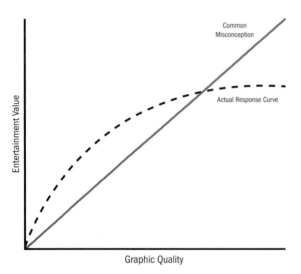

8.1 *More graphic quality isn't always better.*

The common misconception holds that more graphic quality is always better. People don't work this way! The value of almost any commodity to the consumer follows *diminishing returns*: the more you have of it, the less value each increase offers you. There are, of course, plenty of exceptions and special considerations, but in general, more is only decreasingly better.

Notice that I haven't provided any scales on the axes of this graph; our current situation could lie anywhere on this curve. For example, if current graphic capabilities fall well down to the lower left, then increasing graphic quality will still earn us huge benefits in entertainment value. On the other hand, if our situation lies closer to the upper right of the graph, then we are wasting our time pursuing increasing graphic quality. How can we calibrate our graph?

The Lessons of Cinema

We are fortunate to have a sizable database on which to calibrate our graph: the cinema. Over the last century, the movies and television have built up a mammoth database of material to which we can refer.

We can trace the progress of the cinema up the graph. For example, the talkies swept silent movies aside in a matter of two years; it's safe to say that this cosmetic improvement lay on the lower-left portion of the graph, where the benefit of cosmetic enhancements is high. On the other hand, the transition to color movies was considerably slower; the first color films appeared in 1926, and black-and-white remained viable through the 1950s. This slow transition demonstrates that color lay considerably further up the curve than sound.

The next development in cosmetic quality was the use of *special effects*, which I shall narrowly define (solely for the purposes of this argument) as any technique that generates images other than those created on a conventional set. For the most part, this refers to the use of models, bluescreening, and (much later) digitally rendered images. Such techniques were used at the very beginning of the 20th century, but the clay models and miniature spaceships used through the 1950s never attained enough verisimilitude to accomplish much. However, by 1970, these techniques were getting good enough; from *2001: A Space*

Odyssey through the *Star Wars* movies to a variety of movies in the early 1990s, such techniques matured enough to claim a solid place in the movies. The introduction of digitally rendered images in the 1990s permitted even more spectacular results, and now such techniques are well established. But it is important to remember that these techniques are still confined to a subset—a very significant subset!—of the movies. Even when we measure impact in terms of box office dollars, the entertainment value of these cosmetic triumphs remains limited. The majority of movies, and the majority of movie dollars, go to movies that do not rely on such splendiferous cosmetics. Therefore, I think that it is safe to say that the movies are now far up on the upper-right side of the curve.

A textbook experiment was played out for game designers in the summer of 2001 with the nearly simultaneous releases of two major digitally rendered movies: *Shrek* and *Final Fantasy*. These two movies pursued completely different strategies. The creators of *Shrek* concentrated their creative energies on the story; the cosmetic quality of the movie was merely adequate. *Final Fantasy*, on the other hand, perfectly exemplified the values of game designers—indeed, the movie was created and directed by the designer of a successful series of games. Cosmetic quality was the entire point and purpose of the movie; the story seemed almost an afterthought. The people voted with their dollars and the electoral result was a landslide for *Shrek*: It outsold *Final Fantasy* by ten to one. It's difficult to imagine more decisive evidence for the relative value of story and cosmetic quality, yet even today, some game designers insist that *Final Fantasy* was a great movie.

One could of course argue that a movie combining the top-notch cosmetics of *Final Fantasy* with the brilliant storytelling of *Shrek* would do even better, but this argument deliberately obfuscates the lesson of the two movies. A nuclear bomb equipped with a tape recorder that screams insults as it approaches its target would be even more demoralizing than a plain old everyday nuclear bomb, but that doesn't mean that insulting tape recorders are a significant military weapon.

Graphic Realism and the Human Imagination

Some argue that graphic realism stimulates the player's imagination. The relationship between graphic realism and the human imagination is considerably more complex than many designers realize; it works in both directions: Imagination can just as easily be smothered by excess information as stimulated. This basic truth has been a female secret for thousands of years, and most males are too dumb to catch on. Every woman knows that she can be more seductive by careful concealment of her allures than by direct revelation. The sexiest clothing accentuates a woman's curves without actually showing anything. This is best exemplified by a variety of female dances, such as the dance of the veils, the belly dance, or the cruder striptease. The entertainment value of the dance lies in what is concealed as much as what is revealed. Indeed, completely nude female dancers are generally regarded as less titillating than the semi-clothed variety. Graphic realism stimulates the imagination, but it must leave room for the imagination to run free.

The absence of graphic information can be just as stimulating to the player's imagination as its presence.

The game designer must therefore exercise great judiciousness in applying cosmetics. One of the simple but little-recognized secrets of the first smash hit 3D graphics game, **Doom**, was its dark environment. The monsters were poorly illuminated, a trick the designers used to cover up the weaknesses of their rendering technology, but they had serendipitously hit upon a powerful way to stimulate the players' imaginations.

Cosmetic excess becomes injurious to good design when it suggests what is not true. Blood splashes are my favorite example of this. You shoot up the bad guy and gratifyingly

17

Realistic
graphics
must be
matched
by realistic
behavior; if
you can't
achieve the
latter, ditch
the former.

realistic blood splatters all over. However, this blood has no reality other than its splashiness. It remains on the floor and walls, but it is not slippery as one would expect, nor does it coat objects nearby, making them slippery. An even worse blunder is the maintenance of images of dead bodies on the ground after the slaughter. Sure, it looks realistic, but you can walk right over the pile with no additional effort. A swarm of bad guys can charge your machine gun, piling up a mountain of bodies in front of your position, but the newcomers plow right through the pile as if it weren't there.

Cosmetic realism communicates the intended realism of the experience as a whole. Consider, for example, the classic cartoon scene in which Character A foists a stick of dynamite with burning fuse onto unwitting Character B. The dynamite explodes, and when the smoke clears, Character B is revealed singed but unhurt. "Ooo, that smarts!" exclaims Character B. Now, if this scene were played out in full graphic realism, with a real human being and real explosion, it wouldn't entertain. It wouldn't be funny, it wouldn't be exciting, it wouldn't be dramatic; it would be confusing and stupid. The disjunction between the graphic realism and the fantasy unrealism jars the imagination.

The best single gauge for the ideal degree of cosmetic realism is the indirectness of the conflict in the game. Socialization serves to deflect our primal conflicts into more indirect channels; the most direct (i.e., violent) forms of conflict are forbidden. Thus, direct, violent conflict is socially and psychologically unrealistic. Such themes, therefore, require a more cartoon-like presentation. Extreme graphic realism should be confined to games in which the conflict is pursued in the most indirect manner: legal dramas, corporate politics, and the like.

Consider, for example, the examples provided by two movies: *Jurassic Park* and *Shrek*. Believe it or not, *Shrek* is actually the more violent of the two movies. For all the dinosauric violence in *Jurassic Park*, there is actually very little on-screen violence: Only one person is actually killed on-screen: the weaselly lawyer. All the others who die in the movie—the animal handler, the fat programmer, the chain-smoking programming supervisor, and the Aussie hunter—suffer their fates outside of the camera's direct view. Even the sacrificial cow and goat are dispatched off-screen.

Shrek needs no such visual delicacy. We see a scene almost exactly like *Jurassic Park*'s lawyer-meal, only this time it's a dragon eating a prince—and the scene does not shock; it's funny. In addition, we see a graphic torture scene, a character catapulted high into the air and crash-ing through a roof—surely violent enough to kill, but the character survives unhurt. We see four characters smashed under a huge barrel, a bird explode, and a frog and a snake violently abused. In *Jurassic Park*, a boy falls 20 feet; in *Shrek*, the donkey falls 50 feet. *Shrek* has two fight scenes with a number of characters badly beaten up; *Jurassic Park* has no violence between people.

The conclusion seems obvious: You can't use realistic vio-lence in mass entertainment. You can suggest it with realis-tic imagery, turning the camera away at the moment of violence. Or you can reduce the graphic realism and retain the violence. Either way, the basic rule is clear.

This lesson runs counter to current industry wisdom, which extols the most detailed graphic realism in games of extreme violence. This is an understandable phase of an

Match the realism of the cosmet-ics with the realism of the fantasy.

industry still in its youth. There is, to be sure, a permanent segment of the population that revels in psychopathic fantasies, but if the industry is to reach a larger audience, it must cater to the requirements of the larger population.

Other Reasons for Overdone Cosmetics

All the remaining reasons for snazzy cosmetics are wrong-headed, yet they play far too large a role in the thinking of game designers.

Reason #2: To permit the player to show off the superior cosmetic capabilities of his new computer. There was a time when this reason actually sold games. New graphics cards were rare, expensive, and special, and when somebody dumped $500 on one, they were quite willing to pay $50 for some software that would justify the expense. Nowadays, however, most computers come equipped with strong graphics capabilities, and the people who pay extra to get the latest, most powerful graphics capabilities are not numerous enough to justify utilization of those superior capabilities.

Reason #3: To show off the superior technical prowess of the programmer. Again, this was once a major factor. Game designers were programmers, and showing off your talents was one of the perquisites of the job. People appreciated those snazzy graphics tricks, and a number of people developed reputations solely on their ability to produce stunning graphics effects. Nowadays, however, this kind of grandstanding is no longer tolerated. It still plays a role in the thinking of some team members, and subconsciously seeps through the organization, but usually this reason uses Reason #4 as a Trojan Horse.

Reason #4: To keep up with the competition. This argument is nonsense, but it still gets plenty of mileage in some companies. The obvious riposte is the same one that parents use with whining children: If everybody else jumped off a cliff, would you do it, too? If the competition wants to waste thousands of dollars chasing after some stupid graphic, that's their business. If you can't demonstrate that the graphics are justified under Reason #1, then aping the competition is a waste of time and money.

Reason #5: To provide the player with images and sounds that are intrinsically pleasing. This one is a bit tricky, and requires careful distinction from the valid arguments that arise in Reason #1. Perhaps the best way to understand the flaw in this reasoning is with a variation on the old *reductio ad absurdem* argument. Consider the Mona Lisa. Now, there's a nice painting, and it certainly is pleasing to gaze upon. So, why not interrupt the game action every now and then and show the player a picture of the Mona Lisa? Sure, it sounds ridiculous in this context, but there are plenty of games out there that commit pretty much the same blunder. If the image or sound in question advances the play of the game, then run with it; if it's just a pretty picture, lose it!

Incremental Accretive Design

This is the practice of starting with an existing design (usually a big hit by the competition) and adding some tidbit to make it better. It is the primary method by which new games are produced. Now, most of the pressure to stay conventional comes from publishers who reason that God favors the product with the bigger bullet list, but this book is for designers, not publishers, and so I shall concentrate on the problems on the designer side.

The first factor behind incremental design is simple laziness. Some young hot-shot plays Game X and greatly enjoys the game, so he decides to build the same game, only better. The thought process is simple: How could I make Game X even better? The young designer always thinks in terms of adding some new feature to the existing design, some additional twist or complication that would make the game more complex and therefore, in the designer's mind, more interesting.

The flaw in this reasoning is that it assumes the same level of experience in the playing audience. To appreciate the new, improved Game X1, the audience must have mastered Game X. The game aficionados who loved Game X will indeed love Game X1, but lesser players will find Game X1 intimidating. Take this process through several iterations, with Game X2, Game X3, and so on, and you end up with ridiculously complex games that appeal only to the aficionados. Then some brave soul comes along with a new, clean design, and the cycle starts all over again.

Design is not an accretive process! Piling on more features does not necessarily make the game any better—it just makes it more complicated. Some designers seem to revel in features, shoveling more and more gew-gaws into the game, as if the size of the pile of features is a measure of the quality of the game. Incorrectissimo! Making a game bigger doesn't make it better; it just makes it...bigger.

Subtraction is just as important an element of good game design as addition. Truly great design is always characterized by a stripping out of unnecessary detail, and this is true of all forms of media, not just games. Da Vinci deliberately left out details of the Mona Lisa's face to more clearly show that enigmatic smile. Michelangelo's statue of David knowingly smoothes out some details of musculature and erases some natural wrinkles in the skin to enhance the sense of bodily perfection. Shakespeare's Hamlet overlooks lots of important details about its protagonist to sharply delineate the dramatic conflict of the play. And every teacher knows that the only way to help a student learn is to give him carefully measured doses of truth, leaving out confusing details in the early stages.

Yet there are few games that show any flair for simplification. Sid Meier's **Civilization** is one; Sid was so brutal in his simplification of history that I sometimes wince at the game's inaccuracies. Yet the result of Sid's design parsimony was one of the greatest computer games of all time.

I can see many places in that game where a lesser designer would have succumbed to the temptation to pile it on; Sid's discipline in cutting out the dirt should be emulated by all designers.

Conceptualizing by Topic Rather Than Content

Improving a game design requires *both* addition and subtraction.

A young game designer once told me with obvious pride that he was working on a "King Arthur game." I wasn't cruel enough to point out that he had already blundered from the get-go by thinking of it as a "King Arthur" game. But the fact is, the topic of a game has little to do with the core design problems. Consider, for example, the various kinds of "King Arthur" books and movies. There's Disney's *The Sword in the Stone*, a saccharin family drama; John Boorman's deep and mysterious movie *Excalibur*, with its flamboyant sex scenes and its animal-like armor; T.H. White's *Once and Future King*; Marion Zimmer Bradley's *The Mists of Avalon*, a feminist rendition of the legends; Mark Twain's *A Connecticut Yankee in King Arthur's Court*, a clever social satire; Mallory's *Le Morte D'Arthur*, presenting the French reworking of the earlier Celtic legends; and of course, the original Celtic versions, as partially recorded in the *Mabinogeon*, with their deeply symbolic, almost Jungian psychology. With all these versions of the legends floating around, it doesn't mean much to define anything in terms of "King Arthur." The topic could be used for anything.

Novice game designers, in their earliest conceptualizations, think of a new game in terms of its topic rather than its system. They talk about building a science fiction game, a fantasy game, a wargame, and so on. Some even go so far as to define their game by the graphic technology, referring to their concept as a "first-person game." Whenever you launch your game project in this way, you have already doomed your efforts to failure. Indeed, you really haven't decided anything. To say that you're going to do a "science fiction game" is about as informative as insisting that you're going to build an "electronic game."

This kind of nomenclature is useful for marketing purposes, because marketing people can't be asked to think in terms of the fundamentals of game design. But you're not a marketing person—you're a game designer. You must use the nomenclature most relevant to the problems you face.

Concentrate on the problem that *really* lies at the core of your game: its interaction. Is the interaction going to be a matter of fast reflexes? Deep strategy? Complex logic? Intuition? Human insight? Random trial and error? What's the challenge of the game? How will the player interact with the game? *What does the user do?* These are the crucial questions, and so at the very outset of the game conceptualization process, you must concentrate on these questions. After you have answered these questions, then you can ask yourself what topic best serves these goals? Then and only then can you decide the topic. Don't be dishonest with yourself—if the topic really is the initiating concept in your thinking, then you simply don't understand game design well enough to do a good job.

It is certainly possible to be inspired by a topic, and use that inspiration to guide your conceptualization process. For example, I have always held the ancient Celtic versions of the Arthurian legends in awe, because they rumble with deep wisdom. For years I have had a vision of designing an Arthurian game. However, my very first step after the inspiration is to ask myself, "What is it about these legends that inspires me? What is the substance, the message, the concept that I want to convey?" For me, that substance is the problem of leadership. How do you lead people to greatness when they're caught up in petty disputes? How can you inspire them to look beyond the needs of the moment and see the glorious vision you can see on the horizon? These were the ideas that I wanted to express in the game; I still have not figured out how to accomplish this, so the game remains unbuilt. Perhaps some day, I'll pull it off.

Storyboards

Storyboards have been a standard tool in the game designer's kit. Their primary value lies in pitching the game to executives who don't understand interactivity. The basis for this lies in the vanity of people (especially executives) in the games biz. Storyboards are what people use for making movies. If *we* use storyboards, then we must be as hoity-toity as the movie people. Or something like that.

What, exactly, does a storyboard do to help organize and understand the project? Certainly the screen sketches showing the various screens in the game are useful, but we used to do that long before we used storyboards. Every game designer must prepare a complete collection of the screen layouts required at every point in the game. But there's a huge difference between a pile of screen layouts and a storyboard: The storyboard communicates sequentiality, which the screen layouts do not. In other words, the storyboard suggests that the various screens will come one after another in a specified order.

Now, you as game designer may realize that in fact the order of screens is not cast in stone, that there will be lots of variation in the order of screens. But when you nail down that sequence by using a storyboard, you are implicitly imposing that sequence on every member of the team. The implication is that the player will not have as much freedom during the course of the game, that the player must follow the assigned path through the game.

Conceptualize your design in terms of its challenge, not its topic.

20 LESSON

Lose the
storyboards.

Consider the evolution of programming practice. Back in the bad old days, we wrote spaghetti code because we had GOTO statements that made it easy to jump all over the program. In the early 70s, computer scientists had figured out that the GOTO statement was the cause of much programming anguish and began urging programmers to write "GOTO-less" code. And programmers did restrain themselves, but the temptation to use that handy-dandy GOTO statement was too great, and the use of that statement continued.

Then came the second generation of high-level languages, such as C, Forth, and Pascal, that simply excluded GOTO. At first, programmers were a little put off by this strange new style of programming, but after using it for a while, they realized that everything they could do with a GOTO statement could be done just as well in the new languages, and the resulting programs were much easier to understand and debug. They knew that GOTO-less programming was superior, but they really couldn't absorb the message until the mind-biasing tool was taken away from them.

Storyboards do to game design what GOTO statements did to programming: They encourage a way of thinking that's just wrong for the task. At their most fundamental, games are interactive, and a storyboard is an anti-interactive construct.

Over-Reliance on Tools

Tools are great; tools are wonderful. Some of my best friends are tools. The gargantuan effort required to create a modern game would be impossible to complete without an extensive library of tools. Hurrah for tools!

That said, let me now point out the dark side of tools, for those who are seduced by the dark side become the Darth Vaders of game design—more machine than man.

There are four fundamental properties of all tools:

- **Capital cost:** It takes time to build a tool, time that is not itself productive.
- **Greater efficiency:** A tool permits a task to be completed in less time.
- **Narrower application:** A tool is designed for one specific task.
- **Learning time:** Every tool requires some time to learn to use it properly.

Consider, for example, the simple task of digging a deep, narrow hole for setting a post into the ground. At the simplest and quickest level, you could claw at the soil with your bare hands, moving it out a handful at a time. There's no time wasted on building a tool, but your work proceeds slowly. You could, of course, (1) take the time to build a shovel and (2) enjoy the greater efficiency that this would confer upon your efforts, but (3) unlike your hands, which can be used for a great many tasks, the shovel is good for little more than digging dirt. And of course, (4) it takes a few minutes to get the hang of using a shovel to greatest effect.

Now let's move up a notch. You build a double shovel, a device with two narrow shovel blades, two shovel handles, and a swivel connection. This hand tool (1) costs a little more to make, because it has two shovel blades and some extra mechanical connections, but (2) it is definitely more efficient at digging post holes, so the work goes faster. Of course, (3) this specialized shovel can't be used for general dirt-digging pur-poses; it can be used only for the narrower task of digging post holes, and (4) this shovel is trickier to use and takes some time to master.

Okay, let's go big time. You're gonna get yourself a post hole auger for your tractor. This baby (1) costs hundreds of dollars, but it (2) wowie zowie—it can punch a post hole into the ground in seconds.

Unfortunately, (3) it couldn't possibly be used for anything other than digging post holes, and (4) you better take some time learning how to use this monster or you're gonna punch a hole through your foot.

Now, the greater capital cost of a tool can be offset by the increased efficiency of the work it does—but only if the tool is applied so many times that its cost is offset by the multiple small savings of using it. For any one-shot task, handwork is *always* faster than using a tool. A shovel is more efficient than using your hands only because, to dig a hole, you must claw at the ground many times. If you wanted to dig a divot-sized hole just once, you couldn't justify the purchase of a shovel for the task; it would be easier, cheaper, and quicker to just claw the divot out of the ground with your hands.

Thus, tool use in game design is only effective when the tool is used many times for a repetitive task.

> A quick terminological digression: There are cases where you might profitably purchase a special-purpose chunk of software that you integrate into your own code. For example, you might wish to purchase a library of 3D graphics routines for inclusion in your game. You might object that, in this case, the library is used just once, for a single application, and so refutes my claims about tool use requiring multiple applications to be cost-effective. The trick here lies in the fact that you are purchasing a library, not a tool. You don't use a library in the same manner that you use a tool; it's a different beast and obeys different laws of utilization. None of my comments in this section apply to software libraries.

NOTE

The dark side of tool use is that, in your eagerness to make the tool cost-effective, you start to distort your approach to design problems to make them fit the special capabilities of the tool. The old saw that beautifully expresses this idea is, "When you've got a big enough hammer, everything starts to look like a nail." A big, expensive, powerful tool warps all of its users to thinking in the same way, engendering a homogeneity of thought into an entire community. If this homogeneity of thought clarifies thinking on a complex problem, then it is useful, but we must always be vigilant against the subtle influence that a tool exerts on our thinking.

Every tool is like a road: It takes you somewhere quickly and easily. A truly fine tool is like a freeway: It gets you there especially quickly. Of course, like a freeway, a fine tool attracts a great many users, all of whom end up going to the same place, and if you take the freeway, you end up at a crowded beach. It's a big world out there; if all you ever do is stay on the freeways, you won't see much of it. Sure, it's good to take the freeway to the general area, but few roads or freeways lead to mountaintops; ultimately, the good designer does not shirk from the effort of getting out of the car, donning hiking boots, and setting off across rough ground to reach that special place that nobody has ever visited before.

A prime example of this problem is the "level editor": a tool used to lay out the levels in games such as first-person shooters. They're certainly a good idea; laying out levels without a level editor is a tedious and boring task. Indeed, I wrote a little map editor for my first big hit, **Eastern Front (1941)** that was functionally the same as a level editor. However, look how the existence of level editors has distorted the evolution of first-person shooters. By making it easy to build big complex levels, designers started providing their games with lots and lots of big complex levels. By itself, that's not a bad thing, but the ease of providing value through level creation distracted designers from other, possibly more interesting directions of development.

Take weapons, for example. There are all sorts of possibilities for wild and crazy weapons in first-person shooters. How about a weapon that shoots both forward and backward simultaneously? Wouldn't that be handy when you're surrounded? Or a weapon whose impact increases with range, encouraging long-range fire? Or a weapon that requires time to build up to full strength? I used both of these ideas in an early game design—howcum nobody has tried something like this in modern

22

The tool has a strong influence on the weak-minded; we must be wary.

first-person shooters? The problem is, it's so easy to offer value by providing lots of different levels that it's not cost-effective to offer value by providing lots of different weapons.

Or how about monsters? I can imagine a hundred different monsters to put into a first-person shooter. A monster that slimes you so that you move more slowly for a few min-utes, bogged down with monster slime. A monster that bounces up and down three times, then explodes, forcing you to time your exposure but duck at the right instant. A barrel-shaped monster that's indestructible and rolls about, crushing the unwary—easy to avoid but impossible to kill. These are all simple, almost obvious ideas, but they and hundreds of other ideas have not been explored in first-person shooters because it's too easy to use a level editor instead of thinking up something really new.

What's especially interesting about these examples of mine is that I haven't played a first-person shooter since **Doom II** (although I did look at **Half-Life**). There must be scores of first-person shooters that I've never seen, and here I am shooting off my mouth about ideas that have "never" been implemented. For all I know, every single one of my ideas could have been done already. But such is my confidence in my theoretical analysis that I can make such extreme statements with serene confidence. Either some-body will make me eat crow by pointing out my error, or I will appear to be blessed with godlike omniscience. It's all done with theory, my boy.

the education of a game designer

If you're young and hoping to become a game designer, you'll need a good education. Here are my recommendations for what constitutes that education.

Get a Degree

First, get a bachelor's degree at a reputable college. The degree serves three purposes:

- First, it establishes your credibility in the eyes of employers.
- Second, it gives you a saleable skill that you can use to launch your career.
- Third, it will teach you how to learn.

These are some of your options:

- **Technical school:** These schools provide students with a highly focused, narrow education concentrating on the specific skills necessary for success as game programmers. There are a number of schools that operate under this philosophy, and they are turning out a goodly number of graduates each year. These graduates will find good positions as programmers and will play important technical roles in many games projects. Some of these will likely become great game designers, but it will not be due to their schooling. The reason for this is simple: almost all their coursework is in programming. As I stated in the introduction to this book, game design and game programming are different fields.

- **Computer science plus game design:** Computer science departments all over the country are rushing to bring game design into their own fold. Most of the early efforts have started small, basically little more than a regular bachelor's degree program in computer science with an emphasis on graphics techniques and a few special courses thrown in. With the passage of time, I would expect these programs to broaden, adding more courses from the arts and humanities, as well as special courses specifically about game design (as opposed to game programming).

- **Cinema (or media studies) plus game design:** The flip side of the computer science approach is the media studies approach. An existing media studies program is broadened somewhat to include computer games. These programs have suffered from the same difficulties that beset the computer science programs: With a dearth of expertise on games in particular, they are forced to approach game design circumferentially. Moreover, these programs are just as weak in the science and technical areas as the computer science programs are weak in the arts and humanities. Academic institutions in the USA are still hobbled by a certain amount of "two cultures" antagonisms—the science and engineering side and the arts and humanities side just don't understand each other. These difficulties hurt both sides when it comes to game design.

For some reason, the European academics are not so deeply caught up in these "two cultures wars." I have seen several academic programs at different European universities that achieve a good balance between the science and engineering side and the arts and humanities side. The students seem to be comfortable with both programming and artistic considerations. This model, I think, will work better in the long run.

Eeeny, Meeny, Miney, Mo

So, how do you choose among these options? If your true interest is primarily in games programming, then the technical school or a program at a computer science department will likely serve you best. If you take this approach, however, you must be under no illusions that you will become a game designer. You will likely become a good games programmer and you might—*might*—become a game designer if you continue your self-education to make up for the gaps in your education.

If you are less interested in the technical side, then you should pursue a media studies degree, but you should still supplement your degree program with some courses on programming.

Don't get a job in the games industry unless you really, really love games.

Lastly, you should seriously consider the possibility of studying in Europe. There are a number of programs at European universities that tackle software design in a genuinely multidisciplinary style. Moreover, you need not worry about language problems: Many of these programs are taught in English as the "best common denominator" language.

Unrealistic Expectations

All over the world, millions of kids aspire to be game designers. Many are so intent that they go to special schools for game designers. What's sad about this is that very, very few will ever be game designers. The games industry can support perhaps 10,000 creative workers, the vast majority of whom are programmers and artists who will never design a game. This industry cranks out a few hundred games a year; that means that there are only a few hundred working game designers. Moreover, people in the games industry are paid substandard wages because there are always plenty of eager young kids ready to replace the old pro who's getting tired of living on macaroni and cheese. The only ones who climb high enough in the hierarchy to become game designers are those who are brilliant, talented, and willing to endure a lower standard of living for years.

Education Versus Schooling

Mark Twain once wrote, "I never let my schooling interfere with my education." Schools can give you a good orientation and equip you with important skills, but the larger task of acquiring an education takes a much bigger commitment than merely attending school, getting decent grades, and graduating. Education is a lifelong process; it is unlikely that you will emerge from college with an adequate education to become a game designer. You'll need to learn a great deal more than what you can learn in college. I therefore describe an educational program for prospective game designers that will, I think, give them what they need to excel in this tough job.

Good game designers are broadly educated to be comfortable in the world of ideas. They are intellectual jacks-of-all-trades, capable of exploring any field that might become relevant to their designs, and their education gives them a large stock of different ways of thinking about problems.

There are four broad areas that a prospective game designer should learn. They are covered in the following sections.

Systems

Game design requires the creation of systems that are interesting and fun to play with. The world is full of systems. A good game designer should learn about many different systems to provide source material for designs. Here, in order of priority, are books that will teach you about various systems:

- *The Way Things Work* by David Macaulay. Required for two reasons: first, the book explains all the basic technology of our civilization, which you should know about, and second, the visual presentations are themselves instructive in graphical technique.

- Guns, Germs, and Steel by Jared Diamond. Magnificent! Explains how Europeans were able to conquer the world—they had all sorts of biological advantages.

- *Connections* by James Burke. The videos are better than the book, but either way, they teach you some important lessons about the nature of discovery.

- *River out of Eden* and *Climbing Mount Improbable* by Richard Dawkins. Detailed explanations of interesting aspects of evolution theory. Again, handy for understanding complex systems behavior.

- *A History of Warfare*, *The Mask of Command*, and *The Face of Battle* by John Keegan. Three works from the finest military historian of our times. Military systems have their own logic; using those concepts to illuminate game design problems can prove useful.

- *Six Easy Pieces* and *Six Not-So-Easy Pieces* by Richard Feynmann. Excellent rigorous introduction to some basic concepts in physics. Extracted from the full three-volume set, *The Feynmann Lectures on Physics*, which would make an ideal followup for the more ambitious student.

- *Bully for Brontosaurus* by Stephen Jay Gould. Delightful essays on paleontology and evolution. For that matter, almost any of Gould's books are worthwhile reading.

- *The Rise of the West* by William McNeil. A brilliant explanation of Western history from the very beginning. A strong sense of cause and effect pervades the work.

- *Balance of Power* by Chris Crawford. Explains in detail the ideas and algorithms behind my biggest hit game.

- *The Story of Law* by John Maxcy Zane. Rather old, but still a good basic history of the human struggle to nail down what it means by right and wrong. Law is educational as an attempt to precisely express some very fuzzy ideas; good games often tackle fuzzy ideas, too.

- *Archaeology and Language* by Colin Renfrew. Explains how the Indo-European languages came to dominate much of Eurasia.

- *The Structures of Everyday Life*, *The Wheels of Capitalism*, and *The Perspective of the World* by Fernand Braudel. Dense reading, but these books provide a detailed and fascinating view of the crucial transitional period in Western capitalism from 1400 to 1700. Lots of good ideas about how complex systems behave.

- *Writing Systems* by Geoffrey Sampson. Various technologies for writing language. Useful in terms of designing user interfaces.

- *The Origins of English Words* by Joseph Twadell Shipley. A dictionary of the Indo-European roots of English words. Did you know that "Catherine" and "castrate" come from the same root? The connections between all sorts of seemingly different words will surprise you. I'm not sure what this has to do with game design, but the book fascinated me.

- *Diplomacy* by Henry Kissinger. A history of modern balance-of-power diplomacy in all its fascinating twists and turns. Diplomacy is another complex system that can help inform your design processes. Think about game interactions in terms of balance-of-power diplomacy.

- *How to Make War* and *A Quick and Dirty Guide to War* by James Dunnigan. War has a logic all its own, and Dunnigan's nuts-and-bolts approach shows how to organize big complex efforts.

- *The Descent of the Child* by Elaine Morgan. Evolution in terms of infant survival.

- *Song of the Dodo* by David Quammen. Island populations and gene pools.

- *At Home in the Universe* by Stuart Kaufman. A brilliant explanation of some very complex systems behavior. Advanced material; don't tackle it until you have mastered the basic principles of evolution and chemistry. Will Wright's **SimCity** was partly inspired by cellular automata theory; so how about a game based on autocatalyzing sets?

- *The Origin of Species* by Charles Darwin. The single most brilliant book in all of science. Probably best to read an abridged version, as the original proved its case with mind-numbing detail after detail after detail.

- *The Federalist Papers* by Alexander Hamilton and James Madison. A bit of a slog, but it's useful to understand the complex reasoning behind one of the landmark documents of history.

What Makes People Tick

You cannot entertain people if you don't have a clear understanding of what it is to be human. There are a number of routes to understanding the human condition. Evolutionary psychology is useful. On the other hand, I don't much care for rat psychology (the "hard" version of psychology that emphasizes quantitative experiments). It proves many things that are of little value to game designers. Great literature also reveals much of the human condition. Ultimately, however, much of this is a matter of wisdom, not reading.

- *Homo Ludens* by Johan Huizinga. The definitive work on human play.

- *Hero with a Thousand Faces* and *The Power of Myth* by James Campbell. How mythology affects the human mind. Most games have some subconscious element of mythology to them; you should understand the basic forces at work.

- *The Story of Civilization* by Will and Ariel Durant. Yes, all 11 volumes. They're an easy read and lay out the basics of (mostly Western) history. You've got to know the basic scheme of history if you're going to put anything else into context.

- At least three plays by Shakespeare. He's just too important to miss.

- *The Moral Animal* and *Non-Zero* by Robert Wright. The biological history of morality and cooperation. Very useful for understanding some of the most important social systems that govern human behavior.

- *The Prehistory of the Mind* by Steven Mithen. Explains the concepts of mental modules; you'll need these concepts to appreciate the way that various forms of challenge interact inside the human mind.

- *Walden* by Henry David Thoreau. Everybody should read this as they struggle with early adulthood.

- *Language & Species* by Derek Bickerton. The co-evolution of language and humans.

- *The Iliad* and *The Odyssey* by Homer. The most important fundamental myth of our civilization. If you don't know these, you can't really appreciate a great deal of what has happened since. Be careful to get a modern prose translation; there are plenty of archaic translations, and some that translate the original Greek verse, which is a bit too artsy for most of us.

- *Huckleberry Finn* by Mark Twain. Twain was the greatest American author, and this was his masterpiece. It contains many fundamental elements of great storytelling.

- *Death, War, and Sacrifice* by Bruce Lincoln. Ancient themes of mythology

- *The Code of the Warrior* by Rick Fields. The nature of masculinity. It's nice to understand your customers. Can you explain why big torsos are such powerful indicators of masculinity?

- *When Wish Replaces Thought* and *Why Men Rule* by Steven Goldberg. Lovely, politically incorrect, rigorous thought on social problems.

- *The Acts of King Arthur* by John Steinbeck. The best modern rendering of the classic legends.

- *The Socratic Dialogs* by Plato. All you really need are the four dialogs dealing with the trial and execution of Socrates: Euthyphro, Apology, Crito, and Phaedo. You'll get two big things out of them: an appreciation of the "Socratic method," a powerful form of reasoning, and the power of simple truth.

- *Beyond the Hero* by Allen B. Chinen. How a man grows up.

- *Life on the Mississippi* and *A Tramp Abroad*. Two more classics by Mark Twain.

- *Poetics* by Aristotle. If you want to entertain people, you must understand the basics of stories. This work lays them out so well that it still dominates much early discussion of narrative.

- *The Meditations* by Marcus Aurelius. Stoicism will help you cope with your boss.

- *The Origins of the Modern Mind* by Merlin Donald. Traces how the mind evolved. Not the brain—the mind. Good combination of psychology and biology.

- *The Western Canon* by Harold Bloom. An overview of the most important literary works of Western civilization. It's not as good as reading all those great works themselves, but who's got time for *Beowulf*?

- *Touched with Fire* by Kay Redfield Jamison. Human creativity and manic-depressive illness.

- *The New Testament* by various authors. No, I'm not a Christian. However, this is the most influential book in Western history, so it makes sense to read it. But don't use the old-fogey King James version with its "thee's" and "thou's"; find a modern translation.

- *The Folktale* by Stith Thompson. Definitive study of how folktales developed, the common elements in folktales, and all the variations in folktales across cultures.

- *Studies in Words* by C.S.Lewis. And you thought he was a fantasy writer! You wouldn't think that so much could be said about a single word, but there it is.

- *The Sea Wolf* and *The Call of the Wild* by Jack London. To jerk you out of the lab and back into a more primitive mental state.

- *Billy Budd* by Herman Melville. Good versus evil in a way that's utterly alien to that notion in computer games.

Communications

A good game designer knows how to express the ideas of the game clearly and powerfully. This requires an appreciation of linguistics and the visual arts, among other things.

- *Understanding Comics* by Scott McCloud. Uses comic book methods to explain comic books, an important medium of expression for game designers to consider.

- *The Design of Everyday Things* and *Turn Signals are the Facial Expressions of Automobiles* by Donald Norman. These books will open your eyes to just how badly most things are designed. You will learn the all-important concept of "affordance."

- *Visual Explanations* and *Envisioning Information* by Edward Tufte. These are the premier works on how to present information clearly through the visual medium. These books have an excellent reputation, but I confess that they fell short of my expectations.

- *The Art of Interactivity Design* by Chris Crawford. Lays out basic principles of interactivity.

- *Game Design Theory and Practice* by Richard Rouse. A more nuts and bolts approach to game design than this book offers; very thorough, and includes interviews with top designers (including me!).

- *Cambridge Encyclopedia of Language* and *Cambridge Encyclopedia of the English Language* by Richard Crystal. Understanding language is crucial for understanding the nature of human communications. Communicating with humans without using linguistic data structures is like interfacing to a computer through its mouse port instead of through the USB or Ethernet. These two books make great reading, and they really cover the ground.

- *The Art of Human-Computer Interface* by Brenda Laurel. Random collection of essays, some good, some bad, one by me! Lots of good ideas about user-interface concepts.

- *The Alphabet Effect* by Robert Logan. The role of alphabetic writing in the development of civilization. Handy for understanding methodologies for expression.

- *About Face* by Alan Cooper. A detailed examination of the basic components of computer interfaces.

- *The Art of the Comic Book* by Will Harvey. A medium very close to games.

- *The Liveliest Art* by Arthur Knight. A quick, easy history of the cinema. So many game designers compare games with the movies that you should at least be educated about the real thing.

- *The Origins of Writing* by Senner. How writing got started.

- *The Humane Interface* by Jef Raskin. Delightful, eccentric rants on the failures of computer interface design.

- *Computers as Theater* by Brenda Laurel. A quirky, brilliant exposition of a completely different approach to the human-computer interaction. Brenda speaks a different language, which you'll have to adjust to, but it's worth the effort.

In addition, there are a number of movies that teach much about communications. I'd like to offer a few older works that you should see, not primarily for their dramatic power, but for their creative example:

- *City Lights* and *The Gold Rush* by Charlie Chaplin.

- *Rear Window*, *North by Northwest*, *Vertigo*, or any of Alfred Hitchcock's great works.

- *Koyaanisqatsi*. A movie that tells a story with no characters, no plot, and no dialog!

- *High Noon*. A simple tale, cleanly and powerfully told. The unifying element of the clock is particularly striking, especially at high noon (ahem!).

- *The Red Balloon*. Another simple tale well told.

- *Excalibur* by John Boorman. This surrealistic representation of the Arthurian legends gets closer to the heart of those legends than anything else.

Programming

Despite my insistence that programming and game design are two distinct activities, the effective game designer must still possess basic competence as a programmer. Perhaps that will change in a few decades, but for now, it remains the case.

- *Code Complete* by Steve McConnell. Good programming practice. Programming is a lot more than just getting the code working, and this book explains how.

- *Algorithms* by Sedgewick. You've got to know all the basic algorithms; here they are. Knuth is the standard work in the field, but this is more compact. Read Knuth if you want to understand this material in greater depth.

- *The Art of Computer Programming* by Donald Knuth. The classic in the field of computer programming. Covers algorithms and data structures. Not for the timid, these three books are dense with ideas.

- *The Mythical Man-Month* by Brooks. Old, but still true: Throwing more people at a project that's behind schedule only makes things worse.

Periodicals

Education never stops; you should always be learning. Here are two periodicals that will help you keep up with the ever-changing world:

- *The Economist.* Thoreau wrote, and this is a poorly-recalled paraphrase, "The majority of what men call news is merely idle gossip. If we read of one ship lost in a storm, one revolution in Spain, or one cow run over on the Western Railway, we need never read of another; the principle is the same." On any scale of sensationalism versus real news content, American television news is at the bottom; it is nothing more than a collage of plane crashes, war victims, and sound bites. American newspapers and newsmagazines are better but still overly dependent upon reaching the gut rather than the mind. *The Economist,* however, is a serious newsmagazine that concentrates on the forces that are really shaping our world. Most American news is embarrassingly parochial; you'd never know from it that there are other countries in the world, unless they're enemies. *The Economist* has a truly international outlook. It's more expensive than other newsmagazines, but it's worth it.

- *Scientific American.* A good way to keep up with what's going on in the world of science. Unfortunately, *Scientific American* has dumbed down in the last decade, but it is still the best digest of the progress of science. *Science News,* a weekly, is also good, but not as in-depth as *Scientific American.*

Exercises

Reading and watching aren't enough; you must also try your hand at a variety of active tasks.

- **BASIC STAMP:** This is a computer on a chip that you can program in the BASIC language. You can hook up LEDs (little red lights), buzzers, stepper motors, and all sorts of other electronic devices to sense and control the world. You can purchase a variety of kits that include all the accoutrements you need to get started. You'll learn a great deal about digital logic at the hands-on level. Alternatively, you might consider one of the many robotics kits for students; they are more expensive and more detailed, but you learn more.

- **Writing:** Join interesting newsgroups and try your hand at writing good contributions to the newsgroups. Don't just toss together random rants—compose serious essays on the issues discussed. Do your own writing offline and make sure that you include in each of your posts at least one fact that you had to look up. Don't pay any attention to the foolish flamers and random ranters you'll encounter; concentrate on engaging the brighter members of the group in serious discussion of intricate issues. Your objective should be to learn how to express your thoughts in a clear and convincing manner.

- **Programming:** Keep writing programs after you've learned the basics. Build micro-games that try out interesting algorithms or systems. Don't worry about graphics or sound; concentrate on getting an internal system operational. If you can play with your system using simple blips, beeps, and clicks, that's good enough for the educational purpose.

- **Self-probing:** Take up some mildly dangerous hobby: motorcycling, skateboarding, surfing, skydiving, rock climbing, or skiing. Measure yourself against your own limits. Can you accurately gauge the limits of your abilities? How close can you come to those limits and still be absolutely, positively certain that you are not exceeding them? Can you calmly assess risk and make sound judgements when your youthful cockiness goads you to push harder?

- **Manual creativity:** Make things with your hands. Build wooden structures; make pots; carve wood; polish rocks; build gardens or fences; make model airplanes or railroads; pour concrete; repair cars or motorcycles. Get your hands dirty.

- **Social education:** Break out of that suffocating circle of people who are just like you; all they do is reinforce your false conceptions. Make friends of people you wouldn't normally make friends with: fundamentalist Christians, old people, factory workers, artists, skinheads, leather-clad motorcyclists, gays or straights, waitresses, people from different ethnic groups, somebody who doesn't speak your language well. It's especially useful to make friends with a foreigner. Sure, they're different, and sure they have lots of attitudes you disagree with. So what? They still have something useful to teach you. Concentrate on discovering the commonalities you share and diplomatically pass over your differences. One good tip on

Learn
everything
you can.

getting started: no matter who they are, no matter what their culture, asking them about their family will always break the ice. Family is one absolute universal. Swap family stories.

- **Observe:** The world is full of surprises to one whose eyes are open. I recently visited a submarine museum. All the other visitors wandered through the submarine rather quickly, but I took the time to notice and wonder about details: where did that pipe go? Why were there so many valves on that pipe? How are the batteries connected together? I had a lot more fun than the others, I think, because I combined observation with wonder. When you drive down a street, look at the houses. Why are they built the way they are? Can you tell which houses are older and which are newer? What can you tell about the occupants just by looking at the outside of the house? When you're in the country, can you tell which way the water flows across the land? Why are the trees spaced the way they are? Look at the sky. Its color changes from day to day—can you notice the changes? Watch clouds move, grow, and shrink. Why do they do that?

games I'd like to build

games I'd like to build

Over the years I've come up with all sorts of strange ideas for games. Many of these ideas I have since discarded, but there remain some ideas that seem worthwhile. What with my many projects, I don't have the time to implement the ideas, so I've decided to place them before you, not so much as specific proposals, but as incitements to creativity. Take these ideas and run with them.

Galilean Relativity

Most people know about Einstein's theory of relativity; few people know that Galileo came up with a kind of slow-motion analogue of it. He reasoned that, until you know about something happening, it might as well not be real for you. In other words, events happening in the New World right now would not be known in Europe until several months later, so it was better to think in terms of the lag being a kind of reality. Galileo showed that this view of reality had some practical benefits. But the idea never took off.

This could provide the basis for a nice game. I actually started building just such a game, calling it **The Last of the Incas**. It was based on the final struggles of the rebel Inca leaders against the Spanish. There were several such flare-ups, and it is conceivable that a truly determined and well-led effort might have succeeded in ejecting the Spanish from Peru. What made these struggles interesting was the slow speed of news travel in the rugged terrain of the Andes. Often, a military force would set out for a destination without realizing that it had already been captured by the enemy. My game factored this into the display: The dispositions you saw on the map were based on your latest information about them; they could be wildly out of date. Traveling closer to one area gave you more up-to-date information about it, but also made your information about distant areas even less reliable. The game played rather like a modern information war—by controlling road junctions, you could blind your enemy and concentrate your forces on his weak points, capturing them before he even knew they were in trouble.

Napoleonic Cavalry

This is another strategy wargame that takes the ideas of the previous game one step further. I have seen few Napoleonic wargames that captured the essence of Napoleon's technique, which was to use cavalry to blind the enemy while sending the main army along a variety of routes, converging them on the true objective at the last moment. All movement in those days was road-bound, and the road network in Europe was thin enough that it constituted the primary constraint on strategic movement. Cavalry, however, could move cross-country, so Napoleon would send out swarms of small cavalry bands that would serve as Napoleon's eyes, and turn back enemy cavalry so as to blind the enemy. This screen of cavalry could be two hundred miles wide; behind it, Napoleon's army would crawl like so many ant trails spread over a huge area. As he developed a clearer idea of the enemy's dispositions, Napoleon would start to concentrate his armies in such a way as to cut the enemy's supply lines. If all went well, the enemy would find himself surrounded before he even realized what Napoleon was up to. It was every general's dream: victory through maneuver.

Such a game would also show the benefits of central position. If an enemy's army splits up too much, and you keep your armies in a central position, your information comes in faster than your enemy's; in a war of maneuver, this gives you an advantage.

Napoleon in Space

Okay, so most people find all this historical stuff boring; let's jazz it up with a science fiction theme. Sure, there are plenty of space-based **Empire** clones, but how about one in which ships and news travel at the speed of light rather than infinitely fast? Information about the progress of the war reaches you only as quickly as light can travel, so you can be completely in the dark about important developments until it's too late. It's a good idea to position yourself close to the action so that you can get reports more quickly, but this places you in some peril; moreover, it moves you further away from other sectors. This gives a natural advantage to smaller, weaker empires; they can mount raids on distant corners of the big empire and pull them off before the big player knows what hit him.

Attack of the Cellular Automata

The computer game of **Life** (first created by Tom Conway) spawned the whole field of study of cellular automata. Will Wright used cellular automata to build **SimCity**. However, I always thought that it might be fun to fight a war with cellular automata. In this game, the playfield would be a standard array of cellular automata, and the two players would occupy opposite corners. The goal of the game is simple: destroy the enemy's fortress. You do this by launching gliders in his direction. He fends off your gliders with his own. Both of you have the ability to place standard units near your fortress. Gliders are one example; glider factories are another. But you can also place defensive units such as crosses and stars that act like temporary walls. The most important units you can place are "resource factories." These are very expensive, stable units that generate "resource points." These resource points are spent every time you place a unit; if you don't have any resource points, you can't place any units. So you must build and protect your resource factories.

Using standard game of **Life** rules, the defense would always have a large advantage over the offense, so some tweaks would be necessary to balance the system. There are plenty of ways to do this. One design solution would be to permit players to modify the rules of individual cells by hitting them with special weapons. For example, one could build a "bomber glider" set to detonate after a specified number of generations; when it explodes, all the cells within the blast radius are modified in such a way as to prevent enemy activity from taking place in those cells for a set period of time. Players could thereby build a safe channel that could be traversed by their own gliders only.

Bomber gliders could affect their targets in a variety of ways. The basic rules of cellular generation could be altered to render an area dead or overproductive. A dead area blocks activity, while an overproductive region generates lots of dangerous radiation.

Volkerwanderung

This German word describes the historical period from about 200 AD through 600 AD when different peoples ("volk") wandered ("wanderung") all over Europe, fighting and conquering. What strikes me about this period is the blending of peoples and cultures. France, for example, was Celtic with Roman cultural elements, and then it was overrun by Germanic peoples; the France of today still harbors many Celtic elements. England, on the other hand, was less deeply Celtic when the Romans arrived, and the Germanic invasions eliminated a great many Celts; this, along with the later Norman invasion, led to a population with strong Germanic elements colored by rare Celtic elements.

In this game, the player would represent a higher-level abstraction than we see in most games: a culture, as represented by its language. The player might represent Celtic culture, in which case his goal is to maximize the use of Celtic language throughout Europe. Merely conquering other peoples is not enough; a player must also outbreed them. The verbs of the game establish the culture's proclivities toward various cultural elements: the warrior tradition, respect for authority versus respect for the individual, the rule of law, exaltation of agricultural productivity, admiration for art and learning, and so forth. The player can freely increment or decrement these values, but there are limits on the rate of change a culture can absorb.

Each volk in the game is composed of some mix of the three fundamental cultures: Celtic, Germanic, and Roman. Each of the three players gets to control each volk in proportion to the fraction of that volk that he owns. Thus, if the Lombards are 50% Germanic, 30% Roman, and 20% Celtic, then the Celtic player's commands have 20% weight, and the Germanic player's commands have 50% weight. The actual policies that a volk applies are the weighted average of the commands given by the individual players.

A volk grows in population in proportion to its agricultural output. But a volk can influence other volk by several means. It can attack another volk, in which case the victorious volk absorbs the losing volk. When this happens, the population proportions change in a manner that reflects the actual populations of the two volk and their cultural distributions, with a weighting factor in favor of the victorious volk.

This game would have strong historical value, but it would also be fascinating as a game because the player's identity is so diffuse. To a greater or lesser extent, each player's identity exists in each of the actors (the volk).

Third-World Dictator

The player is the dictator of a small third-world nation; his goal is to survive for twenty years. The key structural element of the game is the ministry, a primary governmental department. Each ministry is headed by a minister, has a budget that the player sets each year, is broken down into departments headed by deputy ministers, operates under the player's directives, and yields results that can be readily examined. There are eleven ministries, ranging from Defense and Education to Trade and Transportation.

The game is played in one-year turns. At the beginning of each year the player receives a budgetary report from the Ministry of the Treasury, specifying total revenues available for the year and last year's budget values. The player then adjusts these budget values. The player also sets policy by means of directives to each ministry. For example, the directive to the Ministry of Internal Security might give the player seven different levels of repression for dealing with dissent, ranging from "ignore them" and "monitor their activities" to "make some of them disappear."

The politics of the game revolves around factions. Each minister belongs to a faction; that minister will use the ministry to further the interests of his or her faction. If a minister becomes too ambitious, the player might decide to replace that minister with a less threatening one. Of course, sometimes the most loyal ministers are not too competent, and their ministries will then perform poorly, raising the level of popular discontent.

Thus, the player must juggle the ministries to ensure that his ministers are loyal and his enemies are impotent, to keep the people reasonably happy, to deal with those who aren't, and to keep the military from staging a coup. All in all, the game offers a host of challenges.

Lies

"Oh, what a web we weave when we seek to deceive!" It's always seemed to me that this web might form the basis of an interesting game. I designed such a game once, using a contrived situation in which eight jewel thieves spy on each other and attempt to determine which one of them currently possesses the jewel. Knowing who has the jewel makes it possible to steal the jewel. The thieves can also tell each other about the whereabouts of third parties at specified times, but these statements might easily be lies. The game provides the player with a handy-dandy visual tool I called "Visi-Lie," which graphically showed all the logical relationships among the various observations and statements that the player has collected. This game plays rather like a vastly expanded version of the old boardgame **Clue**. Indeed, a nice variation could be built around a murder mystery. The central design problem is to provide different agendas for each person so as to encourage lying without obvious causes for the lying.

Spies

Along the same line as **Lies**, this game would place the player in the role of a spy caught up in a confusing world of espionage and double agents. The player attempts to unravel truth from deception as he inter-acts with other people. We'd certainly need some sexy female spies as well as plenty of money sloshing through the game. Most of the game-play would revolve around conversations with other agents in attempts to catch them in lies. These lies would then have to be correlated with actual observations. Tailing another person would be an important task, for it might reveal meetings that expose true relationships. Of course, some of those meetings can also be misleading. And there has to be some item of great value—a microdisk, in standard spy-movie parlance— that everybody is seeking. The important thing with this design is to avoid chase scenes, shooting, and explosions, as they will undoubtedly drag the game down into a first-person shooter.

The Wheels of Commerce

Fernand Braudel, the great French historian, wrote a book with this title in which he explained how mercantile capitalism developed in Europe during the period 1500–1800. It's a fascinating book, although perhaps a little too eggheady for most people. I think that it provides the basis for a great game. The mechanics of trade back in those days were

nowhere near as well developed as they are today, and the legal structures to support trade just didn't exist, so merchants were (metaphorically) more likely to pack a six-gun than a briefcase.

The player in this game would have to make choices as to the type of
merchandise to deal in and where to get it. Your ship leaves Amsterdam
with its load of textiles and sails for Sweden, where it trades the textiles
for lumber, which it carries to England to trade for coal before returning
to Amsterdam. At what point should merchandise be converted into
cash? And what about the problems of international finance? You can't
just carry lots of coin around with you—that makes you a target for
pirates and robbers. Better to get letters of credit that can be redeemed
at the desired location. But how do you know those letters of credit will
be honored? And if you think that currency speculation in the twenty-
first century is wild and crazy, you should see how it worked in the
sixteenth.

Another big issue is market intelligence. You keep agents in most of the
major ports, and they'll write you if prices for any particular good suddenly become attractive—but letters move slowly in this world, and those
prices could change by the time your ship arrives. Suppose a colleague
tells you that cotton prices in Egypt have collapsed—now is the time to
grab tons of the stuff. Is he genuinely sharing good fortune or does he
want to distract your attention from silk prices in Istanbul? There's plenty
of room for rich gameplay in this situation.

Corporate Politics

Here's a game I've wanted to do for a long time. Corporate politics can
be intense and hard-fought. The player starts as a manager at a large
corporation with the goal of promotion to the top. The first question to
ask about the design, as you already know, is "What are the verbs?"
and here is precisely where the toughest problems in the game arise.
Political behavior in a corporation is closely tied to the specifics of

business activity. You can't design a game with a generic, one-size-fits-all "stab in the back" verb. The specifics of the stab in the back are essential to making it understandable.

The solution to this problem is to build an elaborate business story that unfolds in a linear and predictable fashion. This is a tale of interactions with outside agencies: other businesses, banks, the stock market, government agencies, and so forth. Within this tale there are many possible actions that each member of the corporation can take; the player will be but one of those members. Thus, the outside forces are fixed and immutable and the internal reactions to those forces are the battleground of the executives.

Evolution

There have been a number of attempts to design games about evolution, but none seem to have hit the nail on the head. They are either tedious or not really about evolution. Unlike many other design problems, the verb set here seems to be obvious: The player must select phenotypes to produce a fitter species. The core problem, it seems to me, lies in the set of phenotypes presented to the player. The problem is complicated by the unavoidable interrelationships among many of the phenotypes. My first decision was to limit the game to land vertebrates; this greatly reduces the number of phenotypes the player has to deal with, and it concentrates on the kind of animals most people are familiar with. After some work, I came up with a design using one set of phenotypes and another set of genotypes. Here is the phenotype set:

- **Speed:** Fleetness of foot
- **Agility:** Ability to jump and change direction quickly
- **Metabolic efficiency:** Caloric requirements per kilogram of body weight
- **Digestive efficiency:** The efficiency of extracting nutrients from food sources
- **Digestive range:** Types of foods digestible

- **Weight**
- **Height**
- **Armor:** Defensive apparatus such as horns, scales, and so on
- **Weaponry:** Teeth, claws, and so on
- **Sensory acuity:** How good the eyes, ears, and nose are
- **Social intelligence:** Ability to cooperate with others in the same species

The set of genotypes is as follows:

- **Musculature:** Overall strength
- **Cerebellar size:** Fineness of control of musculature
- **Muscular efficiency:** Power output per kilogram of muscle
- **Digestive tract size:** Directly affects digestive efficiency
- **Armor**
- **Weaponry**
- **Sensory**
- **Social intelligence**

You will note that many of the genotypes match closely with phenotypes. However, there's a trick: Each genotype contributes positively or negatively to several phenotypes. For example, musculature increases speed, maneuverability, and agility, but it also increases weight and decreases metabolic efficiency. If you build a carnivore with lots of strengths (say, plenty of speed, maneuverability, agility, weaponry, sensory acuity, and social intelligence), then the poor thing will be huge and have monstrous caloric requirements; it'll starve if it doesn't eat at least a cow a day.

So here's how the game works: At the outset of the game, early evolution has produced two competing biochemistries, one controlled by the player, the other by the computer. Each of these biochemistries has produced just two animals: one herbivore and one carnivore. Although the biochemistries are somehow incompatible, they both can eat the same plants and grasses, and the carnivores can digest the meat of both kinds of animal. In other words, there are two evolutionary teams: the player's critters and the computer's critters.

The environment in which the players compete is a mix of grasslands, savannah, and forest. The two teams have the same set of genes for corresponding creatures, and the overall system is in balance with each creature pursuing an environmentally stable strategy. However, all four critters are optimized for life in the grasslands. In other words, there are just cows and lions. Each species consists of a certain number of individuals.

The player's basic verb is "speciate," which splits a species into a main group, which is unchanged, and a small splinter group of 100 individuals, whose genes the player can alter as part of the speciation process. However, the player can change only a single gene for each speciation act, and the player can speciate a species only when it has at least 1000 individuals. The player also gets to name the new species.

The new species must now compete in the environment against all the other species. Critters play no favorites—they'll happily wipe out another species on the same side if it's to their advantage. This is not necessarily bad; the player wants to set up a healthy ecosystem with herbivores providing food for carnivores.

The goal of the game is to achieve maximum gross nutrient extraction in a specified number of turns (shorter for beginning games, longer for advanced games). Maximum gross nutrient extraction means hogging the nutrients provided by the plant life. Those nutrients come in many forms: leafy tissue, seeds, and fruits. Players must therefore build a broad range of herbivores capable of getting all those goodies, but players must also build carnivores to harvest the herbivores better than the computer's carnivores do. Suppose, for example, that at the outset of the game, the plant life is generating 100 units of nutrients every turn, the cows on both sides are each harvesting 20 units of those nutrients (for a total of 40 units), and the lions on both sides are also each harvesting 20 units of cow nutrients each turn (but 20 nutrient units of lion die off each turn, too). This is a stable system; every turn, 20 new units come into the animal system, pass through the cows and lions, and leave the system. The player and the computer each have a score of 40 points. Suppose now that the player creates a new species with better digestive efficiency, and it can now harvest 25 units of plants, but nothing else changes. The player now has 45 points each turn. Of course, the lion populations of both sides will grow slightly to take advantage of the greater number of cows, until the system stabilizes again.

There are all sorts of directions this design could expand in. For example, the simple predator-herbivore model could be vastly expanded into all sorts of other types of critters. How about bugs, or scavengers, or birds? I'd love to introduce changing environments as ways to challenge species, and the occasional giant meteor could certainly inject lots of chaos into the game.

The Self-Modifying Game

Back in the good old days, we programming cowboys had a trick that's seldom used these days: self-modifying code. One segment of code rewrote another segment of code. This was frowned upon because it made debugging particularly difficult. How could you tell where the problem was arising if you couldn't know which version of the code was actually executing?

Nevertheless, there were some situations in which self-modifying code was useful. One of these was anti-piracy. If self-modifying code was difficult for the programmer to debug, imagine how tough it would be on a pirate! I used that trick twice, and I still smile at the thought of some poor teenage geek running through code, trying to figure it out, and then encountering a piece of code that has changed behind his back. Knowing the way these hackers think, it was certain to send avalanches of "that does not compute!" waves rippling through his brain.

There were also a few cases where self-modifying code could save a few bytes or a few cycles of code, but they were seldom worth the effort. Besides, you couldn't use self-modifying code with a ROM cartridge. All in all, it just wasn't a good idea.

But self-modifying code has always held a fascination for many programmers, and it seems to me that this fascination could carry over nicely to game design. What would it be like to play a game in which the rules changed while you played?

The idea is not original to me; it's been done a number of times. Mathematicians and game theorists have toyed with the idea for years; Douglas Hofstedter discussed such games in *Metamagical Themas*. While most self-modifying games are really exercises in mathematical cleverness, **Cosmic Encounter** is genuinely fun. Two of my other milestone games, **Illuminati** and **Magic the Gathering**, have mild self-modifying elements in them.

If we wish to be liberal with our definition of self-modification, we could say that **Pac-Man** has a self-modifying element. When the player eats a power pill, the tables are turned on the ghosts, for now the player can dispatch them by chasing them down. For a short period of time, the roles reverse. This is a kind of rules change.

The problem with self-modifying games is keeping a lid on them. How does one permit rules changes while ensuring that nobody can get a lock on victory with some simple trick? Previous games have accomplished this by restricting rules changes to particular cards that must be played to alter the rules. The players are not allowed to make up any old rule change; they must confine themselves to the set of rules changes that are pre-defined for them. This tends to keep the rules changes rather modest. But I think that the computer offers us a great opportunity to design much richer self-modifying games.

We must be clear to differentiate self-modifying games from variable scenario games. Such games permit the player to make rules modifications at the beginning of the game; most of the times such modifications exist for handicapping purposes or to explore variations on the game. The differentiating factor is the ability to change the structure of the game in the middle of gameplay and the fact that these changes are meant to be an intrinsic part of the gameplay.

The simplest form of self-modifying game does nothing more than change parameters critical to the game. Some variable scenario games permit a certain amount of this during gameplay, but this is primarily for real-time adjustment of play balance. If the player is getting clobbered, he can request a really big gun. Indeed, some games do this automatically; if the game detects that the player is doing poorly, it adjusts one or more game parameters to make things easier for the player. This is not what I mean by a self-modifying game.

What I mean by a self-modifying game is one in which the rules change during play of the game. Of course, we all know that data and process are interchangeable, and since rules are really just processes, rules can also be treated as data, and therefore my claim that parameter-changing games don't count as rules-changing games is not strictly correct. Nevertheless, to convert changeable rules into changeable data requires a degree of abstraction that most people find noisome.

Of course, such abstraction need not be foisted on the players; the program might well change parameter #27 from a 6 to a 7, but the player might experience this change by discovering that his shotgun is now shooting marshmallows.

The trick, of course, is that the changes to the game must be related to the behavior of the player. A simple way to accomplish this would be to set up a series of parallel universes, giving the player the ability to jump between universes that retain the same map, but in which the rules of play are different. Suppose, for example, that we have a standard first-person shooter. The player is stalking through the blue universe when suddenly he is confronted by a hook-nosed warblestomper! Egad! Those things are impervious to all gunfire! Thinking fast, the player hits his Universe Jump button, and finds himself facing the same hook-nosed warblestomper in the orange universe. Here, gunfire is just as useless against warblestompers, but gravity is ten times stronger, and the warblestomper's great mass renders him immobile. With great effort, the player climbs the stairs to a point overlooking the warblestomper and then drops a coin onto the monster, which slices through him like a bullet. But look! Now there's a Muscle-skito flying towards him! Time to change universes!

In general, this kind of environmental change is the easiest way to implement self-modifying games. It makes much more sense than a game in which rules appear to change arbitrarily. The other way to pull it off is the method used in **Magic the Gathering**: use magic. However, magic seems to me a ploy used by insufficiently imaginative designers. It's rather like the cartoon of the scientist working on a huge mathematical derivation who has obviously hit an impossible obstruction. There's a gap in the equations, with an arrow pointing to the phrase "And then a miracle happens!" followed by the remaining formula. Miracles are a cheap way out, and after a while the arbitrariness of magic confuses the player. It's better to have a complete, consistent system that the player can grasp as a whole.

Mooser-Gooser

Necessity is the mother of invention. We seldom apply this handy-dandy aphorism to our work, because necessity is seldom a concept we apply to entertainment. However, when my good friend Laura Mixon found herself working a three-month contract in San Francisco, with her family remaining in Albuquerque, her sadness at being isolated from her husband and her little girls quickly became a matter of deep concern. She phoned home every night, but conversation just wasn't enough. She wanted something more, some way to spend time with them. One evening we spoke just after she had conversed with her family, and she was feeling particularly homesick. I tried to empathize, but never having had children, I was doing a bad job of it. "Can't you make me a computer game that I could play with my kids?" Laura asked. Thus was **Mooser-Gooser** born.

It didn't take long to establish the basic design concepts. At one end of an Internet connection is a parent wishing to spend some time with a faraway child; at the other end is a child whose conversational skills leave much to be desired, but who loves to play games. The trick, I realized, is to build a two-player game with asymmetric skills required of the two players. My design assumption was that this game was for parents of small children; the ten-year-old probably doesn't need parents intruding into their videogame playing. But smaller children, say, six years old, are a different matter. They can't automatically outperform their parent; they'll need some help. Yet, the game could not take the form of parent guiding the child at all times; children need some sense of their own power. The child must have some power, too. This in turn implies a third player: Mooser-Gooser the dog, named after my dog Moose, a large, lovable lunkhead. The child gives orders to Mooser-Gooser. Thus, we have three players with three different sets of capabilities. The parent is larger than the child, able to reach higher, climb over taller obstructions, and to lift heavy things. The child is smaller and so can crawl through small holes that the adult can't negotiate. Mooser-Gooser, when properly instructed, can jump over gaps and retrieve objects. He can also run fast if need be.

This provides the basis for a great platform game. Parent, child, and Mooser-Gooser must negotiate a series of vertical mazes, overcoming lots of obstacles. They must pool their special capabilities to tackle each problem. Sometimes the child will crawl through a small hole and drag a ladder back through it so that the parent can climb over the obstacle. Sometimes Mooser-Gooser will jump over a gap carrying a rope so that the parent can fashion a bridge using the rope as the starting point.

Sometimes the parent will lift the child over a tall wall. Sometimes they'll both be able to get past an obstacle, but Mooser-Gooser won't, and they'll have to devise a means of getting Mooser-Gooser past it.

A tough problem arises from the possibility of virtual injury. We must challenge the two players with obstacles, but we cannot permit anybody to suffer virtual injury in this game. Nobody can fall, be crushed, or otherwise hurt. Yet how can we provide an interesting set of obstacles without imposing some risk? I came up with two solutions, neither of which completely satisfies me.

The first solution makes missteps impossible. Mooser-Gooser won't jump a gap unless he can do so successfully. If ordered to jump too large a gap, he simply paces back and forth at the edge whining. This requires a somewhat different input structure. Instead of giving the players full motion freedom with a mouse, we would instead give them chunky verbs. For example, motion verbs would be handled by clicking on a destination icon, perhaps a blinking star. Thus, the child need not have ideal motor control; he simply clicks on the desired destination and his avatar moves there. We can then prevent accidents by offering only those destinations that can be safely reached.

The problem with this approach, as with all such "precluded input" systems, is that it frustrates the player who cannot see how to achieve the desired goal. It is structurally no different from the infuriating word processing program that will not permit you to carry out your desired task because "you haven't done something else yet." Of course, we could argue that, unlike a word processing program, the whole point and purpose of this game would be to solve puzzles. Nevertheless, I remain uncomfortable with this solution.

The second solution is a literal *deus ex machina*. Should somebody misstep, an angel appears, flies down, catches the unfortunate, and flies them back to the point of departure. If the parent doesn't like angels, this agent could be a fairy godmother, the ghost of a departed loved

25

There are a million great game ideas just waiting to be implemented.

one, or their tax accountant. My discomfort with this approach mirrors our universal distaste for all *deus ex machina* solutions.

Mooser-Gooser could be a great game. Surely the need is there; between traveling parents, divorced parents, and parents with limited visitation rights, there are plenty of people who could appreciate the opportunities opened up by such a gentle, warm-hearted game.

So What Does All This Mean?

This chapter attempts to demonstrate that games don't have to follow the same tired old conventions. Here were 13 ideas, none of which follow any of the current conventions of game design—yet each one could be made into a compelling game, even a hit if well implemented.

storytelling
storytelling

Games and storytelling have a long and twisted history. Brenda Laurel was the first exponent of storytelling in computer games; she wrote a number of influential works on the theoretical problems. The game design community seemed to like the idea of stories mixed with games, but could never figure out how to do it. They especially liked the idea of making games more "cinematic," but few had any idea of what that entailed.

Adventure Games

There were plenty of early, blundering attempts in the general direction of storytelling. The adventure games of the early 1980s made an attempt in this direction. Although they were really just extended groups of random puzzles, they were often organized along the lines of a story. InfoCom pushed things forward in the mid-80s with a series of artistically impressive adventure games. **Trinity**, **A Mind Forever Voyaging**, and a well-done adaptation of **Hitchhiker's Guide to the Galaxy** all showed how much could be accomplished within the limited confines of the text adventure genre. However, text adventures were overtaken by graphic adventures, which tended to be weaker on story, and the promising initial effort led nowhere. (The LucasArts graphics adventures provide an important exception; they pushed the story aspect harder than most graphic adventures. Sadly, despite their great commercial success, they failed to inspire the industry to follow their lead.) Nowadays, text adventure aficionados prefer the cognomen "interactive fiction," but in fact, the genre remains nothing more than a series of obscure puzzles stitched together under a single storyline. The most successful of these to date is the **Myst** series of graphic adventures. They boast glorious graphics, a well-done storyline, and a better-than-average set of obscure puzzles.

Some enthusiasts claim that adventure games like **Myst** and its sequels constitute genuine interactive storytelling. To say this with a straight face requires a considerably expanded definition of interactive storytelling. The story in an adventure game is fixed and complete; there is nothing for the player to do other than to experience the story. **Myst** worked well because the story was presented in a fragmented form that required the player to piece it together to understand it. But there was no interaction whatsoever between the player and the story. No matter what the player did, it was always exactly the same story. The most interactivity he could hope for was to experience different fragments of the entire story—in which case, the experience was unsatisfying because the story never came to a conclusion.

> As a historical side note, I should point out that the idea of presenting a fragmented story for the player to piece together was not original to **Myst**; I believe that Rob Swigart created the first such adventure game sometime around 1988.

NOTE

Sadly, despite many years of dedicated work by a cadre of devoted followers, adventure games have failed to deliver anything more (in the way of storytelling) than the early InfoCom games. The genre has its appeals, but storytelling is not one of them.

Backstory

From earliest times, computer games were provided with a backstory, the dramatic context in which the game takes place. This was often presented in part on the back of the game box and fully presented at the beginning of the manual. "The evil Klogg empire has sent its squadrons of Death Fighters to attack Earth. All resistance has been overcome save for a single Earth Fighter; now it's your job to stop the Kloggs!" This was followed by the now-standard line, "The fate of humanity is at stake!" Gee, with stakes like that, who could resist? Unfortunately, the reality of the game always fell far below the promise of the box. Its cover might show a muscled man fighting off dastardly monsters while a woman equipped with physiologically impossible breasts clings to his knees, but the game itself would have little more than orange squares moving around randomly, with a purple square (that's the player, bent on saving humanity) darting about emitting little blue dots that hit orange squares and make them disappear. The incongruity between the lurid text and imagery of the box and the clumsy graphics on the screen was laughable to all but the game players.

Backstory continues to hold its place in games, if only because they *do* require some sort of dramatic context to explain the events taking place. A great deal of sage advice and erudite writing on the subject has smitten the games industry; would that it had some significance. The fact is, backstory is simply not part of the game; it's mere window dressing. The quality of the backstory has no significance to the game itself; a weak backstory cannot ruin a strong game, and a strong backstory cannot salvage a weak game. Some of the biggest hits in the history of games— **Space Invaders**, **Pac-Man**, **Civilization**, and **The Sims**—have no backstory whatever.

Cut Scenes

The lurid graphics of the game box first migrated onto the computer in the form of *splash screens*, single screens presented at the outset of the game with its title and provenance. These screens were progressively gussied up with ever-better graphics, until they were quite swishy affairs. The next logical step was to integrate some of those flashy splash screens into the game. Cinematronics was one of the early perpetrators of this behavior, mixing great-looking stills with less-than-great-looking game screens. As the practice spread, it acquired the name *cut scene* to differentiate it from the splash screen.

Although there were many interesting variations on the idea, the scheme that best exemplifies it was the big hit of the early 90s, **Wing Commander**. This was a reworking of the Atari game **Star Raiders** for the PC, with cut scenes added. The player would fly out for some first-person space combat, at the end of which he returned to base where a new cut scene advanced the overarching story one more step. If the player survived enough missions, the entire story would be revealed, cut scene by cut scene. It may sound rather lame today, but back then, this was heady stuff.

The next step was the, video cut scene. In the early 90s, getting good full-screen, full-motion on the computer screen was a major technological hurdle. One of the earliest solutions was worked out by Graeme Devine, who teamed up with Rob Landeros to build a game using this great new technology. The result was a hugely successful Franken-game, **The 7th Guest**. This game spliced a series of nicely done puzzles into another series of video squibs that advanced the story. The story didn't have much to do with the puzzles, but the technology was so impressive that most people didn't care—they could see real video on their computer screens! The process continued with a number of later games such as the **Final Fantasy** series and the **Metal Gear Solid** series, and it has maintained some popularity.

Integrated Cut Scenes

The next step in this snail-like evolution was the presentation of the cut scenes using the same graphics engine as was used for the game itself. **Half-Life** pioneered this technique. This greatly smoothed the transition for game to cut scene. The jarring effect of jumping from one graphics style to another graphics style was eliminated; the experienced smoothly flowed from game to story and back again. The story itself remained functionally isolated from the game; nothing that happened in the game affected the story itself. This required some story jury-rigging. The easiest arrangement was to simply kill off the story with the player; should the player die, then there was no opportunity to see the rest of the story, which makes sense because the player was the protagonist anyway. You can't tell a story with a dead hero. The designer had to hamstring the game so that it marched along a narrow path leading to either victory or death; these were the only two story developments permitted in the game itself. Later, a few designers embellished this concept by adding a handful of endings and a corresponding number of game developments that would send the player to one of the pre-defined conclusions.

Despite their clear superiority, integrated cut scenes don't solve the problem of interactive storytelling, because they do nothing to make the story interactive. The stories in such games are still fixed, with little or no opportunity to respond to the player. The story and the game remain isolated from each other; these designs are shotgun weddings.

Here Come the Academics!

By the mid-90s, many computer scientists had decided that storytelling was an exciting research area, and some interesting work was being done. The games community continued to pursue its cut-scene approach, but the academics were trying a completely different tack. Actually, they were trying a number of completely different tacks.

Agent Technology

The idea here is to anthropomorphize a hunk of software. When attempting to design a big, complicated software system, let's think of that system as a little man who single-mindedly pursues our desired task. What would that little man think? What would be his motivations? How would we implement his desires? Computer users first saw agents as little "help wizards" who would pop up on the screen and offer assistance. The concept was sound, but the implementation succeeded only in annoying millions of people.

While software agents as "intelligent help systems" or "proactive user manuals" weren't much of a hit, a number of people realized that they might be useful in a narrative context. Joe Bates at Carnegie-Mellon University developed this concept with the Oz project; that project was followed by more ambitious efforts by Barbara Hayes-Roth at Stanford and Joe in his new startup. While the results so far are interesting, nobody using this technique has generated anything that can be called interactive storytelling. Agent technology has utility in a variety of fields, but it's still not a technology for interactive storytelling.

Story Generation Systems

The concept here is quite old: Can we write software that generates stories? The first such effort, **TaleSpin**, was built in the 1970s, and it was very impressive at that time. Then came **Brutus**, a system narrowly focusing on betrayal as a narrative schema. Brutus was an impressive demonstration of AI techniques, but as a technology for interactive storytelling, it suffered from two problems: First, it could handle only betrayal, with no indication that other themes could be addressed, and second, it offered no handle on the problem of achieving interactivity. **Brutus** generated a story using parameters supplied by the user, but the system was intrinsically inimical to interactivity; it plotted out the narrative arc in a single pass.

A variety of other systems are also under development, but have received little attention. Certainly a great deal of talent is attacking this problem, and I expect to see a great many interesting experiments in coming years.

Role-Playing Games

Players of these games have always placed high value on the quality of the storytelling. Indeed, the original role-playing game (RPG), **Dungeons & Dragons**, invented by Gary Gygax and Dave Arneson, thrived on the storytelling talents of the person running the game for the players (the Dungeon Master). However, computer RPG's were able to develop every aspect of the genre *except* the storytelling; over the years, these games have become ever richer in their combat systems, in the richness of detail of the worlds they offer, and in many other ways. But the storytelling aspect of computer RPG's has continued to languish. Many RPG players bemoan this problem, and a number of worthy attempts have been made to address it. So far, however, the genre has not generated any major new ideas about how to integrate storytelling with games.

In some ways, the emphasis on character development has impeded progress in storytelling with RPGs. The central premise of these games is that the player steadily builds his abilities by acquiring wealth, tools, weapons, and experience. This emphasis on character development tends to work against the needs of dramatic development—dramatic twists and turns clash with the prevailing tone of steady advancement. Fortunately, this impediment is not fundamental to the RPG genre; it is a cultural expectation rather than an architectural necessity. While this cultural expectation impedes the development of storytelling in RPGs, there is nothing stopping bolder designers from pushing against this constraint. While RPGs at present have little to show in the way of storytelling prowess, I suspect that we may see some interesting developments in the field.

The Real Problem

Despite many interesting developments, storytelling and games are still far apart, and I am pessimistic about the likelihood of the two ever merging. This is not to say that interactive storytelling has little future;

my point is that we are unlikely to see anything impressive emerge from the games industry in the matter of storytelling. The real problem lies in the heart and soul of the industry. The games industry is a bastion of techie-geek triumphalism; it has no truck with those soft-headed artsie-fartsie people. In their hearts, games people believe that any problem can be solved with sufficient attention to technical detail.

When in the summer of 2001 two movies, *Shrek* and *Final Fantasy*, competed for ticket sales, and *Shrek* outsold *Final Fantasy* by ten to one, the computer games people were nonplussed. How could a graphically inferior product like *Shrek* have more appeal than a state-of-the-art work like *Final Fantasy*? The notion that *Shrek* had a better story and more interesting characters simply never caught on with these people. They just didn't *Get It*. Their worldview is literalist in a logical, physical, and spatial sense. When they sit down to create a game universe in their computer, their first act is to set up the spatial coordinate system and the map of their world. Then they populate it with physical objects and endow those physical objects with physical properties obeying physical laws programmed into the virtual universe. All very neat and tidy.

A storyteller setting out to build a virtual world would use a completely different approach. Her first task would most likely be to create a set of characters. Then she would endow those characters with dramatic traits. I doubt that she would ever get around to worrying about the spatial relationships among the various stages on which her dramatic action would take place.

This is the essential difference between game designers and storytellers: The game designers see the universe—everything!—as a gigantic physical system that need only be simulated with sufficient fidelity to achieve any goal. The notion that you can define the universe in human terms seems utter nonsense to them.

This mental fixation leads directly to the current idiocy gripping the imagination of the game design world: that stories can be tucked into games like any other components. To them, drama is just one more physical system to be simulated, like ballistics or optics. A game is a collection of interacting subsystems: a 3D engine, a physics engine, and, oh yes, a drama engine, too. We'll just start with the same old shoot-em-up, puzzle-solving, resource management game and stuff a little drama in there as well. Hire some Hollywood expert to write up something pretty and mash it into the pile, right?

Of course this cannot work; it's trying to pose a question in the wrong frame of reference. Figuring the dramatic content of a bullet ripping through a monster's flesh is as futile as calculating the distance from MacBeth's castle to the witch's cave using the lines of dialog in the play—and just as silly. In order to understand story, you have to be a Romantic with a capital R. And let's face it: There are no romantics, even with low-ercase r's, in this business. Games people will never, ever *Get It*, because they are stuck in a worldview that sees human emotions as mere "parameters," rather than the fundamental drivers of human experience.

Tackling the Problem

Someday, interactive storytelling will surely flower into the mass market of interactive entertainment that games have failed to achieve. The trick to accomplishing this great goal is to make a break with the past. In both marketing terms and design terms, there is no evolutionary path from games to interactive storytelling. The people who pull this off will start with a completely new technology and approach a completely new market.

The design break is easy to conceptualize and immensely difficult to build. What is the fundamental component common to both story and interactivity? Answer: choice. Aristotle placed choice at the core of story; choice reveals character. And choice lies at the heart of interactivity; a user makes a choice with a keyboard or mouse, and the computer responds to that choice.

26

LESSON

It's the
verbs,
stupid!

Verbs are the vehicle of choice in the same way that money is the vehicle of wealth. Whenever we make a choice, we are choosing between verbs. We don't choose between Door #1, Door #2, and Door #3; we choose between *going through* Door #1, *going through* Door #2, and *going through* Door #3. We choose between *kissing* the girl goodnight or *shaking* her hand goodnight. We choose between *clicking* this button or *scrolling* that window.

Here's the killer problem in interactive storytelling: We need thousands of verbs. Open up your favorite novel and count the pages. Now count how many sentences there are on the average page. Multiply the two counts together and you get the total number of sentences in your novel—and each and every one of those sentences has a verb. That's how many verbs you need for good storytelling.

The problem is ameliorated by the frequent re-use of verbs. The single verb "tell" will appear hundreds of times, often in the form of synonyms such as "explain," "say," "relate," "object," and so on. A novel with tens of thousands of sentences may need only thousands of verbs.

Unfortunately, thousands of verbs are still a great many. Can you imagine designing and balancing a system involving such a huge number of verbs? Those verbs don't fall into some simple pattern or system that makes it possible to put them in a simple database. It won't do to prepare a table of each verb's effects on affection, charisma, strength, agility, and so forth; in drama, the effects of different verbs are unique to each verb. Each verb must be custom-programmed.

Any programmer can tell you that any programming problem can be solved with either a code-based approach or a table-driven approach. To use my own terminology, one can use either a process-intensive approach or a data-intensive approach, or any combination of the two. In general, when you have many variations on a single theme, it's more efficient to use a table-driven approach.

Interactive storytelling requires revolutionaries, not evolutionaries.

We see this process in games programs. The big parts, like level maps and weapons characteristics, are all table-driven, while the verbs, being few in number, are always handled with code. Games programmers often build custom tools for manipulating the huge databases required in some games: level editors, map editors, character editors, and so forth. But the verbs themselves are always handled with custom code.

This won't work with interactive storytelling, because interactive storytelling demands too many verbs for a customized approach. We must therefore create development environments that combine a database system with a programming system. Think of it as a database manager for verbs with an embedded programming language for interactive storytelling, all highly optimized for the problems specific to interactive storytelling.

We'll also need a new class of storyteller: somebody who understands interactivity as well as story, and who does not shirk from the minor programming demanded by the development environment.

As you can see, all this will require major breaks with the past. We need new technology, new creative talent, and a new marketplace. It's going to be a tough slog—but what revolution wasn't a tough slog?

random sour observations

random sour observations

You would never guess it from my comments in this book, but I have a reputation for, shall we say, outspokenness. That reputation is mostly on the mark, although it is often colored by the anger of those whom I have skewered. My particular talent is not for detecting problems—anybody can bitch—but rather for phrasing my criticisms in a style that hits hard. I hold euphemism and tactful ellipticity in contempt; integrity demands the expression of the truth in the clearest and most compelling terms. I am no heartless monster; in discussions of a personal nature, the feelings of my interlocutor are my primary concern. But in the world of ideas, feelings have no place. I would abandon a discredited idea with ruthless disloyalty, and I assault faulty ideas with barbaric ferocity. Playing intellectual hardball would not, by itself, have earned me a reputation for ferocity. My crime is applying my talent for language and metaphor to such discussions.

Viewed from a distance, some of my more colorful expressions are truly funny. I once condemned the solitary, unsocial aspect of computer games by comparing them with inflatable dolls. It was the ideal metaphor, capturing the pathetic and slightly sick nature of computer game playing. The metaphor hit home because it contains a solid germ of truth; it infuriated people because it demeans their enjoyment of games while simultaneously questioning their manhood.

This chapter is a potpourri of such observations on those aspects of game design that don't fit into any other chapters. Perhaps it should have been entitled "Crotchety Crawford Crapola." Readers whose sense of humor exceeds their sense of identification with ideas will chuckle over this chapter; all others will be outraged.

Massively Multiplayer Monsters

One of the most interesting ideas to emerge from bringing the computer to games was the massively multiplayer game, in which hundreds or thousands of people play together via the Internet. The field is still young, but most of the basic parameters have now been set.

These games are handicapped by what is to me a killer problem: No player can truly play. The games are necessarily egalitarian—we can't have a single player dominating the game or making all the important decisions. Beginners have just as much right to have fun as the old pros—their money is just as green. Accordingly, the old pros must make some concessions to the beginners; they simply can't mow down the beginners and grab their goods, even though it would be easy to do so. The decision-making process must therefore be broken down and distributed among many players; everybody gets an equally small share of the overall decision-making pie. Being a cog in a machine is necessary in real social environments, but it's not very playful.

So why are they so successful? With one important exception, these games are little more than structured, goal-oriented chat rooms, and their popularity parallels the success of chat rooms. They provide a meeting place for people of like interests to chat and meet new friends. They are, of course, more than simple chat rooms, because friends can participate in adventures together. Much the same experience could be provided by any structured, goal-oriented chat room: chat room quiz shows, chat room debate tournaments, and so forth.

The major exception to which I refer is team behavior. The best examples of this are the air combat massively multiplayer games, such as the old **Air Warrior** game on the GENIE service. In this game, dozens or hundreds of players take to the air, each player piloting one aircraft (or helping man a bomber), with entire air squadrons battling it out. In these games, there is no overriding presumption of egalitarianism. A rank beginner can happily accept a lowly position as a gunner, while old pros need not compromise their talents to give beginners a fair chance. Besides, any beginner who insists on piloting a hot fighter will likely be shot down in the first few minutes anyway. However, he still provides some benefit to his team, if only by forcing the enemy to waste some ammunition shooting him down.

Licensed Games

MegaMovie Studio will soon be releasing their big summer movie, *Big Bob Broadshoulders*, and they want a game to go along with the movie. The project has wended its way through layers of bigshots and has landed on your shoulders. You must now design a game about Big Bob Broadshoulders. My advice is simple: Grab any plausible existing game design and re-create it with Big Bob cosmetics. Use lots of Big Bob images, stills from the movie, and sound grabs of some of Bob's more distinctive pronouncements. Get the studio to film a few snippets of video for direct inclusion in the game. The game itself could be anything: **Tic-Tac-Toe**, **Monopoly**, **Space Invaders**, or **Quake**. It really doesn't matter what game you choose, so long as it gives you plenty of opportunity to slap in lots of Big Bob cosmetics. Use an already-established, absolutely conventional design; the only place to exercise any artistic energy is in the insertion of Big Bob cosmetics.

The one thing you *don't* want to do is waste time and energy trying to get creative with the game design. This will only cost money and cause you grief. Consider the economic realities: Nobody is going to purchase a **Big Bob Broadshoulders** game for the creativity of the game itself;

28
LESSON

Build
licensed
products for
money, not
creative
challenge.

they are buying it solely because of the brand. Any exertions you make to give them creative design are wasted; they don't want creativity, they want Big Bob. Moreover, the licensor retains veto power over your design. Licensing people have no sense of good game design; all they know and care about is maintaining the value of their brand. Never forget that the greatest bomb in the history of videogames was **E.T.**, which was approved by Steven Spielberg himself. The primary role of licensing people in the game development process is necessarily negative. They can proscribe certain features as incompatible with the Big Bob brand, but they can never suggest anything useful. Therefore, your primary problem is to create nothing that these people could disapprove of. Stick close to what already exists, and you're safe; wander away and you'll spend months fighting a losing battle.

New Input Devices

Let's face it—the input devices available to us are pretty boring. Whether it's keyboard plus mouse on the PC or gamepad on the videogame, there's a need for something more. Unfortunately, none of the ideas that I have seen in these many years has been worthwhile.

Brainwave Headband

The absolute worst idea was the "brainwave headband" (also known as the Atari MindLink). Atari experimented with this idea in the early 80s. The concept was simple: Control the computer with your thoughts! A headband with simple detectors would detect your brainwaves and pass the results on to the computer. Such a device was built and actually worked after a fashion; you really could play a videogame using the device. However, the device picked up muscle control neuron activity just as easily as it picked up brain activity, and so it was easier to control it with head muscles than with brainwaves. During intense gameplay, players tended to scrunch their eyebrows around to control the headband, leading to excruciating headaches afterward. The product was never marketed.

Exercise Cycle

A close second in overall stupidity was the "Atari exercise cycle." The idea here was to combat the rather tawdry image of videogames by building a videogame into an exercise cycle, providing good, healthy exercise while you played your videogame. Two design strategies were explored: meandering and fleeing. The meandering strategy offered a screen of pleasant, beautiful bicycle paths among trees. As you cycled along, the scenery changed. This design strategy failed for two reasons:

- First, the sensory input was always much inferior to the real thing.
- Second, it wasn't much fun.

The second design strategy suffered from a completely different problem. What we imagined here was a Tyrannosaurus Rex chasing the player, whose video screen functioned rather like a rear-view mirror. The player had to pedal faster to escape the monster. This was all good fun, and seemed a viable product, until somebody asked what would happen should one of our customers suffer a heart attack while playing. Oops—back to the drawing board.

Nowadays, with better graphics capabilities, products using the first strategy have finally come to market.

Force Feedback

One early idea that did impress me was the "force feedback joystick." This little doodad was a joystick with powerful electromagnets built in that allowed the joystick to fight back against you. The demonstration game that the research team put together for this device was quite impressive. It was nothing more than a fishing game. The joystick acted rather like a fishing pole. The rules were simple: the fish would tug at the line, causing the joystick to jerk in one direction. If the player allowed it to travel all the way to the end of its travel in that direction, then the fish broke the line and got away. The fish was programmed to wait random intervals and then jerk in random directions. The kinesthetic aspect of the experience was uncannily realistic; feeling that stick jerk around in your hands really created the impression of a living thing fighting back.

A variation on this is the "force feedback mouse," a mouse with a device that provides extra friction under software control. This could be used to create a tactile sense of boundaries (e.g., the user feels a slight bump when moving out of a window). This simple addition to existing mouse technology provided a useful enhancement, and there were several unsuccessful attempts to market such a device.

The killer problem, of course, was enticing enough software developers to support the device. Even without this problem (suppose, say, that Microsoft builds support for the device into Windows), there are still serious problems. First, the resistance must be tactile, not just visual. It would be simple to build mouse software that slows the cursor down slightly on encountering bumps, but this would provide mere visual feedback; the power of the idea comes from the kinesthetic feeling of the mouse in the user's hand. Unfortunately, mechanical mice are rapidly being replaced by optical mice, which don't offer any possibilities for tactile feedback.

Eyeball Tracker

A particularly exotic input is the "eyeball tracker." This little doodad watches the eye of the user and figures out where it's looking. The algorithm is surprisingly simple: You need merely compare the iris with the cornea; the offset of their centers gives you an accurate indicator of the direction in which the eye is looking. The problem is made difficult, however, by the rapid motion of the eye, which jumps around wildly in compiling a complete internal representation of the scene. With fast enough processing, this problem can be overcome. But even then, there remains the much more subjective task of determining the user's intentions from his eyeballs. Humans are capable of furtive glances, blank stares, sidelong glances, nervous peeks, and all manner of other visual behaviors; what is the poor computer to make of all this activity?

Microphone

The one alternative input device for which I have high hopes is the microphone. The hardware is cheap, the software for voice recognition is well-developed, the machine cycles required are now available with the current crop of CPUs, and most computers now have microphone input jacks. It is a simple matter to integrate voice commands into existing software; indeed, for a transitional period, voice commands could merely duplicate existing keyboard-driven commands.

The power of voice commands lies in two factors:

- First, voice is a completely different input channel. The user can use it while continuing to use the hands for mouse, keyboard, or game controller.

- Second, voice is familiar to users, and we often use voice in conjunction with our hands.

The objection is often raised that voice input is subject to external noise emanating from other persons nearby. I give this objection little credence. Most computers are used privately; loud nearby conversations would be just as distracting to a user working on a spreadsheet as to the computer trying to hear and understand that user. Moreover, the use of head-mounted, noise-canceling microphones dramatically limits the ability of others to interfere. At this moment, thousands of drudges crowded together in telephone solicitation sweatshops are carrying out thousands of simultaneous conversations in close proximity without noise problems. They could just as well be talking to computers with just as little interference.

Specialized Input Devices

There remains a number of interesting input devices custom-designed for particular games. The most impressive of these is the set of pads provided with **Dance Dance Revolution**; they permit the player to dance with the game, with the player's dance steps becoming inputs to the game. This was a brilliant use of specialized hardware to extend the expressive reach of a game far beyond the traditional. Such specialized input devices are expensive and impose considerable risk on the company placing them on the market; nevertheless, as **Dance Dance Revolution** shows, such an approach can produce successful products.

The Sims

During the 1980s, I employed considerable irony in self-deprecatingly referring to myself as "Zee Greatest Game Designer in Zee Universe." However, since then, Will Wright has demonstrated such a powerful combination of imagination, abstraction, background research, and design perspicacity that I have long since yielded the olive branch to him. His masterpiece, **The Sims**, is without doubt one of the greatest achievements in computer game design, and it has rightly enjoyed huge success.

These things said, I cannot resist the opportunity to take a few sour pot shots at this great work. I offer my complaints not to detract from the reputation of this great game but to demonstrate that even the very best of games have flaws.

The most obvious mistake was the inclusion of urination and defecation in the game. What possible benefit do these features bring to the design? They offer no interesting challenges to the player; it's not as if a character's bladder will explode should the player not walk them to the bathroom often enough. This is distracting realism: It offers nothing in terms of gameplay. It's rather like Leonardo da Vinci carefully painting the fly crawling across the Mona Lisa's face.

In contrast to this over-precise simulation, there are some ghastly errors of omission. This was most powerfully driven home to me when I played with the demo version of the game. It showed a little girl being haunted by a spook who would pop out of the walls in obvious "Boo!" behavior. The frightened child would flee to another room, where the spook would eventually find her and repeat his routine. This went on through half the night. Eventually the child wandered into her parents' bedroom. "Aha!" I thought to myself. "She'll crawl into bed with Mommy for some com-forting." But no, such behavior is beyond the depth of the world of **The Sims**. The little girl simply collapsed at the foot of the bed and fell asleep on the floor. I was mystified. But the coup de grâce was yet to come. Morning came, Mommy sat up in bed, yawned, stretched, and stood up. She then commenced her morning routine by walking over to the bathroom for her ablutions—stepping over the prostrate form of her daughter to get to the bathroom. Now, to my way of thinking, the rela-tionship between mother and daughter deserves far more attention than such things as going to the bathroom or washing the dishes.

To be fair to Will, I must point out that the algorithms required to man-age emotional relationships are much more difficult to handle than those required for urination or home maintenance. Still, the incongruity of the detailed simulation of minor details and the complete absence of information about much more important family matters leaps out at me. Perhaps Will was wise to draw a line and insist that he wasn't going to get sucked into the morass of human emotion—but if so, perhaps he shouldn't have built a game about human behavior.

Nevertheless, I raise my goblet in honor of Will Wright and **The Sims**.

Short-Term Thinkers

The games biz seems to have a greater concentration of short-term thinkers than any other industry. Consider the timber industry, for example. These people are cutting down the forests that provide their livelihood. However, they recognize the problem and take steps to ensure their long-term survival: seedling plantings, selective logging, and so forth. They have not yet achieved full sustainability, but they do seem to be thinking at least a few decades into the future.

The same thing goes for all sorts of industries. Steel makers invest heavily in new technology that will not generate profits for years. MacDonald's funds a variety of research efforts in universities; quite a few industries provide serious financial support to education because they know that they will need well-educated workers in the next few decades. And of course, the research programs carried out within most high-tech companies typically consume 10% of profits.

Contrast this with the short sightedness of the games biz. I was unable to locate a single games publisher supporting any kind of long-term research effort. A few games publishers that are embedded inside larger companies, such as at Microsoft and Sony, can point to some corporate-level funding projects for education, but none of these are devoted to games issues. Here is an industry with gross sales of $6 billion that cannot scrape up any money to support any kind of long-term research or education. The get-rich-quick mentality has such a solid hold on the minds of the games industry that nobody is thinking about the long term.

Consider, for example, the problem of violence in games. For purposes of this discussion, let us consider this solely as a public-relations problem. How does the industry address the problem? By dismissing the complaints contemptuously, wrapping themselves in the First Amendment, and spending money on lobbyists. This kind of stonewalling behavior just doesn't work in the long run—as many other industries have learned the hard way. If they had wisdom, industry executives would create a steady stream of high-profile "noble games"—games that embody messages that capture universal admiration. True, such games will not make much money. They might even lose some money. But in the long run, games like **The Sims** do more for industry public relations than stonewalling.

The contrast between the gutless conservatism of games industry executives and the considered risk taking of Hollywood executives is striking. The decision makers who make the basic decisions about what games to publish seem to think on a level one notch above accountants: They look at last year's sales and use those numbers to choose this year's products. Why do stockholders pay these people executive salaries for this kind of middle-manager decision making?

Hollywood, by contrast, makes product decisions on a more rational basis. Sure, they use focus groups and accountants in the process, but they factor a lot of other considerations into their big spending decisions. Sometimes an executive will have nothing more than a gut feeling that a movie idea, while unorthodox, will sell. The history of Hollywood glitters with long-shot projects that hit big. It's not that these people are always right; their history includes plenty of big-budget flops like *Heaven's Gate* and *Waterworld*. That's why it's called "risk." One way or another, Hollywood as an industry is able to generate a steady stream of unorthodox ideas that blossom into new product lines. The games industry has not.

Hollywood uses a pyramid system for generating product. At the base
of the pyramid is a large collection of movie-making wannabees: bright
young talents eager to show their skills. Part of the genius of the
Hollywood system is that it has found ways to keep these people alive
and to sample their talents. Those who pass the lowest-level cut find
a variety of funding sources to help them continue to ply their trade.
There's not much money, but it's enough to keep them in business. The
more talented individuals are able to rise to the top of the pyramid,
gaining access to greater amounts of funding. From the point of view of
the individual, the system is brutal and often unfair. But from the point
of view of the industry as a whole, the system is successful in providing
a steady supply of new ideas and new talent. The games industry has
nothing remotely like it. I don't wish to romanticize an ugly and fero-
ciously competitive industry; Hollywood has plenty of warts. But on this
one problem of fostering creative experimentation, the games biz has
lots to learn from Hollywood.

Everybody's a Game Designer

Games are for kids, right? They're simple, easygoing fun, right? Ergo,
anybody should be able to design them, right? WRONG! It takes lots
of training and years of practice to become a good game designer.
Surprise, surprise. Game design, like any other serious activity, requires
expertise. Yet this simple lesson is lost on just about everybody. I don't
know how many times I have seen executives butt into the game-design
process, imposing their personal opinions on game designers who have
had years of experience. I've seen QA testers try to pass off their own
opinions on game design as bug reports. Beginning game designers at
their first Game Developers Conference have waylaid me in the halls to
lecture me on my purported design mistakes.

Such problems are usually little more than irritations, but when prac-
ticed by executives, they can have serious consequences. For example,
in January of 2002, four executives launched an online games company

with a novel revenue model. They offered substantial cash prizes to players who won their game. In truth, it was really a puzzle, not a game, but that's not relevant to this tale. What was striking about their company is that they didn't include an experienced game designer in their executive staff. They had a CEO, a marketing person, a CFO, and a CTO—but *no* game designer. Obviously, they figured that they could design the game themselves. The result was predictable: Their product was boring, very few customers signed up, and they pulled the plug after just two months on the market.

We can laugh at these clods because they wasted only their own money, but it's a different story when some sophomoric executive ruins a product by trying to play game designer. One of these jokers even boasted to me once that his ignorance of game design was a strength: Untainted by conventional thinking, he could think outside the box better than experienced game designers. Can you guess how his company came out?

On this point I will offer a word of praise to the larger games companies. The executives of established games companies seem content to leave the game design to, well, game designers. Perhaps they're just too busy cutting big deals, or counting their stock options, but one way or the other, they've got the right idea.

A variation on this is the programmer who thinks he can design a game because he can write a program. The most celebrated exponent of this view is John Carmack, creator of **Doom**, **Quake**, and other bloodthirsty exercises in nihilism. John is reported to have declared that "game creation is 99% programming and 1% game design." His declaration is certainly consistent with his design philosophy, because he has no design philosophy. He simply implements other peoples' game designs better than they do. The ploy has made John rich, famous, and widely respected among games programmers, so I cannot dispute its efficacy. Indeed, if you're as good a programmer as John Carmack (and as bad a designer), then you should do the same thing.

Be advised, however, that the super-duper graphics algorithms that made John's fame have now been supplanted by superior algorithms implemented directly in silicon. Nowadays, any clumsy slob of a programmer can simply use a few hardware calls to perform amazing graphics tricks far beyond anything John built his reputation on. No dummy he, we can be certain that John Carmack has stayed ahead of the game, developing even more brilliant algorithms always better than what the hardware can do. Someday soon, however, video display hardware will become so powerful that John and his acolytes will find themselves clawing for marginal performance gains that nobody cares about. ("Brand X models only 10,000 hairs on a person's head, but our technology offers 20,000!") Meanwhile, the real game designers will still have plenty of exciting challenges on their plates.

Hollywood Envy

For some reason, games people look to Hollywood as their nirvana. They love to insert moviemaking terminology into their discussions of game design. Storyboards are de rigeur among many games people, even though they really don't add anything to the design process. The word "cinematic" seems to be more common in game design discussions than "interactivity," even though the latter is central to game design and the former is peripheral. And when games people need somebody to write dramatic prose, it's got to be a screenwriter with Hollywood experience, not some mere novelist or playwright.

If the reader will indulge my attempt at psychoanalysis, I suspect that what's going on here is some kind of attempt to break out of the geeky clodishness that so immures games people. Despite the bravado of declarations of geek pride, the sad truth is that hunks, not geeks, get the girls. To put it bluntly, geeks don't got no glamour. But Hollywood—now *there's* glamour for you! Could you imagine yourself at the "Games Oscars," emerging from the limousine to the popping of flashbulbs, walking up the red carpet with a starlet hanging on each arm, smiling that devil-may-care smile that makes beautiful women swoon? Can you see the moment when you accept your award while millions watch and celebrities applaud...Hey! Wake up, you dreamer! Back to the keyboard!

Young Males

Young men are the most dangerous and inventive creatures on the planet. A huge portion of the sum of human creation, be it artistic, technological, literary, or scientific, is attributable to young men. They have the drive, the reckless ambition, and the energy to pull off astounding feats. They are also the most dangerous driving group on the roads. They are far and away the largest source of violent crime. They are poorly socialized, testosterone-poisoned, and so driven that they have no sense of the possibility of failure.

It's no surprise that the field of computer gaming was created by young males. Nobody else would have had the balls to pour years of labor into a field that didn't exist, confident of eventual triumph. Nobody else would have plunged into a task about which he knew nothing whatever.

I was one of those early testosterone-poisoned fools. I didn't know anything about game design—hell, nobody did. That didn't stop me; I figured I would just make it up as I went along. I proudly, grandiloquently blundered my way forward, refusing to acknowledge my many failures but somehow learning from them. The huge database of idiotic mistakes I compiled now provides me with a sound foundation for game design wisdom.

The game design industry, however, has long since passed out of the early pioneering days. A multi-billion-dollar industry cannot operate on macho conceit and arrogance; it needs guidance by steadier, more prudent hands. Yet the industry remains dominated by young men. Partially it's a matter of turnover; there are so many young male fools willing to "break into the games biz" for a pittance that it's just too easy to dump overpaid oldsters and replace them with fresh young (and cheap) faces. Here's an industry that is twenty years old, in which the average creative worker has fewer than five years of experience.

The costs of this cheapness are evident everywhere we turn. Not least is the weak sense of community culture. With so many people coming and going, there is little opportunity to develop a stable set of community values. There are no calm older guys to rein in the young hotheads with cautions that "we don't do it that way." This in turn leads to an industry weak in moral constraints.

The contrast with the book publishing industry is striking. The book people have all been around for years and years; some of the publishers are more than a century old. Many are based in New York City and they all know each other. Untoward behavior is quickly reported through the community grapevine; jerks and rogues are shut out. Competition is certainly not lacking; these people operate on tight margins and sweat every nickel. But they do so with a sense of decency and honor that is entirely missing from the games industry. As with Hollywood, the book publishing industry has its own special set of warts, but on the matter of industry values, the games industry has much to learn from the book publishing industry.

The games industry has been evolving a mechanism for coping with this problem: It has bifurcated into two groups, the publishers and the developers. The publishers are staffed with older fellows who have stuck around for a while. They have their own internal culture that guides them. The young men are all routed into the development houses, where their barbaric behavior is channeled in productive directions. The development houses come and go with a velocity that would astound conventional corporations. I have given up keeping track of development houses; their lifetimes are too short to make the effort worth the candle.

The games industry is an industry by, for, and of young males. This is great for young males, but if and when the industry decides to grow up and out, it will need a broader talent base.

Sleaze

The worst consequence of the domination of the games industry by young males has been the steady descent of aesthetic standards. In the early Atari days, games were meant to be family fun—clean, upbeat, even cute. There were, of course, always those who sought to make money by appealing to the more sordid interests. One of the first of these was a videogame for the Atari 2600 entitled **Custer's Revenge**. In this sublime work of art, the player as General George Custer must cross the playfield, avoiding a snowstorm of thorny tumbleweeds that threaten to injure his exposed and erect member. On the opposite side of the screen waits an Indian maiden tied to a post. A successful traversal yields the rewarding opportunity to rape said maiden with a series of upward thrusts with the joystick. The storm of outrage generated by this deliberately provocative "game" played right into the hands of its sleazy purveyor.

Such games were surprising exceptions to a prevailing attitude that games should provide happy, clean fun. Nintendo reinforced this attitude with its early enforcement of "family values" in games for its platform.

The first-person shooters broke the dam. The very first, **Castle Wolfenstein**, copped a nasty attitude with its deliberately glorified killing. Victims cried out "Meine Liebe!" as they died; blood spattered as they fell. The lead designer, John Romero, continued to develop this vicious style with the enormously successful **Doom** and its many sequels. Each game showed more gore more realistically. One hit game of the early 90s, **Mortal Kombat**, seemed to take special pleasure in gore, concluding each victory with the yanking out of the loser's spine. The material accompanying the games reeked of an ugly nihilistic attitude toward killing. All this was, of course, billed as satire or pure fantasy, but the bloody-minded style took hold of the industry. I recall an ad for a game in the mid-90s featuring a man holding a gun lying in a bathtub full of blood. Smelling the scent, the industry advanced the cause with more blood-soaked shooters like **Half-Life** and **Grand Theft Auto**. The third installment in the latter series boasted an especially vicious style, offering players the opportunity to hire and then murder a prostitute. As I write this, the newest sleaze game, **BMX XXX**, is generating plenty of consternation among industry outsiders, intense jealousy among competitors, and even greater anticipation among players.

Compounding the problem is the approbation that the industry bestows upon such products. A prudent industry would treat sleazy products with harsh disdain, but the games industry cannot conceal its delight in sleaze. **Grand Theft Auto III** won industry awards despite the damage it did to the industry image.

Industry insiders protest that they are merely offering the players what they want; they are not imposing values on players but responding to values already inculcated in youths by a sick society. This is self-serving circumlocution. The games industry is not passively responding to values imposed upon it by a ruthless marketplace; it has selected its own audience, driving away most who do not revel in blood-soaked killing. By offering such games, the industry has attracted the kind of audience that demands them—thereby reinforcing the cycle.

The result of this profound strategic marketing blunder is an industry that is steadily descending into ever-deeper sleaze. The only solution is to take a deep breath, devote a large amount of money to breaking out of this self-imposed pit, and pay the price of developing a healthier marketplace.

tonktics

tonktics

NOTE

The next 14 chapters tell the stories of the games that I have designed over the course of my career. I'll not be dragging you down memory lane with endless tedious tales of code breakages and deadline headaches. The purpose of these chapters is not to produce a history of my efforts, but to illustrate some of the more interesting design issues raised in actual practice. Much of my time during the years covered by this history was devoted to uninstructive drudgery; there's no point in burdening you with such dreck. Instead, I'll be flitting through the years, picking out interesting vignettes from the larger story. These will, I hope, fill out the skeletal theory presented in earlier chapters with flesh-and-blood examples of the messy application of the grand principles. Besides, some of the stories are fun.

In the summer of 1974, I was working on my master's thesis on visual binary stars. The thesis, "A Catalogue of Dynamical Parallaxes of Visual Binary Stars," was mostly a matter of computer programming, with judicious assessments of the occasional oddball binary star. Consequently I spent a lot of time at the university computer center. While working there one afternoon, I ran into a chap who was attempting to write a program that would play a boardgame called **Blitzkrieg**. It was a strategy wargame, using division-sized units maneuvering across continental-sized maps. I was skeptical of his project; it seemed to me that the task of creating algorithms for planning such movement was likely impossible. Nevertheless I was intrigued, and for the next few years mulled over the problem.

After graduating, I taught physics at a small community college in Nebraska. In my spare time, I played board wargames and continued to wonder if it might be possible to program a computer to play a wargame. The problem of programming a strategy wargame seemed too difficult, but a tactical wargame of armored combat was a simpler proposition. With tanks, there are only a few combat units, each moving and fighting separately. Each one need only establish a simple line of sight to shoot at an enemy. Terrain considerations seemed simple enough. As I mused about the problem, I broke it down into sub-problems, writing down my rough approach to each. In this way, I convinced myself that the overall problem could in fact be solved.

Map

The first sub-problem was the map representation. This problem had two components: terrain representation and hexgrid computation. A hexgrid

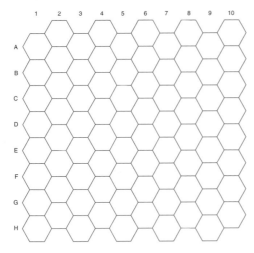

is commonly used in wargames because it allows more precise directional alignment of units and doesn't have the problems with corners that a rectgrid (such as is used on a chessboard) imposes. A hexgrid looks like what's shown in Figure 13.1.

Each hex in the hexgrid can contain terrain of some type: trees, hills, depressions, rivers, lakes, open ground, etc. After much wasted effort trying to computationally define all these terrain elements, I realized my error, an error that is fundamental to all game design: I was thinking in terms of data, not process. That is, I was so busy thinking about what terrain *is* that I failed to think in terms of what it *does*. If we think about terrain in terms of its operational properties, it really is quite simple. All terrain has just four basic properties:

13.1 *A hexgrid.*

- It can block the line of sight into its hex.
- It can block the line of sight through its hex.
- It can prevent motion into its hex.
- It can impede motion into its hex.

I treated all four properties as binary, so with just four bits of information, I could record everything I needed to know about a hex. Thus, what I was previously calling a plain hex is really just a hex whose terrain value is, in binary terms, just 0000. It doesn't block the line of sight, prevent motion, or impede motion. A lake hex has a binary value of 0010; it can prevent motion into its hex, but otherwise is just like a plain hex. Trees are a little trickier: They have a binary terrain value of 1101, because they block the line of sight both into and through the hex, as well as impeding (but not preventing motion).

You might wonder why there's a difference between blocking the line of sight *into* a hex and blocking the line of sight *through* a hex. The difference becomes apparent when you consider a hill hex as compared with a tree hex. A hill hex has a binary terrain value of 0101: it blocks the line of sight through its hex, but not into it, and it impedes but does not prevent motion into it. Imagine a tank climbing onto a hill hex. It can climb the hill, but it slows down doing so, because the hill is steep. More important, once on top of the hill, it can see far and can also be seen from afar. The line of sight can be traced into the hill hex. However, if the tank is behind the hill, then it cannot be seen; the hill blocks the line of sight through the hex (but not into it!).

Now, imagine the same tank in a tree hex. The trees block the line of sight through the hex just like the hill blocks the line of sight. A tank hiding behind a tree hex cannot be seen. But the trees also block the line of sight into the tree hex; a tank hiding in the trees cannot be seen. What's important here is that the tank can see out of the trees but cannot be seen. That's tactically valuable, which is why so many tanks spend so much time lurking around in the trees.

This system thus permits sixteen different types of terrain, some of which are nonsensical:

Blocks LOS* Into	Blocks LOS Through	Prevents Motion	Impedes Motion	Label
0	0	0	0	Open ground.
0	0	0	1	Rough ground.
0	0	1	0	Lake.
0	0	1	1	Nonsense value.
0	1	0	0	Nonsense value.
0	1	0	1	Hill.
0	1	1	0	Mesa? I never used this.
0	1	1	1	Nonsense value.
1	0	0	0	Depression (a "hole").
1	0	0	1	Rough ground depression.
1	0	1	0	A lake in a hole? Useless.
1	0	1	1	Nonsense value.
1	1	0	0	Really high grass?
1	1	0	1	Trees.
1	1	1	0	Impassable forest.
1	1	1	1	Nonsense value.

*LOS = Line of sight

You will note that five of these values are nonsense values and four more are silly or useless. Thus, more than half of my values are wasted; I could have gotten away with using only three bits of data. However, deciphering all these values would have been more trouble than it was worth; I stuck with this simple scheme because it was easy to compute with.

Calculating Line of Sight

The next problem was figuring the line of sight through a hexgrid. Imagine the situation: Tank #1 is at coordinates C4 and Tank #2 is at F9. Can Tank #1 see Tank #2? To put it in more computationally rigorous terms, can Tank #1 trace an unblocked line of sight to Tank #2? See Figure 13.2.

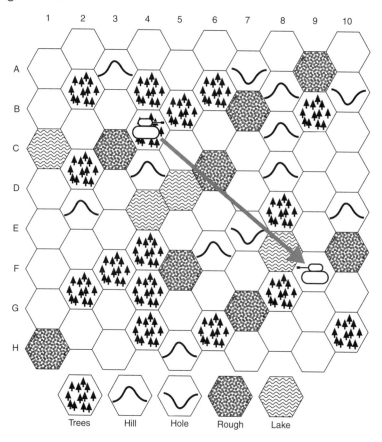

13.2 *Determining line of sight (LOS).*

The solution to this problem turns out to be rather complicated and mathematical, so I will not delve into its gory details. The problem was exacerbated by the requirement to operate in an 8-bit CPU with no hardware multiplication or division; everything had to be done with logical operations and simple addition and subtraction of 8-bit integers. It happens that computer scientists had solved a similar problem years before, but I, having no training in computer science, simply had to re-invent this wheel for myself. Sad to say, the solution was not discovered by game programmers for quite a few years after me. Roger Keating in Australia discovered it not long after I did, but there were plenty of wargames as late as 1982 whose designers still hadn't cracked the problem. Nowadays, with floating-point hardware multiply-divide capabilities, this kind of problem is so simple that it's silly to discuss, but back in the 1970s, this was a serious challenge.

Planning Moves

The actual planning of moves turned out to be easier than I had antici-pated. Each tank planned its moves on a simple system based on an incremental approach. It merely asked, "Would I be better off in one of the six adjacent hexes than in the one I'm in right now?" If so, it moved to that adjacent hex; otherwise, it remained in place. This required a calculation of the "tactical value" of each hex, which in turn depended on a number of factors. Each factor gave the hex a point value:

- If the hex blocked the line of sight into itself, it earned 8 points.
- If the hex was easy to enter, it earned 2 points.
- If the hex was closer to the enemy, it earned 6 points.
- If the hex was further away from the enemy, it earned −6 points.

These simple rules were not by themselves good enough; I discovered that tanks would often oscillate between two hexes. So I added another rule that specified that, if the hex had been occupied recently, then it lost 4 points. That helped dampen out oscillatory movement. But there were still problems when the computer's tanks had not caught sight of any enemy tanks. I resolved this problem by two stratagems:

- First, I assigned each side an objective hex that required that side's tanks to move across much of the map. In moving toward their objectives, the two sides' tanks were bound to run into each other.

- Second, I set up a system of strategic movement based on flanking movement. Every computer tank had a primary objective and a secondary objective. The secondary objective was calculated to be halfway between the starting position and the objective, but offset laterally. This allowed the tanks to approach their objectives by a flanking movement.

At the outset of the game, each tank took as its primary objective the geographic objective assigned to its team. The tanks would all move toward their secondary objectives, some of which would be to the right of the geographic objective, and some of which would be to the left of the objective. However, as soon as contact was made with the human, the computer tanks all modified their objectives. The sighted human tank became the primary objective, and each tank chose a secondary objective to flank the human tank on the right or the left, depending on the circumstances. Thus, the entire computer tank force began an encircling movement. As soon as a second human tank was sighted, the nearest computer tanks would modify their objectives to take it into account. And of course, if a tank was close enough to get a good shot at the human, he'd take it.

Initial Programming

Convinced that I really could get a wargame running, I set to work writing the program. This was 1976; all I had to work with was the IBM 1130 at the school where I was teaching physics. It had, I believe, 8K of memory and a hard disk with virtual memory. After hours I would insert my hard disk cartridge, fire up the computer, and go to work on the program. It was written in FORTRAN, an old computer language used for scientific calculations. All input and output were made through a Selectric typewriter. The computer would type a line of text specifying the situation, and then I would type a string of characters specifying my move. No graphics, no sound, no nothing: just a typewriter. I had a mapboard next to the computer console on which I placed little tanks to represent the two sides, and I would translate the coordinates on the typewriter paper into the positions on the map.

I still remember the sense of elation I felt when, during one of the early games, the computer got the upper hand and chased my tanks all the way across the board. I made a fighting retreat, with one tank lying in wait while the others bounded back. I was able to pick off the computer tanks one by one, and by the end of the game, I knocked out the last enemy tank with my last tank. Only then did I notice that it was after midnight. This may well have been the first hexgrid-based computer wargame played anywhere.

In May of 1976, I hosted a small wargame convention and several dozen people came. There they had the opportunity to play the first version of **Tanktics**. People were mildly impressed, but the game experience didn't have the richness of the boardgames available at the time. It seemed to them an interesting oddity.

Enter the KIM-1

I continued polishing and tuning the game on the 1130, but I was already turning my attention to a strange new technological development: microcomputers. It's difficult for people these days to appreciate just how exotic microcomputers were back then. Only a tiny number of people, perhaps a hundred thousand in all, were even aware of the technology. But those of us who caught the bug were passionate in our optimism for this technology. I realized that I'd have to make the jump, so I set to work teaching myself digital electronics and microcomputers.

After a few months, I bought myself a KIM-1 single board computer for $249. That was a lot more money than it seems; adjusted for inflation, it comes to $750 in today's money. This baby was packed with features: an 8-bit, 1MHz 6502 CPU with all of 1K of RAM. It had two 6520 Peripheral Interface Adapters, a machine-language monitor, a 21-key keypad, and a 6-digit, 7-segment LED display. It took me a few weeks to learn 6502 machine language; pretty soon I was ready to transfer **Tanktics** from FORTRAN on the IBM 1130 to machine language on the KIM-1. Unfortunately, 1K of RAM wasn't enough for the program, the tanks, and the map, so I had to trim it down. I ended up with a tiny map, just 16 hexes high by 16 hexes wide, with a single type of terrain: forest. Each side had one tank. And this wasn't human versus computer: It was human against human! I carefully divided the keypad so that one player used one side of the keypad and the other player used the other side. Each player read three of the six LED digits. This was enough, however, to communicate the game's events.

The best part of the game was that it provided blind play: Neither player knew what the other was up to. This, however, did create a problem. It's pretty hard not to notice what the other player is up to when you're sharing a calculator-sized keypad and display. My solution was, as Mr. Spock used to say, crude but effective: I draped a bedsheet down from the ceiling, taping it down to the keypad so that each player could see only his half of the computer. The two players had their own little mapboards that they used to represent the game. Being left-handed, I took the right side of the computer; my opponent had to be right-handed to use the left side of the computer.

This two-player version of **Tanktics** was fun, but I soon lusted for more power. And so, in the summer of 1977, I ordered my first memory expansion kit. For just $149 I got a card with 4K of RAM! Of course, it was a kit, not a complete card. I spent hours and hours soldering RAM chips onto that board. There were 32 of those little chips, each of them with 16 pins. Along with all the addressing circuitry and the capacitors on each chip, there were more than 600 joints that had to be soldered—and a single mistake could fry the board. Nowadays, the same amount of money will buy you 64,000 times as much memory, and you don't have to solder anything. Yes, those were the good old days.

After building the memory board, I built an interface circuit for it and built a big box for my KIM-1, including a power supply. (I nearly burned down the physics lab while testing it—the lab had defective wiring.) I designed and built a pair of "tiny terminals," each with its own calculator-style keypad and a set of sixteen seven-segment digits, as well as an interface board for them. Now I was set! By early 1978, I had programmed **KIM-Tanktics**, a huge leap over previous efforts. This was a two-player, blinded game (each player could see only the data on his own tiny terminal). Each player had his own map and his own game pieces, and a small screen sufficed to block his view of the other player. With eight tanks per side and a large map, there was plenty of opportunity for interesting games. I expanded the game, permitting a variety of tank types and scenarios.

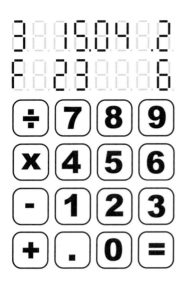

13.3 *Tiny terminal.*

Input and Output

Back in those days, we were so constrained by hardware limitations that we had to think long and hard about what could and could not be expressed through the hardware. For example, the tiny terminal looked something like what appears in Figure 13.3.

Here's what the display means: The "3" on the upper left means that you are looking at the current situation for your Tank #3. It is at map coordinates 1504 and facing in direction 2 (upper right). The "F" means that it is currently engaged in firing at an enemy tank. After firing, it will move one hex in direction 2, then another hex in direction 3. It has 6 rounds of ammunition left.

The keys on the keypad take the following meanings:

1-8 Subjects or objects of commands

   x command FIRE

   - command ORDERS

   = command REPORT

   . command CLEAR LAST ORDER

   + command CLEAR ALL ORDERS

      commandROTATE LEFT

   9 command ROTATE RIGHT

Linguistic Input

This crude system permitted some surprisingly rich play, largely because the core input structure was linguistic: Orders are sentences. A player would enter "4x7" to say "Tank #4 ordered to fire at enemy Tank #7." The display shown in Figure 13.3 was obtained by merely pressing the "3" key; any additional keypresses would have been added to its orders queue shown in the second line of the display.

The orders queue is the trickiest part of the user interface. Each tank may have up to five orders in its queue at any given time. This limit was imposed by the display; I could have stored more orders for each tank but then they would have been invisible or the display would have become cluttered. The problem was that the orders queue was constantly in motion: As orders were executed, the orders queue would shrink, and as orders were entered, the queue would grow. This made for some programming difficulties, and I never quite got the display refresh system working properly. There were too many processes going on at once: orders coming in from the player, movements by the tank under examination, and movements by other tanks. Under some circumstances, the player would end up looking at an out-of-date orders queue. With modern software, multiple process management isn't much of a problem, but when you're working in machine language, it can become quite a headache.

Thus, a typical conversation between player and computer might look like this:

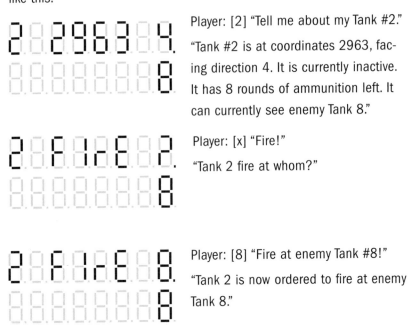

Player: [2] "Tell me about my Tank #2."

"Tank #2 is at coordinates 2963, facing direction 4. It is currently inactive. It has 8 rounds of ammunition left. It can currently see enemy Tank 8."

Player: [x] "Fire!"

"Tank 2 fire at whom?"

Player: [8] "Fire at enemy Tank #8!"

"Tank 2 is now ordered to fire at enemy Tank 8."

Of course, if the player were in a hurry, he could simply punch [2x8] in rapid succession to order Tank #2 to fire at enemy Tank #8.

Sound Effects

In 1978, Texas Instruments had just released a sound-effects chip that could be programmed to generate a variety of sound effects. Of course, the programming was done primarily by wiring capacitors and resistors of certain values onto certain pins. It was clumsy but good enough for my needs. I purchased one and built a board for it, setting up a trigger line from my KIM-1. Then I added some software to the program to trigger the sound chip whenever a tank fired its gun. I fed the chip's output into a small speaker and, by golly gee, it really worked! Whenever a tank fired, a nice throaty explosion sounded on the speaker.

I decided to surprise my friend and playtester Mike, so I fed the output of the sound chip directly into my stereo system, which faced the table on which the KIM-1 sat. I invited Mike over to play a few rounds with a "new improvement" I had made on the software. We sat down, the game began, and we both started frantically maneuvering our tanks, searching for each other. The surprise, it turned out, was on both of us, because Mike saw my tanks first. He entered a fire command before I even suspected that we had made contact. Unfortunately, I had miscalculated the impedance matching of the chip to the stereo, and so the resulting explosion was enough to knock us both out of our chairs. As we staggered to our feet, I asked, "What do you think of the new sound effects?"

Showing It Off

It was now the summer of 1978, and I was so proud of my system that I drove it around to a variety of wargamers' conventions, showing it off. Most of the gamers had not dreamed that such a thing was possible and were quite impressed. However, as with the older version of **Tanktics** on the IBM 1130, they found the game lacking in the richness that boardgames provided. My claim that **Tanktics** offered true blind play, just like the real world, fell on deaf ears. Nevertheless, there were a few wargamers who had purchased some of the early personal computers, primarily the Commodore PET, and they urged me to re-write **Tanktics** to run on their machines. I thought the problem over and decided to accept the challenge.

Porting

In September of 1979, I bought myself a Commodore PET. I paid $799 for this technological wonder, boasting a 1MHz 6502 CPU, the same as in my KIM-1, 4K of RAM, a tape cassette storage system, a keyboard, and a video monitor. The world was agog at the amount of power Commodore could deliver for so little money. (Corrected for inflation, the money I paid for the PET is now worth about $2000. Think of how much computer you can get for that nowadays.) The keyboard wasn't the real thing; it had tiny flat keys crammed together, and touch-typing was almost impossible. The video monitor wasn't a true bit-mapped monitor; it could display only 24 lines of 32 characters. But it was a huge advance over the single row of six characters on my KIM-1, or the two rows of eight characters on my tiny terminals. Moreover, it included a good implementation of BASIC in its ROM, making programming a much simpler task.

However, the PET could not support two-person play as my custom-built KIM-1 could; I would have to revert to the old single-player version of **Tanktics** on the IBM 1130. That was written in FORTRAN, but the PET required BASIC. My friend Dave Menconi offered to do the translation. Meanwhile, I converted some of the important routines from the KIM-1 to run on the PET; these would run much faster in machine language than in BASIC. After a few weeks, I integrated Dave's code with my own, and after a few weeks more, I managed to get everything running.

This version of **Tanktics** was still a pure text system: The player referred to a large printed map using coordinates from the computer. On-screen graphics were still out of the picture on personal computers.

Production, Marketing, and Sales

I had a few hundred copies of the map printed up, and I made cardboard counters using blank counters and rub-on numerals. I copied cassette tapes on my PET and labeled them by hand. I typed up a manual and had it photocopied. For the cover I drew a cute little picture of a PET with tank treads and a cannon emerging from its screen. The PET was so big and bulky that the rendition looked pretty good. I can't draw, but I can use a ruler and compass, which were all I needed for this simple line drawing. I folded the 34×22" map into quarters, and stuffed everything into a Zip-Lock bag. That's how software was made in the late 1970s.

For marketing, I prepared my own ad (see Figure 13.4).

There weren't many actual computer magazines in those days; *BYTE*, *Kilobaud*, and *Creative Computing* were the only ones I knew and they covered all kinds of computers. I found two user-written newsletters for the PET and put full-page ads in each; I think I paid $50 for the privilege. Then I sat back and waited for the orders to pour in.

And pour in they did! I sold my first copy of **Tanktics** on December 31, 1978, and over the next year, I sold 150 copies of **Tanktics**! At $15 a copy, that represented over $2000 in gross income. Marketing and cost of goods sold came to under $1000, so I ended up making over $1000 on this, my first software endeavor. By today's standards, that's not much, but back then, it was impressive.

Introducing

TANKTICS

If you've gotten tired of playing children's games on your PET, consider TANKTICS, the most sophisticated computer game available. TANKTICS is a computer game which simulates armored combat during World War II. You command a force of up to ten tanks; your mission is to take and hold an assigned objective. Opposing you is the PET itself, armed with twice as many tanks as you have. The PET's tanks are just as fast and powerful as your own, so to win you must maneuver your tanks more shrewdly than PET. This isn't easy — PET's sophisticated software allows PET to play a very good game. To beat PET, you must carefully judge the effects of terrain, range, and individual tank facing as you plan your move. You must consider and utilize the element of surprise, for you do not know the position of an enemy tank unless one of your tanks can see it. TANKTICS is a "think" game rather than an "action" game, so you have all the time you need to plan your move. In sum, TANKTICS provides a tense and challenging game that can be played many times without losing its richness.

 With each game of TANKTICS, you get: 1) tape cassette containing TANKTICS program in two segments (1.4K machine language segment and 5K BASIC segment); 2) 31 playing counters; 3) 17" x 22" map depicting the battlefield; 4) 8 page player's manual explaining how to play and giving tactical hints.

 TANKTICS is now available for shipment. To order, send check or money order for $15.00 (Calif residents add 6% sales tax) to:

**PLEIADES Game Co
202 Faro Ave
Davis, CA 95616**

Please allow one to three weeks for personal checks to clear the bank.

13.4 *The ad for Tanktics.*

The game even garnered a review. Robert Purser's *Computer Cassettes Review* had a two-page review of the game; he spiffed up his review with a professionally-drawn picture of a sexy girl wearing a beret, straddling the cannon of a tank (ahem!). Although Robert liked the game and recommended it, he ranked it below another game he had seen, **Android Nim**. This TRS-80 program was nothing more than the game of **Nim** implemented with little robots built out of the TRS-80 character set. The robots were constantly in motion, turning their heads this way and that. When the player eliminated a robot, it disappeared in a cute graphic. Robert was enchanted by the graphics of **Android Nim**; while he confessed that **Tanktics** offered richer gameplay, he still preferred **Android Nim**.

Thus began the bane of my career as a game designer: graphics versus gameplay. From the very beginning, I was a gamer seeking ever-richer and more interesting gameplay, fighting a world more interested in cute graphics. This conflict plagued every single project I worked on; in some cases, I managed to satisfy the graphics crowd without compromising gameplay, but most of the time, it was a frustrating battle.

Avalon-Hill

As far as I was concerned, **Tanktics** was a finished product and I was ready to move on to new projects. However, in 1981, Avalon-Hill, a board wargaming company, was just entering the computer wargaming field. They offered me a contract to publish **Tanktics** for a variety of platforms. I took the PET version, spiffed it up a bit, and it was ready to go. I ported this version over to the Atari. A friend, Bob Smith, ported it to the TRS-80, while another friend, Todd Frye, ported it to the Apple II. These guys did this work for a share of the royalties, which never amounted to much, but not for any sharp dealing on my part. This Avalon-Hill version shipped in a beautiful box with a gorgeous map in late 1981. I think I earned a total of perhaps $10,000 on it; I don't recall how many units they sold, but it was certainly in the thousands.

Fade Away

Avalon-Hill continued to sell **Tanktics** for a number of years, but the lack of graphics was a severe weakness; the development of good on-screen maps quickly made the game obsolete. Interestingly, though, the game-play wasn't surpassed for quite some time. Armored combat wargames couldn't match **Tanktics'** variety of tank types, richness of terrain, or complexity of combat results calculations for several years. Nevertheless, by 1985, **Tanktics** was dead. The game has been so completely forgotten that Interplay recently published a game under the same name, completely unaware of the original. When I searched the Web recently for "**Tanktics,**" I got some 1700 hits for the Interplay game. Narrowing the search to my game yielded just seven hits.

Results

Tanktics was the first commercial computer strategy wargame. While there were a number of games sold in 1978, all were simple affairs; none approached **Tanktics** in game depth or AI. This game was the state of the art in 1979, but when Avalon-Hill released the second edition just two years later, it was already obsolescent. Things were moving rapidly in those days. Even so, **Tanktics** was reasonably successful by the standards of its day. I think it sold some 10,000 units, good results in 1981. It had the bad luck to come out simultaneously with **Eastern Front (1941)** and so was lost in the excitement. But I am pleased with the overall result. As my first real game design, it came out well.

legionnaire

legionnaire

In February of 1979, besotted with the success of **Tanktics**, I resolved to design a new game, a design that would take proper advantage of the capabilities of the Commodore PET computer. **Tanktics**, after all, had been designed to run on an IBM 1130 and was therefore clumsy to use on a personal computer. I wanted something that would really shine in the luxuriant environment of these powerful new personal computers.

I looked at a variety of possibilities: a Battle of the Bulge game, an Eastern Front game, and a Waterloo game. I toyed with designs for these, but nothing seemed to come out well. For three months I fiddled around to no avail. At last, frustrated with my lack of progress, I simply sat down and tossed together a hexgrid map display using the PET's graphics character set. You see, the PET did not offer a pixel-addressable display; it was pure alphanumeric. You had 24 rows with 40 characters on each row, and that was all. Graphics were built up from special "graphics characters" provided by the operating system: horizontal, vertical, and diagonal lines, dots, squares, stars, and so forth. I used the various line components to assemble a hexgrid map. Of course, each of the line segments filled an entire character space on the screen, so the only usable screen space was the empty character space inside each hex. This meant that I had about as much screen space devoted to hex edges as to hex content—not an efficient use of precious screen space. I had a lot to learn back then.

With a map in place, it seemed right to put in some units. Obviously, my combat units would have to be displayed as single characters. The small size of the display limited the game to eight units for the player and

29
LESSON

Never build
a technology
and then go
looking for
a game to
fit it.

eight for the computer. The player's units were marked as
the numerals 1 through 8; the computer's were the same
numerals in inverse video (black where white normally is
and vice versa).

Next, I slapped together a movement system using much
the same sentence structure I used with **Tanktics**. To command units, the player simply pressed the key corresponding to his unit, and then gave it movement orders in the
same 1-6 directional rose system that I had used in
Tanktics. The player could enter multiple orders, delete
some, and enter more, just like **Tanktics**. In other words,
I simply threw together a screen-based version of the
basic mechanics of **Tanktics**. All I had to do now was
design a game to fit this nifty display system.

A Record-Setting Blunder

I had just committed one of the worst—and most common—mistakes in game design: I had built a technology
and then went in search of a game. "Let's get some code
up and running, then we'll get to designing the game!" I
can smile indulgently at my younger self, as I was probably
the first game designer in history to make that mistake.
With all the experience we've developed in the 25 years
since that day, you can't justify such self-indulgence.

I didn't realize the error of my ways at the time; indeed,
my evil twin insists that everything came out fine in the
end, and so there's no reason to dwell on it. But I'm not so
confident that **Legionnaire** was a solid design; I'll explain
some of those design problems later. For now, though,
here's the lesson (Lesson 29).

The first problem bit me in the butt almost immediately: The units couldn't move at a perceptible rate. If they did move at, say, one hex per second, then the game would be over in less than a minute. Moreover, the player wouldn't have any time to plot a strategy; the game would play like an arcade game without any of the nice graphics. I needed to slow down the pace of the game. But this in turn meant that a unit might take five or ten seconds to make its move. How would a player know which of his units he had already ordered to move? They looked the same moving as just standing around with their hands in their pockets. I had no additional screen resources to expend on the problem.

After much design agony, I stumbled on the idea of internal animation. While waiting for the player's input, the computer would sweep through all the units, briefly replacing each one with a symbol indicating which way it was preparing to move. If it wasn't going anywhere, it didn't animate. Of course, given the slow execution speeds of computers back then, this animation taxed the machine to its limits; it took a perceptible fraction of a second to execute the loop. Remember, the computer was not redrawing the entire screen; it merely redrew one character for each unit! We were a long way from full-screen, full-motion, first-person graphics displays. The result of this scheme was a frenetic display that was hard to read. There was plenty of on-screen activity to distract your eye, but it normally wasn't important. When you *did* want to find information about a unit, you'd have to wait a second or so before it animated to show you its intentions.

All in all, it was a completely unsatisfactory solution. Given the primitive state of game design back then, I could get away with it, but **Legionnaire** could have been a much better game had I designed it as a game first and a program second.

Play non-
electronic
games, too.

Disruption

On the plus side, I included a nice disruption system. When units fought, they suffered both permanent losses (dead and wounded) and disruption of the unit's cohesion, which had the short-term effect of lowering the unit's combat effectiveness. All units slowly recovered from disruption effects. If you pulled a unit out of combat and let it rest for a few minutes, it would come back up to full strength.

The real value of this design feature lay in its effect on strategy in the game. Units could not be left in combat for long periods of time; they had to be pulled out to rest and recover. This in turn required that other units be ready to take the place of the retreating unit, all of which required careful planning. Better still, the disruption rules sharpened combat. Your own units were not the only ones suffering from disruption; so too were the enemy's. When a unit was badly disrupted, one more big attack could finish it off before it had a chance to recover. This encouraged a kind of desperately offensive play that was loads of fun. No matter how bad the situation was, there was one best way to handle it—Attack!

I will happily deny authorship of the concept; the credit for that goes to Simulations Publications, Inc., and probably Jim Dunnigan. Their **Thirty Years War** game system had introduced this approach to disruption in the early 1970s. I did nothing more than carry it over to the computer and make it work in a real-time environment.

This, by the way, illustrates an important rule of good game design: You need a strong background in games to be a good designer. And when I say games, I mean *all* games, not just computer and videogames. All through the 1980s, and even today, a small group of old-time board wargamers have made a disproportionate contribution to the evolution of game design, largely because of all the good ideas they stole from other fields of game design.

Terrain

The game included terrain of a sort: A few hexes were blacked out and impassable. These added much to the game, even though there were typically only two or three such hexes. Since every unit moved at the same speed, units could use such impassable hexes to block enemy movement, to guard flanks, or to channel an attack.

Sales

Designing, programming, testing, and debugging **Legionnaire** required all of four months; I put the game on sale in May of 1979. Since it did not include an expensive map, I could not in good conscience demand as much for it as I did for **Tanktics**. I therefore sold the game for $10. I sold about a hundred copies.

First Draft Design

In May of 1982, I started thinking about the possibility of making a new version of **Legionnaire**, but I moved forward very slowly because it was a home project. As an Atari employee, I dedicated most of my time and creative energy to my project for Atari Research, the **Excalibur** design. However, in odd moments on evenings and weekends, I would occasionally turn my thoughts to the **Legionnaire** problem. My earliest design document dates from June of 1982. Here is a neat version of that document; I have added line numbers to make subsequent discussion clearer:

New Legionnaire Specs

1. Map: Rectgrid, scrolling.

2. Terrain: Clear (brown), forest (green), slope (orange).

3. Romans: Red military symbols alternating at 2Hz with background terrain.

4. Barbarians: Blue symbols alternating at 2Hz with background terrain (if seen by player).

5. Unit count: 16/side.

6. Object of game: Destroy enemy, especially leader.

7. Romans start game in three encampments, each of different size.

8. Barbarians start scattered about.

9. Barbarian algorithm:

10. Strategic: For each target, determine "projected strength" as

11. PS = SumOfBarbarian(strength/distance)/SumRoman (strength/distance).

12. Tactical: Determine confidence level from own strength, neighbor's strength, Roman proximate strength.

13. Player-missile graphics: Cursor, eagle, barbarian leader.

14. Roman units: Infantry, 10th Legion (elite), cavalry, light infantry.

15. Input: Joystick has three modes: scroll, move cursor to select unit, specify unit orders. Change states with button (Roll).

I offer this document as a textbook version of a concept document for a game design. In 15 lines, it lays out all the basic concepts of the design. It specifies all three critical components of any interactive design: input, processing, and output. Moreover, it specifies those components in terms of the primary design constraints:

- The five basic colors permitted by the Atari display system are each specified in lines 2, 3, and 4.

- The initial conditions of the game are laid out in lines 7 and 8 (probably too much detail in that).

- The core algorithm for the barbarian AI is worked out in lines 10 and 11, while a subsidiary algorithm is presented in less detail in line 12.

- The allocation of crucial player-missile graphic resources is presented in line 13, while the basic types of units are declared in line 14.

- In line 15, the basic input structure is laid out.

Note also the parameters that are *not* specified. The size of the map is one such parameter; it's not central to the design of the game, and it will ultimately be determined by the unit count, which *is* specified. I take a completely functional approach to the graphics, specifying them only in terms of what information they convey and how. I do not specify anything about the prettiness of the graphics; that's not a central problem in the design. Once I know how the graphics will *function*, I can approach the problem of making them pretty.

Still, the document has its flaws. There really wasn't any need to specify the object of the game; that's obvious. It should have said more about the combat system or the mechanics of leadership. But the best indication of the quality of this design document is the fact that, except for lines 7 and 8, the game came out pretty much the way this document specifies—and this was months before I began programming.

In July and August, I wrote two more detailed documents specifying some of the design options in front of me. I considered but rejected the possibility of using the crude

31

LESSON

Begin each project with a one-page specification of the gameplay.

graphics of the original version so that the program would run on the Apple and the TRS-80. I was undecided on the fundamental question as to the scale of the game: Would it be a strategic game or a tactical game? And I fretted about getting the fog of war into the game without making it unplayable.

In September of 1981, there was a big wargame convention in the Bay Area where I live. I attended, and so did Eric Dott, the CEO of Avalon-Hill. We were eating dinner one evening when he asked me about my plans for future work. I mentioned my speculations about a new version of **Legionnaire**. I also mentioned that I thought I would publish it through the Atari Program Exchange. "But you have a contract with us for it!" he protested. Greatly surprised, I asked him what he meant. It turned out that my contract with Avalon-Hill for **Tanktics** also granted them rights to **Legionnaire** as well. I was deeply embarrassed by my oversight, instantly apologized, and assured Eric that I would certainly honor our agreement.

At this point, the reader may wish to skip ahead to Chapter 18, "Eastern Front (1941)." The remainder of the story took place after I developed **Eastern Front (1941)**, and some of the material in that chapter bears on this discussion. In a sense, the Avalon-Hill version of **Legionnaire** was almost a new game design. Nevertheless, I have placed its design history here so that the continuities with the earlier version will be clearer.

NOTE

Much had changed in the 30 months since I published the original **Legionnaire**. The Commodore PET was obsolete. Although Eric Dott had asked me for a version of **Legionnaire** that would work on the Apple II as well as the Atari, he had also expressed a strong desire to have the scrolling map technology that made **Eastern Front (1941)** so appealing. I told him flatly that he couldn't have it both ways; the Apple II could not scroll anywhere near as well as the Atari. We both dropped the subject, figuring that we'd cross that bridge later. The Atari 800 was my obvious target machine, so I went to work on the design with somewhat more determination. This time, I approached the design problem more intelligently. I spent plenty of time establishing my design goals before writing any code.

My primary concern lay with the problems of combining a real-time game with a scrolling map. Most of the map would be out of view; action taking place there would not be visible to the player. I considered a dual-view system with a grand overview and a main map for orders entry, but that idea collapsed when I realized that the grand overview map would use tiny colored squares for the military units. It simply couldn't communicate the essential information about the game. Eventually I realized that, with a low unit count, most of the battle would take place on a single screen. Nevertheless, one of the weaknesses of the final game lay in this problem. Occasionally, a few units would wander out of the field of view and be forgotten by the player. Much later the player would stumble upon the units. While this problem was not fatal, it was nevertheless a design mistake on my part.

By early October, I had settled on several decisions: playability over realism, the use of disruption in combat, the importance of slope effects, and the maintenance of reserves. But I couldn't seem to pull the design together; my design notes from those days express much vacillation and pessimism about the design. Realizing this, I made one of the best design decisions I have ever made: I stopped working on the project.

Game design is at its innermost core a creative act. Creativity cannot be forced. You can work on a problem as much as you want, but effort alone can never overcome a creative mental block. I turned my attention to other tasks and simply forgot about **Legionnaire**.

32
LESSON

When you're creatively stumped, don't try to force it; do something else for a month or two.

In mid-December, I had cleared out my other tasks, so I turned my thoughts back to **Legionnaire**. Sure enough, the answers seemed clearer then. I wrote it all down on one page:

Legionnaire: *Final* Design

Tactical scale: (Same as original Legionnaire).

Rectgrid with overlarge battlefield and scrolling map. Battle fought on a portion of the map.

Standard **Eastern Front (1941)** order entry. Real-time execution.

Unit types: Infantry, cavalry, and Caesar.

Units are animated: Alternate unit type icon with motion arrow icon.

Combat system: Same as in original **Legionnaire**.

Unit count: 10/side.

Facing counts heavily!

Slopes and slope effects—yes.

Graphics scheme: Background color is tan, contour lines black, trees green, Romans red, barbarians purple.

Character sets: Contour lines: 48. trees: 8. special: 8. no character set DLI.

Player-missile graphics: Cursor, objective, arrows, and attack animations.

This document is not as complete as the first one, but it represents the decisions I had made over vexed issues, not the complete design.

The reference to slopes and slope effects requires some explanation. I wanted to explore the role of slopes in this design. All of my previous terrain systems had presumed that the contents of each hex were essentially independent of the contents of its neighbors. Terrain was therefore a collection of different icons scattered about a map. But ancient combat took place at a much smaller spatial scale than modern combat. Battle was literally hand-to-hand, whereas modern combat always takes place at some distance. Under such circumstances, the macroscopic terrain has little effect on combat. A forest of trees cannot block your view of an enemy standing directly in front of you; and you can't take cover behind a tree under such circumstances. What does matter is any height advantage you might have. If the slope places you six inches higher than your enemy, you can smash your sword down on him with considerably greater force, and he is commensurately weakened in the same fashion. Moreover, much ancient combat involved simple shoving. Like an inverted form of **Tug-of-War**, the two sides locked shields and shoved until one side collapsed onto the ground, where they were easily killed. If you have the upper hand over your enemy, it's a lot easier to knock him down.

But how to represent slopes on a computer screen? The angle of slanted or curved surfaces is particularly difficult to communicate; the human eye relies on fine differences of texture of the surface to detect its inclination and curvature. Such texture control requires pixel-by-pixel shading algorithms, which were beyond the reach of even the Atari. I needed something better.

This is not a new problem; mapmakers have struggled with the representation of slopes for hundreds of years. There are several schemes: splash lines, watershed lines, and topographic lines. I settled on the last of these. I briefly considered designing an algorithm to generate the terrain for each game, but after a few fruitless attempts, I gave up.

And so in January of 1982, I set to work on the programming of **Legionnaire**. With a clear design in my head and complete mastery of my hardware, I had a rough prototype up and running by the end of February. Here's a task list from March, presenting the tasks I had yet to tackle:

Task List

1. Variable disruption response rates—better leaders rally the men faster.

2. Caesar's legion rallies nearby legions.

3. Must put in orders display arrows!

4. Need strong indicator that a unit has been selected.

5. Combat should be very similar to **Eastern Front (1941)**, except make a clang sound instead of a machine gun.

6. Add sound of marching feet. Put in half-character animation to show motion better.

7. Need more complexity in gameplay.

8. Make combat facing-dependent.

9. Add variable number of barbarians?

10. Variable number of Romans [real leadership challenge with more units].

11. Player must scout for enemy—line of sight rules?

12. Add barbarian leader who can rally barbarian units.

13. Scenarios: Destroy barbarians, cross the board, breakout and escape, defend.

14. Apply cursor wink to barbarians.

15. Variable speed for different units.

16. Recovery from disruption is too rapid.

17. "Clang" sounds like "buzz."

18. Barbarians don't retreat—they stand and die.

This is a good example of how I develop a game. As it comes together, I make a list of incomplete features, display problems, ideas for improvement, and so forth. As I resolve each problem, I check it off. All of the items on this list are checked except for items 2, 11, and 12, which have X's next to them, and items 7 and 13, which have dashes next to them. The X-ed items are features that I decided to reject after further reflection. The dashed items are ideas that I liked, but resolved to defer until later in the project, when I might have more time. This, by the way, is a healthy way to deal with feature creep. Instead of tossing in features as they occur to you, you should implement only those features that you are certain will cost little time and are unquestionably worth the effort. Anything that is questionable should be put on the list of desirable features. Later on, when the project is behind schedule, you can show the list of desirable features to the Powers That Be and suggest that these could be added to the game if only you were given more time.

I had difficulty getting the barbarian AI to work well against experienced players. This is a common problem in game design. The usual response is to simply grant the computer some special advantage that makes up for its stupidity. I could have used the standard solution in this case: set the pace of the game so fast that the greater intelligence of the player could not be brought to bear effectively. However, I decided against this and opted instead to give the computer twice as many units as the player. After all, I reasoned, the Romans were outnumbered in most of their battles against the barbarians. However, this was the lazy solution; had I taken more pride in my work, I would have dedicated some time to sharpening the AI.

The playtesters, both those at Avalon-Hill and my own playtesters, got their first crack at the game on March 1. I was not surprised when they reported a number of problems; I was aware of these. The playtesters were all experienced, and so they were able to look past the obviously

33
LESSON

Defer unanticipated but desirable features until late in the project.

34 LESSON

If you're not passionate about it, the best you can achieve is competence.

incomplete sections of the game and assess what was actually there. I continued to implement final features, correct bugs, and fine-tune the game all through March and April. By early May, all the bugs had been expunged and the gameplay was well tuned. I was getting tired of spending my nights and weekends on **Legionnaire** while I worked on **Excalibur** during the day. I was experiencing burnout. Nevertheless, I pressed on in that last surge of energy just before deadline day. On May 30, I shipped the final version of **Legionnaire** to Avalon-Hill. They published it six weeks later. Things went a lot faster back then.

Conclusions

Neither the original version nor the Avalon-Hill version of **Legionnaire** was a great game. Like all of my games, it had a great many clever ideas, but clever ideas don't ensure great designs. The games were certainly competently designed and executed; nobody had any complaints. The reviews of the games were uniformly positive. Certainly by the standards of the day, both versions of **Legionnaire** were of better quality than most of the competition. Both games played rather like a thinking man's arcade game. I'm not ashamed of the overall results; I did a good job with both of these designs. But there was no lightning bolt of genius in the design; I never felt any passion for it. Every creative person must grind out a great many works, some of which will be turkeys, some of which will be merely competent, and a few of which will be masterpieces. **Legionnaire** was no turkey, but it was certainly no masterpiece. It was good experience for me, but I would have spent my time better had I moved on to something that fired my imagination.

wizard

On September 4, 1979, I began my career as a professional game designer at Atari. The new Atari Home Computer System (HCS) with two models, the 400 and the 800, was just coming out, and all the game designers wanted to work on those machines. Management therefore ordered that everybody who wanted to work on the home computers must first complete a game on the game machine, known as the Video Computer System (VCS). I therefore set to work learning the innards of the VCS.

VCS Technology

It is traditional for old timers to regale young-uns with improbable stories of the immense difficulties they faced as young-uns, the better to impress upon young-uns just how cushy their lives are. I shall not refrain from indulging myself in this matter, for indeed, my tales should give pause to younger game designers.

The VCS, internally known as "Stella" and designated the 2600, was not the first programmable home videogames machine—Fairchild deserves the credit for that. Nor was it the best home videogame machine. However, it had the best combination of getting to market early with good technology, and with strong marketing, it dominated the market. However, its computing and display resources were appalling. Inside was a 6507 processor (a trimmed-down version of the classic 6502) running at 1.2MHz and a special interface chip called the TIA (Television

Interface Adapter). It was also equipped with a luxurious 128 bytes—not kilobytes, not megabytes, just plain old everyday bytes—of RAM. There was no internal operating system of any kind; every scrap of code available to the system had to be inside the plug-in ROM inside the cartridge that the customer purchased and plugged into the VCS.

Are you choking on your coffee yet? The worst is yet to come: There was no bitmapped display system. You didn't simply write bits into some bitmap defining the display. Instead, Stella displayed one line at a time, and you changed the line display in real time.

To appreciate the trickiness of all this, you must understand the basics of CRT (cathode ray tube) operation. The CRT operates by shining a beam of electrons onto a special surface on the inside of the screen. The electrons hit the surface and excite the atoms there, causing them to emit light. The image is built up in three ways:

- First, you control the intensity of the electron beam to make the spot brighter or dimmer.

- Second, you sweep the electron beam across the screen in a special pattern called a *raster* (see Figure 15.1).

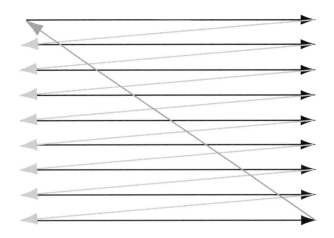

15.1 *Schematic representation of a raster scan display.*

The electron beam starts at the upper-left corner of the screen and sweeps to the right, brightening and dimming to make the scan line of the screen brighter or dimmer. When it reaches the end of the scan line, it quickly jumps back to the left side of the screen and drops down by one scan line, as indicated by the gray arrow. Then it scans to the right again, repeating the process for each scan line in the display. Thus, if you have a 640×480 display, it uses 480 scan lines each broken into 640 separate pixels. At the bottom-right corner of the screen, the beam retraces its path to the upper left corner, as indicated by the diagonal gray arrow. During the periods where the beam is retracing, it is turned off so that nothing is drawn on the screen; those times when it is retracing horizontally are called *horizontal blanking* (HBLANK) and *vertical blanking* (VBLANK).

- The third dimension of control is color; this is accomplished by making fine adjustments in the position of the electron beam so that it will hit the red, green, or blue portion of the pixel. Fortunately, at the programming level, this was not a direct concern; the TIA took care of this for you.

Now, the timing of all this is critical. In the VCS, each horizontal line took exactly 76 machine cycles of CPU execution time; vertical blanking was much longer, giving you about 3000 machine cycles. You programmed the display by loading up the TIA with data for the contents of one scan line. It transferred that data from its input registers to its internal buffer and then sent the signal out to the television. While it was busy doing this, you could reload the data registers with the display data for the next scan line. However, you had only 76 machine cycles to do so; this didn't permit a lot of time for snazzy display calculations. The entire display data structure for the VCS was as follows:

- **Playfield:** 40 bits of simple on-off data, indicating whether the corresponding portion of the scan line was to be displayed in foreground color or background color. In other words, this was a black-and-white display, except that you could change the actual color values of black-and-white to, say, green and purple, or red and blue, or some other pair. But either way, you had only 40 horizontal pixels to work with.

- **Playfield colors:** As I mentioned, you could specify the fore-ground and background colors from a set of 256 colors. You could also change the values of these colors from one scan line to the next, so that your black-and-white display could be green and purple for the first ten scan lines, red and blue for the next 40 scan lines, and so on. If you were really clever, you could change the values of these registers in the middle of the scan line, giving you not two but *four* glorious colors to work with! Of course, your timing had to be perfect to pull this off, and you also expended eight to twenty of your precious machine cycles pulling off this trick.

- **Players:** This is confusing terminology. The player here was not the actual person playing the game: It was a graphic image meant to be highly maneuverable that would almost always be used to depict the player's piece on the playfield. You had two of these. Each was an eight-bit wide chunk of binary pixel data, with its own color registers for foreground and back-ground, just as with playfield. Players were special in two ways: First, they were displayed at four times higher resolution than the playfield; and second, they could be moved around hori-zontally by changing the value in a single register.

- **Missiles:** These were single-bit versions of players. They were meant to be the bullets that players shot at each other.

Thus, to put a display up on the screen, you had to write a tight little routine called the *kernel* that stuffed information into the various data registers of the TIA, keeping track of which scan line you were on and changing the values as the beam moved down the screen. If you wanted a more intricate display, you'd need to change the registers more often, which required more machine cycles. But if you took more than the max-imum of 76 cycles per scan line, your display would get out of synch with the television, and the screen would turn into pixellated garbage. Most VCS programming was a battle to squeeze maximum display intri-cacy into 76 cycles, and VCS programmers knew the cycle counts of all the 6502 instructions by heart. It was part of the daily office routine to

hear an anguished cry from an office down the hall: "77 cycles!"—
another programmer would have to completely redesign his kernel.
(Actually, there were not one but two female VCS programmers at Atari
during my tenure there: Carol Shaw and Carla Meninsky.)

So I hope that you're properly impressed with just how hard it was to
design games back in those days. Did I mention that we had to walk
twelve miles through the snow to get to work each morning?

Designing the Game

Once I figured out the basics of VCS programming, I set to work. Since
programming the VCS was so difficult, management didn't place any
constraints on a designer's early work; you just developed any idea that
came into your head, and only after you'd gotten something working
would management take a look at it and offer suggestions. Much later,
when the game was taking clear shape, the marketing people would
come into the picture.

The central notion I wanted to develop in my design was the idea known
elsewhere as *fog of war*: You don't know where the enemy is, but he's
coming to get you. All other games at the time kept you fully informed
as to the location and movements of your enemy. This, it seemed to me,
deprived the game of important elements of suspense. So I decided
to build a game in which you must fight an enemy who can hide
behind walls.

This required a carefully designed playfield: It had to provide lots of
walls to hide behind, but also permit occasional long lines of sight. I
spent a lot of time tuning the playfield to get the right balance. My final
result looks like what appears in Figure 15.2.

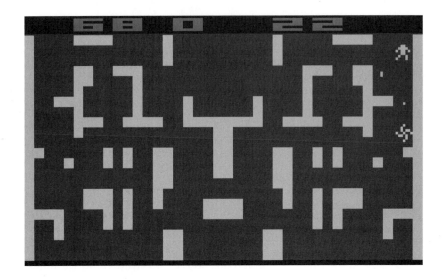

15.2 *The final result.*

Note that this is a reflected playfield: The two horizontal halves are reflected images. This saved me 58 bytes of ROM space, a significant savings in a 2K ROM. Did I mention that the entire program, display tables, sound tables, and so forth had to fit inside a 2K ROM?

It didn't take a design genius to figure out that there would be two players, one for the human player, and one for the computer. I gave them asymmetric properties to sharpen the conflict (and to lessen the difficulties of computer AI on a 2K cartridge). The computer player—henceforth the monster—would simply pursue the human, shooting at him whenever he got a clear line of sight (LOS). The human would run around, evading the monster and getting off shots as best he could.

Since I didn't have the resources to build an AI smart enough to plot paths through the maze, the monster needed the ability to move through walls, but I saw no reason to give the human the same ability; this would be an advantage of the monster. Thus, the monster could, in effect, see through the walls, but the human couldn't. But this created a problem: It was mightily disconcerting to have the monster suddenly pop out from a wall when you least expected it. I'm quite proud of my solution to this problem: I equipped the monster with a characteristic sound that grew louder as it drew closer. To really make the player's hair stand on end, I needed a creepy sound. This was none too easy to do: The TIA's sound capabilities were optimized for gunshots, explosions, and so forth. After much experimentation, I fashioned a believable heartbeat sound. This turned out to be one of the finest elements of the game. When the monster was out there, steadily bearing down on you, the rising sound of its heartbeat raised the tension to unbearable levels.

Asymmetric Combat

Once I had decided upon this fundamental asymmetry, it seemed natural to extend it to the combat system. Sure, both sides would be shooting at each other, but they didn't have to be shooting with the same weapons. Again, I'm rather pleased with the asymmetric system I came up with. The monster's gun, in keeping with its poor AI, simply shot as fast as it could. Because there was only one missile per player, I could show only one missile in flight at any given instant, so the rule was simple: Neither side could fire a shot while a bullet from its gun was still in flight. At close ranges, then, players could machine-gun each other, but at great distances, shots were few and far between.

Since this was imposed upon me by graphic constraints, I decided to run with the idea and build it into the game design. The monster would shoot bullets with small, fixed destructive value; its best tactic was to get close to the player. Accordingly, the human's best tactic should be to engage the monster from great distances.

I therefore established the simple rule that the destructive power of the human's bullet increased with the distance it traveled. I then extended the rule to give the player even richer tactical considerations: The destructive power of his bullet was proportional to the amount of time between pressing the button down and the bullet's impact. The player did not simply push the trigger button to shoot at the monster; he pressed and held it down and the bullet began building up strength, accompanied by the sound of an ominously rising tone. When he released the trigger button, the bullet would fire. This could not go on forever; when the bullet reached its maximum strength, it automatically fired. There was no need to aim in this game; bullets automatically traveled directly toward their target.

The result was completely original gameplay: the player was constantly in flight from the monster; should the monster ever get really close to the player, its machine gun fire would quickly end the game. The player had to keep his distance, but also had to shoot back, so he would start building a bullet, get it up to maximum strength, and then jump out into the open to let loose a devastating shot. If the monster was where he expected, the trick worked. If not, the player was in trouble.

Lines of Sight (LOS)

To make all this work, I needed to trace clean lines of sight. This, it turns out, was no simple matter. Be warned: The next few pages are tediously technical. If you want to avoid the gory technical details, skip ahead to the line that says, "If you're a non-technical reader, you can resume reading now."

Still with me? Good for you! Now, those simple 8-bit processors had no hardware multiply/divide capabilities. All calculations were carried out with 8-bit addition and subtraction. How can a program trace a straight line from point (x1, y1) to point (x2, y2) without any concept of slope (ΔY divided by ΔX)?

I couldn't just cram a software multiply/divide library into the game: There wasn't enough ROM. I needed a fast algorithm that required little ROM or RAM. It was precisely this difficulty that forced all shooting games on the VCS to use simple angles for shots: horizontal, vertical, or 45-degree diagonals. A few of the snazzier games also handled 30-degree and 60-degree shots because they had slopes that were simple 2:1 ratios. But a general-purpose line calculator? That seemed impossible.

Such an algorithm had already been invented, but I was too unschooled to know of it; I had to re-invent this wheel. As it happens, the route I followed to do so provides an interesting tale. After many long walks in the parking lot, trying to figure out a solution, it one day dawned on me that the Maya Indians had faced the same problem in designing their calendar. The critical task facing any calendar maker is the determination of the exact length of the year, which is approximately 365.24220 days. Unfortunately, the Maya did not have the concept of decimals in their mathematics, nor did they have fractions, so they had no way to express this number. They knew that the length of the year was a bit more than 365 days and decidedly less than 366 days, but that was as far as their mathematics could take them. Until one day when some Maya genius came up with a way to express it: There are 1461 days in four years (1461 divided by 4 is 365.25). With further refinement, they were able to figure out that there are 14,975 days in 41 years, and so on. This system allows you to express ratios with as much resolution as you require, and permits running calculations of slope using just integers.

Here's how my algorithm worked: Let's say that we want to trace the LOS (which is exactly the same as the path of a bullet) from the player at (20,30) to the monster at (30,57). ΔX is 10 and ΔY is 27. Now we carry out a brute force division of 27 by 10; to do this, we subtract 10 from 27 until the remainder is less than 10. This happens just twice, so we conclude that the slope is at least 2; the next higher integer is 3, so the true value of the slope is between 2 and 3. Our basic algorithm, then, will be to sometimes take a jump of 3 steps in Y for every one step in X, and other times take a jump of 2 steps in Y for every one step in X. The problem is to figure out when to take which jump. (See Figure 15.3).

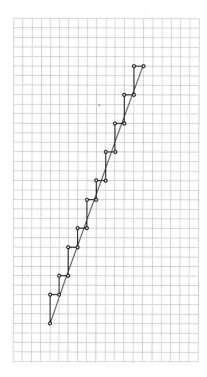

We have to start somewhere, so we'll pick one of the two jumps. Since the remainder of the previous division was more than half of the divisor (27 mod 10 gives 7, which is more than 5), we'll start with the bigger 3:1 jump rather than the smaller 2:1 jump.

So we take three steps in Y followed by one step in X. Our bullet moves along the path (20,30); (20,31); (20,32); (20,33); (21,33). Our cumulative path so far has taken us 3 steps in Y and 1 step in X; these cumulative values will become important soon.

15.3 *Tracing a LOS.*

Now we must decide whether to make a 3:1 jump or a 2:1 jump. If it were 2:1, then we would have a cumulative motion in Y of 5 and a cumulative motion in X of 2; if instead we take a 3:1 jump, then the cumulative ΔY will be 6 and the cumulative ΔX will be 2. Now, the temptation here is to calculate slopes of the two possible lines, but we can't do that because we don't have fractional division. Instead of dividing down to small values that will be fractions, we will multiply up to large values that will be integers. So let's extrapolate our values upward. How far must we go? We will simply ask, how many cumulative ΔX's are there in the final ΔX; that's how far we must extrapolate our ΔY. So, with each jump, the cumulative ΔX will be 2. There are five 2's (the cumulative ΔX) in 10 (the final ΔX), so we want to see how five cumulative ΔY's compare with the final ΔY. The big jump would yield a cumulative ΔY of 6, while the shorter jump would yield a cumulative ΔY of 5. Multiplying these two values by 5 yields 30 and 25, respectively. Which is closer to 27? The value coming from the shorter jump, so that's the jump we want to take this time.

Now we repeat the process. Unfortunately, we encounter a problem here: We can't extrapolate our Δ values with integers. Our ΔX values will each be 3, and 3 does not divide integrally into 10. Put in mathematical terms, 10 modulo 3 is nonzero. What now?

The solution relies on the fact that, of the two possible jumps (3:1 or 2:1), the 3:1 jump is the "majority" jump—we know from the final ΔY:ΔX that the 3:1 jump will be taken more often. Therefore, a close approximation is to use that jump to fill in remainders. Here's how it works: We go ahead and divide 10 by 3 to get 3, but we make a note of the remainder of 1. Then we extrapolate each of our cumulative ΔY's by three, and then we add one more majority jump to each ratio, to account for the remainder. Here's the calculation:

- 3:1 cumulative ΔY:ΔY is 8:3.
- 2:1 cumulative ΔY:ΔX is 7:3.
- Multiply 3:1 cumulative ΔY:ΔX to get 24:9.
- Multiply 2:1 cumulative ΔY:ΔX to get 21:9.
- Add one 3:1 jump to 3:1 cumulative ΔY:ΔX to get 27:10.
- Add one 3:1 jump to 2:1 cumulative ΔY:ΔX to get 24:10.

Aha! The 3:1 jump gets us closer to the correct 27:10 value; that's our choice. We then continue this process all the way along the line,

Here's a table showing the calculations for each jump. I used an alternating choice when the two choices were equally close to the ideal value of 27.

Current Position	3:1 cum $\Delta Y{:}\Delta X$	Extrapolated $\Delta Y{:}\Delta X$	Make Up Deficit	2:1 cum $\Delta Y{:}\Delta X$	Extrapolated $\Delta Y{:}\Delta X$	Make Up Deficit	Final Choice
(20,30)	3:1	30:10	30:10	2:1	20:10	20:10	3:1
(21,33)	6:2	30:10	30:10	5:2	25:10	25:10	2:1
(22,35)	8:3	24:9	27:10	7:3	21:9	24:10	3:1
(23,38)	11:4	22:8	28:10	10:4	20:8	26:10	2:1
(24,40)	13:5	26:10	26:10	12:5	24:10	24:10	3:1
(25,42)	16:6	16:6	28:10	15:6	15:6	26:10	2:1
(26,45)	18:7	18:7	27:10	17:7	17:7	26:10	3:1
(27,48)	21:8	21:8	27:10	20:8	20:8	26:10	3:1
(28,51)	24:9	24:9	27:10	23:9	23:9	26:10	3:1
(29,54)	27:10	27:10	27:10	26:10	26:10	26:10	3:1
(30,57)							

(The algorithm I actually used was a bit more complicated and efficient than this one, but I figured that this example was befuddling enough, so I kept it simple.)

In this way I was able to calculate either the trajectories of bullets or the LOS. Of course, to calculate the LOS, you must determine whether it intersects any solid objects, in which case it is blocked. Here I pulled a simple trick: The TIA chip also provided collision detection between moving objects and playfield (collision detection tells you when one graphical object is superposed over another), so I simply ran a bullet from the monster to the player and checked collision detection to see if the LOS was blocked. In other words, the LOS was checked by shooting invisible, harmless bullets from the monster to the player; if there was no collision detection, then the LOS was good and the next bullet was for real.

If you're a non-technical reader, you can resume reading now. For the player graphics, I used a simple stick man whose legs wiggled about as he moved. For the monster, I used a rotating spiral; along with the thump-dump, thump-dump of its heart, it was robustly creepy.

Somewhere along the way, I decided to add a topic to the game. All along, I had simply followed the logic of game. From the starting point of hidden players, everything else flowed naturally. But having concocted this screwball situation, I needed some plausible context. What the hell, I decided, it might as well be a wizard fighting a monster; after all, wizards can do anything. The wizard's bullet became a fireball; the maze became a dungeon, and poof, that was all there was to it.

The logic of the game dominates; pick a topic to fit it.

Disposition and Conclusion

I finished **Wizard** in early January of 1980; it took exactly four months from the time I joined Atari to learn the VCS and finish the game. Even by the quick standards of those days, this was considered fast. We sent the program over to marketing and, my dues paid, I set to work on a program for the HCS. About a month later, marketing was ready with their comments.

They liked the game, but it didn't fit well into the product line. Atari had been making the transition from 2K ROMs to 4K ROMs, and the new 4K ROM products were gobbling up all the sales; 2K games just couldn't sell. I had been required to build a 2K game because they weren't sure of the future of 2K ROM games when I started, but by the time I finished, they were sure that such games had no hope in the marketplace. Still, they liked the design; could I re-design it to take advantage of 4K? Perhaps some snazzier graphics, better sounds, or more game options?

I had a hidden agenda: I was already well into my project for the HCS, and I found the HCS much more interesting to work with then the VCS. I really didn't want to revert to that Neanderthal machine. Besides, I had a perfectly solid argument, which I used to foil the marketing people: You don't just take a 2K game and add another 2K of padding to get a 4K game. The game would have to be completely redesigned from scratch, and the end result would be a completely new product. I couldn't guarantee a fast delivery and I couldn't even promise that the game would play like a souped-up version of the 2K game. I would just start over and do the best I could. For political reasons I was unaware of at the time, the marketing people decided not to press the matter. **Wizard** was buried in the Atari archives.

Few people have ever seen **Wizard**. There appears to be a version of it floating around on the Web, and it supposedly can run on the various VCS emulators available for PCs. It is certainly not one of my best designs, but I am nevertheless pleased with it. It's a solid design that takes good advantage of the platform and delivers a gaming experience that was otherwise unavailable at the time. It's a strong demonstration of good design in a tight environment: I set a clear gameplaying goal (hidden movement), and I achieved it.

energy czar

energy czar

In early 1980, having met my obligation to design a game for the Video Computer System (VCS), I eagerly set to work learning the Home Computer System (HCS). It was quite a challenge; the documentation was fragmented and not very helpful. At the same time, I was casting about for a game idea. I proposed to my supervisor, Dale Yocum, that I build an educational game on energy/environment/economics issues. As it happens, I had built a crude version of such a game and declared it on my Inventions and Patents agreement with Atari, so it was technically my property. He agreed that, if I could build a game good enough to pass muster with marketing, then Atari would pay me $2,000 for my rights to the design. I set to work on initial design considerations and then made my first design presentation to the marketing staff.

The marketing people at Atari had a tough job. They had to sell home computers into homes that didn't know what a computer was. They had to work with geeky programmers who saw all software as a gift bestowed on users by beneficent programmers who knew what was best for users. And they had absolutely no market history on which to draw; this was completely virgin territory.

One of the few decisions that they were confident in was the decision to clearly differentiate the home computer from the videogames machine. They did not want the HCS to be dismissed as a toy, nor did they want it cannibalizing sales of the VCS. So the rule was simple: no more games. A bunch of games had been produced for the HCS during its design phase, including **Star Raiders**, which was what we now call a "killer app"; people were willing to buy the computer just to play the game.

This and the other games provided a strong starting library; now we had to flesh out the line with serious applications. Therefore, marketing made it known that for the time being, it would approve no more games proposals.

Dale and I had therefore agreed to present the design as an "educational simulation," not a game. I was understandably nervous on the morning of the presentation; I had 30 minutes to make my case to these strangers. Still, my experience as a public speaker served me well, and in my allotted time, I made all the important points. At the end of my presentation, the VP of marketing, a brilliant and thoroughly likable fellow named Peter Rosenthal, fixed me with a hard stare and asked me, "Is this a game?" I gulped; I could see the suspicion in his eyes. "No, no," I assured him. "It's an educational simulation!" I declared with hopeful confidence. "I don't know," Peter mulled skeptically. "It sure looks fun to me." I was dismissed and waited in anxious helplessness for several days. Then one day Dale came into my office and announced the good news: The project had been approved.

The basic design was ridiculously simple: It was just a small set of coupled first-order differential equations—Lunar Lander writ large. The player could set taxes or subsidies on each of several different energy sources: oil, coal, natural gas, nuclear, solar, and wind. The taxes gained from one energy source could be used to subsidize another. Each energy source generated a certain amount of pollution. The player then balanced the tax structure to obtain the best combination of energy prices and low pollution.

The program was written entirely in BASIC. I had the skills to write it in Assembler, but it was so much easier to work in BASIC that all of us just assumed that we'd use BASIC. The program did nothing more than display bar graphs of the various numbers coming out of the simulation.

I jazzed it up a little by adding sounds as the bars were drawn. Right at the end of the project, while marketing was reviewing it, I figured out display list interrupts on the Atari and how to set them up in BASIC. This enabled me to draw the bar charts in many different colors.

The only interesting design lesson from this project was the fight I had with my supervisor, Dale Yocum, over user friendliness. At that time, I was very much the programming geek. I clearly recall an unpleasant meeting with Dale where he picked through my software, demonstrating points of confusion. What would happen if the user did this at such and such a point? What if he did that? The problems he was citing were all matters of input bounds, such as if the player typed a 9 when the largest admissible value was a 5, for example, or a D when the only meaningful inputs were A, B, or C. I thought his objections were silly—if the user were serious about using the program, it was reasonable for me to demand that he read the manual. I didn't say it, but I was giving voice to one of the oldest cop-outs used by programmers: the disdainful command "RTFM!" (Read The Manual!) Programmers seem to feel that, having laid down the rules and regulations of the program, they have satisfied their responsibilities; any user too lazy to read and obey those rules and regulations deserves everything he gets. And I was right there with them, my nose in the air and my self-righteousness waving proudly.

Dale was endlessly patient with me, trying to explain that paying customers shouldn't have to undergo such treatment; our job was to make their experience as pleasant and rewarding as possible. I wouldn't budge. So Dale appealed to my vanity, pointing out that poorly human-engineered programs were a dime a dozen and that only a few could boast truly clean user interfaces. It didn't work; my stubbornness exceeded my vanity. In the end, Dale had to order me to fix the problems.

36

Young program-
mers can
be stubborn
asses.

I have come a long ways since then, and I now embrace user friendliness to a degree that goes well beyond what most programmers are comfortable with. I'm also more open to suggestions that I don't like hearing. But it's important to remember that, in my own youth and the youth of the industry, the concept of user friendliness was poorly developed and had little support.

scrom

scrom

Before I became a professional game designer, I was a "Mr. Science."
I went to high schools all over the state of California, putting on shows
about energy policy issues for entire student bodies. After each show,
I'd go into classrooms and talk to students about energy policy. To
improve my classroom presentations, I wrote two little simulations on
my computer: One simulated energy policy decisions and later became
Energy Czar, and the other simulated nuclear power plant operations.
When I started working at Atari on the Home Computer System (HCS),
the marketing people were eager for educational software, so I wrote
Energy Czar. Since they were eager for more, I set to work adapting my
nuclear power plant simulator to the Atari.

The original simulation did nothing more than figure out the heat flow
through the plant. It used simple physics equations to calculate the
temperatures at various locations inside the plant and presented all the
numerical results in a big, dense display crowded with numbers. As a
physicist, I appreciated having all the numbers at my fingertips, but my
boss, Dale Yocum, took one look at that screen and said, "We have to
work on the user interface." The task was clear: convert a screenful of
numbers into a pretty picture of the nuclear power plant, using just a
few numbers as labels at critical points. Moreover, I had only four colors
to work with, including background. I was able to add a few more colors
by clever use of player-missile graphics (see Figure 17.1).

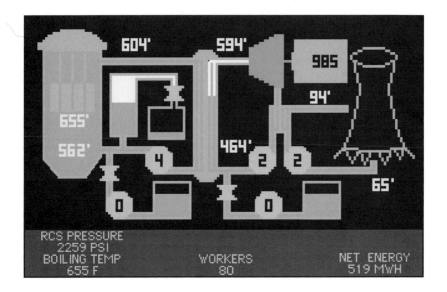

17.1 *Scram* screen.

With **Scram** I committed the most common error in game design: I used the display as the foundation of the design. Most beginning game designers make this mistake, and I was a beginner back then. It's easy to understand how we fall into this error. When struggling with a new task, the mind gropes for some solid foundation on which to build, and most beginning designers think of a computer game in terms of the visuals rather than the play.

This problem is so simple, and yet so fundamental, that it deserves some elaboration. Here's an experiment to try: Ask somebody to point to their computer. Odds are they will point to the monitor, not the CPU. The monitor is, after all, the locus of their attention during the interaction of playing the game; it is the primary sensory manifestation of the game. Yet the monitor is only a peripheral. The computer itself is a flat, square chunk of plastic and silicon buried deep inside the box. Ask a child to point toward himself, and he will respond by pointing toward his approximate center of mass—his chest. Ask an adult the same question and you'll see a finger pointing at a face—the face we present to the world.

What's so wrong with this mental fixation is its failure to appreciate what's important about computers—they compute! A computer is NOT an image-generation device; it is an interactivity device. A game is not a sequence of pictures; it's an interactive process. What we see on the screen is not the substance of what we get from the computer; it is only the visual expression of the deeper, more subtle process that we seek when we turn on the computer.

It is therefore a mistake to design a game by first sketching out the screen display. That screen display is a vital component of the game, but it is not the essence of the play experience. The starting point of game design must be the nature of the play experience, not the visual experience.

Design your games as play experiences, not visual experiences.

Input Structures

Once I had my screen laid out, I set to work figuring out how the user could control the power plant. Having gotten the problem backward by laying out the screen before settling on my input structure, I was now in a bind. I could figure no clean way to control the power plant with a joystick and cursor. Being young and impatient, I simply barged through the problem with a wretched solution. The game offered eight controllable devices: four pumps (the orange octagons), three valves (the orange X-shaped objects), and the reactor core. Clearly the player would somehow use the joystick to select one of those eight objects, press down the joystick button, and actuate the joystick up or down to adjust the device. But how, exactly, should the joystick select one of the control devices?

This may seem a ridiculous question to a generation raised on mice. Put the cursor on it and click, right? Not so fast, young-un. Back in those days, we didn't have mice, and we didn't use cursors much except for maneuvering through text. Moreover, joysticks are nowhere near as handy as mice for moving cursors around on the screen. I considered using the joystick to move a cursor, but decided that users would find the experience uncomfortable. We didn't have standard conventions for what a user could click on. It seemed likely that the user would scroll around the screen randomly clicking on things that didn't do anything, growing ever more frustrated. I therefore decided to implement a "jumping cursor" as opposed to the "sliding cursor" that is the standard nowadays. My jumping cursor would have only eight possible positions to occupy: one for each controllable device. A single step of joystick movement would jump the cursor from device to device. It was clean and simple, but fatally flawed.

Look again at the screen display. The eight controllable devices are not laid out on a clean rectgrid. Moving from one to another requires horizontal movement in some cases, vertical movement in others, and diagonal movement in still other cases. How was the player to know how to get from the auxiliary feedwater pump to the reactor control rods?

My design simply papered over this problem; I cobbled together a table of jump destinations. When the player used the joystick, the cursor jumped to the location that seemed best. The spatial fidelity of the system was cockeyed, but people were so unfamiliar with cursor-control systems that they didn't seem to mind. In short, I fudged the problem and got away with it.

Oh Yes, It Was Supposed to Be a Game, Wasn't It?

Having botched the design strategy and perpetrated a crappy input structure, I was now ready for the finishing touch of incompetent design: I was going to make a game out of it!

I have already pointed out that good game design requires you to design the play experience first and build the design outward from there. My bungled design was so far gone that there is no need for further preaching on this matter. I shall merely observe that, having already built a simulation, a display, and an input structure, I had zero design flexibility to actually make the software fun. All the player could do was operate the power plant, turning pumps on and off and opening and closing valves. Whoop-de-doo! Of course, I was too young and eager to engage in the type of navel-gazing that allows one to notice outrages against common sense and decency, so I blithely cobbled together the following lame-brained scheme.

The player's nuclear power plant would be visited by occasional earthquakes, which would shake the plant (here I employed a clever graphics effect, amazing myself even more with my brilliance, and failing utterly to recognize the true nature of the problem). Each earthquake would break some component of the power plant, but the screen would not show the damage directly. The only valid data the player would have was the temperature data; an analysis of the rate of change of temperatures in various parts of the plant would permit the player to deduce the nature of the problem. Dispatching repair teams to the damaged component would effect a repair, but the supply of repair teams was limited, so a faulty analysis could be disastrous. The player scored points for keeping the reactor running at full power for the longest possible time.

38
LESSON

Sometimes the most brilliant design stroke is to kill the idea.

Coda

All in all, **Scram** was a stupid game devoid of entertainment value. But it was loaded with clever graphics stunts (I even showed the water flowing through pipes with little moving bubbles) and boasted plenty of good sound effects: rumbling earthquakes, clanging metal, insistent klaxons, and so forth. I could hide behind the fact that software in those days was mostly bad. Indeed, at about the same time that we released **Scram** for the Atari HCS, somebody else released a game called **Three Mile Island** for the Apple II. This may be hard to believe, but **Three Mile Island** was considerably inferior to **Scram**. As a simulation it stank, its display was dull, its input structure was completely confusing, it had no sound effects, and the gameplay was, astoundingly, even worse than **Scram**'s!

But I couldn't get away with such excuses. I screwed up the design of **Scram**. If I had it all to do over again, I would start my design process by asking myself, "What is fun and interesting about nuclear power plants?" The answer, of course, would be "Not much," and I would walk away from the idea of building such a game.

About six months after **Scram** was released, there was a minor accident at a nuclear power plant in upstate New York, and Ted Koppel of *ABC Nightline* decided to devote his show to the problems of nuclear power plant safety. As a pleasant wrap-up for the show, he sent his San Francisco area reporter, Ken Kashiwahara, to interview me. He obtained permission from Atari to interview me and we got together in a demo room on the Atari campus. Remember, this was all on a tight schedule: The decision to devote the show to nuclear power plant safety was made in the morning, and the show would air that night.

There were four of us in the demo room: Ken, his cameraman, myself, and a suspicious Atari public relations person who made sure to keep me on the straight and narrow. I was quite nervous and kept glancing over at the PR person for reassurance that I wasn't about to get myself fired. Ken figured out what was going on and put me at ease by suggesting that, prior to the interview, we just run through the basics while the cameraman got the lighting perfect. He asked me to talk about the game and I happily obliged, losing myself in the fun of explaining all the cute features in the game. Warming to my subject, I laughed and giggled as I fought earthquakes, struggled with steam voiding, and eventually melted down the reactor. Having explained the operation of the game to him, I handed him the joystick and suggested he give it a try.

"No, thanks," Ken answered. "We've got our interview."

Stunned, I stared uncomprehendingly. "But, but, aren't you going to do the interview?" I pleaded.

"We left the camera running while you were talking. You did great!"

The PR person was furious at being tricked. I grinned in admiration and tried, badly, to echo the PR guy's mortification. Ken Kashiwahara sure was a smooth operator. That night, viewers were treated to the sight of Chris Crawford bouncing up and down in his chair, laughingly pointing at the screen, and twittering in his best choirboy voice, "Oh no, Mr. Bob! Steam voiding!"

eastern front (1941)

In August of 1980, I saw a wonderful bit of software (I believe it was written by Ed Logg) for the Atari Home Computer System (HCS) that set up a huge map and smoothly scrolled through it. The map was done with character graphics, but the HCS had the ability to change character sets, so it was not difficult to use graphic character sets to assemble a map or larger image. I realized that this opened up a world of possibilities for wargames. No longer would we need to squeeze the entire map onto a single 320×192 screen; now we could have huge maps. I sat down and wrote a routine that duplicated the functions of the original demo, then designed a custom character set for map use, and finally assembled a map using that custom character set. The result was astounding: a smooth-scrolling map that was four screens wide by four screens high.

It may be difficult for designers brought up with modern PCs to appreciate just how exciting this was. We had been confined to single-screen, low-resolution displays; the best we could do to add more information was to jump from one display to the next. This smooth scrolling map was absolutely revolutionary!

The Scrolling Map

Other
people can't
see your
vision; you
have to
make it
happen
yourself.

I was busy working on **Scram** at that time, so progress on the scrolling map was slow. I was also helping outside software developers with their needs for technical support for the Atari hardware. In November of 1980, I was promoted and given the task of setting up a group that would provide technical support for external software developers. I immediately began approaching software developers in the Bay Area, giving them photocopied documentation, software demonstrating how to take advantage of various features of the Atari computers, and so forth. Despite the clear superiority of the HCS, many programmers had a strong emotional attachment to the trusty old Apple II, which they knew inside and out. The scrolling map demo was the most powerful demo I had. Programmers' eyes would bug out when they saw that. Even then, though, some people just wouldn't budge from their loyalties. I especially remember a visit to a wargames company. As the *piece de resistance*, I dangled the scrolling map demo in front of their eyes, and enticingly suggested all the new possibilities this could open up for wargaming. But no, they were too wedded to the Apple II. They were building *real* wargames, not childish videogames.

I was deeply disappointed by their rejection; it seemed that nobody was willing to develop this wonderful technology into a game. Very well, I decided, if nobody else will accept this challenge, then I shall have to do it myself. I would build a wargame using scrolling map technology.

During December 1980, I began serious design work. I refrained from putting fingers to keyboard or pencil to paper; I wanted to get a clear vision of the game before

I plunged in. I took many long walks alone at night,
considering the fundamental properties of the game. Above all, I concentrated on the player's experience. What should it feel like to play the
game? Would it be a complex logical problem? A matter of recognizing
weak spots in the enemy line and exploiting them? What should the
pace be like: fast and clean, or slower and more deliberate? All through
December I mused over the game, and then in early January, I put my
ideas down on paper in a single-page design document.

Eastfront Game Preliminary Description

Map: 64×64 squares

Unit count: 32 German corps, up to 64 Russian armies

Time scale: "Semi-time" of one week/turn. German enters moves for
the next week (meanwhile, computer figures Russian move). When
player is ready, play proceeds in real time.

Human interface: Map window on screen. Joystick input scrolls map
and players. Putting unit under crosshairs activates it and orders
arrows show. Then holding down button while twiddling joystick enters
next order. Arrows (player-missile graphics) pop onto screen showing
orders. Space bar clears orders. Releasing button resumes scrolling.

START button starts turn.

Colors:

Background:	Brown
PF0:	Green (forests)
PF1:	Blue (rivers, lakes, seas)
PF2:	Grey (German units, cities)
PF3:	Red (Russian units)
P0–P3:	Pink (orders arrows)

[Not enough color! Use DLI's or time-multiplexed color.]

I worked on my game at home on nights and weekends; I enjoyed the work because my work at Atari involved less and less programming and more and more management issues. It was pleasant to concentrate on the simpler problems of programming rather than the messy personnel issues that crowded my days at work.

The end result of this work was a beautiful scrolling map (see Figure 18.1).

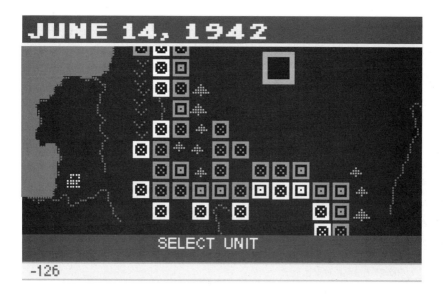

18.1 *Eastern Front (1941) screen display.*

Once I had a scrolling map, I needed some military units that could move around on the map, so I went to work on those. After a month's time, I had units that I could select with the joystick and give orders to; not much later they were executing those orders, marching all over the map.

I had all the mechanics necessary for a wargame, but this program was by no means a wargame yet. It needed two major components: a combat system and AI for the computer player.

The Combat System

Combat was no big deal; having worked with combat systems for board games, I knew most of what I needed to do. Terrain considerations were the least of my concerns: I'd just double defensive strength in dense terrain and behind rivers. Facing considerations were important: Units being attacked from the flanks or, worse, from the rear, would suffer a loss of effective defensive strength. What I really wanted to focus on was the disruption element. When units fought, they would suffer both casualties and disruption. The casualties were never replaced, but the units would slowly recover from their disruption. This meant that there were two forms of combat strength: muster strength and combat strength. The former was the full strength of the unit based on the number of men and weapons it possessed. Combat strength was the actual working strength at any given moment, based on how badly disrupted the unit was.

Here I made a classic mistake: I allowed old ways of thinking to influence my design. In boardgames, combat was always resolved in a single roll of the dice. I built my combat resolution algorithms to do the same thing, never realizing that there were plenty of other possibilities opened up by the computer. I thought that being able to do simple arithmetic was a big enough improvement. However, I quickly ran into a fatal problem: My combat system was unable to take proper advantage of disruption. Since each combatant got exactly one crack at its opponent, the disruption it inflicted would not be of any significance unless another unit also attacked the enemy unit immediately after the first battle. This kind of one-two punch had been an important part of **Legionnaire**, but that game had an open battlefield in which units could freely maneuver. In this game, the units were packed together more tightly and so arranging a one-two punch was more difficult.

I wasted far too much time on this problem before the solution came to me: break the battle up into a series of micro-battles. When Unit A attacks Unit B, don't resolve the combat with one formula based on

Always be
on guard
against the
tendency to
think in the
old ways.

their relative strengths; instead, fight a series of tiny battles, each of which inflicts casualties and disruption onto both units. The advantage of this scheme was that the benefits of disruption of the defender could be enjoyed by the attacker. On the very first micro-battle, the defender would likely suffer some tiny disruption, which, in turn, would make it slightly weaker in the next micro-battle. In this way, two closely-matched units would not batter each other into splinters; one would gain the upper hand sooner and break the morale of the weaker, forcing it to retreat. This scheme for multiple micro-battles worked much better than the old-style, single-step battle system.

AI

Although **Eastern Front (1941)** is remembered primarily for its scrolling map, I can take no credit for that; it was built into the hardware. The design element of which I am most proud is the AI for the game. At a time when many wargames were still being written in BASIC, my design boasted two major innovations.

The first of these was the threaded execution. All of the I/O was executed during the Vertical Blank Interrupt (VBI), a routine that executed once each 60th of a second, synchronized with the vertical blank period of the television set. This was the only good time to mess with the display, as changes to the display while the beam was drawing it were likely to yield irritating rips or tears in the image. So I set up all I/O through the VBI routine, which meant in turn that the mainline program—the one that executed in the absence of interrupts—could operate in the background while the player worked in the foreground. In other words, even as the player was entering his own orders, the program was figuring the Russian move.

The more important innovation, of course, was the algorithm for planning the Russian move. This time, I told myself, I was going to solve the problem of figuring a front line. My initial plan had been to start at one edge of the map, select the closest Russian unit to begin the line, and then somehow trace a line through other Russian units to the opposite edge of the map. This idea broke to pieces against a nasty problem: what to do if the line were broken? If the Germans achieved a complete breakthrough, would my algorithms break down and lead to a total collapse of the Russian position?

This led me to think of the line from the point of view of individual units. Since they might be operating in some isolation, it would be necessary to think of each unit as a fragment of a line; my algorithm then needed only to find a way to link together such fragments.

At the time I was designing the AI, there were no *zones of control* (ZoC) in the movement system. The concept of the zone of control was developed for board wargames way back in the 1950s. In such games, each unit projected a zone of control into each of the squares (or hexes) adjacent to it. Movement from one ZoC square into another ZoC square was forbidden. With ZoCs, you didn't need a solid front line; you could hold the line with a thin string of units. Yet you could still concentrate lots of units in the spaces to mount an offensive. It was a winning idea, and most board wargames used it. Yet I chose not to use this design construct in **Eastern Front (1941)**. I had initially believed that my unit densities were so high that it would not be difficult to trace a continuous line.

All this meant that my algorithms should be directed toward gap-filling in the line. The overall course of the line, I expected, would remain intact through the game; I needed only find a scheme for plugging holes that might develop.

One of the big questions that bedevil many designers is the problem of whether to design the AI to be bottom-up or top-down. In a top-down design, the AI system starts off by looking at the grand strategic situation, figuring out what needs to be done, and then trickles these decisions down to the individual units. In a bottom-up design, the AI is applied to the individual units without any central coordinating authority. Each unit follows its own nose in planning its move. This type of AI, when it works, yields what is called *emergent behavior*. When it doesn't work, it yields what is termed a *turkey*.

I decided on the latter course because I expected that Russian units might face chaotic situations where they would need to think for themselves. Besides, this allowed me to break the problem down into smaller steps that could be addressed in increments, so that the program would not need to complete some monstrous calculation before it could begin the turn.

For this discussion, I will present the system I used in the final version, which used a 5-wide square for analysis. In the initial design, I used only a 3-wide square; later on, it occurred to me that I could improve the overall quality of the AI by simply extending the 3-wide square notions into a 5-wide square. I am proud to say that my code had been so cleanly written that the conversion from 3-wide squares to 5-wide squares went smoothly. So here is what my 5-wide square might look like under analysis (see Figure 18.2).

The five rectangular symbols with crosses in them are standard military symbols for infantry units.

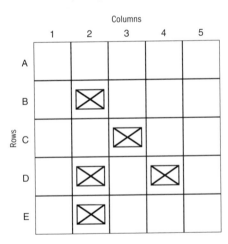

18.2 *Grid for AI computation.*

The first problem to tackle is, what is the direction of the front line? Does the line trace right to left, or up and down? Given the fluidity of the Eastern Front, I could not assume some standard direction; German units sometimes found themselves attacking toward the west. My answer to this problem was simple and clean: danger is a vector, not a scalar. When evaluating its tactical situation, each unit must first evaluate how much danger it finds itself in and the overall direction from which that danger emanates. The algorithm calculates the overall danger coming from each of the four cardinal directions, and then evaluates the strength of the defensive position against that danger. This is done for each of the four cardinal directions, so the 5-wide square above is, in effect, rotated through each of its four possible orientations.

The details of the algorithm are quite messy, especially because I didn't have hardware multiplication and division. I made use of doubling and halving by the simple expedient of shifting a byte to the right or left, but if I wanted 16-bit precision, I had to carry the bits between the low byte and the high byte. The thrust of the algorithm is to assign points for each column that is occupied, with adjustments for the straightness of the line. This is done by looking at vertical offsets between pairs of units; in a good line, those vertical offsets are minimal. Thus, points are assigned to each square, representing the overall utility of the unit positioning itself there. The unit simply selects the best square and plots a path to it.

The algorithm had a nicely convergent behavior: Each unit determined its objective square, taking into consideration the objective squares of every other unit. As the algorithm ran through more and more iterations, it converged on an ideal move for the Russian player.

"No plan survives contact with the enemy"—so goes the military adage. Such was the case with the behavior of units in **Eastern Front (1941)**. Their carefully laid plans were based on the assumptions that the Germans would all cooperatively remain in their original positions. The fact that those Germans did in fact move wrought havoc with the

Don't panic.
Take the
time to
evaluate
the design
as a whole.

Russian plans—but then again, the Russian moves did exactly the same thing to German plans. It's an unavoidable problem in war. My AI made no attempt to anticipate German plans.

Looking back at this old assembly language code from the vantage point of twenty additional years of experience, I see only a few improvements to make. The code ran fast, so I could have stepped up to a 7-wide square to get even better coordination of behavior. The code was insufficiently documented, although I was able to figure out its workings even after twenty years have passed. In particular, I should have given more labels to my constants. The incidence of mysterious values ("LDX #$97", for example) detracts considerably from the cogency of the code.

Tuning

When I first tried it out as a game rather than a program, I instantly realized that I had created a turkey of the highest order. The game was slow and tedious; the Germans slogged through the Russian line with all the excitement of a World War I infantry offensive. I was heartbroken; I had expected that the game would need tuning, but I didn't expect it to be so terribly bad.

At this point, my design instincts served me well. First, I took a long walk to think about the design in the largest possible terms. I refused to start throwing patches at the problem; I wanted to characterize the problem precisely, to put my finger on exactly what was wrong with the design. Some good ideas came to me, but I still refused to act on them; I wanted to be sure of my next move. After two days of intense cogitation, I had my answers.

Four related problems turkified my game:

- There were too many units for the player to handle.
- It took too long to play.
- There was little opportunity to maneuver.
- The Russian AI was too stupid.

I resolved upon three solutions. First, I would introduce zones of control into the game. This dramatic change would have no effect on the Russian AI, and it would permit the second change: a drastic reduction in the unit count. With zones of control, fewer units would be needed to hold a solid line. My third solution was merely a decision to proceed with a feature I had already determined to put into the game: logistics. Units were required to trace a clear line of supply back to their home edge of the map; if not, they were "out of supply" and their combat strength was halved. This would make encirclements an attractive ploy.

After carefully considering all possible implications of these changes, I set to work. It took me just three weeks to complete these changes. When I brought the new game up for the first time in mid-June, I knew that I had a winner. The game still had plenty of rough spots, but as a designer I could see that they were blemishes, not structural defects.

It required another eight weeks of playtesting and tuning to get the game just right. I spent much of that time expunging trivial bugs, juggling the reinforcement schedules for the Russians, and fine-tuning the AI algorithms. I also had a number of friends playtest the game. They all had lots of suggestions; I rejected the great majority of these suggestions and eagerly embraced a minority of them. My playtesters were mystified by my reactions to their ideas. Some suggestions I dismissed instantly without any further discussion; it seemed that I was a stubborn ass. But other suggestions I would pounce upon enthusiastically. "What was the difference?" one of them asked me.

Most suggestions are additions; some are embellishments, some are corrections, and some are consolidations. The additions are new features; those I dumped instantly. You don't add new features to a game during playtesting. If the game needs major improvement, then it should be redesigned; if it doesn't need major improvement, you shouldn't go adding features this late in the design cycle. Embellishments are improvements on existing elements in the game; these got a few seconds' consideration. Again, the burden of proof falls on the embellishment; if I can't see a compelling reason for adding the embellishment, then I don't want to mess around with it. Corrections fix clumsy aspects of the design; these I relish. My only concern in hearing such suggestions is that they constitute genuine corrections, that they really do fix a problem in the design. If they do, then there's nothing to discuss; it's a go. Lastly, consolidations are ways of bringing two dissonant aspects of the game into harmony; these I also embrace. It's rare that a playtester sees some deeper connection that escaped me, but when they do, I grab the idea and run with it as if it were my own.

Herein lies a small lesson concerning open mindedness and the ownership of ideas. Some people think that open mindedness requires a designer to hear out every idea, to give every suggestion its day in court. This isn't noble; it's stupid. Seriously considering every idea that drifts by isn't a sign of open mindedness; it's an indicator of indecisiveness. A good designer has already thought through all the basics of the design and so should be able to reject a great many ideas without much consideration, knowing that they are incompatible with the heart of the design. To put it another way, you should already have considered most of the ideas that are put to you; if somebody surprises you with an idea you didn't think of, you should consider it a warning sign that you haven't thought through the design carefully enough. If the great majority of ideas that are offered you have already gone through your mill, you should have no problem rejecting them without much consideration. Other people will consider you a narrow-minded prima donna for doing so; let them. Your job is to build a great design, not gratify your co-workers. Be courteous, but concentrate on doing your job.

Conclusion

Eastern Front (1941) was released in August of 1981. It was an immediate hit, sold very well, and garnered a number of awards. It propelled me into the forefront of the gaming industry; I was suddenly Mr. Big Shot. None of this, of course, served to inflate my ego, which was already at maximum inflation. I handled it all with a graciousness derived from my utter certainty that this was the natural and proper order of things. The game also earned impressive royalties (for the time); I think that total royalties amounted to some $40,000, which was more than my salary.

In 1982, we published the source code for the game, including detailed explanations of how it all worked. I am confident that this was the first time anybody had published source code for a major game. I wanted to show people how it was done. The source code, although rather expensive, sold well.

Eastern Front (1941) was one of my best works. It incorporated bold innovations, technical excellence, and a clear design vision. What more can we ask of a great game?

42

LESSON

Humbly obey the Muse of Design; ignore the Harpy of Politics.

gossip

In late 1981, Dr. Alan Kay recruited me into Atari Research and challenged me to dream. Most people take a lazy approach to dreaming. They put their feet up on the desk and engage in idle mental forays for half an hour, and they call it dreaming. To me, dreaming is a much more deliberate and difficult process. Dreaming is hard work!

I see dreaming as occupying a middle ground between fantasy and planning. A fantasy is the free indulgence of human desire, unconstrained by the limitations of reality. A plan reduces human desire to a pedestrian statement of objective, and then posits a sequence of steps that will attain the objective. Fantasy springs from human desire, where planning hews to reality. Dreams live in the gray zone where fantasy merges with planning. Where a fantasy spreads its wings and soars off into space, and a plan plods along earthbound, step by bitter step, a dream takes a running start and leaps as high as it can to gain a handhold by which to hoist itself up.

Fantasies and dreams both create alternate universes. A fantasy's alternate universe is unconcerned with the real universe. It is a desirable universe, but not an attainable one. A dream creates an alternate universe that is both desirable and attainable. That requires the dreamer to sketch out all the ramifications of his dream, to create a complete and consistent universe. A fantasy universe can be fragmented or inconsistent, because human desire is often fragmented and inconsistent, but a dream universe cannot be so self-indulgent. A good dream universe is a complete image, not a partial sketch. Every detail of the ideal is clearly specified, every consequence worked out. Only when we know precisely where we're going can we begin planning how to get there.

So, under Alan Kay's prodding, I set to work on my dream. It took me a year and a half to give it form. I wrote the first edition of this book, *The Art of Computer Game Design*, as part of my process of forging my dream. By 1983, I had my dream:

> I dreamed of the day when computer games would be a viable medium of artistic expression—an art form. I dreamed of computer games expressing the full breadth of human experience and emotion. I dreamed of computer games that were tragedies, games about duty and honor, self-sacrifice and patriotism. I dreamed of satirical games and political games; games about the passionate love between a boy and girl, and the serene and mature love of a husband and wife of decades; games about a boy becoming a man, and a man realizing that he is no longer young. I dreamed of games about a man facing truth on a dusty main street at high noon, and a boy and his dog, and a prostitute with a heart of gold.

What elevated these thoughts from fantasy to dream was the identification of the central problem: the concentration of computer games on things rather than people. I wrote an essay entitled "People, Not Things!" in which I bemoaned the fact that all computer games were about things, not people. "You chase things," I noted, "and things chase you. You acquire things, expend things, utilize things, shoot at things, but it's always things, things, THINGS! There are never any real people in our games!" My goal was clear: I must perforce design a game about people.

But how? Given the wimpy hardware available to me in 1982, I had difficulty imagining a game about people. So I got down to basics. If the game is about people, it has to be about their behavior. More specifically, it has to be about their behavior toward each other. After much random flailing about, I hit upon the earliest expression of Crawford's First Rule of Software Design (Lesson 43).

43

The answers to this question tell you everything important about the design. The user's choices and actions lie at the essence of any software design, not just games. You can describe a word processor in a thousand ways, but the best description provides a list of what the user does: type words, edit them, and print out the results. The user of a spreadsheet enters numbers and formulae, and then fiddles around with those numbers and formulae to explore various scenarios.

Always ask, "What does the user do?"

My little rule, simple as it might be, offers vast utility. It can sniff out a design error in a flash. Pick out any piece of badly designed software and ask the magic question, and you'll get an answer that reveals the fundamental flaw. The old checkbook balancing programs of the early 1980s were utter failures, but the personal financial management programs of the 1990s were big successes. Why? Because the checkbook balancing programs allowed the user to do nothing more than enter the amounts on bank checks and then print out the results—that's not much better than doing it by hand with a calculator. The personal finance programs, in contrast, allowed the user to enter all financial data, categorize it, prepare budgets and compare them with actual spending, and use the data in tax returns. These are useful things to do, which is why many people like to use such programs.

And so I asked myself, "What should the player of a people-style game do?" The obvious answer is that the player should be able to do social actions with other people. So what do people do to and with each other? The answer to this question is as vast as the range of human culture, so I needed to find some clean, simple subset of human behavior, some set of actions that form a closed set of actions. After much trial and error, I hit upon the answer: gossip. People love to gossip about each other.

Of course, gossip is a complex behavior requiring the use of language; there was no way I could get the full range of gossip behavior into a computer. But I *could* get a tiny subset of it in place: the declaration of affinity. A great deal of gossip boils down to statements of affinity: "I like Jane," "I hate Tom," and so forth. Such statements have a pronounced effect on the listener, serving to alter the listener's own affinities. After all, if your best friend tells you that he likes Mary, then you are likely to be more favorably inclined toward Mary.

Even at this simple level, gossip behavior offers all sorts of interesting possibilities. For example, it works in reverse: If your best friend tells you that he hates Mary, then you are likely to be less favorably inclined toward Mary. And if someone you loathe is Tom's best friend, you are likely to be less favorably disposed toward Tom. This behavior also feeds back to the speaker: If your best friend tells you that he likes Tom, then your estimate of his friendship will diminish.

This can all be summarized by a simple statement: "People like people who like people they like, and vice versa versa versa." (I put in the extra "versas" to cover each of the different "likes" in the statement.) The idea can also be presented in mathematical form:

$$CA\ [Listener, Speaker] = DA[Speaker, Object] \times A[Listener, Object]\ /\ K1$$
$$CA\ [Listener, Object] = DA[Speaker, Object] \times A[Listener, Speaker]\ /\ K2$$

where

- CA is the change in affection.
- Listener is the person hearing the gossip.
- Speaker is the person speaking the gossip.
- Object is the person being gossiped about.

- DA is the declared affection.
- A is the absolute affection.
- K1 is some constant greater than one, say, 10.
- K2 is some different constant greater than one.

Now, these are simple differential equations, but they apply individually to each member of an entire group of people, and so the overall behavior of this system of equations can be complicated.

All the hard work lay in getting up to the point where I realized that gossip restricted to declarations of affection could provide the basis for a game. From that point forward, it was easy. I wrote a quick version in BASIC in one day; it lacked graphics, but the game was playable. Much tuning would be required, but the gameplay seemed solid. It was a ridiculously simple game, but then, so was **Pong**. This game was to people-games as **Pong** was to videogames.

AI

I had an excellent play-mechanic in hand, but now I needed some AI to control the computer people. How were they to respond to the gossip they heard?

At this point, it is worthwhile to point out the obvious: The solutions I describe never came quickly. I can't remember the many trials and errors I pursued, but there were quite a few. Weeks rolled by while I struggled with these problems. The gap between problem and solution in this book is often just a line of text, but in the real world it was much greater, and the eventual solution was nowhere near as clear as I present it here; most of the time I bumbled towards it in a reverse Drunkard's Walk (that's an old mathematical problem), eventually getting myself to the street light.

The solution that I eventually chanced upon relied, once again, on an analogy with the real world. In this case, I imagined the social system in the game to be rather like a set of springs tied together. Each person

44

LESSON

With enough
imagination,
you can find
models to
solve any
problem.

represented one node; seven springs, one for every other person, were tied to that person. Each spring had a "desired length" given by the affection that the one person held for the other. Now, if you tried to build such a system, you'd get a tangled mess, but in the pure mountain air of software, tangles don't exist. The idea is that each spring pushes two people apart or pulls them together; if you let the system "relax," the springs will all push and tug at each other until each person is in his optimal social position relative to the others. Good friends are close; hated enemies are far away.

This imagined environment could easily be simulated on the computer, and it suggested the solution: Each person should attempt to reduce the spring tensions around him. If one spring pulls him one way and another spring pulls him the other, he'll seek to release the tension by moving toward or away from somebody else. The calculation for all this is not difficult; it's a simple physics problem. So, with a snap of my fingers, the AI was ready to go.

Implementation Woes

I had just taken on a summer intern for my group; my intention had been to let him poke around with the other members of the group, helping out as possible. He had great skills as a graphics programmer and this little design needed nothing more than some graphics tacked onto it. Well, yes, it would have to be converted from BASIC to assembly language, but it was such a short program that I anticipated no problems. So I assigned the **Gossip** project to the summer intern.

Things went swimmingly at first. He had the game screen up and running in no time. There were eight people in two rows across the screen, each one shown with head and upper torso only (see Figure 19.1). They looked rather like the panelists on a game show. The person on the upper left was the player. Beside each player was a little telephone.

19.1 **Gossip** *main display.*

I congratulated the student on his rapid progress, and suggested that he get to work on the algorithms, but he wanted to finish up the graphics first. So he went ahead and added the remaining graphics, as well as some delightful sound effects. The gameplay was simple: The player would use a cursor to designate a person to be called. Pressing the button would select that person, whose telephone would ring with an appropriate jangling sound and the handset jiggling on the telephone base. The person called would pick up the handset with a simple three-step animation, hold it to his or her ear, and say something like

"Air-oh?", which was the best that could be done with the primitive sound capabilities of the day. Then the player would use the cursor to designate another player, the one whom he wished to gossip about, and press the trigger button again. This would highlight that person; at the same time, the player's face would undergo a simple seven-step animation.

There were five of these animations. In one, the player had a big smile on his face and nodded his head up and down vigorously. The next, selectable by the joystick, had the player's face nodding up and down a bit less vigorously and with a merely pleasant smile. The third showed the player's face motionless with a blank look. The fourth showed the player frowning slightly, and nodding his head from side to side. The last showed the player looking quite angry, yanking his head from side to side most emphatically. The player would select the facial expression that reflected his feelings toward that individual, and then press the trigger button. One piece of gossip had been completed.

It looked and sounded really great; I was quite pleased. Just three weeks had passed and all that remained to be done was to implement the behavioral and AI algorithms, which, as I wrote earlier, were a piece of cake.

But my summer intern just couldn't hack it. Try as he may, he simply could not get a few simple equations to work in assembly language. Being a lousy people manager, I failed to intervene to walk him through the code problems; I simply couldn't believe that anybody could be so brilliant with graphics and so utterly incompetent with simple arithmetic. Pig-headedly, I urged him on with affirmations that the problem was trivial.

It's a measure of just how bad a manager I am that this situation per-sisted for three months before I finally put my summer intern out of his misery. I had figured that he'd go away at the end of the summer anyway, so I swept the problem under the rug. But he never did go back to school, and so I had to bite the bullet and let him go. Fortunately, he found a position elsewhere in Atari.

I turned the problem over to another subordinate who fixed it and got the program running in about a week. With a little tuning, we had the whole thing ready to ship within a month of the departure of the summer intern.

Conclusions

Gossip had the bad luck to be published in 1983, just as Atari was beginning its death spiral. With all the chaos of the layoffs, jobs like publishing games proceeded at a snail's pace and without much in the way of verve and élan. There is some question as to whether it ever appeared in the sales catalog; I myself don't know. I don't even know its sales figures; it seemed that, every time I called someone to ask, that person had been laid off. I'm sure it sold poorly; few people recall the game.

But **Gossip** deserves a place in history: it was the first computer game about people instead of things. It opened up all sorts of interesting possibilities for further development. Games in which the gossip mechanics are extended to cover additional modes of expression. Games with larger groups. Games with gossip augmented by other dimensions of behavior. Sadly, nobody else ever followed up on these ideas; even today, the most people-oriented game on the market, **The Sims**, boasts a level of interpersonal interaction no higher than that offered by **Gossip** in 1983.

Yeah, sure, if it ain't broke, don't fix it; but if it *is* broke, fix it NOW!

excalibur

excalibur

Gossip was a pure design exercise; I never intended it to be a product. I desired only to demonstrate that a game addressing social interactions could be built. Underlying my efforts here was a much grander ambition.

I had been inspired by John Boorman's magnificent exposition of the Arthurian legends in the movie *Excalibur*. I wanted to create something as noble as Boorman's film. The Arthurian legends seemed to be the ideal vehicle for my efforts. These legends have played such an important role in Western literature because they have carried just about every basic dramatic theme and idea. Starting off as a defeated people's wistful legends of past glory, they were modified by the French troubadours to suit the ideals of courtly love fostered by Elizabeth of Aquitane.

Later, Thomas Mallory gathered up the many bits and pieces and forged them into a unified whole in his great classic, *Le Morte D'Arthur* (which, by the way, played a major role in standardizing English, because it was the first widely read book written in English). But Mallory's version had a heavy-handed style, with as much violence as a modern videogame.

In the nineteenth century, there was a grand revival of Arthurian romance, with less blood and more brooding. Then Mark Twain the Impertinent put his hand to the legends and came up with the magnificent satire *A Connecticut Yankee in King Arthur's Court.*

In the mid-twentieth century, two more Americans took the legends in two other directions. Walt Disney created a children's entertainment with *The Sword in the Stone*, while Lerner and Lowe produced a classic love triangle in the musical *Camelot*. Times changed, and Marion Zimmer Bradley wrote *The Mists of Avalon,* a feminist take on the Arthurian legends.

Throughout these many evolutions, the legends served their artists well. Marion Zimmer Bradley's feminist version is just as rich and robust as Mallory's masculine version. The Arthurian legends have become an entire body of literature embracing all the important dramatic themes of Western civilization; they can be molded to serve any artistic purpose. I therefore resolved to build my dream on this vehicle. In particular, I wanted to create a work about the nature of leadership: How can a leader overcome the fissiparous tendencies arising from personal ambition, jealousy, and possessiveness in any group in pursuit of a grand goal for the group as a whole? Watching the insane combination of anarchy and overbearing dominance at Atari, I couldn't help but wonder what makes a good leader. My game would explore these dilemmas.

I decided early on that the game would consist of a number of sub-games. This was an ambitious idea back in 1982. Most games then had a single main screen and a single challenge. The idea of combining several smaller games into one larger game is now common. I don't know if **Excalibur** was the first published game to do so, but it was certainly one of the earliest.

Camelot

The castle at Camelot was presented as a series of highly ornate menus. I used a huge Old English font; it was quite striking in those days. Unlike modern menus (remember, this was before the Macintosh), the player moved a cursor up and down along a wide path and clicked the joystick button when his cursor was lined up with the menu entry. By exiting the top of the screen, the player could access the next "room" (menu). Each room had the menu listings on the left, the broad vertical band traversed by the cursor in the center, and a characteristic display on the right. Thus, the Treasury room showed Arthur's wealth and offered him opportunities to increase or decrease tax rates. The Great Hall showed the knights in their social relationships, with menu items on the left permitting Arthur to grant money, bestow honors, or even banish individuals. The Map Room showed the other kingdoms of England and permitted Arthur to learn more about their strengths and weaknesses. Merlin's Room permitted the player to consult Merlin and occasionally ask his assistance in clobbering enemies.

There was a minor technical innovation in Merlin's Room: the use of a temporally dithered image for Merlin's face. Given the low resolutions available to us in those days, we couldn't do much with faces. It occurred to me that I could dither temporally as well as spatially. The idea was to store the image of Merlin's face as an 8-bit deep bitmap. During display, the software would prepare a random 1-bit version of the 8-bit image, display it for a single frame, and then prepare a new random 1-bit version. By "random 1-bit version," I mean a 1-bit image whose pixels have been obtained by comparing a random 8-bit number with the 8-bit brightness value in the 8-bit deep image. If the random number was less than the luminance of the pixel, then I drew a white pixel in its location; if the random number was greater than the 8-bit luminance value, then I drew a black pixel. Even with the slow processor, the algorithm ran fast enough. The result was a haunting, shimmering image that was undeniably a face.

The Interpersonal Subgame

My theoretical work had convinced me of the importance of interpersonal factors. Much work on the problem had yielded **Gossip** as a design study, and the result was good enough to integrate into the overall design.

Gossip provided a firm foundation on which to build, but it lacked context. Characters in **Gossip** adjust their feelings in response to each other's feelings, but there was no underlying dynamic to support these relationships in the first place. I needed a mechanism for creating conflict, a stage with some props on which my characters could develop disputes that could provide fodder for the **Gossip** engine.

Game design, like any form of software design, turns on the three fundamental steps of interactivity: listening, thinking, and speaking. A computer game listens to its player through joystick or mouse and keyboard, it thinks with its algorithms, and it speaks to the player through its monitor and speakers. Good game designers must keep all three factors in mind while struggling with difficult design decisions. It was the conjunction of these three requirements that made the task of designing some sort of interpersonal relationships game so difficult. How was I to show the emotionally significant interactions among the characters? I knew I could probably figure out some decent algorithms, but how was I to get input from the player about emotionally significant actions?

Gossip provided no help here. I couldn't have Arthur telephoning his knights to exchange catty remarks about others. After months of hand-wringing, I came to the conclusion that no ready solution to the problem existed; interpersonal relationships are pursued with too much complexity to be reduceable to the simple input structures available to me on the 8-bit, 1MHz machines of the day.

Nevertheless, I was determined to come up with something, so I resolved to insert the **Gossip** engine into the design as a primarily autonomous and low-interactivity system (Figure 20.1). The display showed a group of shields, each shield bearing the distinctive crest of each knight of the Round Table. In the center of the area was a shield representing the player, King Arthur. The other shields were scattered around King Arthur in an arrangement that reflected their cumulative feelings. A good friend would nudge up close to Arthur, while a sworn enemy would stand in a far corner. Of course, the knights also had relationships among themselves, which tended to tug and push knights into different locations.

20.1 **Excalibur** *interpersonal subgame.*

Arthur's only options in this display were to bribe the knights with either money or honors. Money came out of Arthur's limited treasure chest; honors to one knight diminished the value of honors already handed out to others. That was the best I could come up with.

Diplomacy

The player also had to worry about the other fifteen kings of Britain (see Figure 20.2). Each king had diplomatic relationships with each of the other kings; attacking one king might well bring another into battle against you. The player could also demand tribute from another king, or pay it, if necessary.

20.2 *Diplomacy screen.*

The Strategic Map

The overarching goal of the game was for the player to unify Britain, initially under the rule of 15 other kings. For this portion of the game, I designed two fairly conventional subgames. The first was a strategic game showing a huge scrolling map of England. This in itself was no big deal; I had done scrolling maps in two previous games, and there were no important innovations here.

One minor technological problem arose from our memory requirements. Even with a fully loaded Atari 800, the game simply wouldn't fit into RAM. I had expected this and developed a system for swapping different modules in and out of RAM from the floppy disk. Nowadays this kind of thing is routine, but I didn't have modern memory managers; I had to overlay segments by hand.

The player, upon leaving the castle at Camelot, would appear on the map at Camelot's location. He could then travel around England with his army in tow. When he crossed the border into another kingdom, his knights would immediately set to work ravaging the land, stealing cattle and anything else they could carry away. The enemy king could come out of his castle with his army and fight a battle with Arthur, or remain safely inside the castle. If the enemy did choose to fight, then a third subgame began: the battle.

The Battle Subgame

I had no intention of turning **Excalibur** into a strategy wargame, so I kept the battle scene quite simple. There was no terrain, just a patch of bare ground with the units from opposing sides drawn up in two battle lines facing each other. Each unit was depicted by a shield, using the same crests showing up in the Gossip display. The battle was fought in real time, with units moving at high resolution; that is, they didn't jump from square to square, but instead oozed along at a deliberate pace. The player controlled each unit by clicking on it and designating an objective toward which that unit should move. When a unit attempted to move into a location already occupied by an opposing unit, it instead attacked that unit. Several units could gang up on a single unit, hastening its downfall. There was, of course, consideration for the facing of the defending unit: Attacks from the rear were spectacularly effective, attacks from the side not so effective, and attacks from the front were best defended against. If multiple units attacked a single unit, the likelihood of getting in a flank attack was increased.

The battle subgame also utilized my now-standard concepts of disruption, augmented by a new twist: The breaking point at which a unit's morale would collapse was set by the affection that its leader held for Arthur. In other words, loyal knights stayed in the field longer. Once a unit cracked, it ran until it felt safe. If the danger was merely local and temporary, the unit might recover its morale a short distance in the rear, at which time the player could send it back into battle.

Losses suffered in the battle subgame were carried over into the rest of the game. If a unit was wiped out in battle, its knight was killed and removed from the game. This might seem a good way to get rid of rebellious knights, but recall that such knights lose their morale and run away more easily.

If Arthur won the battle subgame, then he kept his spoils and could resume pillaging, but if he lost it, then all the spoils were lost and Arthur was automatically returned to Camelot in defeat, suffering much loss of prestige with his knights.

The battle could be reversed if another king came to pillage Arthur's territory. In that case, Arthur would enjoy a defensive benefit arising from the local peasantry's contribution to the fighting.

In design terms, the battle subgame is of minor interest. The notion of moving units pixel by pixel rather than square by square (or hex by hex) was novel for strategic games, but absolutely conventional in the videogame world. Order entry, unit display and movement, and combat results were all conventional, although the disruption system was a bit more elegant than in other games. There wasn't much room for complicated tactics, there being no terrain to work with. I had intended it that way, as I didn't want to create yet another wargame.

Overall Course of Play

The player would always start the game with too weak an army to engage in any kind of offensive operations. By setting the tax rate low, Arthur could encourage the growth of population in the kingdom, which would ultimately provide a larger tax base. But too much emphasis on long-term growth left the army too small to defend the kingdom. After building the army to a large enough size, Arthur could hazard an attack on one of his weaker enemies; success here opened the door to more victories. All the while, Arthur had to closely monitor the sentiments of his knights, attempting to placate malcontents.

Arthur's toughest job, though, was to figure out the diplomacy of England. Each of the kings had his own diplomatic attitudes; attacking one king could easily bring a second king into the conflict. Conversely, attacking the enemy of an ill-disposed king might warm relations with the third party—if he didn't attack Arthur's lands during his absence. Most important, a threatening posture toward a weak king might well bring him into Arthur's fold as a vassal, saving the trouble of fighting. And the vassal's army was joined to Arthur's, making a big difference on the battlefield.

The Manual

I wanted to create something especially good for the manual for **Excalibur**, and I conceived the notion of writing a short story to illustrate the principles of gameplay. I'd always wanted to try my hand at fiction, and this seemed the ideal opportunity. But when I first offered the alpha version of the game to the Atari Program Exchange for them to sell, they ruled out my unorthodox plan for the manual. They wanted a conventional manual. Fortunately, I was not required to meet their demand. At Corporate Research, there was no pressure to create actual products. So I went ahead and wrote the manual the way I wanted to, then submitted it with the beta version of the game. I nervously waited their reaction, but when I checked in one day, the producer who had previously rejected my proposal called me into his office and declared, "I lay my writer's pen at your feet." I was astounded. I knew the guy to be a competent and serious individual; my work of fiction couldn't be *that* good. But he seemed to think so, and I garnered a goodly number of compliments from others, so perhaps someday I should enter the lucrative business of writing fiction.

Conclusions

More thought went into **Excalibur** than into any other game I have created. While its interpersonal aspect was completely new and quite innovative, the true achievement of the design lay in the tight integration of multiple subgames. The player had to juggle economic factors, diplomacy, military strategy, tactics, and the loyalties of his underlings. Before **Excalibur**, computer games were single-task challenges that required intense concentration on small, specific problems. **Excalibur** required much more in the way of global thinking, of integrating a large number of disparate variables into one's thinking. This gave the game a "symphonic" quality the achievement of which is the most esoteric challenge of game design.

Most games feel rather like rock songs: a simple melody, some harmony, and a great, pounding, primitive beat. As games have grown larger and more complex, most have simply grown obese, like some ghastly imaginary rock song that goes on and on repetitively for two hours. The same chords, the same melody, the same beat, all pound away at the player with machine-like repetitiveness. A better way to grow a game is to build it like a symphony with several movements, each different melodically, yet conceptually integrated. Many thousands of great songs have been written, but the list of great symphonies has only a few score entries, because that magical symphonic quality is so much harder to attain.

I maintain that **Excalibur** was the first game possessing some symphonic quality. There have been more since then: Certainly **Civilization** is strong in its symphonic quality. All in all, however, the games industry has done poorly in this regard, probably because symphonic quality is so difficult to attain. It requires above all a generalist world view, not the specialist approach that the industry has concentrated on recently. Sid Meier had to bring together concepts from half a dozen fields in order to create **Civilization**. I also had to bring to bear a wide array of knowledge to create **Excalibur**. Not many games people put themselves through the rigors of a broad education.

To design a symphonic game, you must broadly educate yourself.

balance of power

In March of 1984, Atari was in its death throes and I, along with almost everybody else, was laid off. The severance package I received was more than generous; it gave us so much money that I wouldn't need any income for nine months. That would be plenty of time to develop a new game; I set to work considering my options.

It was tempting to do yet another Atari game; I had mastered the platform, my name alone would sell games, and I had a number of good ideas. I built two prototypes, one that I called **Western Front (1944)**, a simple translation of **Eastern Front (1941)** to France. The other I called **The Last of the Incas**, covering the struggle of the last Inca emperor to raise a revolt against the Spanish. I quickly rejected the first option as too derivative. Besides, I was finished doing wargames; they no longer held any creative attraction for me. This decision was, in financial terms, imbecilic. I had a big hit in **Eastern Front (1941)**; a second game in the genre would surely make a bundle of money. Artistically, it was a sound decision: If you've mastered a problem, it's time to move on. This provides us with a useful criterion for establishing motivation (Lesson 47).

The Inca game struck my fancy, but I decided that it was time for me to make a break with the past, to look forward rather than backward. It was time to make the jump to a new machine.

47

LESSON

Sequels are for entertainment; they have no artistic content.

Three options lay before me: the IBM PC, the Macintosh, or the soon-to-be-released Amiga. I quickly rejected the first option—nobody played games on the IBM PC in those days. Besides, it was a horror to program and supported only text displays. I interviewed at Amiga, and they offered me a job, but I decided that the Macintosh would do to Amiga what the Apple II did to Atari. Although the Amiga had superior hardware, the Mac's overall design impressed me. I was especially impressed by its emphasis on user interface. Here, I decided, lay the future. Choosing between the Mac and the Amiga was one of the more momentous decisions I ever made, and I made the right call.

So I signed up for the Apple Developer program and ordered a development system consisting of a Lisa computer and a Macintosh. It was very expensive; worse, I had to wait for two months to get my Lisa. I used the time to think long and hard about my design. I also collected and read a great many books on geopolitical conflict. The most influential of these were Henry Kissinger's two books on his years in power: *White House Years* and *Years of Upheaval*. You are welcome to think ill of the man's politics, but I must insist that his books are illuminating and well written. They certainly had a large influence on my design.

The UnWar Game

I was, and remain, a child of the 60's. Although I never marched in a demonstration, smoked dope, or took any kind of mind-altering drug, I embraced the core values of the 60's counterculture, the most prominent of which was pacifism. War, in that view, was the greatest evil mankind had ever created, and was to be avoided at all costs. As the 1984 electoral campaigns heated up, there was plenty of belligerent talk from the right wing, and a series of alarming events boded ill for the future of peace. And here I was, profiting from the sale of wargames, and contemplating designing even more. It was wrong, and I knew it. But what could I do?

As soon as I had phrased the problem in that form, the answer was obvious: I would design an unwar game, a game about the prevention of war, a game about peace. After weeks of feckless hand-wringing, it all became perfectly obvious once I had phrased the question in the right terms.

Now, there have been plenty of "nice guy" games in which players are encouraged to love each other, be nice to the little bunnies, and throw away their weapons. Unfortunately, these "cooperation" games all share one crucial problem: They were BORING! Recall Lesson 10: A game, like a story, must have a conflict.

The taxonomy of play in Chapter 1, "Definitions, Definitions," shows that games are a form of organized conflict. So my task was to design a game that was full of conflict, but lacked war. This is not so difficult a challenge as it might seem at first. As von Clausewitz noted in *On War*, "War is the extension of policy to other means." In other words, it is an extension of geopolitical conflict, not the first manifestation of it. War arises when conflicts between nations cross the line from peaceful into violent expression. Hence, there can be plenty of conflict in an unwar game—it's just not violent conflict.

I found my theme song for the project in Peter, Paul, and Mary's rendition of Bob Dylan's "Blowin' in the Wind." The killer line was this:

Don't struggle to find the answer, struggle to find the right question; the answer will then be obvious.

How many deaths will it take 'til he knows
that too many people have died?

This project pushed me to my emotional limits; listening to that song
gave me the strength to carry on.

Early Efforts

My first written reference to this design comes from April 1984, just
after I was laid off by Atari. I called the game **Arms Race**, and here is
the complete description:

> This is...the game I have been wanting to do for a long time. I propose
> a game that shows why the US and the Soviet Union are locked into a
> dangerous balance of terror. You are the President during the entire
> 40-year span of the game (1960–2000). All you have to do is get to
> the turn of the century without igniting Armageddon. It's not easy. The
> game is actually about geopolitics, not the arms race per se. You are
> tied into numerous alliances with small countries the world over. The
> complex web of obligations is constantly being strained by the petty
> disputes of the small countries. The small squabbles can erupt into
> war at any time, and the danger always exists that events could suck
> you into a major confrontation with the Soviet Union. The central
> question of the game, then, is to ask whether the US and the USSR
> can carry on a global rivalry without eventually getting themselves into
> a nuclear war. The answer, of course, is that they can do so only by
> rigorously constraining and reducing the scope of that conflict.
>
> The game would use a smart map that presents a great deal of infor-
> mation about nations and their relationships in graphical format.
> Icons would show treaty obligations, military status, bases, and so
> forth. Animation would be used in much the same way as other
> Macintosh software uses animation: to show relationships.
>
> This game would be serious, it would be very educational, and I think
> it would grab a great deal of attention. It would not be action-packed,
> but I think that the launching of Armageddon would be far more
> wrenching in this game than **Missile Command** ever was.

As I set to work designing the game, I took some time to study the
Macintosh and develop an appreciation of its strengths and weaknesses. I laid these down in a long letter to a publisher. I concluded

that the black-and-white display would have less sensory "heat" than the color display of the Commodore 64, the dominant machine at that time, and therefore that Mac games should be more cerebral. Moreover, I suspected that the market of Macintosh owners would be a more serious, more adult group demanding a more mature style of game. I also felt that the mouse, a new input device at that time, was not ideally suited for fast action games; it was better suited to discrete choices than continuous input.

There was more in the letter, but the key point here is important: I took the time to consider the precise strengths and weaknesses of the platform on which I proposed to work. These careful considerations paid off; later, after **Balance of Power** was published, several reviewers complimented the game for its deep "Mac-ishness."

By May I was deeply caught up in design details. I toyed around with a number of possible titles: Arms Race, Annihilation of Mankind, Stopping the Madness, Thwarting Armageddon, Man's Last Decade, The Extension of Policy, Words vs. Bombs, and Policy. Plainly, these are all lame titles compared with the final title, **Balance of Power**. So where did that great title come from? The CEO of Mindscape during my first meeting with him. He just pulled it out of a hat.

In accordance with my most sacred rule of software design ("What does the user *do?*"), I set down my verb list at the outset:

- Arm insurgents.
- Provide shelter to insurgents.
- Give economic aid.
- Give military aid.

- Sell weapons.
- Apply trade sanctions.
- Intervene militarily.
- Sign mutual defense treaty.
- Hold summit meeting.
- Set military spending level.
- Carry out a military demonstration of strength.
- Declare war.
- Blockade.
- Establish/break diplomatic relations.
- Set rhetoric level.

The correspondence between this list and the final list of verbs is striking. Seven of these verbs did not make it into the final verb list—but
some of them did make it in altered form. The primary difference
between this list and the final list is that the final verb list segregated
the verbs into groups organized by degree. The basic verb groups in the
final version related to insurgency, government stability, and treaty relationships, with a special group of verbs related to the state of alertness
of your own military.

The primary area that I cut from this list was trade. The problem with
trade is that it's slow and undramatic. Trade sanctions slowly strangle
an enemy's economy. A python may be just as successful a predator as
a lion, but we don't see many football teams named after pythons.
I reluctantly decided to strike trade considerations from the design.

The Rubber Map

One idea on which I fixated was the "rubber map." I was inspired by two
books, *The State of the World Atlas* and *The War Atlas*. These presented
world maps showing a great many factors, such as arms sellers,

weapons spending, relative wealth, trade power, and so forth. Some of these maps were distorted in such a way as to indicate the relative standings of different countries in various dimensions. For example, the National Income map showed Japan as huge and Greenland as tiny. I thought that this would be an excellent way to graphically present a great many complex relationships. And so for weeks I struggled with algorithms, trying to find a fast scheme for reshaping nations to any desired set of sizes. After six weeks of effort, I gave up; I just couldn't come up with anything fast enough.

Thank You, National Enquirer

Some months before, while waiting in a supermarket checkout line, I observed that the headlines in the *National Enquirer* appeared to be designed by a combinatorial algorithm using standard components such as Elvis, flying saucers, revolutionary new diet plans, freakish babies, secret things, etc. Reflecting further, I realized that indeed a great many headlines have a formulaic quality to them. Perhaps, I mused, someday I would write a headline generator program for harried editors.

Now that fantasy came back to me, and I realized that I could put that crazy idea to work in my design. I could have a headline generator that would present events to the player in terms of news stories generated by combinatorial algorithms. The basic form of my sentence template looked like this:

Subject Verb Direct Object Degree

51

LESSON

Know when it's time to throw in the towel on a feature.

Here, Subject referred to the country that was taking the action, Verb was the nature of the action taken, Direct Object was the country upon whom the action was being performed, and Degree was the intensity of the action. Thus,

USA offers $100 million in economic aid to Panama.

would have USA as the subject, Panama as the direct object, "offer economic aid" as the verb, and "$100 million" as the degree. Of course, internally these were represented by simple numbers: index values for the countries, verbs, and degrees.

Over the course of time, I embellished the headline generator. First came embellishments to the presentation of the subject. There were two of these: leader name and capital name. The code could substitute "Washington" or "President Reagan" for "USA." Naturally, I made these substitutions available for the direct object. Extending the idea, I added the name of the insurgencies of every country.

Representing degrees of action was easy in most cases: I needed strings for how much money, how many troops, or what kind of treaty was being signed. However, there was one kind of headline that posed more complex problems: the headline describing domestic events. For example, it was important to provide information on the progress of the insurgency. For such headlines, the basic template was this:

{Insurgency of country X} {is in this state of development}

In other words, it was just a subject and a statement of degree. This, I found, could quickly become boring. "Panamanian insurgency grows more powerful" just doesn't make for exciting reading. So I developed a scheme for providing some variety and color. Here's an example:

0*Anti-government guerrillas*Forces opposed to the government*% fighters*Members of the %*

0* launch a series of attacks on* fight with government troops in* carry out attacks on* take control of*

1* isolated villages* several remote towns* two provincial capitals* the outskirts of @*

3*. *

52

LESSON

Here's how the system works:

Fantasize. Play what-if games. Ask silly questions. Why aren't cows green like grass?

- The first character, a numeral, denotes the method by which one of the succeeding text segments is to be selected.

- A value of 0 says that the segment is to be chosen randomly.

- A value of 1 indicates that the segment is to be chosen based on the rank index passed to the headline routine.

- A value of 3 indicates that there is no choice to make, and that the first and only segment is to be used.

- Segments, it should be obvious, are delimited by asterisks.

There are also text variables that are replaced by strings specific to the country. For example, the percent sign (%) indicates that name of the insurgency, while the ampersand (@) indicates the name of the capital. Thus, if we use Peru as our example, then we might get any of the following headlines:

Members of the Sendero Luminoso fight with government troops in several remote towns.

Anti-government guerrillas carry out attacks on the outskirts of Lima.

Sendero Luminoso fighters launch a series of attacks on two provincial capitals.

Pretty cute, huh? But even this became tiresome after a while, so I added a provision for multiple templates for each situation. This did the job; the headlines had enough freshness and color to achieve the needed sense of realism.

The sentence generator proved to be one of the most important ideas to emerge from the **Balance of Power** project. In particular, the text variables concept proved amenable to considerable elaboration. I developed and refined this technology through many of my projects, especially for **Siboot**. It later became the basis for the concept of substories that I developed for my work in interactive storytelling. It also set me thinking about the nature and role of language, which has been a fruitful line of inquiry for my research. And it all started from a whimsical fantasy in a supermarket checkout line.

Research

Meanwhile, I was reading everything I could lay my hands on. In all, I acquired and read about 15 books as part of my research, and consulted another 12 that I had already acquired and read. These books addressed many elements that I put into the game: the mechanics of insurgency and coups d'etat, global power structures, and so forth.

Among these were *The War Trap* by Bruce Bueno de Mesquita, which presented a mathematical analysis of how countries get themselves sucked into wars. The ideas in this book suggested a great many algorithms, but in the end, I didn't use them. Nevertheless, reading the book proved beneficial to the project, as it clarified my thinking on a number of issues.

Also useful was *Essence of Decision: Explaining the Cuban Missile Crisis*, by Graham T. Allison. This book brought home to me the dramatic nature of superpower confrontation, and was the inspiration for what eventually became the Crisis feature in the game.

Not all of the books were directly useful to the creation of the game; indeed, there was very little that I found that I could simply lift out of the book and insert into the game. But all that reading stimulated my thinking on the problems of the design; ultimately, I think that it was an important factor in the overall success of the game.

Building the Map

While I was doing all this reading, I kept myself busy with a simple project that consumed plenty of time. I needed a map of the world that I could fit into the Mac's 512×342 screen. Nowadays we'd just scan something in, doctor it a bit, and voila!—there's our map! Unfortunately, we didn't have scanners back then, nor did we have photo manipulation programs. Besides, I needed more than just an image; I needed a digitized map with individually addressable countries. In other words, I needed a data structure for each country that defined its boundaries. I had to have graphics of each and every country in the game.

My solution was simple and straightforward. I placed a wall map of the world onto the floor and taped semi-transparent graph paper over it. I then traced the borders of the countries onto the graph paper, conforming my tracing lines to the gridwork of the graph paper. Then I pulled out my tape recorder and set to work. "Germany," I would announce. "Starting coordinates 189 X and 118 Y." Then I would launch into a long monologue tracing the border in directional steps: "One north, two west, one north, three west, two north, one west, four north..." and so on until my tracing of the border had completed the circuit of the country. Then I would move to the next country.

In each
project, do
at least one
special task
by hand.

When I had finished all the countries, I sat down at the computer and entered the data as strings. I'd type in the name of the country and the coordinates of the point of origin. Then I'd listen to the tape recording, typing in the steps: N2WN3W2NW4N.... As you might imagine, it was a slow and tedious process. This became the source data for my country images. During program initialization, the code read in all that data and converted it into manipulatable graphics objects. All in all, it took me about a week to create the map this way.

I'm sure this primitive technique leaves you agog, half-expecting me to follow up with tales of walking five miles through the snow each day to get to school. But there's an important lesson here. The tool shapes the hand of the user; or, to use the more common expression, "If you've got a big enough hammer, everything starts to look like a nail." Nowadays we've got tools up the wazoo, tools to handle every aspect of game development. Many times, when a team starts working on a completely new project, the first thing they do is set to work building tools for the project. This is good, but it is possible to go too far with tools, as I pointed out in Chapter 8, "Common Mistakes."

Memory Headaches

In 1984, when I was working on **Balance of Power**, the Macintosh had just been released and was equipped with 128KB of RAM. This was twice what most computers had in those days, but I couldn't seem to fit the game into the available space. The graphics weren't the primary factor: they cost only about 15K. Part of the problem lay in the number of countries and the vast amounts of information I maintained about each country: the text strings for the country name, capital, leader, insurgency, and so forth. The code itself was also sizable, and of course, some of the RAM was taken up by the operating system.

Before the Macintosh, programmers simply took over the machine and all its RAM. The operating system was really nothing more than a set of utilities. But the Mac changed all that. We cowboy programmers had to learn to live under the operating system, abiding by its rules and using its systems. It was hard on us; the same mentality that enabled us to succeed in the Wild West atmosphere of early personal computers now chafed under the rules and regulations of the Mac operating system. Many of the cowboy hotshots of the 8-bit era couldn't adjust to the new regime and dropped away. Fortunately, I was blessed with the intellectual and psychological agility to adjust to the New Order.

An important lesson lies buried in this experience. My advantage lay in an unorthodox approach to technology. Most technical people take a shotgun approach to technology, memorizing mountains of technical details. That huge heap of knowledge constitutes the expertise on which they build their careers. Since that expertise is their basis of competitive advantage, technical people, and especially programmers, take much pride in the size of the pile of facts that they have stuffed into their heads. This has the pernicious effect of rendering programmers insensitive to the demands that technology makes upon its users. Programmers revel in the arcana that torture users. But what goes around comes around; the mind that is stuffed with bucketsful of technological trivia becomes bloated and slow-moving; the inertia created by all that expertise

55

LESSON

Take no pride in facts memorized, but in ideas grasped.

retards further learning. Programmers are mostly young because they reach their mental capacity sometime after their 30th birthday, after which they ossify.

My advantage I owe to my physics professors, who ground into my stubborn skull the single question, "What is the *essence* of the problem?" Always dive down into a problem and get your hands on the deepest issue behind the problem. All other considerations are to dismissed as "engineering details"; they can be sorted out *after* the basic problem has been solved. And so I have equipped myself with a bloodthirsty drive to purge all facts from my mind. If it's a principle, I want to understand it; if it's a fact, I want to forget it. Facts clutter the mind; ideas organize it. If I can fit a fact into the larger structure of my understanding, then I can retain it; otherwise, it slips from my mind like water from a steel cage. I can't remember names, faces, or telephone numbers, but I can absorb new ideas even into my fifties (although I'm starting to slip).

Making It a Game

The game took shape during the fall and winter of 1984; by early 1985, it had reached an early alpha stage. All the important features were in place, considerable debugging and polishing remained, and some housekeeping functions still needed work. But one problem towered above all others: The game just wasn't entertaining. It functioned well as a simulation, but it didn't grab the player. I struggled with this problem from January until it was completed in July. The problem broke down into several sub-problems.

First, there was too much information for the player to assimilate, and little of that information was truly significant to the player's decisions. The solution to this problem was to simplify the game by lobotomizing all countries save the two superpowers. My original intent had been that the petty wars between minor countries could drag the two superpowers into a nuclear war, but in practice, I found that minor countries generated lots of petty activity in addition to their minor wars. The only way to clean up the game was to reduce the minor countries to the status of pawns. Note, however, that in the process, I concentrated activity onto the two super-powers. That sharpened the conflict and improved the game.

Another problem was that the critical information wasn't immediately obvious to the player. Fortunately, an easy solution to this problem presented itself: instead of expecting the player to go looking for it, I shoved it into his face. At the beginning of each turn, the news display popped up unsolicited and presented the most important news item. This required that I develop a criterion for the "importance" of each news item. It wasn't difficult; all I had to do was assign a native importance to each verb and then adjust that native importance by the intrinsic importance (power) of the countries affected.

The third sub-problem was the most subtle: The information needed to be organized for the player. Months of effort went into sorting it out, adjusting font sizes, reorganizing screen layouts, and, most importantly, layering the information by priority. My proclivities as a control freak were to give the player as much information as possible, but I failed to realize that too much information can be just as uninformative as too little. And so I struggled through the basic problems of graphic design.

In the end, there was no breakthrough. No single idea or alteration transformed the game into the award-winning design that we shipped. A slow, tedious process of playtesting, polishing, and tuning, spread over six months,

Polish, polish, polish! Take a minimum of six months after alpha for polishing.

was required. For reasons outside of my control, publication of the game was delayed by four months, during which time I continued to polish, polish, polish. I now believe that this extra polishing was the most important factor in the success of the game.

Publisher Woes

I had no publisher when I began work on **Balance of Power**. 1984 saw the collapse of the videogames business, and publishers were dropping like space invaders. They were too terrified to take a game like **Balance of Power**. Months dragged by and my agent couldn't find any takers. Our savings were running low and I was beginning to worry about making ends meet. Fortunately, in early January of 1985, Random House agreed to take the game. I met with the publisher and we saw eye to eye. We signed a contract, I got an advance, and my financial troubles were over.

But then the publisher handed the project off to an editor and things started to go downhill fast. That editor and I had been preordained in some distant past to do battle. He was a good person, but his particular weaknesses found perfect syntony with my own, and together our clash reverberated to ever-greater amplitude. At one point, I fixed him with a cold eye and asked: "You don't know anything about games, computers, or geopolitics. Why are you the editor for this project?" My question was right on the mark, but he didn't blink. "Because that's my job," he shot back. We were both right, and in our incompatible correctness, we failed spectacularly. After just three months, Random House pulled out of the deal, and I was suddenly in worse financial straits than before.

That was the second-worst period of my life. We were facing financial ruin. My wife, losing patience after I had played freelance game designer for a year, demanded that I get a "real job." Nobody wanted the game. At this point, any rational person would have coldly calculated the odds and taken my wife's advice. But I was possessed by my noble ideals and absolutely certain of the greatness of the design. I ignored all advice to the contrary and pushed on.

The angel that descended upon me was Scott Mace, a columnist for
InfoWorld. Somehow he learned of my predicament and did a two-part
story on **Balance of Power**. That story in turn was read by a junior producer at a new startup in Chicago, Mindscape. That producer knew me
from my reputation and forwarded the *Infoworld* story to his boss with a
strong recommendation that Mindscape acquire the game. And they did.
I was saved.

I Get by with a Little Help from the Press

Balance of Power was published in September of 1985. It attracted a
great deal of press attention. In particular, the *New York Times Sunday
Magazine* assigned David Aaron, Deputy Assistant to the President for
National Security Affairs from 1977 to 1981, to write a story about the
game. Aaron wrote a long piece that concluded as follows:

> ...**Balance of Power** is about as close as one might get to the cut-and-
> thrust of international politics without going through confirmation by
> the Senate.

That story was reprinted in newspapers all over the country, and sales
started climbing. By the time the IBM PC port was ready in the fall of
1985, publicity had grown and sales really took off. My game became a
big hit, generating some $10 million in sales—this at a time when total
sales of all video and computer games put together amounted to about
$500 million. I earned huge royalties on it and my wife, who had urged
me to get a real job, never questioned my career choice again.

The Wheel of Fortune

During my latter years at Atari, I became known as "Mr. Atari" among
user groups and developed quite a reputation. I was a big shot and, as
befits my youth, it went to my head. I actually started to believe the
adulation that splattered all over me. But then Atari collapsed, and

57

Fame don't
mean shit.

overnight I became Mr. Nobody. I couldn't understand why I was so suddenly passé. For two years I labored in solitude, ignored and unadulated. But then **Balance of Power** became a big hit and I was Mr. Bigshot again. This time I was a little more suspicious of the capriciousness of fame; this round lasted about eight years, largely because I added a number of games and the Computer Game Developers' Conference (CGDC) to my fame portfolio. But once I left the CGDC, the crowd turned its back on me and once again I find myself bereft of the screaming masses of nubile nymphs. *Miser me*! I suspect, however, that once interactive storytelling gets rolling, I'll be back up there in the spotlight with flashbulbs popping and a starlet on each arm. And if that does happen, I'll remember Lesson 57.

patton versus rommel

I started working on computer games because I wanted to build a better wargame. Wargames had been the focal point of all my early efforts. I thought that I had left all that behind me when I began work on **Balance of Power**. But as I was finishing up my unwar game, I started casting about for my next project. I liked the people at Mindscape and wanted to do another project with them, but we couldn't seem to agree on anything. Meanwhile, Electronic Arts, which had turned down **Balance of Power**, expressed an interest in doing a genuine wargame. At the time, there were two acknowledged masters of computer wargame design: Roger Keating and myself. Roger was in Australia, and I was in the Bay Area with EA. That made me the logical choice.

At that time, before **Balance of Power** had actually been released, I had no idea how successful it would be, and EA's track record for turning out hits was a strong incentive. So I agreed to build a wargame for them. They didn't care what the content was—that was my decision—but they did know that they wanted it to have "Patton" in the title. "Rommel" would be good, too. Unfortunately, Generals Patton and Rommel never actually confronted each other in battle. Nevertheless, I decided to compromise historicity for marketing by building a wargame about the Allied breakout from Normandy in July and August of 1944. Patton led the American armies, but Rommel was back in Germany recovering from wounds suffered during an American air attack. For the purposes of the game, we simply declared the fantasy that Rommel was not wounded and that he led the German armies.

To Hell with Grids

At that time, wargame designers were wasting a lot of breath arguing over the relative merits of hexgrids and rectgrids. (See Chapter 13 "Tanktics," for an explanation of hexgrids.) The rectgrid was better suited to the computer, but traditional boardgames had always used hexgrids. Some wargame designers sneered that wargames with rectgrids were not the genuine article; real wargamers played with hexgrids. I had started off using hexgrids in my very first computer game design (**Tanktics**), but had shifted to rectgrids for **Eastern Front (1941)** and was convinced of their greater utility. However, I tired of the whole stale debate. Why should we have *any* grids? It seemed rather silly to have military units hopping across terrain like frogs. Shouldn't they move in a smooth series of tiny steps? That, I decided, would be the first element of my design.

But this led to a problem: How do I specify the terrain at various locations? In conventional wargames, each square or hex contains some specified terrain type, which affects movement and combat. How could I have terrain if I didn't have squares or hexes into which to put it?

The solution, obtained after much fretting, was ridiculously simple: "What you see is what it is." The map *is* the terrain (see Figure 22.1).

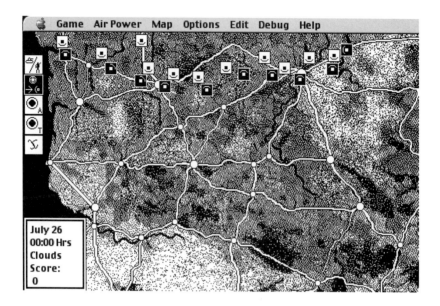

22.1 *Patton Versus Rommel.*

The idea here is simple: The darker the terrain, the denser it is and the more it impedes motion. I could get away with this because the terrain in Normandy is basically flat; the density of woods and the bocage is the only militarily significant terrain. Therefore, I showed that density by the darkness of the terrain on the map.

This made terrain calculations ridiculously simple: The unit only had to count the number of black pixels in the map square underneath it. Some special calculations were required for road movement; the algorithm had to trace the roads to figure out whether a unit could gain the movement benefits of moving along a road. But this was not so great a headache. With this simple innovation, I could move the units smoothly across the map, a pixel at a time.

My next innovation was to extend the concept of unit posture even further. With **Eastern Front (1941)**, I had three modes: attack, defense, and movement. For this game, I decided upon five modes: light defense, strong defense, probing attack, major attack, and road mode. I also used eight directions of facing; these innovations made the mechanics of battle more interesting, I believe.

And of course, I retained the same disruption system I had used in previous wargames; I believe that disruption systems permit more movement on the front line without ridiculously high casualties.

Geometric AI

A standard problem in computer wargames is figuring the line. The military units of each side line up along the frontline and duke it out, attempting to penetrate the enemy line and hold their own line. The first task for the AI to perform is to figure out where the line is. This is not so easy a task. Consider the map shown in Figure 22.2 of opposing units in two ragged lines:

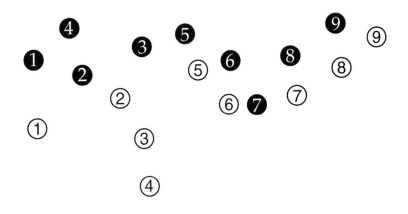

22.2 *Units of opposing sides.*

There are difficult judgments to make about this line. For example, should the black line be drawn 1-2-3-5 or should it include unit 4? That is, should unit 4 be treated as a member of the front line or a reserve unit? How far back or forward must unit 4 be to be excluded or included?

Black unit 7 provides us with another quandary. Is it part of the black line, or should it be treated as a unit cut off behind enemy lines? We could draw the black line as 5-6-7-8-9 or 5-6-8-9. Which is better?

One would expect that the line would be built according to the proximity of units. That is, the line is a sequence of units in proximity to each other. This creates problems of its own. For example, white unit 2 is closer to white unit 3 than white unit 5; this would pull the line through 3 and on to 4. Then the line would have to double back on itself to get back to white unit 5. Obviously, proximity alone is an insufficient criterion for building the line.

I tackled these problems with a sequence of algorithms. The first algorithm draws not a line but a polygon. The polygon is constructed as follows:

1. Start with an arbitrarily chosen unit; call it UnitA.

2. Choose the closest unit and draw a line to that unit; call it UnitB (see Figure 22.3).

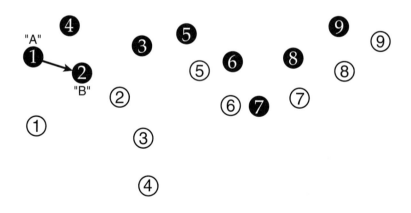

22.3 *A line to UnitB.*

3. Now choose the closest available unit to UnitB and draw a line to that unit (see Figure 22.4).

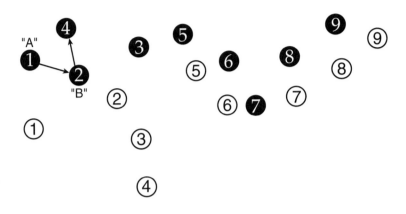

22.4 *A line to the unit closest to UnitB.*

4. Continue until all units have been chosen; then draw a line back to UnitA (see Figure 22.5).

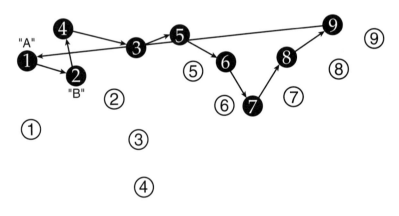

22.5 *Returning to UnitA.*

5. While drawing the polygon, keep a running sum of the line lengths; this is equal to the circumference of the polygon (see Figure 22.6).

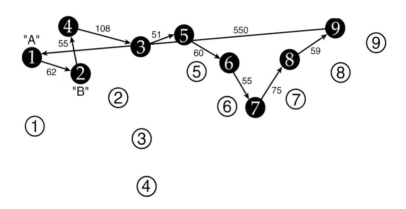

22.6 *Distance of line lengths to calculate circumference.*

6. Store that circumference.

7. In like fashion, draw every possible polygon and select the polygon with the smallest circumference. This is the most convex polygon and is the best initial choice for building the line. It may seem excessive to draw every possible polygon, but with only a few dozen units the number of available polygons is within reach and some elementary pruning methods can make the computation reasonable.

8. The next step is to convert a polygon to a line (see Figure 22.7). This is done by anchoring the easternmost and westernmost ends of the polygon to the edges of the map. We sweep along the polygon looking for the easternmost and westernmost units in the polygon and snip the polygon at those units, extending the line to the edges of the map. A few complexities arise if we want to be able to have the line go to other map edges, but these are complexities of detail, not fundamental algorithmic issues.

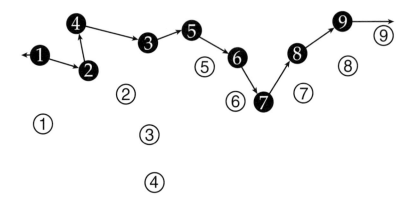

22.7   *Convert the polygon to a line.*

9. The next task is to clip out tight bends in the line (see Figure 22.8). This is done by a simple sweep down the line, looking at groups of three points. With each group of points A, B, and C, we calculate the distances AB, BC, and AC. If AB+BC is greater than twice AC, then the bend in the line introduced by unit B is too great and B is removed from the line. This is a very simple test, yet it works quite well in play. Its only weakness is that it does not consider the significance of enemy units. In the sample line presented earlier, black unit 7 would be included in the line regardless of the presence of white units 6 and 7.

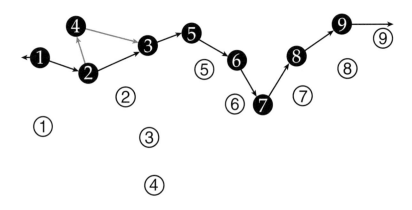

22.8   *Clip out bends in the line.*

Looking Over Your Shoulder

The most difficult algorithm in the project arose from the need to check behind units to make sure that they are not in danger of being cut off. Since the military scenario in **Patton Versus Rommel** presumes a wide-open battle with fragmented lines for both sides, I could not rely on a simple-minded search for any unit behind the line. To be threatened, a unit had to find an enemy unit in its own rear. This raised many tricky problems. Exactly what constitutes the rear area of a frontline unit?

My solution makes use of the sketch shown in Figure 22.9 (not drawn accurately).

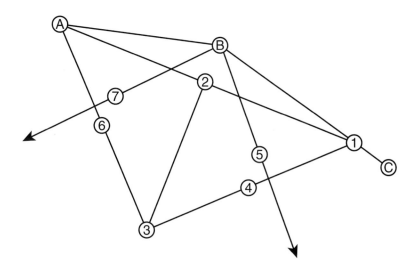

22.9 *Calculating the rear area of a unit.*

Units A, B, and C are frontline units; we are considering the rear area of unit B. We first calculate Point 1, the point on the line connecting B with C that is as far from B as A is from B. This makes triangle A, B, Point 1 an isosceles triangle. We then calculate the midpoint of the baseline, Point 2. This is easily done by averaging the coordinates of A and Point 1.

Now comes a cute trick: The perpendicular to a line is easily calculated by taking the negative inverse of its slope. This allows us to calculate the perpendicular to the line Point1–Point 2. The significance of this perpendicular is that it points toward the rear of Unit B. Now, we could get very messy here with the problem of getting our perpendicular to pass through Point 2. It would involve the equation for a line with a given slope passing through a given point, and it would be ugly. Fortunately, we don't need the full-blown equation; all we need is a single point, Point 3. For reasons to be seen later, we desire this point to fall on the perpendicular at a distance equal to the distance Point 1–Point 2. Rather than belabor the argument, I shall simply show the code to calculate Point 3:

```
DX = X2 - X1;
DY = Y2 - Y1;
IF ((DX>0) && (DY>0)) OR ((DX<0) && (DY<0)) THEN
{
DX = -DX;
DY = -DY;
}
X3 = X2 - DY;
Y3 = Y2 - DX;
```

In this code fragment, I use "X#" to refer to the X-coordinate of the #th point, and similarly for Y. DX and DY refer to delta-X and delta-Y. (Delta-X is the difference in X-coordinates; delta-Y is the difference in Y-coordinates.)

Note that the negative inversion of the slope is handled by reversing and negating the coordinates in the last two lines of the code fragment.

Now that we have Point 3, things get easy. Point 3 forms two isosceles triangles:

A–Point 2–Point 3
Point 1–Point 2–Point 3

I shall begin with the latter triangle. We can bisect the segment Point 1–Point 3 by averaging their coordinates; this yields Point 4. Since the triangle is an isosceles right triangle, the line Point–Point 4 lies at 45 degrees to line Point 2–Point 3. Unfortunately, Point 4 is not quite what we need, as it yields a line based on Point 2, and Point 2 is displaced from Unit B. This is easily corrected by creating Point 5, a point displaced from Point 4 by exactly the amount that Unit B is displaced from Point 2. This means that the line Unit B–Point 5 runs 45 degrees out from the line to Unit B's rear.

A similar calculation yields Point 6 and Point 7. With the two 45-degree lines produced by these computations, we can define a triangular region bounded by these lines as the rear area of Unit B. Any enemy unit placed in this area constitutes a threat to Unit B. To determine whether an enemy unit falls inside this region, we perform some analytic geometry:

```
AX = XB - X5;
AY = YB - Y5;
BX = XEnemy - XB;
BY = YEnemy - YB;
CX = X7 - XB;
CY = Y7 - YB;
DX = XEnemy - X7;
DY = YEnemy - Y7;
IF (((AX * BY) - (AY * BX)) < 0) AND
(((CX * DY) - (CY * DX)) < 0) THEN
{Yes, he is behind us!}
```

This last IF-statement makes use of the equations for the two lines. The inequalities express the notion that the tested point falls on a particular side of a line.

By modern standards, this is pretty clunky stuff, but given the weakness of the CPUs in those days—no, we didn't have floating point processors—this algorithm's ability to carry out complex geometric calculations without resorting to trigonometry was important.

Results

Patton Versus Rommel was released in mid-1986. It was ported to several other machines and sold moderately well, but it was certainly not a hit. As far as I was concerned, it was the last wargame I would ever design. There were some interesting ideas in it, but wargame designers didn't seem to take much note of those ideas. In particular, I had hoped that the elimination of grids would be applied in other games, but few wargame designers seemed interested. And indeed, when I reluctantly decided to create one last wargame (**Patton Strikes Back**), I went back to the rectgrid system.

My deal with Electronic Arts proved to be the source of some chagrin. They had presented me with a 55-page contract, obviating every possible means by which I could let them down. Apparently, at the end of each project, the lawyers interviewed the producer to discover any procedural problems, and then wrote a new paragraph into the standard contract to ensure that the problems wouldn't arise again. The result was a tedious and picayune contract, but I suppose that they were burned enough times to adopt a defensive stance. I certainly did not resent their careful protection of their interests; I just hoped that this mound of legalese was not designed to screw me.

Sadly, I turned out to be wrong. After a year or so of sales, EA decided that **Patton Versus Rommel** was nearing the end of its product life, and decided to squeeze a last bit of revenue out of it. They made it a promotional item for some of their internally generated games. Buy our new game and get **Patton Versus Rommel** for just 1 cent more! This cleared out their inventory and boosted sales of their new products. However, their contract with me specified that I was to get a per-centage of their net revenues on sales of my game. Thus, for each of those copies of **Patton Versus Rommel** that they sold, they paid me a fraction of a cent in royalties. It was a clever way to enhance their own profits and clear out inventory—and I was the only loser in the deal. And it was all perfectly legal.

58

LESSON

Publishers hold all the cards; designers are lucky to get whatever they can.

siboot

siboot

On Christmas Eve, 1985, I suffered a sad tragedy. While doing some morning chores outside, I spied our cat, Bootsie, whom I had not seen in several days. His absence was no cause for alarm; Bootsie was a bit of a loner and would often take off for several days. This time, however, I noticed something odd about him. Stepping closer to investigate, I perceived with horror that his lower jaw was hanging loosely from his head; something had broken his jaw.

I gathered him up into a basket and dashed off to the veterinarian, who upon examining Bootsie declared his condition hopeless. However, before recommending euthanasia, the vet offered to call a colleague who specialized in such injuries. A few hours later, he called me with the news that the colleague was willing to take a look at Bootsie. It was more than an hour's drive away, and I had plenty of time to contemplate the scenarios that were likely to arise. I knew that most of them concluded with euthanasia, and I struggled with tears as I tried to explain the situation to Bootsie, who was lying quietly in his basket on the passenger seat. Bootsie stared back at me with eyes clouded by pain. My fears were realized; the specialist declared Bootsie's injuries beyond repair. I therefore authorized euthanasia and drove home with his shrouded body.

Bootsie's death hit me hard; his mangled face still haunts me. For more than a week, I was unable to concentrate on my work. I was finishing up **Patton Versus Rommel** for Electronic Arts; the work was mostly mindless bug-fixing that required little creative energy, and so my creative juices

59
LESSON

Design springs from the heart.

were flowing in new directions, seeking new outlets. They mingled with the horror and sadness of Bootsie's death, and the brew simmered for several weeks. And then one day, whilst driving—I remember the exact spot on the road where it happened—the result boiled up out of my subconscious and shot into the open air. **Talk to the Animals** would be my next game. If only I had been able to talk to Bootsie, to explain the situation, to express my horror at his injury, to comfort him—if only. The world is a sad place, and sometimes we cannot speak to those whom we must. But what if there were a world in which we could Talk to the Animals? Why couldn't I create such a world?

A Lesson for Designers

Herein lies an immensely important lesson for game designers: Design springs from the heart. If all you want to do is screw around with code, you might create some great programs, but you'll never design a good game. Games people bravely talk about their work as art, but what springs not from the heart is mere cleverness; claiming it as art is idle vainglory and pretension. You as a designer must look honestly at yourself. If you measure your manhood by the elegance of your code, then aspiring to game design will only lead you to failure. Seek your grand achievements in the arena of your true love, coding. Game design requires a designer with something to say, a designer with fire in the heart, not just fire in the belly. Eagerness and ambition can never substitute for genuine passion.

First Draft Proposal

The central problem of **Talk to the Animals** lay in the language. How could I design a language that would permit the kinds of interactions I wanted between the player and the characters of the game? It was obvious to me that I could not use natural language; researchers had been struggling with the problem for years and had not come close to solving the problem on big computers, much less a little personal computer. This led to the conclusion that I would have to invent my own little language. I needed a system of subjects, verbs, direct objects, and so forth that would permit the player to Talk to the Animals.

Now, there already existed a solution to the problem of using language in games: the parser. Indeed, one of the more successful games companies in the industry at that time was InfoCom, famous for the powerful parser that lay at the heart of its excellent adventure games. These games allowed the user to type a sentence in normal English; the parser would then figure out what the sentence meant. The problem, unfortunately, was that parsers were notoriously obtuse. The great majority of sentences that a reasonable person might type would confuse the parser.

Sometimes it was a matter of vocabulary; I experienced this problem in a particularly frustrating form. In the adventure, I had entered a room and read the detailed description of the room, which included a mention that there was a rock lying on the table. I typed "Pick up rock," to which it replied, "I see no rock here." It then re-listed the room description: "Big green room. There is a rock sitting on the table." I was beside myself with fury. I attempted many adroit schemes for laying my hands on that rock, but failed until I typed "Pick up stone." The computer responded, "You now have the stone."

More often, though, the problem was more fundamental; you simply weren't allowed to carry out the great majority of actions that you might contemplate. If you wanted to move the table to the kitchen so that you could stand on the table and look on top of the refrigerator, that would likely not be possible. If the designers of the adventure game did not intend for you to carry out an action, the words for that action would not be included in the parser, and the only way to establish this was through tedious trial and error. A typical fragment of an adventure game might read like this:

> **You are in the outer entryway. There is a door leading into the main room of the building.**
>
> **Open door.**
>
> **The door appears to be stuck.**
>
> **Kick door.**
>
> **The door shakes but remains stuck.**
>
> **Throw rock at door.**
>
> **The door shakes but remains stuck.**
>
> **Use knife on door.**
>
> **The door shakes but remains stuck.**
>
> **Shoot door with gun.**
>
> **The door shakes but remains stuck.**
>
> **Set fire to door with matches.**
> **The door appears to be inflammable.**

And so on and on and on. The difficulty here arises from two facts:

- First, the working vocabulary of the game is much smaller than the working vocabulary of most people. The odds are low that any word you choose will actually do something in the game.
- Second, the working vocabulary of the game is hidden from the player—you don't know what the magic words are. You just have to guess.

For all these reasons, I had rejected the parser approach immediately. My solution would have to use a small subset of the English language— that was unavoidable. I just needed some way to make that subset obvious to the user and broad enough to handle all the situations in the game. The solution hit me in the face as I was traversing an airport. All the iconic signs for restrooms, departures, arrivals, restaurants, and so forth provided the perfect model. Some sort of iconic system—that would be my model.

The First Proposal

It was time to assemble my thoughts; I set to work writing a proposal. It led off with a tiny story about being marooned with a little creature called a Siboot ("Bootsie" with the syllables reversed). The player, a business traveler, was on board a spacecraft that lost an engine on takeoff and crashed several hundred miles from the spaceport, leaving only the player and a Siboot surviving. (Oddly enough, the day after my publisher received the proposal, the Space Shuttle Challenger was destroyed by an engine failure on takeoff.) The core concept of this first proposal was the Interspecies Iconic Language card, which was a table of icons that could be used for simple communications by simply pointing at icons in sequence. This would be simple enough to implement on a personal computer. At the time, however, I had no idea of what those icons would actually represent.

The second major concept of the proposal was a journey from the crash site back to civilization. The many difficulties encountered during this journey would force the player to cooperate with the Siboot, and, I expected, induce him to develop a rapport with the Siboot.

The third major concept was the use of episodes in the journey. I expected to create a large set of incidents or episodes that would randomly arise during the journey to safety. I anticipated creating about a hundred such episodes and exposing the player to about twenty during each playing of the game. This, I estimated, would provide plenty of material for multiple replayings.

Design Essays

I set to work on this concept, but progress was slow. I was attempting something completely new and different; almost every aspect of the game had to be invented from scratch. I groped about, attacking problems willy-nilly. To help sort out my thoughts, I decided to write daily design essays. Now, I have long known that an effective way to develop your thinking is to write it down. The arduous task of articulating your thoughts forces you to confront minor ambiguities, reject sloppy ideas, and tighten everything up. For example, I wrote *The Art of Computer Game Design* as an exercise to organize my own thoughts on game design. Now I decided to make the concept part of my routine. Every day I would write a single-page essay presenting my thoughts on some design problem. Taken together, these essays do not comprise a design document. They do not form any continuous narrative, nor are they consistent; ideas tackled in one essay are often modified or rejected in a later essay. I made a point of not reading the previous day's essay before writing one; I feared that it would exert too great an influence on my current thinking. The essays were not primarily historical documents for later consultation; they were the by-product of an intellectual exercise. It was the exercise in disciplined thinking that was important, not the actual written result.

I did consult my essays at regular intervals, but only when I wanted to step back and trace the progress of an idea. I would read an entire week's essays, or even a month's, to remind myself of insights forgotten or mistakes not to be repeated. Sometimes, an offhand remark in an essay would trigger a new idea to explore.

Here's one of the essays:

Thoughts on the Word Set

I'm having some problems deciding what types of words should be included in my word set. These words will decide the nature of the interactions between the characters, and I am having difficulty resisting the obvious choices. For example, consider groups of words associated with locations. I could have verbs such as go, stay, and associated pronouns such as here, there, and away, and nouns such as tree, camp, trail, and whatever other specific locations I wish to include in the set. The problem is, what would such words do for the game? Here I come back to the central design problem of the day: How do I get interpersonal interaction instead of just resource management?

It would be easy to make the game just a big puzzle. The group must explore the world to find the machine gun lying in the cave that will save them from a monster. But how can I get some interaction among these characters? I don't want it to be just a matter of finding the machine gun and mowing down the dinosaur. I want them to spend their time worrying about each other.

For example, if there is a machine gun, I would rather have it accidentally go off in Gardbore's hands, and nearly hit Chris, and then let Chris yell at Gardbore. That's interaction; mowing down helpless dinosaurs isn't.

Or how about this: They find a water hole. Kendra wants to drink, but Siboot warns that the water is bad. Kendra and Siboot argue.

What if I just prepare a very small sample scene and see if I can make it work? But how would I handle artificial personality? Maybe I could play act that part out, playing the roles of all characters in the group. My test is to see whether the scene and the language are adequate to make a game.

Yes, that's it. To work!

I wrote nearly 200 such essays.

The essays traced a zig-zagging course as I struggled with the many difficult problems I encountered in designing this unconventional game. Here are some of the issues I struggled with and my final resolutions for them.

60

LESSON

Write design essays to clarify your thoughts.

The Cast

I had initially intended that the game would have just two players: the human player and the Siboot. The human would learn to cooperate with the Siboot despite their difficulties in communicating. I later decided that this was too small a cast; I needed more characters to achieve rich dramatic interaction. I therefore added several new characters. This permitted me to bring conflict within the group; with only two characters, much of the conflict would take place with external actors. By moving conflict into the group, I permitted a wider range of dramatic conflict.

The Journey

My initial concept had relied upon the journey from the crash site to safety. A standard literary device, the journey provides many opportunities for a variety of adventures. I eventually learned, however, that the kind of adventures made possible by the journey format were too disparate in nature. I could find no common basis on which to build standard algorithms for the adventures provided in the journey format. I would have to write each and every adventure as a unique experience. This created a problem for repeat playings.

Suppose that I created a hundred unique adventures. If the player experienced all one hundred adventures in a single playing of the game, then a second playing would confront him with the same one hundred adventures, and they would have no surprise value and little entertainment value. Now, I could have reduced the number of adventures that a player would experience in a single game. Thus, if the player experienced only 50 adventures per game, then he could play two unique games—still not enough to be sustainable. By reducing it to just 10 adventures per game, I could extend the replayability to ten games—but then the player would not experience much in any single game.

This is a common problem in many games, and I had long before recognized the fundamental nature of the problem as well as its solution, but many people still have problems grasping it. Games people, in general, seem to have an intuitive appreciation of the problem, but their under-standing seems to lack the depth to realize its full implications. Multimedia people, on the other hand, don't seem to have begun to get a grip on the problem. I've been shouting this concept from the rooftops for at least fifteen years now, but my rooftops seem to be too far from the population centers.

Economies

Another idea that dominated my thinking at this time was the notion of economies. In my thinking, an economy was any system of related quantities whose values could change in response to character actions. The most obvious economy is an object economy, consisting of various items that can be found, taken, carried, transferred to other characters, or used to carry out tasks. But there is also an economy of relation-ships: affection, trust, fear, and so forth.

There is also an economy of information: Facts known to some players that can be shared with other players—under the right conditions. I was certain that a single-economy game would be boring; what I wanted was a game with at least three economies. The relationships among those economies would permit a broad and rich array of relationships among the characters. This thinking was fruitful in my efforts; explaining exactly how it worked its way into the final design must wait until I describe some other matters.

Intransitive Combat Relationships

Plain old everyday transitive combat relationships are what you see in almost all games. If my gun is bigger than your gun, and your gun is bigger than Joe's gun, then my gun can really whomp on Joe's gun. This means that bigger is always better, and the guy with the biggest gun will beat everybody else. It seems perfectly natural and reasonable, but it's often not very fun, especially if you're the guy with the little gun.

Intransitive combat relationships are weird: My gun can beat your gun, and your gun can beat Joe's gun, but Joe's gun can beat my gun! You might recognize this as just the rock-scissors-paper relationship. It's so weird that most game designers have steered clear of it, which is a shame, because I think that a whole slew of games could be built using different intransitive combat relationships systems.

For **Siboot**, I designed the following combat system: Each player began the game with some random number of each of the set rock, scissors, paper. I didn't call them that. In **Siboot**, they were the three auras: tanaga, shial, and katsin. So one player might begin the game with three tanagas, six shials, and three katsins, while another player might have four tanagas, three shials, and five katsins. The goal of the game was to amass an equal number of each of the three auras. Players gained and lost auras in dream combat, during which each player chose an aura from his collection and matched it against his opponent's aura, with tanaga beating shial, shial beating katsin, and katsin beating tanaga. Now, if you knew how many auras a player possessed, you could pretty well guess which aura he'd play, and then you could beat him. So the game really boiled down to acquiring information on other people's auras—information that could be gained only in trade with others.

The result is a much more interesting game. Regular rock-scissors-paper is boring because it's completely arbitrary. You have no way of knowing which piece your opponent will play, so it's just a wild guess. But this variation allows you to make reasonable predictions as to what another player might do—if you know enough about him. If your knowledge is incomplete, then you have to make guesses. And you also have to guess whether an opponent knows your aura set well enough to anticipate your moves. All in all, it's a fascinating combat system because it integrates logic with intuition.

Intransitive combat relationships can be extended in many different directions. You could provide variable numbers of each piece, but make one piece rarer (and therefore more valuable) than the others. You could have them reverse their relationships at specified times or conditions, so that the player with lots of scissors might suddenly find himself running from the paper people. Or you could extend the number of dimensions in use. A four-way intransitive circle offers lots of fascinating possibilities. If A beats B, B beats C, C beats D, and D beats A, what does B do to D, and what does A do to C? You could have them stand off, or you could have them switch. In other words, if A plays against B, then the owner of A captures the B, but if A plays against C, then the owner of C gets the A and the owner of A gets the C.

You could extend to five, six, or even seven dimensions, but it would get very messy. Figure 23.1 shows why.

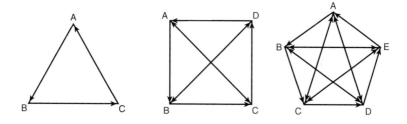

23.1   *Intransitive relationships get complicated with more dimensions.*

Another trick would be to have, in effect, armies of rocks, scissors, and papers. This was actually done back in 1984 in **The Ancient Art of War**. Infantry was rock, cavalry was paper, and archers were scissors. You could extend the system by creating three types of terrain, in each of which one type of unit is invulnerable or perhaps very strong. Combining terrain with a four-dimensional system could produce fascinating gameplay.

61

Experiment with intransitive combat relationships.

The Inverse Parser

I had rejected the notion of using a parser at the outset of the project. My initial concept was that people communicated by pointing to icons on their Interspecies Iconic Language card, which would be reproduced on the Macintosh screen. The player would click on icons to communicate. I soon realized that the icons could not be clicked on willy-nilly—I had to impose some sort of ordering scheme on the player's actions. In other words, I needed to create a syntax.

Here my designer instincts served me well. Rather than try to create a syntax based on natural languages, I instead set out to create a syntax based solely on word order. This, it turns out, was a crucially important decision. Had I attempted to mimic natural syntax, I would have been caught up in a great many difficult problems. For example, natural syntax makes heavy use of "function words." These are articles such as "the," "a," "an," prepositions, and conjunctions, that serve no direct semantic purpose but instead specify the relationships among the meaningful words in the sentence. They're the glue that bind the words in the sentence. Computationally, they can be a real pain in the butt, but I avoided the need for Designer's Preparation H by simply skipping them. In the same way, I avoided all use of conjugation and declension, those special endings that we tack onto nouns and verbs to indicate how they function in a sentence. Instead, I concentrated on just one simple mechanism for syntax: word order.

Fortunately, I had one other advantage in this problem: a two-dimensional display instead of the one-dimension medium of sound that spoken language uses. For example, consider this simple sentence: "I put it in the box that was broken by the dog." You have no problem understanding that the box referred to was damaged by the actions of the dog. But what about this sentence: "I put it in the box that was broken by the fireplace." In this case, you have no problem figuring out that the box was broken and was positioned close to the fireplace. After all, fireplaces can't break things, and dogs aren't useful as positional indicators because they move around, so you can disambiguate the sentences easily enough. But if you're a computer and you don't know anything about dogs, boxes, and fireplaces, then you could never figure out which meaning applied.

Now look at the two sentences as they might be displayed graphically (see Figure 23.2).

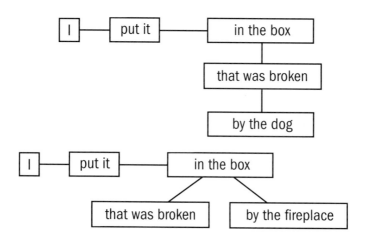

23.2 *Two-dimensional display disambiguates one-dimensional language.*

A two-dimensional representation of a sentence shows its structure more clearly. At this point, I took a wrong turn. I was so enamored of the idea of graphically representing the language that I got carried away and tried to include special connector icons that would indicate the nature of the relationship between two adjacent words. I wasted lots of time designing a clever system with vertical lines, horizontal lines, slanted lines, and so

62

LESSON

Always delete clever ideas that don't add to the design.

forth to indicate all sorts of special things. Then reality caught up with me: I realized that people can stick two words together without all those function words. Indeed, all of the function words can be stripped out of the graph of the sentence, and it is just as computable as the first version (see Figure 23.3).

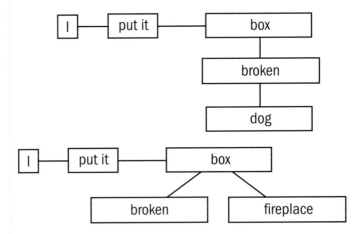

23.3 *"Look Ma, no function words!"*

So I threw out all the clever little connector icons.

At this point, I had a collection of word icons and a scheme for placing them on the screen to organize them into a sentence. I had been thinking solely in terms of output: how the game would talk to the user. But then I had a stroke of genius, so simple and obvious that I didn't even recognize it at the time. I decided to make the input system the same as the output system. Actually, this idea had been implicit in my earliest concepts for the game. The Interspecies Iconic Language card that I had imagined was an intrinsically bi-directional communication device. I had not realized the vast implications of the idea at the time.

I simply plugged ahead, devising an input scheme in which the user clicked on icons with the mouse to build his sentence. The killer problem I faced was this: How was I to show the user all the icons in the word set? There were too many to fit comfortably on the screen, and I was anticipating making many more such icons. Somehow I needed to pare down the list of words. I needed an algorithm that would figure out which words were appropriate to choose from in any given situation. What I needed was an inverse parser. So I invented one.

So what, exactly, is an inverse parser? The easiest way to understand an inverse parser is to compare it with a conventional parser. The user enters a string of commands or keystrokes and the parser takes apart the string, identifies the basic components, and figures out whether those components fit together in a meaningful way. If so, it executes the command. If not, it issues an error message and the user must try again. A good deal of algorithmic complexity is required to parse some commands, requiring big hunks of code. Good parsers take years to build.

For the inverse parser, we simply invert the process. First the computer does lots and lots of work figuring out which commands are available given the current context; then it presents that list to the user, who selects one from the list. The inverse parser gobbles up tons of machine cycles, because the computer has to apply all of its syntactical tests to every possible word. By contrast, the regular parser is more parsimonious, because it applies only those syntactical tests that are called for by the user's actual input. But what the hell, machine cycles are cheap and brain cycles are expensive: Let the computer do the work!

Although the inverse parser requires lots of machine cycles to do its job, it doesn't require any extra code. The same code that checks the string *after* the user inputs it can check a potential string *before* the user inputs it. It's the same code executed in the opposite order.

NOTE

I later learned that my concept of the inverse parser had already been patented by Texas Instruments back in 1980. It is obvious from their patent that they did not realize the full extent of the implications of the concept. Their implementation of the concept was much narrower than my own. But the basic concept of narrowing words from a set based on context was theirs.

An inverse parser for a natural language would be a horribly complicated affair, because natural languages are so messy. In particular, they permit all sorts of word orders. All sorts of word orders are permitted by them. Word orders of all sorts are permitted by them. They permit word orders of all sorts. Gack!

But my language had a specified word order, and that made all the difference. There were 128 words in my language, so I created a 128×128 array of flags, requiring just 2K of memory (which was still precious in those days). The flags indicated whether word X could be followed by word Y. So if the user had already clicked on word X, then the inverse parser needed to scan only the X-row in the matrix. If the Yth column of the X row contained a value of 0, then the inverse parser concluded that word Y was not an appropriate successor for word X, and eliminated it from consideration. But if that value were a 1, then the inverse parser concluded that word Y was an appropriate successor for word X. With one simple trick, I had eliminated vast amounts of complexity from my inverse parser.

There were, of course, plenty of other considerations as to what words were appropriate in any given context, and I had to write Boolean formulas for each consideration. But it was no special matter to include those Boolean formulas in the code.

The Display

Figure 23.4 shows what the display looked like.

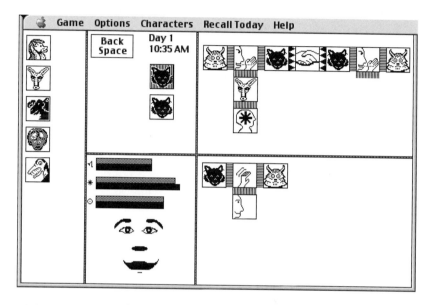

23.4 **Siboot** display.

There are five panes in this window. The pane in the lower right shows you, in the iconic language, what your interlocutor has just said. That sentence is this: "Wiki greets Vetvel pleasantly." Wiki is the dark-faced fellow in the upper left of the pane; Vetvel is the horny character. You play the role of Vetvel.

The pane in the lower center shows you Wiki's state of mind. The three bars show you his three mental attributes, tanaga, katsin, and shial, roughly corresponding to fear, affection, and trust. During the course of a conversation, you can see how these values change in response to your actions. The face underneath is an interesting solution to a resource problem. There are eight characters in the game and each character can show nearly a dozen faces. That would require nearly a hundred separate drawings. There simply wasn't space available for so much graphics. Instead, I opted for a generic face showing only the most critical elements of the face. Like a happy face, this generic face can be applied to anybody.

The pane in the upper center shows you the date, time, your location (Wiki's house) and the other person present (Wiki). It also presents the editing commands for the sentence you are preparing to say, which, in this case, is BackSpace. The sentence that you are building appears in the upper-right pane. It's the most complex form of sentence available in **Siboot**; it says "Vetvel offers to tell Wiki the amount of Gardbore's katsin if in return Wiki tells Vetvel..." The sentence is unfinished. You the player must fill in the name of the character about whom you wish information. The available characters are shown in the left pane; you simply click on the icon to insert it into the sentence.

Interstitial Stories

The initial proposal had posited a series of custom stories, each one tracing some incident during the course of the journey. While I ended up abandoning the journey concept, I retained the concept of the custom stories and developed it into a new idea I called *interstitial stories*. These are stories with variable parameters that can be used in different contexts. They are not at all the same as cut scenes, which are fixed mini-stories inserted at designated points in a game.

Interstitial stories can be used almost anywhere; cut scenes obey a precise schedule. Interstitial stories serve a number of useful purposes:

- Providing color with little dirt
- Enhancing character development
- Giving the player a different set of challenges
- Providing feedback

You probably don't recognize my use of the terms "color" and "dirt"; they're obscure terms from old wargame designs, but they're so useful to game designers today that I still invoke them.

Color is the sense of realism or completeness that improves the sense of immersion. Games people love to add color to their games. "Look, the splashing blood can even get into your gun and make it slippery and harder to use! What realism!" The problem with color is that it always brings a certain amount of dirt with it.

Dirt is created by special rules that the player must commit to memory. Sure, it's more realistic to have the blood splash into your gun and gook it up, but now the player has to remember to stand back from exploding monsters. So the question that game designers must always ask themselves is this: "Does this feature add enough color to make it worth the dirt?" This is what makes interstitial stories such a good feature; they provide tons of color while imposing zero dirt. The color comes from the fact that you're not constrained by the graphical limitations of your game; you can present interstitial stories in text, which can describe anything. There's no dirt because the interstitial story is a one-shot affair. The player experiences the story, makes his response, and then forgets it.

Evaluate each contemplated feature by its color/dirt ratio.

Figure 23.5 shows the screen display for a sample interstitial story.

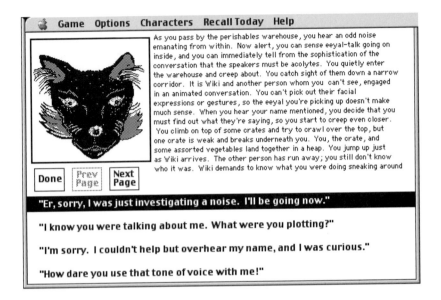

As you pass by the perishables warehouse, you hear an odd noise emanating from within. Now alert, you can sense eeyal-talk going on inside, and you can immediately tell from the sophistication of the conversation that the speakers must be acolytes. You quietly enter the warehouse and creep about. You catch sight of them down a narrow corridor. It is Wiki and another person whom you can't see, engaged in an animated conversation. You can't pick out their facial expressions or gestures, so the eeyal you're picking up doesn't make much sense. When you hear your name mentioned, you decide that you must find out what they're saying, so you start to creep even closer. You climb on top of some crates and try to crawl over the top, but one crate is weak and breaks underneath you. You, the crate, and some assorted vegetables land together in a heap. You jump up just as Wiki arrives. The other person has run away; you still don't know who it was. Wiki demands to know what you were doing sneaking around

Done   Prev Page   Next Page

"Er, sorry, I was just investigating a noise. I'll be going now."

"I know you were talking about me. What were you plotting?"

"I'm sorry. I couldn't help but overhear my name, and I was curious."

"How dare you use that tone of voice with me!"

23.5 *Interstitial story.*

And here is the source file for this interstitial story:

As you pass by the perishables warehouse, you hear an odd noise emanating from within. Now alert, you can sense eeyal-talk going on inside, and you can immediately tell from the sophistication of the conversation that the speakers must be acolytes. You quietly enter the warehouse and creep about. You catch sight of them down a narrow corridor. It is % and another person whom you can't see, engaged in an animated conversation. You can't pick out their facial expressions or gestures, so the eeyal you're picking up doesn't make much sense. When you hear your name mentioned, you decide that you must find out what they're saying, so you start to creep even closer. You climb on top of some crates and try to crawl over the top, but one crate is weak and breaks underneath you. You, the crate, and some assorted vegetables land together in a heap. You jump up just as % arrives. The other person has run away; you still don't know who it was. % demands to know what you were doing sneaking around spying on $. You reply: \

\

"Er, sorry, I was just investigating a noise. I'll be going now."

D2+dT4-tP% shakes ^ head skeptically and lets you go.

\

"I know you were talking about me. What were you plotting?"

T4-t50E-BD4-dA6-aP% grows furious, shouts at you, and stalks off.

20D-BD4+dP% laughs and says, "You fool, we weren't plotting anything!"

P% says, "Oh, dear, we weren't plotting anything!"

\

"I'm sorry. I couldn't help but overhear my name, and I was curious."

D2+d40-BP% looks unconvinced. "Sure", @ says, and @ walks away.

P% yells, "Get out of here!"

\

"How dare you use that tone of voice with me!"

T4-tD8-dA4-aE40-BP% looks chastised and retreats without saying a word.

P% shouts at you angrily and stalks off.

\

The special symbols such as %, @, and $ are *substitution variables* that direct the program to substitute the name of another character or his/her appropriate pronouns. This allowed me to use a story with any character. The four paragraphs following the main paragraph are the menu options available to the player. Each of these, in turn, has several possible responses by the other character. The odd text string at the beginning of each response is a calculation of the likelihood that the character will choose that response as well as a calculation of how the player's decision has altered the character's attitude towards the player. The individual characters might be read as keystrokes for a RPN calculator. (If you don't know what an RPN calculator is, don't worry; it's a technical detail that technical people will appreciate and non-technical people really won't care about.) For example, the first such text string is D2+dT4-t. The first four characters (D2+d) mean this:

Load the dominance that the character feels for the player into the accumulator. Now load the number 2. Add. Store the accumulator into the dominance that the character feels for the player.

In other words, add 2 to the character's feeling of dominance over the player. The next command, "T4-t," subtracts 4 from the trust that the character feels for the player.

This primitive system allowed me to program simple calculations directly into each story file, without altering the program code itself.

I also used the stories to provide feedback to the player, and I myself was the character who delivered the feedback. Here's an example, used when the player fails to get down to business with another character:

> Suddenly the door flies open. In charges Chris Crawford. "No, no, no! That's not the way I intended you to play this game at all! You've got to mix it up more intensely with the characters! You, %, I taught you better than that! Come on, now, show some FEELING! And you, player, what do you think you're doing anyway? Just kinda messing around in a half-witted way? You're acting like this is some sorta game or something! You clod! Don't you realize that this is ART?" He pauses, glaring at the two of you. You both look down at the floor; % scrapes the floor with ^ foot. "All right, people! One more time, with FEELING!" He stalks out, slamming the door behind him. So, are you going to be good? \
>
> \
>
> "Yes, I promise to be good and play well."
>
> " PThank you."
>
> \
>
> "What's going on here?"
>
> " PThat depends on what you want to be going on here."
>
> \
>
> "This guy is really screwy."
>
> " PYou think I'm screwy? I've got your money!"

\

"Go to hell, Crawford!"

" C4PA cloud passes over the sun. The earth shudders."

\

Please note that the final option, in which the player curses me, generates a response "C4." This calculation modifies a key game variable that, in effect, makes it harder for the player to win the game. So there!

In the end, I was able to cook up only some 40-odd interstitial stories. All in all, they definitely improved the game. A few players were a little put off by my appearance in the game, but the great majority took it in the spirit of good fun.

I recommend use of interstitial stories with several restrictions.

- First, they must not be used at fixed points in the game, like cut scenes. If your purpose is to interweave a fixed story through a game with cut scenes, then you have missed the point of interstitial stories, which are standalone anecdotes. They can be told at different points in the story with different characters. Of course, you are free to narrow their range of applicability to take advantage of context. For example, I wrote several interstitial stories that might appear only after the player had lost in mental combat. Indeed, there were very few interstitial stories that could be told at any time during the game; almost all had some sort of special contextual restrictions.

- Second, I believe that each interstitial story must be made flexible to apply to a variety of settings, and that this requires the use of text variables such as those I used in **Siboot**. You can cook up any system you want, so long as you do have a system.

- Third, interstitial stories must be interactive. Merely dumping some cute little anecdote on the player is a waste of everybody's time; set up some sort of conflict and let the user make a choice. That choice, in turn, must be meaningful; it must affect the outcome of the game. Otherwise, your interstitial story is not genuinely interactive.

Use intersti-
tial stories
to add color
and flavor to
the game
with little
dirt.

The Novella

The final design was weird enough that it required some explanation. I did so with a novella, just as I had done with **Excalibur**. It presented the history of the world in which the player found himself, doing so in a series of short vignettes. I'm proud of that novella. A professional writer I am not, but I dare to say that as a work of fiction, it was passable. Even then, a more conventional manual was still required to explain the mundane aspects of the game, such as how to save and load games.

Conclusions

Siboot was published in 1987 by Mindscape under the title **Trust & Betrayal: The Legacy of Siboot**. It was not a commercial success; I believe that only 5,000 copies were sold, and Mindscape never ported the game from the Mac to the PC or any other platform. Nevertheless, I consider **Siboot** to be my best game design. No other game has ever leapt so far out into unknown regions of game design and actually worked. No other game boasted as many significant innovations as **Siboot**: intransitive combat relationships, an inverse parser, a working language of interaction, dream combat, an information economy, general-purpose deal making, and functional, dynamic emotional relationships among characters. Indeed, in the fifteen years that have passed since the publication of **Siboot**, there have been just a handful of games that have successfully implemented any of these innovations, and none that have done so with a majority of these innovations.

If **Siboot** was indeed such a hot design, why was it a commercial failure? I believe that **Siboot**'s failure can be attributed to several factors. First was Mindscape's decision not to port **Siboot** to the PC platform. This was a borderline judgment call. At the time, PC games outsold Mac games by about four to one, so we would likely have sold some 20,000 copies for the PC. Given the economics of computer games at the time, this would have been only slightly profitable, and if it did worse, Mindscape could have lost money. Mindscape's worries about the unconventional nature of the game combined with **Siboot**'s poor initial sales to yield a pessimistic estimate of its chances. Had Mindscape been bolder, they would probably have made a little money on the deal, but they decided to cut their losses with the Mac version.

The killer question, of course, is, "Was it fun?" Innovation doesn't make a game great; it still has to entertain. There is no simple answer to this question. There is no denying that many people were enchanted by **Siboot**. This was the first computer game with characters who were emotionally real, characters you could relate to, understand, and interact with emotionally. One player wrote me to tell me how upset she had been to betray Locksher. He was such a nice fellow, and she felt so guilty about doing it. Another fellow posted a message on a bulletin board expressing his deep anger that Kendra had betrayed him. How could she do that to him, he raged, after all he had done to help her! There's no question that a good number of people found the game immensely entertaining. But the geekier players who revel in man-to-man shootouts were frustrated by the lack of violence. "There's no action in the game," one fellow complained on a bulletin board. "All you do is run around talking to people!"

The decisive factor, though, was the unconventional nature of the design. Now, 1987 was the most crucial year in the history of computer games. In 1984, the industry had collapsed and many companies went out of business. During 1985 and 1986, the industry reconstituted itself in a new image. The simple hand-eye coordination games that had been the foundation of the first games boom of 1979–1983 were out of fashion. The industry needed to find a new identity, and during the crucial years of 1985–1987, it tried on a number of hats, examining itself in the mirror of the marketplace to see what hats looked best. At first, the industry veered away from the childish videogames and experimented with a broader range of possibilities. The Infocom adventure games, while still puzzles, offered a richer experience and more mature themes than traditional adventure games. Dan Bunten's **M.U.L.E.** offered great fun without an iota of violence. My own **Balance of Power** showed that a deep game about geopolitics could become a huge hit. Games were reaching out to new and considerably larger audiences.

It seemed that computer games were about to emerge Phoenix-like from the ashes of videogames and blossom into a true mass medium. **Siboot** pushed this trend to its most extreme limit, and Mindscape, the distributors, and retailers lost their nerve. **Siboot** went too far; there were easier sales to be made with more traditional products. The failure of **Siboot** marked the end of the wildly experimental phase following the collapse of Atari in 1984. I did not recognize it at the time—I don't think anybody did—but the industry was committing itself to becoming a smaller, high-profit hobby rather than a mass medium.

That's where it is today. Computer and videogames are now a narrowly defined entertainment form avidly pursued by a subset of the mass market. It's easier this way for everybody. Marketing people know exactly whom to advertise to, what the ads should look like, and so forth.

65

Retailers know exactly how to stock their shelves. Producers know precisely what sells, and designers don't have to sweat being innovative; they need only apply the latest technology to the time-honored standard designs. It's a comfortable arrangement, and it works well. Thousands of satisfied employees grind out products for millions of happy, well-defined customers. The system works; everybody makes money.

But it's not a mass medium, and it never will be.

Limit your-self to one major innovation per game.

guns & butter

guns & butter

Over the course of the 1980s, a public-domain game by the name of **Empire** gained a loyal following. I am told it was created back in the 1970s, before there were microcomputers. After bouncing around university computer centers for years, people starting porting it to microcomputers.

Over the years, various programmers had steadily improved the game with each design iteration. By the late 80s, there were several commercial versions of **Empire** for the Mac and PC. Dan White had produced a version for the PC, and somebody else had done one for the Mac. But these designs had clung closely to the core concept of **Empire**.

During the years 1988 through 1990, the three best game designers in the world each set out to build a conquer-the-world style game based on the classic game **Empire**, but going well beyond its basic design. Those three designers were Sid Meier, Dan Bunten, and me, and the contrast among these three designer's approaches is illuminating. Each designer set out to create a fun game, but each of us had our own notions of fun.

Sid's was the closest to the conventional gamer. He wanted a game that offered lots of different strategic approaches, lots of variables to keep track of, and a broad strategic integration. When he looked at **Empire**, he saw a game with a crude economic model, a simplistic military model, no real terrain factors, and no technological factors. He resolved to create a game with more complex versions of each of these models. Note that he did not set out to create more realism; Sid's goal was more intricacy of internal relationships, and he readily bent reality to suit his design goals (as he should have). His result, which came out last, was **Civilization**, and it was a huge hit.

Dan emphasized social interaction. He looked at **Empire** and saw a boring solitaire game. He was convinced that you would never get interesting competition from a computer. For really interesting interaction, Dan believed, you simply had to have another human being. He wanted a game with two players pitted against each other, with lots of opportunities for sneaky dirty tricks, cooperative play, and socializing. He produced a two-player telecomm game (the two players connected directly with each other over the phone lines using their modems) called **Modem Wars**. That game was a commercial flop, although it did attract a small avid following.

My approach was, unsurprisingly, the most intellectual of the three. I looked at **Empire** and saw a stupid game that said nothing about how the world worked. I wanted a game that would allow the player to explore the interplay between economics and military power. I was sick and tired of games that emphasized clever generalship. Didn't gamers realize that World War II was won in the factories of Detroit, not the battlefield of Kursk? I wanted to show that economic power is the true source of military power.

Designing the World

My first task was to create a world. I had already decided that, like **Empire**, my game would create its own custom world for each playing. I anticipated that this could create a nasty problem. My world-creation algorithms would be quite complex and could conceivably create nonsensical worlds. In such cases, I would need to re-create the nonsensical world and track down the programming bug that led to the mistake. Yet, if the algorithms relied on random numbers to create the world, then I would have no way to re-create the world. I solved the problem by asking the user to provide a name for the world; this name became the seed for the random number generator, guaranteeing repeatable results should they be required.

My map system relied on provinces rather than a grid of squares. Such grids, called rectgrids (see the discussion of various grid systems in Chapter 13, "Tanktics") are ubiquitous in computer games; even if you can't see the rectgrid, it's there. Somewhere inside the program there are little X's and Y's denoting the position of every object and character in the game. I find such all-encompassing convention offensive to my creative sensibilities. If everybody does it, then surely I must find another way. And indeed there are plenty of other ways to organize space on a map: polar projections, hexgrids, triangular coordinates, and so on. But the most interesting, and I believe the most flexible, approach uses provinces: irregularly shaped splotches of territory treated as single spatial units. I therefore designed the map as a collection of such provinces. This innovation improved the game, I believe.

As I had decided not to include naval factors in my game, map generation would be greatly simplified by the lack of islands. I need create just one huge continent. Map generation began with placement of the capital cities of the various provinces. This was a purely random process—save for the obvious provisions that cities not be too close to the

66

LESSON

Don't be such a square! Think about alternative ways of organizing space in your design.

edge of the map or to each other. The second step was the placement of roads between some of the provinces. Note that, at this point, adjacency between provinces had not been established.

Having decided on roads, I then set about establishing the spokes that connected the cities. Imagine a cluster of points on a map; obviously, they can be connected in many different ways (as shown in Figure 24.1).

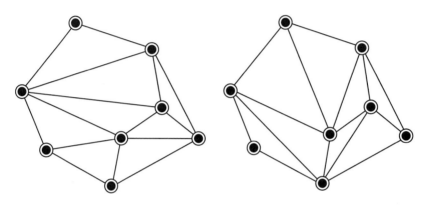

24.1 *Different spoke systems.*

How is the computer to decide upon the best configuration of spokes? The most effective algorithm, I believed, would minimize the total lengths of all spokes. However, when I wrote up this algorithm, it took far too long to run. The reason was that there were up to 64 cities in the game, and the number of arrangements with 64 cities was astronomical. Now, I could have worked out a good pruning algorithm that would have permitted me to explore only the best few thousand arrangements. However, I chose an alternate route, based on a simple-minded scheme using the angles between spokes. It was a clumsy algorithm, and required a certain amount of tweaking, but it ran quickly and yielded acceptable results. In the immortal words of Adam Osborne, "Adequacy is sufficient."

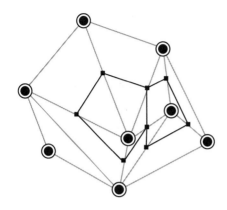

24.2 *Connecting the midpoints of spokes.*

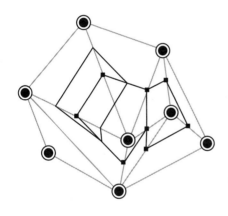

24.3 *Building terrain polygons.*

Building Provinces

Having created the spokes connecting the cities, it was a simple step to make the provinces: I needed only to connect the midpoints of the spokes, like what appears in Figure 24.2.

Of course, such borders are unacceptably polygonal; they needed further cosmetic work. This I did by wiggling the lines as I drew them. I used random numbers to determine how far to wiggle the line in the X and Y dimensions as I drew it.

Adding Mountains, Deserts, and Forests

The next step was to add terrain such as mountains, deserts, and forests. I applied another polygonal algorithm here, defining a polygon that straddled the border between provinces (see Figure 24.3).

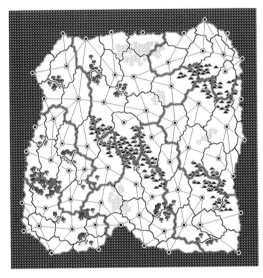

This polygonal region would then be randomly spattered with little mountain, forest, or desert icons. The random positioning of these mini-icons masked the purely geometric shape of the algorithm and produced a suitably blotchy look. The end result of all these manipulations looked like Figure 24.4.

24.4 *Final map.*

Naming Names

Another interesting problem that arose during the development of **Guns & Butter** was the problem of creating names for the various provinces. Most game designers have approached this problem by compiling long lists of names for use in the game; I wanted something better. I found it in some algorithms developed as part of research in computer science. The easiest way to understand these algorithms is to recall the old Edgar Allen Poe story about breaking a code using frequency analysis. The code breaker knew that e is the most frequently used letter in the English language, followed by t, then s, and so forth down to x, the least frequently used letter. By comparing these known letter frequencies with the letter frequencies in his coded document, he was able to break the code.

Now take this process a step further. What if we could compile a table of frequencies of all letter pairs? How often does the letter pair aa occur in English? How about ab, ac, ad, and so forth? There are 676 such letter pairs; it would be a simple matter for a computer to scan a large English document and produce such a frequency table.

Now take it several steps further. Build frequency tables of letter triplets; there are 17,576 such triplets. We can even build a frequency table for letter quadruplets; there are only about half a million of those, no big deal for a computer to build.

The value of all this frequency-table building lies in turning the tables around and manufacturing words from them. For each letter of the English language, we have a frequency value that we can express as a number between 0.00 and 1.00. The sum of all the individual frequency values will be exactly 1.00. Now we pick a random number between 0.00 and 1.00. We start at the first letter in the frequency table, a, and compare its frequency value with our random number; if it is greater than the random number, we then use the letter a as the first letter in our new word. If the frequency value of a is less than the random number, then we move to letter b and add its frequency value to the frequency value of a, comparing the sum with the random number. Again, if the sum is greater than the random number, then we select b as our letter, but if it is less, then we move on to c, adding its frequency value to the sum, and so on until we have selected the first letter in our artificial name. Now we pick another random number and use it to select a letter pair (using the already-chosen letter as the first letter of the letter pair) from the letter-pair frequency table. Now we repeat the process with the third letter. After that, we use the letter-quadruples frequency table to select letters to complete a sliding quadruplet of letters.

The algorithm actually used was a bit more complex than this because it had to take into account some special considerations for the beginnings of words, and it had to terminate words neatly, not just cut them off. But these additional complexities are tedious and do not add to the instructional value of this tale.

This algorithm can be used to generate any kind of sequence: musical notes, sequences of aerial maneuvers, moves in a game, etc.

I used one other trick to make the scheme work: I did not use English place-names as my source document for building my frequency tables. Instead, I used Mongol-Turkish place names. These are sufficiently unfamiliar to most Americans that I could get away with the occasional badly formed word. Here's a sample of the output of my name generator:

Murcherv, Baika, Koka, Baqabaidzh, Ildak, Alik, Orgingu, Kunkononog, Laqchokor, Adiqaibud, Mongandoda, Oghardaqta, Taisak, Kanbor

Interestingly enough, when I used place names from England, the results weren't so convincing—people are too familiar with English place names to accept concoctions like "Grodgich."

First-Person Firing Squad

Back in my Atari days, first person games were rare and prized. Most games were third person—you saw the action from a third-person perspective, with your little tank, man, or airplane running around on the screen just like all the other tanks, men, or airplanes. But in a first-person game, you saw the action from the point of view of your character. This was a much greater technological challenge and was seldom adequately implemented until the arrival of **Doom**.

Nevertheless, as early as 1980, game designers at Atari were avidly discussing the possibilities of first-person games. One wag suggested a **First-Person Firing Squad** game; I thought the idea had merit so I slapped something together in BASIC. Four little stick-figure men marched from the right side of the screen toward the center while a stick-figure commander waited on the left side of the screen. When they reached the center, the commander raised a hand and beeped "Halt!" Two more beeps enlivened an animation of the soldiers turning to face out from the screen, and the text "Left face!" appeared. Next came the command "Ready!" at which the soldiers presented their rifles. Another beep indicated the "Aim!" command, at which the soldiers took aim at the viewer. The third beep, "Fire!" was instantly followed by a loud bang and the screen suddenly going black. I always had fond feelings for that stupid little game, so I decided to build it into **Guns & Butter**. This time, however, the graphics and animation were much better (see Figure 24.5).

Hey, it's just a game! Judiciously chosen levity is entirely appropriate.

24.5 *First-person firing squad.*

The Economic System

The economic system used in **Guns & Butter** was another major innovation. In most military-economic games, the only product of a country's economy is weaponry. The more sophisticated games have technological scales; the player expends resources to climb the technological scale, which in turn grants access to more modern and more powerful weapons. Sid Meier's **Civilization**, for example, used a system in which the player expended resources on scientific research, which in turn produced a variety of discoveries which in turn enabled more powerful weapons or more efficient economic facilities (and some other things as well).

69

LESSON

You must
have a clear
conception
of the cen-
tral conflict
of your
design.

Civilization wasn't on sale when I designed **Guns & Butter**, so it didn't affect my design, but it employed (to my thinking) merely a more advanced form of the same old approach. My reading of history had convinced me that economic, military, and technological advances all spring from the same source: economies of scale. As a society grows more populous, more people can be diverted to more specialized efforts, which in turn permits the development of more efficient tools. Moreover, this population effect can also be achieved by pooling the populations of several countries into a single economic unit. This struck me as an excellent foundation for conflict. Players must cooperate economically if they are to grow powerful, but ultimately, they will go to war. This would, I planned, create a complex, constantly shifting pattern of alliances and conflicts. Here was the central conflict of my design.

The economic system was based on two primary inputs: resources and labor. You may object that this leaves out the third element of the "land, labor, and capital" triad that you were taught in school. My explanation for this unconventional element lies in the fact that the game covers such a large period of time that I can safely assume 100% capital depreciation from turn to turn. This approximation does not address the division between consumerism and capital formation (which, interestingly, **Civilization** does address), but I believed that such division could reasonably be treated as a constant.

Moreover, resources were fixed by the resource base of each country. The player had no control over the availability of resources; each province provided a fixed amount of each basic resource. The player's overall resource base was simply the sum of the resource bases of each province in the country. This, of course, created strong incentives to capture provinces well endowed with resources that the player lacked.

Thus, the player controlled neither capital formation nor resources. This leaves only labor as the element directly controlled by the player. And in fact, the player controlled not the absolute quantity of labor, which comes from total population, but instead the fraction of the country's workforce that is dedicated to each industry. This was quite deliberate on my part; I didn't want to inundate my player in a tidal wave of complex decisions. I wanted my game to zero in on the nature of economic strength, and so I kept the player's decisions tightly focused on the matter at hand.

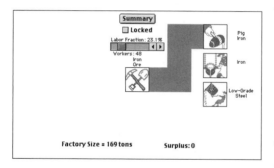

24.6 *Single-factor economic flow diagram.*

The player implemented his decisions with a handy little display looking like what appears in Figure 24.6.

Remember that screens were small back in those days; this display filled the screens of most user's computers. Also, many users still lacked color display capabilities, so the display had to work just as well in black-and-white as in color.

This shows the production of iron ore. The player controls the single scroll bar at top center to allocate a greater or lesser fraction of his work force to the Iron Ore mine. The player has 48 workers at the Iron Ore mine; they produce 169 tons of iron ore, all of which goes to the Pig Iron factory. Now let's follow up that production: The player simply clicks on the Pig Iron icon and jumps to the display for the Pig Iron factory (see Figure 24.7).

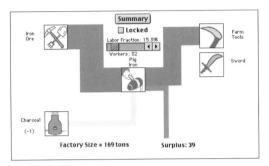

Iron
Ore

Summary
☐ Locked
Labor Fraction: 15.3%
◀ ▶
Workers: 32
Pig
Iron

Farm
Tools

Sword

Charcoal
(-1)

Factory Size = 169 tons   Surplus: 39

24.7   *Multi-factor economic diagram.*

Here's what this screen means. The central element is the large icon in the center: Pig Iron. Pig iron requires two inputs: iron ore and charcoal. The output of the Pig Iron factory can be sent to either the Farm Tools factory or the Sword factory, or some combination of both. In this screen, the player has dedicated 15.3% of his workers, 32 in all, to the Pig Iron factory. This many workers can produce 169 tons of pig iron each turn. They will require, of course, enough iron ore and charcoal to manufacture the pig iron. The output of their factory goes directly to the Farm Tools factory, but that factory has a capacity of only 130 tons, which means that 39 tons of pig iron are surplus and wasted. Clearly, this player should reduce the capacity of his factory; that will reduce the waste. Of course, then there will be too much iron ore, and the player will have to reduce the number of workers at the Iron Ore mine. To do so, he merely clicks on the Iron Ore icon, and goes back to the Iron Ore screen.

This system neatly allows the player to traverse an entire economy, looking at all the inputs and outputs of all the industries. Now, if you have any training in economics, you will likely be impressed by this, because input/output diagrams of economies are huge messy affairs that everybody hates—except they are so useful that they can't be avoided. My design does for input/output diagrams what Excel does for spreadsheets: It makes them fully interactive and instantly modifiable! Boy, was I ever proud of myself.

A great idea it may have been, but it turned out during gameplay that it really wasn't that much fun to work with. Sure, it was clean and easy to use, and you could readily trace the entire flow of goods through your economy, but during gameplay, you really didn't want to spend much time admiring the details of your economy. There really weren't many interesting decisions you could make with your economy. Yes, there was always the fundamental "guns and butter" decision of improving your economy versus developing powerful armies, but that decision didn't require a detailed analysis of the economy. It really could have been made with a single scroll bar. Although the input/output aspect of the game was clean and easy, it just wasn't much fun to play with.

What could I have done to fix the problem? I think that my mistake here was keeping the problem one-dimensional. The entire output of the economic system was divided between just two results: population growth and military strength. Moreover, the algorithms for population growth kept the player's range of options pretty narrow. Thus, the player was faced with just an optimization problem, and not much in the way of serious trade-offs and choices. If I had broken up military strength into several components, then I could have challenged the player to carefully configure his army to make best use of his particular resource base. But I was so concerned with maintaining a clean user interface that I cleaned the most interesting problems in the game right out of existence.

Combat

The combat system I designed for **Guns & Butter** was also quite innovative. My scheme made the military power in each province a continuous variable (as opposed to the discrete military units used in conventional combat systems). In other words, the player could have 4.2 "bangs" of military

Sometimes a great idea just doesn't make the game any better.

The interface serves the game, not the other way around.

power in one province and 2.73 "bangs" of military power in another province. During each turn, the player specified just two commands to the armies in each of his provinces:

- What portion of the army should march off, leaving the remainder of the army to defend the province.

- Which province the specified portion of the army should go to.

If the player directed his mobile armies to move to an adjacent friendly province, they would reinforce the defenses there. If instead he directed his mobile armies to move into an unfriendly province, they would then attack that province.

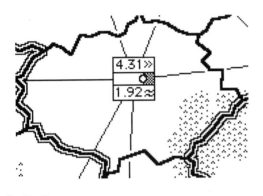

These commands were clean and simple to implement. To specify the portion of the army moving and the portion of the army staying, the player merely slid a small dot right or left in the military allocation box, which looked rather like what appears in Figure 24.8.

24.8 *Military allocation box.*

Specifying the direction of attack required nothing more than clicking on the chosen province, dragging to the destination province, and then releasing the mouse button.

When combat was initiated, the player was treated to a dramatic display showing big black arrows sweeping across the map, representing the attacks of the various armies. When combat was resolved, the attacking player, if successful, would find his mobile army now established in the capital of the newly-conquered province, and the map redrawn to show the new country borders.

The military strategy of the game was its best feature. The strategies available to the player were simple to imagine but intricate in their possible interactions. A player could attack one province from several directions, in which case the attacks would play out in sequence. The first attack might only weaken the defenders, but then a second or third might be successful. To counter this, the defender could launch an attack at the attacker's jumping-off province in the hopes that, stripped of its army, he might obtain an easy victory. Of course, the attacker could counter this by moving reserves from an uninvolved province into the jumping-off province. As you can see, the possible combinations were endless, and provided the player with some fascinating challenges.

The alliance system of the game, on the other hand, was a complete muddle. One of the players would declare an alliance against some enemy, and then try to induce other players to join the alliance. Such an alliance pooled their economic resources, making possible much more efficient and productive economies. I thought that these alliances, being so powerful, would provide lots of ups and downs in the game, as alliances would constantly shift in response to the successes and failures of the different players. In practice, it just didn't work. I put a great deal of effort into this subsystem of the game, and it included many devious and clever algorithms. For example, players could betray each other by breaking off an alliance and forming a new alliance with the enemy. When this happened, the betrayed player developed a distrust of the traitor, which would inhibit any predilections to forming a later alliance with him. In the end, however, alliances simply didn't work out as well as I had hoped. Early in the game, the alliances would work well, but as the game progressed and players betrayed each other, the overall level of distrust built up so high that nobody would trust anybody enough to form an alliance; at that point, the game was won by the biggest brute in the world.

Faces

While I was at Atari Research, I was fortunate to meet Susan Brennan, who had done impressive early work in the algorithmic representation of the human face. Susan's ideas greatly affected my thinking about the importance of the human face in all communications; I resolved to make best possible use of the human face in my future work. Unfortunately, the best I could do with the hardware and storage available was to depict static faces, simply blitting artwork onto the screen. It was nice, but not good enough. But with **Guns & Butter**, I saw an opportunity to apply some of Susan's ideas. For the diplomatic interactions, I realized that it would be useful to communicate the attitudes of the various characters toward each other. A perfect application of faces! I set to work. I started with a "base face," consisting of a set of basic features, each feature consisting of a set of points connected by lines. The first facial feature was its outline, a rough oval defined by about a dozen points.

There were ears, nose, eyebrows, lips, eyes, cheeklines, eye lines, and so forth (see Figure 24.9).

What was special about all of this was that there were no bitmaps whatsoever;

24.9 *Algorithmic faces.*

everything was drawn using lines, regions, and ovals. Now, by itself, a non-bitmapped face is, as you can see, not very good, but what made this system interesting was its algorithmic flexibility. Changing an expression on a face was a simple matter of re-mapping the face points according to a set of numbers defining the facial expressions. I was therefore able, in the highly constrained hardware environment of the times, to display eight different faces with seven different facial expressions. In 1988, when I designed this system, I was way ahead of the rest of the games industry, although the work at various research lab was much, much better. I continued to develop face depiction in later work.

The Ideas Behind the Game

The ideas behind the various game systems are best explained in the appendix I provided in the game's manual. Here is that appendix:

After-Dinner Conversation

"That was an excellent dinner, Florin. Please congratulate your chef for me."

"Thank you, Embert. He certainly did an impressive job tonight."

"That wine—it's Rhenish, isn't it?"

"I have no idea; I have never pursued oenology. YOU are the man of wealth and taste."

"So I have been called," Embert laughed. They had reached Florin's study, a simple room with two comfortable chairs, no decorations, a desk and table, and a fireplace that was not in use. Florin swept up her robe with her arm prior to seating herself.

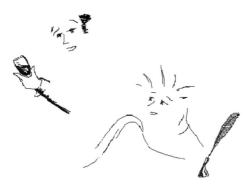

"So tell me, Florin, have you reconsidered that silly theory of yours?"

"To which silly theory do you refer, Embert? I have so many."

"I have in mind your latest perambulations on the economics of cultures."

"Oh, yes, THOSE! Yes, those ideas are particularly pretty, aren't they? I must admit, I DO take special pleasure in the cleverness inherent in those ideas."

"I will surely concede their cleverness—you have always been a dazzlingly creative thinker. But the undeniable cleverness of the conceptual structure in no way alters the simple fact that they are flat, dead, wrong. Impressively clever, yes, but still wrong."

"Well, then, Embert, you will be frustrated to learn that I have indeed reconsidered the matter (largely at your behest), and that I have further developed and even extended the conceptual structure."

"Oh, no! I should have known. Ah well, I suppose that it will supply grist for tonight's discussion. Where DID we leave off last time?"

"As I recall, we had reached an impasse over the role of technological innovation. To plunge right back into it, I reiterate: Technological innovation plays no primary role in the economic development of a culture. I know that you find that assertion incredible, but let me develop the point.

"I am not arguing that technology itself has no impact on economic development; that point should be patent. Rather, I focus more narrowly on technological innovation. Suppose, for example, that we were to inject the knowledge of, say, plows, plowshares, the tri-annual rotation system, and so forth into a Stone Age tribal culture. What good would it do them? They couldn't use the knowledge if we gave it to them. Even if some Stone Age Einstein were able to figure it out for himself, to single-handedly invent plows and harnesses for oxen and the techniques of long-row plowing, it would do no good whatever. A tribal group of a few dozen individuals couldn't afford to use the technology. Who would build the harnesses for the oxen? Who would care for the oxen? Who would make the storage bins for the grain? Who would maintain the calendar so necessary for successful agriculture? It just couldn't be done by a group that small."

"But Florin, you take your argument too far. You argue that technological innovation has no impact on economic development. What about the myriad serendipitous discoveries that have changed so many histories? What about Oersted reversing the wires, or that Phoenician fellow who discovered glass in his campfire, or Smith and penicillin? Surely you will not relegate these acts of intellectual heroism to some statistical dustbin, dismissing them as 'fluctuations?'"

"Indeed I shall, Embert. I readily concede that some discoveries came earlier than they should have, but it is equally true that some came later. The decisive factor was not the earliness or tardiness of the discovery, but the receptiveness of the culture to the discovery. To cite an easy case, the Vikings discovered the New World 500 years before the Spanish, but their culture was not receptive to the discovery, and so nothing came of it."

"But WHY were the Vikings unable to exploit the discovery? (I shall overlook for the moment the fact that it was not strictly a technological discovery.) Was it not because their culture was simply not attuned to colonization, and instead pursued other goals?"

"But is not colonization itself an expression of population? An under-populated culture does not think in terms of colonization. Only when a culture reaches a certain population density does colonization acquire any value. Had Viking culture been more populous, perhaps they WOULD have initiated colonization of the New World. And this argument brings us straight back to my central thesis about population and progress."

"Ah, yes, Florin's direct equation: progress through population. Better living through procreation. I cannot believe you would entertain a hypothesis so easily countered. What about China, a nation swimming with people for so many thousands of years? Or India, a nation equally blessed? What about the Third World nations of the twentieth century? Their exploding populations should have guaranteed sensational economic progress, but in fact the reverse happened. Moreover, the hypothesis cannot even be held to be original; Marx himself zeroed in on expanding markets as the underpinning of capitalism."

"Well, I think that we should dismiss Marx right now. I've never understood the man's theories, especially after the French got ahold of them."

They both laughed.

"But to address your historical observations: Yes, you have a good point about excessive populations. But remember that China's failure was a very near-run thing. They were making excellent progress there for a long time, and I really held my breath when they sent that expedition to East Africa in the 1400s. They came so close, but they lost it. I was really rooting for them. But the Europeans beat them to the punch."

"Yes, I really got you on that one, didn't I? Your genteel Chinese couldn't quite pull it off. They turned inward and lost their edge, overpowering with their stultifying self-assurance even the invading Mongols and Manchus. Your theories certainly fell apart there! Meanwhile, my feisty Europeans set about taking over the globe."

"Yes, you nailed me on that one. What did that cost me? A dinner?"

"A dinner AND that black obsidian orb of yours. I keep it in my meditation tower."

"Ah, yes, I miss that orb. Ah well, I deserved to lose—I was wrong. But this time I am not wrong. I am quite certain that population growth is the primary factor in economic development. I concede that there are many qualifying considerations, such as the degree to which population expansion creates a labor surplus, but I will insist that the core issue in a culture's economic progress is population growth."

"You insist, eh? Do I detect a challenge in that word? Are you leading up to something?"

A wry grin spread over Florin's face. "Actually, no, I wasn't leading, but now that you mention it, I think that I would be willing to try another experiment with you. What will be the stakes?"

"If I am right, I want that perfect feather quill that you keep by your table."

"And if I win, I want my black obsidian orb back."

"Done!"

"Very well, Embert, let us design our experiment. I shall create a planet with four billion different continents."

"Why so large?"

"Because I want a proper statistical foundation for our work. I've always felt cheated by the ways things came out on Earth. You must admit, it really was a fluke."

"A fluctuation, you mean? I thought fluctuations didn't matter."

"They shouldn't matter. Really, didn't the denouement of that experiment leave you feeling dissatisfied?"

"Not I, old friend; I can understand your frustration with an ending that you would characterize as startling, but I found a reassuring irony in it. It was so, so...[he paused, searching for the word]...so very true to form for them."

Florin laughed. "Indeed it was. Although I must say, the line I shall always remember was Hitler's."

"Which one was that? There were so many memorable ones."

"I refer to his comment upon learning that he had just triggered World War II: 'What do we do now?'"

Embert howled uproariously, slapping a thigh. "Oh, yes, yes, that was choice. That was the best." He wiped a mirthful tear from his eye. "You know, I truly outdid myself with him. I zeroed in on the essence of those people, their psychology. He certainly proved a lot of my arguments. Yes, I don't think I've ever done as well as with him. But I digress. We were discussing your new planet. You shall have four billion continents. That is acceptable to me. Why don't we begin immediately with that?"

"Capital idea, Embert." Florin leaned up from her seat and called into the next room: "Gabriel! Bring me my keyboard!"

Gabriel appeared bearing The Keyboard of Creation. With an overly theatrical flourish he placed it on the table in front of Florin. "Will there be anything else, madam?"

"No, thank you, Gabriel. You are dismissed."

"Very good, madam."

Designing a Planet

They set to work, Embert crowding over Florin's shoulder as she fired up the machine.

"Now then, good Embert, what shall our continents look like? Shall they have mountains and forests and deserts and islands and lakes and other good terrain features?"

"Yes, I do think that you should include the mountains, forests, and deserts, as we can make them the choicest locations for acquiring certain resources. Some areas will be well endowed with crucial resources, while others will be cursed with shortages of resources. That will force our protagonists to cope with one person's surplus and another person's shortage. What a lovely way to encourage lively competition!"

"Hold a moment, my warmongering friend. I agree that we do need to encourage territorial disputes by distributing natural resources unevenly, but we must not take it so far that a particularly unfortunate mortal would never be able to get his economy started. We must provide that the mortal cursed with poor terrain still have enough resource that he can get started."

"Ah, my bleeding-heart friend, why must you always soften the harsh realities? If some mortal is cheated by territorial circumstances, why would you want to reverse that verdict?"

"Because it would ultimately make the game less interesting. Do you really want the outcome to be determined by the mere luck of the random number generator? What would that prove? Don't we want to see how cultures interact economically? How could a connoisseur of war like yourself take any pleasure in the sight of a rich and powerful nation squashing a poor and weak one?"

"You are right, of course. Thank you for correcting me. Let us provide a modicum of natural resources to each mortal, augmented by a bounteous supply for those blessed with the proper terrain."

"Well and good, Embert. Now, what about other terrain features? Do we want lakes and islands?"

"I should think not, Florin. I think that we should remove all maritime factors and make this a strictly land-based environment. We have spent months debating the role of maritime factors in the social evolution on Earth, and we never did reach any agreements. It was simply too complex. The transition from a land-centered regime to a maritime regime coinciding with the fall of Byzantium..."

"No, Embert, the transition came earlier than that. Fully 54% of all trade tonnage in 1300..."

"You see, we STILL cannot agree on anything. I must say, at first I liked your ideas about water-borne traffic, and all those rivers and seas everywhere to make certain that the humans would be able to transport things at a very early stage of their social evolution. But we were never able to agree on what it all meant! We debated endlessly and fruitlessly. Let's leave maritime stuff out this time, just for simplicity's sake. Please?"

Florin laughed. "Very well, Embert, I will forego my preference for seaborne activity. Just for you. So, we won't have any lakes or islands or maritime geography. Anything else?"

"How about a few volcanoes spewing lava, and perhaps the occasional earthquake with yawning crevices swallowing people and horses, and..."

"That's another game, Embert."

"Yes, I know. Sorry."

"Very well, I think that we have the physical geography down pat. Now, how about the political geography? Shall we just go ahead with our standard provinces-cum-countries system?"

"I don't know, Florin, it seems so staid. Every planet we've done had provinces making countries. Can't we come up with something better this time?"

"Be my guest, Embert."

A long pause followed. Embert paced about, hands clasped behind his back. Several times he jerked to a stop with a sentence pregnant upon his lips, only to hesitate and swallow the thought. At length, his shoulders slumped.

"Very well, Florin. Provinces and countries."

"If it ain't broke, don't fix it. Now, what about roads connecting provinces?"

"Oh yes, I assumed that we would have some roads. But how many? Should every pair of adjacent provinces be connected by roads?"

"Surely we can do better than that. Let's say that, oh, only half of the adjacent provinces are connected by roads. The others will have no connections other than the simple adjacency."

"Ooh, ooh, we can put the forests, mountains, and deserts into those places where there aren't roads!"

"Capital idea, my man! Yes, let's! And that suggests another simple idea: Attacks down roads are easier than attacks across borders without roads."

"Why, Florin, you've never been one to take interest in the finer points of military technique. I'm pleased to see you taking some interest in the subject."

"Some of your voluminous knowledge on the subject had to rub off on me. Now then, let's see how it all adds up."

Florin had been tapping away at the keyboard as they spoke, translating their ideas into code. Her fingers flew across the keyboard in a grey blur, the lines of code rocketing across the screen. Like a concert pianist reaching the crescendo of her piece, she completed her work with a dramatic flourish and melodramatically pressed the carriage return, then looked up at Embert with a self-satisfied smile. Embert glanced down at the screen, paused, and then looked up at the ceiling. Alarmed, Florin looked back down at the screen. "What!?!?! It refused to compile?!?! What's wrong with this thing?"

"Um, perhaps, dear Florin, just perhaps you made some minor programming error."

Florin's fists clenched and she sat more erect. "You forget, friend Embert, just who I am. Remember, I am omnipotent, omniscient, and infallible." She paused, and then said slowly, evenly, and with great emphasis on each word:

"I...DON'T...MAKE...PROGRAMMING...ERRORS!"

Florin set to work examining the precise nature of the problem. After a few moment's effort, she uttered a triumphant cry and pointed at the offending item. "There, there it is! The language specification calls for this class of records to be infinitely dimensionable, but the compiler writer decided to restrict it to three dimensions and never declared the restriction. Damn that compiler writer!"

"Florin! Do you mean that literally? Do you wish to consign him to my care?"

Florin glanced up, realizing that she had lost her temper. She started to correct herself, then hesitated, thought for a moment. A wicked smile slowly crept across her face. Very softly she said, "Yes...yes...why don't you take him? Truly he deserves it. Yes." She smiled with great satisfaction for a moment. Then she sat up and muttered, "Back to work." It took a few moments to program around the flaw in the compiler. "There. All done now. Let's try it out." Once again she pressed the carriage return to engage the compiler, albeit a little less melodramatically this time. They watched with satisfaction as the program compiled properly and launched. It created the planet and built something vaguely like continents. "Oh my!" Embert exclaimed. "That's not right at all. Oh, dear me!"

"Of course, how silly of me! In my rush to correct that stupid compiler problem, I overlooked that possibility of word overflow on one of the variables. It's all that compiler writer's fault. Will you see to it that he occupies one of the less temperate climes?"

"But of course, my friend. I suppose that we shall have to dispense with this abomination of a planet?"

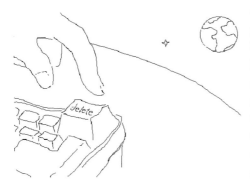

"Yes, yes, let it go." Florin pressed a key. Somewhere in space, a malformed planet exploded into atoms.

On the next try, it came out right. They looked over their new planet with satisfaction.

"Perfect! Perfect! This will serve our purposes admirably! Florin, you've done it again!"

Population Design

"Very well, what shall we do now?"

"I suggest that we consider the population structure of each country."

"There isn't much to consider, is there? Each province has a population and a certain amount of farmland. The farmland is just enough to feed the existing population using the primitive methods available at the beginning of the game."

"Let's give them a small surplus to permit some opportunity for economic growth."

"Very well, a small surplus it is. Now, we shall lump together all the populations in all the provinces to create the labor force for the entire country."

"Embert, is that wise? Shouldn't there be some sort of transportation limitation on the economy of each country? I am uncomfortable with the idea of just lumping everything together without any consideration for transportation factors."

"But Florin, do we really want our subjects to devote their energies to getting the train schedules running smoothly? You know how complex a task that can be. Why tax their little minds with large problems that do not ultimately bear on the matters we wish to explore?"

"I suppose so. It's just that I have always been so fond of trains and boats."

"Well, we can do a Transportation Planet next time."

"Very well. On with the design!"

"We were considering the population of each country. Now, how should that population grow? I suggest that population grow in proportion to food surplus."

"That makes sense. For simplicity, let us declare that one ton of food per person per year will sustain life with no population gain or loss. Less than one ton will lead to population decline, more will lead to growth."

"What should the function look like?"

"Well, we don't want it to be too harsh. Let's allow food supplies to fall to, say, about half a ton per person before we start to get severe population decline."

"Fair enough. On the other hand, though, we shouldn't be too generous with population growth. I certainly don't want anything like a linear function."

"Most certainly not. We can't have them doubling their population merely by doubling their food surplus. Let's put in a nice diminishing returns function—how about a square root?"

Food Functions

"Yes, that should work just fine. Yes, indeed. Now, how about food production? How should we have that work?"

"Well, as I see it, there are three factors that will control food production: acreage, labor supply, and machinery."

"The acreage will be fixed by the stock of provinces in the country. What about the labor supply? I suppose we'll need some sort of function that will permit diminishing returns for increasing numbers of workers per acre."

"You know, Embert, we could greatly simplify matters by freezing that variable."

"What? Freeze the number of workers per acre? That's crazy! Why would you want to do that?"

"Well, in the first place, our experience with Earth indicated some stability in that number across a wide range of circumstances. The only strong exception was the rice-growing culture of East Asia, which had very high labor densities. But the wheat and cereal growing regions exhibited a remarkable stability in the number of workers per acre."

"Toward the end there was a precipitous decline."

"Yes, that's true, but I think we can safely skip that. And think how much it would simplify the system!"

"That's certainly true. Freezing agricultural labor at one worker per acre would eliminate one degree of freedom from the situation. Yes, I'll go for that."

"Good. Now we have just one variable left to tackle: machinery."

"Which is, of course, the dominant one for the purposes of our study. What we need is a sequence of agricultural tools that are increasingly powerful."

"I would greatly prefer to see the progression be one of regular increases in the utility of the succeeding tools."

"Dear Florin, you are certainly being structured this time around. Where are all those creative flourishes you used on Earth, or the baroque creativity you expressed with Lamina? Are you losing your flair?"

"Not at all, Embert. I want a nice, simple planet this time around. We spend so much time arguing the intricacies of the matter that this time, I want something with no intricacies."

"I am hurt, Florin. Have you lost the enjoyment of our discussions?"

Florin leaned back from her keyboard and laughed. "No, no, Embert, that's not it at all. I just want to crucify you this time around, without any intricacies to obstruct my intellectual assault."

"Well and good—I shall be on my guard. To return to the subject at hand: You wanted a simple progression in the increases in utility of agricultural devices. Would a factor of two be simple enough for you?"

"Each succeeding agricultural tool is twice as productive as the previous one? Yes, that sounds straightforward enough. It appeals to my sense of order."

"What shall we call them?"

"We'll make up four or five. It doesn't matter what we call them. The locals won't know the difference."

"I would impose this constraint on the sequence: Not only should the productivity of each tool increase in a regular geometric fashion, but the production cost should also increase geometrically, but at a lower rate. Thus, as the mortals move along the technological curve, they enjoy greater efficiencies."

"Very well. I suppose that we shall want to start off with simple farm tools and move all the way up to tractors."

"OK. I'd like to see iron plows and irrigation systems, but that makes only four. Can you suggest at least one more?"

"Well, we are lacking a tool from the middle Industrial Revolution period. The farm tools and iron plow are pre-Industrial Revolution, and the irrigation and tractor are post-Industrial Revolution. That does leave a historical gap that we must fill."

"Hmm, what about a cotton gin?"

"No good—too narrow in application."

"Very well, how about a steam-driven combine? It will require use of the steam engine. We do have a problem with the steam engine. Its primary application on Earth was for transportation, railroads, and steamships, but you have eliminated transportation considerations, so our planet's occupants will simply skip the steam engine. That seems such a shame. This would correct the problem."

"I like that. We have five agricultural technologies."

"Now it's my turn. We must discuss the weapons technologies that we will make available to our mortals."

"Ah, yes, I knew this would come. Look, I am prepared, with some reluctance, to concede the necessity of conflict, weaponry, and war. But can we make it a little less bloodthirsty this time?"

"But conflict is the acid test of our theories. War is the great judge of societies, the wolf that purges the herd of its weaklings, the cleansing agent that sweeps away all that is false and weak. Look what happened when we held back the barbarians from the Roman Empire. The damn thing slowly rotted, smothering the European peoples with its putrescence. Attila was the best thing that could have happened to Europe, and you stopped him!"

"Now, I've told you before, I only intervened at the Po Valley in 452. I felt that there was still some life left in Rome, and I could not stomach those Huns tearing everything down. But I had nothing to do with the battles of Campus Mauriacus or Nedao. Those were fair fights, good examples of what you call 'the cleansing agent.' It was your Huns who were swept away, fair and square."

"Humph! I suppose so. Still, the Huns had a lot of bad breaks. Attila's death had to be one of the worst."

"Sympathy for the Huns, eh? Sorry, Embert, I don't feel it. Now let me counterattack. If war is such a purifying agent, what about the Great Plains American Indians? Their culture institutionalized perpetual warfare. At puberty, a boy became a warrior, not a man. And the result was an utterly stagnant culture. Those people wasted 10,000 years while almost every other culture on the planet made great strides forward. And don't give me that line about 'lack of resources.' The Indians of the Great Plains were surrounded by gigantic herds of bison, a food surplus that should have touched off a population explosion, but they never could get their population to increase because they were always killing each other. Even sparing the women and killing only males, they still couldn't get a population increase. The direct result of their warlike attitudes was that they were still in the Stone Age when the Europeans arrived."

"That's true, Florin, but recall what the Europeans did to them: They wiped them out! War corrected the problem!"

"I'm sorry, Embert, but you haven't convinced me. I will concede, though, that some amount of warfare is necessary. I think that we can work together within that compromise, don't you?"

"Yes, of course, my good friend. Tell you what—as a gesture of goodwill, I propose that our sequence of weapons stop short of atomic weaponry. No nuclear weapons, ICBMs, ABMs, or any of that good stuff. Let's stop with tanks. I can have enough fun with them. Fair enough?"

"A noble compromise! Done!"

"So we shall have tanks at the top of our sequence and, what, um, swords at the bottom?"

"If you don't mind, Embert, I would prefer not to participate in this part of the design. Feel free to devise any reasonable sequence you fancy."

Embert laughed. "Very well, I shall do so. Let's see, I suppose that we should follow up swords with firearms. What firearms do I want? Arquebuses, muskets, culverins, bombards, field cannons, howitzers—there are so many from which to choose."

"Please don't drag this process out."

"Very well, I shall keep it simple. I shall follow swords with muskets, rifles, cannons, and lastly, tanks. That's five. Good enough?"

"Fine. Now we must move on to what is perhaps the most difficult task we face: the definition of all the commodities used in the economy and the relationships between them."

"I was afraid of this one, Florin. I presume that you want to keep things simple."

"Yes, I think we should strive for the simplest possible structure. Rich enough to demonstrate the principles, but not so messy as to dominate the economic interactions."

"We have agreed on the end products, agricultural tools and weapons. Now, should we work up from raw materials or down from the end products?"

Transcriber's note: There followed a tedious and extended discussion of the merits of nearly 100 different raw materials and intermediate products and their natural interrelationships. The two interlocutors went to great lengths to examine every one of the many millions of mathematically possible combinations. After much trial and error, a coherent set was finally obtained, but not before the patience of the transcriber was exhausted. The transcription resumes at the agreement.

NOTE

"So let's go over it one more time, shall we?"

"Please, Florin, let's!"

"For raw materials, we have lumber, coal, sulfur, iron ore, light metals, heavy metals, petroleum, and nitrates. Agreed?"

"Agreed. My list of intermediate materials now includes charcoal, pig iron, iron, low-grade steel, high-grade steel, gunpowder, explosives, and high explosives. That's still eight, yes?"

"Unless the complexity of this discussion has addled my arithmetic powers as badly as it has yours. What does our list show for machinery?"

"I have steam engine, wire, pipe, electrical devices, ball bearings, diesel engines, and instruments. How many is that?"

"It's only seven, but we can live with it. I just can't accept iron parts as a prerequisite for anything else."

"OK, OK. I think we have it. You have the input/output diagram for it?"

"Right here."

"I must tell you, Florin, I am not at all comfortable with this structure. I'm not suggesting that we should go back over it one more time; I think that we have driven this one into the ground. My fear is that the thing may still have holes in its structure, holes that we will not be able to divine."

"Embert, if I had intended to make flawless economic systems, I would have made them that way. Part of the fun of all this is seeing how it works out, yes?"

"I suppose so. So now let us turn to another bedeviling issue: the mechanics of production. Land, labor, and capital. How shall we balance these factors this time around? I have a truly novel suggestion: Let us dispense entirely with capital in all its forms."

"WHAT!?! Embert, is this another one of your jokes, like that planet with the non-commutative sexual relationships? I felt so sorry for those poor people..."

"Hey, what's the point of creating all those worlds if you can't engage in a bit of levity?"

"Indeed! What about all those particles you kept foisting on the earth physicists?" Florin chortled. "You got them started with the simple proton-electron-neutron triangle, but then came the mesons, baryons, and leptons, and then the neutrinos, and then when they started getting close, you really went wild. Quarks! Those were great! How did you ever think up anything so funny?"

"I don't know what got into me. I considered the whole thing an intellectual challenge, but the little buggers kept going to higher and higher energies, and I had to keep making up new and better schemes to keep them at bay. Once the joke got started, I couldn't stop it—you can imagine what their reaction would have been had they discovered the truth. I'm just glad that they were so good at translating laboratory results into weaponry so quickly. It sure got me off the hook."

"Yes it did. Imagine—a blue quark bomb. Oh, well."

"Well, this time, I am not joking. After all, what is capital but the accumulation of the product of labor? And do not all capital assets depreciate?"

"Yes, but many of the largest capital assets depreciate very slowly indeed."

"HOW slowly, Florin? How long does it take the typical capital asset to depreciate?"

"Well, that depends on the capital asset in question. Some assets depreciate in years, while others take decades."

"There IS a pattern, though. In general, capital assets do not last longer than the average lifetime of the builders. After all, who wants to expend precious resources creating an asset whose returns will not be fully realized in one's own lifetime?"

"There are many cases of societies building capital assets whose lifetime greatly exceeded the life of an individual. The Pyramids, the gothic cathedrals, the great bridges and dams—there are thousands of counterexamples to shatter your claim."

"But every one of those counterexamples was a PUBLIC work, undertaken not for private profit but rather for the public good. Moreover, every one represented an investment too large to be undertaken by private concerns. If we restrict our considerations to business activities undertaken for profit, I think that you will find that my generalization holds water."

"I suppose so. But what is its significance?"

"Just this: If we use a long enough time scale in monitoring economic activity, EVERYTHING depreciates! If we use as a basic unit of time the life span of an individual, then all capital assets will depreciate away in a single unit of time. And that means that they can be ignored!"

"I am not willing to completely dispense with capital; its role in economic development is absolutely undeniable. And how do you explain the accumulation of wealth that is always associated with economic progress?"

"I do not propose the total elimination of capital from the economy, only its elimination from our direct involvement. In effect, each generation creates its own capital. In any real system, the creation and depreciation of capital is an ongoing process. At any given moment, slightly more capital is being created than depreciated, and so the net stock of capital grows. What I am proposing is the artifice of gathering all the creation for a single generation into a single instant at the beginning of that generation, and also gathering all the depreciation for a single generation into a single instant at the end of the generation. This vastly simplifies the behavior of the system from our point of view, does it not?"

"I must admit, it is a brilliant way of simplifying an otherwise knotty problem. I will readily concede that the handling of capital assets is a truly infernal problem. Your scheme does banish that problem. But I must insist that you recognize this as a gross simplification."

"Oh, yes, I will gladly concede that point. A simplification, yes; but one whose clarifying effects make it worth the sacrifice."

"Very well, I accept your proposal. We shall have no capital assets in this planet. The workers build the factory in their youth, use it to make product in their maturity, and decommission it as they retire."

"Very well, we have eliminated capital from our considerations. Now, what about land and labor?"

"We have already established the basic land factors: farmland, forest for lumber, mountains and deserts for other raw materials. I think we are in good shape there. All that remains is labor."

"You know, Embert, I begin to appreciate the novelty of your system. An economic structure dominated by labor. Do you think we should fetch Karl Marx to look in on this once it is complete? He would surely think that he had died and gone to heaven!"

"Please, don't reward my creativity with exposure to that long-winded bore! Don't you recall how we fought over who would be stuck with him?"

"OK, OK, we'll leave Karl out of this. Now, back to labor. How shall we handle it?"

Productivity Functions

"I deem it absolutely essential that we provide a solid basis for economies of scale. Productivity MUST increase as an exponential function of labor."

"Agreed. But there are two issues we must tackle. First, should the proportionality constant in the productivity function be the same for all industries, and second, should the exponent be the same for all industries?"

"Well, let's figure it out. If we use the same proportionality constant for all industries, that implies that workers in different industries would be equally productive. If it takes five workers to produce 1000 tons of coal, then it would take five workers to produce 1000 tons of, say, electrical instruments. That doesn't make much sense, does it?"

"Obviously not."

"So our proportionality constants must differ across industries. I further believe that we must have different exponents. Old technologies, simpler and more labor-intensive, would enjoy smaller economies of scale, expressed mathematically in a lower exponent in the productivity function. Newer and more complex technologies would, I presume, require more in the way of capital and less labor, permitting them to enjoy larger economies of scale, and hence we would want to use larger exponents."

"But aren't you going too far? After all, who will be able to appreciate such subtleties? Do you really think that the mortals will be able to figure out the differences between industries with differing proportionality constants and exponents?"

"Probably not. But even if they don't understand it, the system must still work. The more advanced industries must have smaller proportionality constants and larger exponents so that they are less efficient at smaller scales and more efficient at larger scales. This is an essential component of technological progress. Without it, we would have fifteenth century peasants building digital watches. In effect, my economies of scale theories link with your population theories to ensure that technological progress parallels population increase."

"Embert, you do seem to have quite an infatuation with economies of scale. Is this your latest interest?"

"Yes, I have been quite taken by the notion of late. I suppose that what got me started on this was the realization that economies of scale are nothing more than an operational expression of the essence of toolness. Bigger and better tools cost more but are more efficient. That's just a rephrasing of the notion of economies of scale. It's really quite fascinating."

Technology Transitions

"Florin, I would now like to turn to the difficult problem of technology transitions. It is vital that the mortals move through the technological sequence that we have created in a regular and orderly fashion. I am concerned that this might not happen."

"Come now, Embert, it should be easy. Each technology in the sequence is twice as efficient as its predecessor. That should be motivation enough to guarantee an advance up the ladder."

"Actually, we may have to worry that the motivation might be too much. What if an iron plow is twice as productive as farm tools, and costs only 50% more? Surely our subjects would move immediately to the iron plow."

"But Embert, that is precisely our intention!"

"Yes, but we don't want it to happen too soon. If we fail to adjust the equations properly, we might well see sixteenth century peasants riding tractors."

"I see your point. How can we balance the equations?"

"I believe that we need to use exponential functions to express the economies of scale. To make advanced technologies more productive at the high end of the production scale, we need to give them larger exponents. And to hold their value down at the low end of the production scale, we need to give them small multiplicative coefficients. The trick then will be to balance the system of equations to guarantee that the entire set of equations (one for each technology) fits together properly. I think that it all turns on selecting a good set of crossover points."

"Well, what if we initialize the situation such that the mortals start halfway up the scale with the lowest agricultural technology. That way, they will only need to double output to saturate that technology, and when they make the transition to the next technology, it will automatically be halfway toward saturation (because it is exactly twice as productive)."

"This implies that crossover points will be spaced at neat intervals of factors of two in output. I like that. The only remaining issue is to set the boundary conditions. Just how many workers should it take to handle all this?"

"The boundary condition is established by our initial population and our desired growth rate. If they put all their labor into building agricultural tools at the lowest level, then the labor supply should be just large enough to create enough food to achieve, say, 30% growth."

"Fair enough. This still requires me to balance the system of equations. Ugh! I'd better get cracking."

Military Factors

"You know, Florin, we have been avoiding the all-important issue of military operations. I realize that you find the matter distasteful, but it is incumbent upon us to address it now."

Florin sighed. "Yes, I know, Embert. Let's get it over with now. How do you want to handle this?"

"Well, we have already figured out the source of military power in production. The only tasks are the actual application of military power. First off is the problem of getting the weapons from the factories to the field."

"I would very much like to minimize this element of the system. Can't we just make it happen automatically?"

"Florin, you can do anything you want. Sure, we can make it automatic. How, though, can we ensure that the automatic process makes sense?"

"What if weapons are distributed each turn in proportion to the previous turn's concentration? If you had concentrated forces in one province on turn X, then on turn X+1, weapons will be sent to that province."

"I like it! Yes, that is very clean. OK, so now we turn to problem of combat results computation. Province A attacks Province B; how do we calculate the winner?"

"You do this, Embert."

"Very well, here goes: We don't want to encourage too much attacking, so let's put in some attack penalties. First off, I suggest that the attacker automatically lose 10 firepower points, and the defender fights with an extra bonus of 10 firepower points. This will discourage attacks with small forces. I hate it when somebody wins a victory with trivial forces. I want to see Combat! Battle! Not some petty skirmish leading to conquest. OK so far?"

"I would prefer not to have such automatic bonuses—they won't make sense to the locals. Your proposal presumes a standard calculation of the ratio of attack strength to defense strength. What if instead we use the difference between the two rather than the ratio? That would automatically solve the problem of minimum attack strength requirements."

"Hmm, you make a good point. I suggest that we defer to a Higher Authority on this matter."

"Very well, Embert; you do the honors. I take my normal position."

Embert reached into the folds of his gown and brought out an ancient coin. He flicked it high up into the air with his thumb. Both parties watched it spin higher and higher, just missing the vaulted ceiling, and arc down. Embert's eyes glanced down to catch Florin's attention; he grinned impishly before looking up again to follow the coin as it fell into his extended palm. He slapped it down hard onto the back of his hand.

Then he slowly raised the hand, with coin still covered by the other hand, up to his face. Casting a facetiously suspicious glance at Florin, he raised one finger of the covering hand ever so slightly and peered underneath it for a few long seconds. Then he looked up at Florin, took a deep breath, and announced: "Heads—I win!"

"Very well, Embert: strength ratios with additive penalties and bonuses."

"Next, I think we should have a strong terrain penalty. Let's say that the attacker is quartered attacking across terrain."

"What do you count as terrain?"

"Anything that isn't a road. Attacking down a road, you fight with normal strength, but anywhere else, your strength is quartered. That should force some sense of strategic maneuver onto our subjects."

"Anything else?"

"Hmm...oh, yes, we need a provision for the effects of the battle on the civilians. After all, they are the ones who pay the highest price. I suggest that we reduce the population of the attacked province by the amount of military power that the attacker brought to bear on the province. That way, a big conquest will wipe out the population and dramatically reduce the value of the province. Scorched earth, so to speak."

"Leave it to you, Embert, to remember these fine points."

"Ah, but I am done now!"

Economic Unions

"Good! Now we have one last problem to address, and we are done. How are we going to prevent runaway growth in the eight-nation continents?"

"I don't see the problem."

"Consider the question, at what point does one nation obtain an unshakeable lead over all the others?"

"That wouldn't happen until that nation has 51% of the total resources on the continent."

"No, it would happen much earlier. Remember, we have large economies of scale on this planet."

"I still don't follow you. What do economies of scale have to do with this?"

"Economies of scale in production imply that a 2:1 superiority in population translates into a greater-than-2:1 superiority in production. Hence a nation with 51% of the total population will have much more production than all of the other nations combined. In fact, given the strong economies of scale we have set up for this planet, a nation with only 25% of the total population could still produce more than all the other nations combined!"

"How could that possibly happen?"

"Here, I'll walk you through the numbers. Suppose that one nation has 25% of the total population and the other seven have 11% each. Suppose further that all other factors are equal and that the economies of scale work out to a cubic power in this case. Thus, the leading nation, with a population superiority of 2:1, ends up with a production superiority of 8:1. If all of the smaller nations throw all their production against the largest nation, the combined production ratio is 8:7 in favor of the larger nation. He's got a lock on victory with only 25% of the population base!"

"Mon dieu!" Embert stood stunned and speechless for a moment. "What are we going to do?"

"It's obvious that we must somehow permit smaller nations to engage in some form of economic cooperation that enables them to enjoy the benefits of economies of scale."

"Hold it right there, Florin! Are you about to drag me into some sort of trade scheme again?"

"Well, that was not my intention, but I will point out that trade would solve our problems handily."

"No good, Florin. We've been through this once before, with Planet Hubert. Don't you remember what a disaster that was?"

"But you must admit that trade worked well on Earth."

"That was different. On Earth, we decentralized trade. It was handled by millions of earthlings in millions of tiny transactions. It became a statistical function out of the direct control of the policymakers. It worked well that way. In fact, it worked so well that any attempt on the part of the policymakers to influence the trade process only garbled the process. It was funny, I admit, watching the poor fools struggling with a phenomenon that was out of their intellectual grasp. They'd twist the trade policy one way, and the currency valuations would jerk around to correct the problem, and then they'd try to stabilize the currency, and round and round they went, never getting on top of it. Yes, it was funny. But there was a clear message: Trade cannot be handled by direct control. It's too intricate trying to match up two economies by hand. The matching must be done statistically."

"But wouldn't it be possible to create some sort of statistical arrangement for trade?"

"That's exactly what we tried to do with Hubert. Remember how that came out? We used that central store concept of yours to even out fluctuations in prices and supplies, and so the Hubertans spent all their energies interacting with the damned store! They bought and sold wildly and never noticed each other. And when we started twisting the numbers away from the store, they were unable to form a decent economy. Remember, a stable economy requires a perfect marketplace, and the half-dozen actors we placed on Hubert were insufficient to create a perfect marketplace. We needed a hundred different countries to make that work."

"But, Embert, we NEED trade. Without it, the biggest player will have a lock on victory."

"We need something, I agree, but trade won't work unless there are many countries to assure stable supplies of and demand for every commodity. Without the smoothing effects arising from large numbers of countries, trade breaks down. Admit it, Florin, trade is a statistical concept that works only in large decentralized systems. And such systems are outside the range of the tightly controlled experimental system we are setting up here."

"But do you have any alternative?"

Embert paused. He had been on a roll in his condemnation of trade. Now he had to change gears and was momentarily off balance. He hummed and hawed for a moment. "What if we allow them to directly merge their economies?"

"What?!?! Simply merge their economies, just like that?"

"Well, yes, and why not? We're working at such a large scale here that it seems appropriate to me. After all, are not close trade relationships extended over a long time a form of economic integration?"

"Integration falls well short of union."

"True, but as a simplifying model, union expresses the concept, doesn't it?"

"Let me hear a proposal."

"OK, here goes. We allow nations to merge their economies for single turns. While merged, all their assets are pooled. They enjoy the benefits of economies of scale. They distribute the fruits of their labors, both military and agricultural, in proportion to the labor supply they brought to the pool. At the end of the turn, the union is dissolved."

"Who makes the economic decisions for the union?"

"Its sponsor, the person who declared the union. Anybody who joins a union surrenders economic sovereignty to the leader."

"Why should anybody do that?"

"First, what's the joy in figuring all those economic balances? Second, joining a union makes you stronger than you would be alone. It's worth it."

"It's a radical idea. We've never tried anything like this before."

"Is that any reason not to try now? After all, it's just an experiment, a game. Besides, consider the interesting advantages that accrue from this. Think of all the interesting diplomatic interactions that arise from this system. Consider how quickly a player could rise or fall with the fortunes of his unions. Without unions, the planetary situation focuses on economics and military factors. The unions make it a triangular interaction between economic, military, and diplomatic factors. Now that's interesting, don't you agree?"

"You've convinced me. Let's do it!"

"Done!"

And they did it.

No matter
what the
schedule
says, give
the game
enough time
to get it
right.

Results

Guns & Butter was a collection of clever, occasionally brilliant ideas crammed together with insufficient integration. The input/output charts of the economy should have shown the player the intricacies of a working economy in a way that was easy and fun. The facial displays were a huge technological leap forward. And the diplomatic system could have made the game especially interesting. But these good ideas did not perform well together, and the result was the worst game I ever designed. Sadly, this could have been one of my best games. I attribute my failure to a single blunder: my failure to properly polish the game.

I was in too much of a hurry to get the game done quickly; I should have ignored the deadline and insisted on getting it perfect before I released it. There was a reason for my imprudent haste: I had been approached by another publisher asking me to build an environmental game, but they had a tight deadline imposed by licensing considerations. In order to be certain of completing the environmental game in time to meet their deadline, I had to rush **Guns & Butter**. This was stupid, short-term thinking on my part. With two or three months of careful playtesting and polishing, I could have pulled the pieces together and made the whole system sing in harmony. Instead, to save three months of time, I threw away the year of work I had put into **Guns & Butter**. Not too swift, eh? I paid the price for my stupidity: The game bombed and I never earned a penny of royalties. The advance was all I got from the project.

balance of
the planet

In early 1989, I was approached by Joe Miller of Epyx, asking if I was interested in working on a license they had just secured. The project was a movie entitled *Voice of the Planet*, which was about environmentalism and was intended for release in conjunction with Earth Day 1990. Would I be interested in doing an environmental game?

The proposal struck my fancy. Although I was wary of licensed games, the topic here seemed worthy. I had always felt that **Energy Czar** simply didn't capture the richness and complexity of problems balancing environmental problems with economic issues. It was time to go back and get it right. Besides, my wariness of licensed games was outweighed by the trust I had in Joe; whatever happened, I knew that he would make things right in the end. So I told him that I would put some time into working out a preliminary design.

I already had my vision for the game: the complexity of environmental issues and their entwinement with each other and with economic issues. I wanted to demonstrate that everything is connected, that simplistic approaches always fail. This required a huge system of factors all connected by equations. My central design problem would be coming up with a clean way to pile all the factors into the game and keep the equations organized. Any large system of equations is intrinsically unstable—it takes just one out-of-range value to send the system crashing into psychotic behavior: trillions of fatalities from air pollution, say, or hydroelectric dams generating more energy than the sun, or some other such nonsense. How could I possibly design a system that was likely to remain stable with so much complexity?

Apple had recently released **HyperCard**, its beautiful hypertext-programming-drawing system that offered all sorts of wonderful possibilities. It was quite the rage in the Macintosh community, and although it was quite inadequate for my needs, the concept of hyperlinks seemed an appropriate model for use with environmental problems. After all, environmental topics are all intricately linked in myriad ways—what better model than hyperlinks could I use?

So I resolved to build something rather like a hypertext system, but first I wanted to list the elements that would go into this system. What would each page in my hypertext system contain? The first few dozen came easily, but as the list grew longer, problems emerged. There were problems of overlap: Should sulfur dioxide emissions be subsumed under air pollution or should they stand alone?

Values

By far the most difficult question, though, concerned the problem of values. It was easy to build equations for air pollution deaths and such, but in the end, how important were those deaths compared to the economic benefits of the factories that create the air pollution? In effect, I had to put a price on human life, something that makes all of us queasy. Environmental problems are difficult precisely because they force us to confront such uncomfortable issues. My design problem was to integrate values into the design without creating something that would be dismissed as narrow-minded.

I spent too much time trying to figure out how to be politic in this delicate matter; it seemed that, no matter how I approached the problem, somebody would be able to accuse me, with some justification, of bias.

There *is* no objective, balanced approach to the myriad complexities of environmental issues; ultimately, the core issues are matters of personal values.

It's funny how some of the toughest problems in game design can have ridiculously simple solutions. The challenge is to step far enough back from the problem to be able to see the simple solution. In this case, my problem was embarrassingly easy to solve: I need merely throw the problem right back into the user's face. In effect, I needed to say to the user, "If you have an opinion, put your numbers where your mouth is. *You* declare the values to be applied in the simulation!"

This simple insight dramatically changed the design and catapulted it into a higher level of simulation. It freed me of the responsibility to be absolutely unbiased, although there remained an expectation of being fair. Instead of providing the user with unchallengeable numbers, I needed only provide a range of reasonable numbers from which to choose.

It also changed the simulation in a more profound and more exciting manner. Instead of presenting the simulation itself as the truth, I was presenting it as just that: a simulation. This new design concept challenged the user to understand it as a simulation, not as truth handed down from the almighty computer. It also brought the user into the simulation, thereby providing more direct and intimate interaction between user and computer. In a larger sense, this design innovation allowed me to present my thinking on a deeper level. Instead of coddling the user with false assurances that the simulation was correct, I was making it clear to him that much of what we believe is based on the assumptions behind our thinking.

Another unforeseen benefit of this approach was that it applied broadly, not just to values, but to judgments about scientific truth itself. Who is to say precisely how dangerous a nuclear power plant is? There are plenty of studies that give us an inkling of the answer, but no definitive answer can be found. Why then, could not a user declare any reasonable value for this supposedly objective truth?

Implementing a Value System

There remained the problem of designing some system that would permit the user to assign numeric values to the components of the simulation while preventing psychotic behavior in the system. It's one thing to design a balanced system of equations when the coefficients are all stable—but preserving balance when the user can change the coefficients seemed beyond the realm of possibility.

An even more serious implementation problem loomed beyond this one: How was I to design a system of equations that would be accessible to the average user? I had handled games with complex internal systems of equations, but a system that the average user could handle? That seemed completely out of the question.

The design problem clearly called for linear equations of this form:

Result = Adjustable Coefficient×Input Factor

There might also be a need for additive equations of this form:

Result = Input #1 + Input #2 + Input #3

Such equations permitted the user to adjust the single coefficient to increase or decrease the severity of the phenomenon.

The interesting design problem here is, how did I decide which variables to include and which to reject? A variety of factors affected my decision. Obviously, I needed some form of point system reflecting what might constitute success or failure; this required variables for various forms of points. I also needed to include obvious factors such as nuclear power, coal power, and various forms of pollution. Ultimately, however, the choice of variables to include rested on my familiarity with the issues underlying environmental problems. There was no cook-book method that I can offer you; I simply had to apply my judgment based on my expertise. As it happens, I spent several years working on environmental policy issues during the 1970s, so I required little more than a few books' worth of reading to bring my expertise up to date. Had I lacked such expertise, I would have been reluctant to attempt the design.

Few game topics are closely tied to reality; by placing games in a fantasy environment, designers seldom need to worry about the constraints of reality. There are plenty of exceptions, of course, flight simulators being the most obvious. As the industry advances, game designers will be required to integrate more real-world knowledge into their work. This will in turn make it ever more important that designers bring some real-world expertise into their work. Content experts are invaluable, but they're not enough; the knowledge they offer must be integrated into the overall design, and that integration process can take place only inside the designer's mind. Thus, content experts must be treated as teachers, not direct contributors.

73

LESSON

Know your topic inside and out.

I created the following list of 154 variables for my simulation:

AcidRain	DeathPoints	HeavyMetalDeaths
AveEnergyPrice	DebtForNature	HeavyMetalPoints
BasicResearch	Desertification	HeavyMetalPrice
BeefProduction	DrinkingWater	HeavyMetalSupply
BeefTax	EnergyConservation	HeavyMetalTax
BiodiversityPoints	EnergyDemand	HeavyMetalUse
BioResearch	FallPoints	Housing
Biotechnology	FallsFromRoofs	IndustrialInput
BirthRate	FamilyPlanning	IndustrialOutput
CarbonDioxide	FarmLand	InundationPoints
CFCProduction	FertilizerTax	LakeAcidity
CFCTax	FertilizerUse	LakeHabitats
CoalPrice	FloodDeathPoints	LakeLifePoints
CoalResearch	FloodDeaths	LandAbuse
CoalSupply	FoodSupply	LandAbusePoints
CoalTax	ForestClearing	LifePoints
CoalTechnology	ForestHabitats	Logging
CoalUse	ForestLand	LoggingTax
ComputerGamesPts	ForestLifePoints	LungDiseaseDeaths
ConsumerGoods	FuelwoodUse	LungDiseasePts
Crops	Garbage	MarineLife
CropStrains	GlobalGenePool	MarineLifePoints
CropTechnology	GlobalTemperature	MaterialsDemand
CropYields	Grasslands	Medicines
Dam	GrossGlobalProduct	Methane
DamPrice	GroundwaterSupply	NaturalGasPrice
DamUse	GroundwaterUse	NaturalGasSupply

NaturalGasTax	Price	StratosphericCFC
NaturalGasUse	PropertyDamage	StripMining
NetEnergy	QualityOfLife	Subsidy
NitrousDioxide	QualityPoints	SulfurDioxide
NonrenewEnergy	Radiation	Sustainability
NorthernLifestyle	RadiationCancer	SustainabilityPts
NuclearAccidents	RadiationPoints	Tax
NuclearPrice	RadWaste	Total
NuclearResearch	RadWastePoints	TotalCoalUse
NuclearSupply	RecycledAluminum	TotalNatGasUse
NuclearTax	RecycledPaper	TotalNuclearUse
NuclearTechnology	RecyclingCenter	TotalOilUse
NuclearUse	RenewableEnergy	TotHeavyMetUse
OilPrice	ReservoirCapacity	TroposphericCFCs
OilResearch	RiparianHabitats	UV
OilSpills	SeaLevel	WaterPollution
OilSupply	SeaFood	WaterSupply
OilTax	SkinCancerDeaths	WoodStove
OilTechnology	SkinCancerPoints	
OilUse	SoilErosion	
Overgrazing	SolarEnergy	
Ozone	SolarEnergyPrice	
PesticideDeathPts	SolarEnergyUse	
PesticideDeaths	SolarResearch	
PesticideTax	SolarTechnology	
PesticideUse	SouthernLifestyle	
Phytoplankton	Starvation	
Population	StarvationPoints	

It's a long list, isn't it? You can see why I was so worried about the simulation getting out of control. My next task was to set up a huge dependencies chart showing with simple lines and arrows what other variables were affected by each variable. This chart covered quite a few pages; it took me a while to find clean breaks in the chart so that it could cover many pages without too many arrows departing from each page. Once I had that chart, the only task was to write out one equation for each arrow.

Here's an example: One of my variables was Nuclear Accidents. This was presented to the user with the display shown in Figure 25.1.

25.1 *Nuclear accidents.*

Note that there are two causal factors in this display: Nuclear Technology and Nuclear Use. The former represents the results of subsidized research that, presumably, lessens the dangers presented by these plants. The latter represents the actual number of nuclear power plants in existence. The formula display for this variable, accessible to the user, looks like what appears in Figure 25.2.

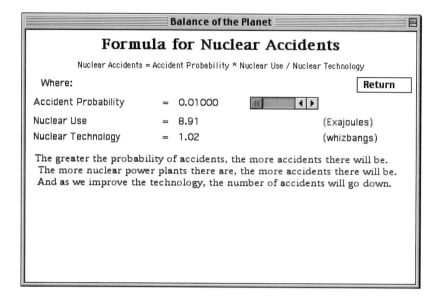

25.2 *Nuclear accidents formula.*

Note how clearly this presents the formula used in the simulation and the three values that go into the formula. It also explains how the formula works. One of the secrets behind the functioning of this game lies in that scroll bar. I pre-programmed it with upper and lower limits that ensured that the simulation would remain within reasonable bounds. In other words, the user was free to alter the values, but only within limits that I felt were reasonable. This restriction was crucial to keeping the entire simulation balanced.

In practice, we found that there were four ways of playing the simulation. The first was simply surfing the web of causality. With 156 different screens linked together, many people were happy just to browse through all the connections. This in itself made an important point about how deeply intertwined environmental and economic issues are. Once users had satisfied their immediate curiosity, they settled down to playing the game, using the coefficients that I had built into the game.

74

Accept
full moral
responsibility
for the
games you
design.

The Politics of the Game

At this point, I must point out that here is where I got to ply
my own political agenda. One cannot develop expertise in a
field without developing some opinions, and I'm no exception. While I wanted to be fair to all sides, I had to plunk
down some values for the coefficients, and those values represented my own opinions about environmental problems.
Although my own values are obvious in this game, the fact
is that *every* game we produce reflects the values of the
designer. The physicist who designs a hydrogen bomb can't
shuck off responsibility by claiming that he was only following orders; there is an undeniable element of personal
approbation required to work on any project. The same thing
goes with game designers: The games that you design reveal
your values. You simply can't avoid it, so you'd better learn to
live with it and take responsibility for your actions.

Higher Levels of Play

The great majority of players were happy to play the game
with my own value system; I encouraged them to try higher
levels of participation and some took me up on that offer.
The next higher level of play involved the concept of political bias. I offered the player several other sets of values
representing certain common points of view, such as
Environmentalist, Oil Company, Pro-Nuclear, and so forth.
Players who tried out these value sets quickly discovered
that the only way to win was to follow the kind of policies
embraced by proponents of each bias. For example, in the
Pro-Nuclear bias, nuclear power plants are safe, clean, and
cheap; building lots of nuclear power plants generates lots
of cheap energy that propels the world economy to new

heights. By contrast, other forms of energy are polluting or dangerous; using these energy forms will lead to much suffering the world over.

The highest level of play invited the player to alter the coefficients in the model. This provided the greatest challenge and required the deepest thought. For example, I am particularly proud of the two formulae shown in Figure 25.3.

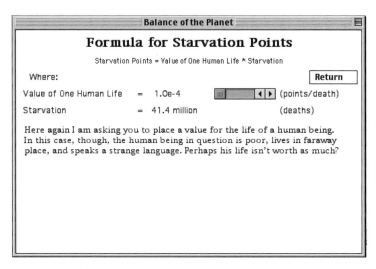

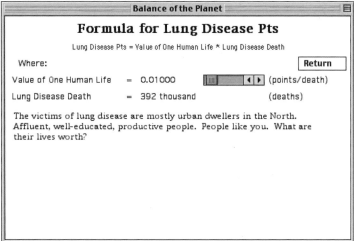

25.3   *Formulas for starvation and lung disease points.*

Forcing the player to explicitly assign point values for human life puts a lot of stress on people, stress that most people avoid by refusing to think about it. This game shoved the problem right into their faces. It turns out that, if you assign equal values to both forms of death, you can never win the game, because the number of people who die from starvation each year is overwhelming.

Balancing the Equations

Balancing large mathematical systems is one of the killer problems in game design. Every game has plenty of interacting subsystems; all too often some unforeseen interplay between two such subsystems can result in psychotic behavior from the system as a whole.

Let's use an imaginary first-person shooter as an example. Suppose that this shooter offers the player a reward for killing Goony-Woonies by equipping each Goony-Woony with one ammo clip, which the player gains by stripping each dead Goony-Woony. Of course, Goony-Woonies are dangerous critters; the player sustains an average of two health points worth of damage every time he fights a Goony-Woony. Fangybirds, by contrast, can be killed only by shooting them with a gun. They carry medicine packets worth five health points. If the cost of shooting down a Fangybird is less than one ammo clip, then the player has a simple strategy: Kill a Goony-Woony, use the clip obtained to shoot down a Fangybird, use the medicine from the Fangybird to heal the injuries inflicted by the Goony-Woony, and you're ahead in both ammo and health.

No game designer would make so glaring a blunder—but that's only because there are only two monsters here to worry about. What if there were a hundred different monsters in the game? How can the designer get such a large system operating with any confidence that it won't have some hidden combination that reduces the game to nonsense?

75

This is no hypothetical problem. The first edition of **Civilization** suffered from precisely this strategy. Somebody discovered a "lock on victory" in the form of a simple strategy, called "The Mongol Strategy," that always won the game. That strategy took advantage of a slight weakness in the balancing of the system of equations at work in the innards of the game. Now, Sid Meier is one of the great masters of complex simulation design; if this problem could nip Sid, you can be sure that it will masticate a mere mortal like you.

Herewith, then, some lessons for balancing large systems.

Eschew sensitive functions like exponentials or hyperbolics.

NOTE

Warning! The following material is highly mathematical! If you don't care for mathematics, skip this section!

Consider the following formula:

Apples = Oranges^2

If the value of Oranges increases by 1%, the value of Apples will increase by 2%. To appreciate the danger imposed by such a formula, think in terms of "excursions." Imagine that your system has settled down to a nice stable configuration, and then one component, say Oranges, wiggles by 1%. That triggers an excursion. At its first step, the excursion is only 1% in magnitude, but on the second step, it has doubled in size. If you have many more of these sensitive functions in your system, the excursion can rapidly grow to outrageous levels.

Dampen excursions with shock-absorbing functions.

This doesn't mean that all of the functions in your system must be lily-livered wimps. You can have volatile functions; you just have to watch them carefully, as they will surely be the source of most of your headaches.

Just as exponentials magnify excursions, inverse exponentials dampen excursions. The simplest, safest shock absorber you can add to your system is a square root function. Let's apply the idea with a modification of our previous example:

Apples = Oranges$^{1/2}$

For this formula, a 1% excursion in Oranges yields a 0.5% excursion in Apples. If your system is hyperactive, jumping around wildly, toss a few square roots in there to calm it down. If you need lots of dampening, use a log function— I guarantee that a log function will take the life out of the most rambunctious system. Just be sparing in its use; the log function is a dinosaur-strength tranquilizer for any system of equations.

Buffer divisors with additive elements.

Everybody knows that it's dangerous to permit the possibility of division by zero:

Apples = Oranges÷Pears

If the value of Pears just happens to reach zero, you get a divide by zero error and your program blows sky high. Most people simply avoid division in any case where the divisor could conceivably equal zero. But there is a way to use division without risking catastrophe. Just add a buffer term to the divisor, like so:

Apples = Oranges÷(Pears + 1)

If you are absolutely certain that the value of Pears can never go below zero, then this modification will protect you from divide-by-zero blues.

You don't need to use lots of snazzy functions. Sure, you can impress your boss with that clever Gaussian function or a Legendre polynomial, but remember: You've got to eat everything you put on your plate. If you stuff some high-falutin' function into your system of equations, you'll have to tune and balance it later. Tuning and balancing requires a feel for the way that functions behave—do you have a feel for Legendre polynomials? You'd be surprised just how much richness you can get out of the four basic arithmetic operators (addition, subtraction, multiplication, and division). If you work with them long enough, you'll develop a feel for how they work together, and you'll find it easy to tune a misbehaving system of equations until it purrs. Top them up with squares to punch up some factors and square roots to tone down others, and you can handle just about anything. Shift a factor with addition or subtraction; scale it with multiplication or division. Combine shifting and scaling in differing degrees to get just about any effect you want.

Some designers like to set up functions like this:

```
IF (x > 23)
        Y = A1 * x + B1
ELSE
        Y = A2 * x + B2
```

This is very dangerous! You have to make absolutely certain that the function itself is continuous across the boundary you have created. That in itself is not difficult, but often designers fail to ensure continuity of the first

Stick to the basic four functions.

Don't use Boolean-modulated multi-part functions.

Use only one mathematical operation per line of code.

derivative of the function, leading to sudden changes in the behavior of the system as a whole. The user experiences these as hiccups; he's making slow, steady changes to the system and suddenly it jumps.

Here's the wrong way to write a big messy formula:

Apples = 43×Oranges + 19×Pears − 27×Kumquats

Here's the right way:

Intermediate#1 = 43×Oranges

Intermediate#2 = 19×Pears

Intermediate#3 = 27×Kumquats

Apples = Intermediate#1 + Intermediate#2 − Intermediate#3

The latter way makes it easy to check those intermediate values during your tuning process. Sure, this latter approach is slightly less efficient than the former approach; why, it probably wastes several dozen billionths of a second of processing time! What many programmers don't realize is that programming efficiency is often at odds with debugging efficiency. When you're poring over the system, trying to find out why it's misbehaving, you need to rapidly check out every possibility. If your problem is that the value of Pears has gone bonkers, you might not see the problem if that value is buried inside a big long formula. But if you use the latter approach and just check every left-hand value, the answer will pop right out at you. Do not underestimate the difficulty of tuning a big system of equations; use every ploy available to simplify that task.

Don't commit "formula grabbing."

Back in my days as a physics teacher, I had to help students past a nasty habit: formula grabbing. It arises when the student doesn't really understand the physics of the situation and desperately grabs a formula from the textbook and stuffs values into it, trying to get some answer, ANY answer. Some people never quite shuck the habit, reaching for a formula out of a book and then ensconcing themselves in a false sense of correctness because they got their formula out of a book. Most of the time, the formula you get out of the book is scientifically accurate but completely inappropriate to the situation you face. If you have to turn to a book to get the formula, then you don't understand the fundamentals of the system well enough to tune that formula later. You're better off using a simplistic approximation that you do understand.

Assert maximum and minimum allowable values for each variable.

For every single variable that the user can experience, determine the range of acceptable values. State those values in the variable declarations in the program and then use assert statements to enforce their proper behavior. Most delinquent systems start with one variable going out of range, and then the rest of the system gets corrupted.

Artwork

The artwork used in the game was unorthodox. In those days, floppy disks were the only distribution medium available, and artwork quickly filled up floppies. To make matters worse, the user community was divided between the color haves and the black-and-white have-nots; in order to sell, the game had to satisfy both groups. Moreover, I needed 156 different images, one for each variable. My solution was to break each image up into a black-and-white bitmap and a color overlay. The color overlay was built up out of triangles; I had to build a special tool for my artist to specify the triangles and their colors. The system worked: The average image required only about 60K of floppy space. Black-and-white images looked good, and so did the color images.

The art style was especially unorthodox. I was dissatisfied with the ultra-realistic style so common in computer games; I wanted something deliberately artistic in intent. For this work, I chose Amanda Goodenough, the creator of such HyperCard classics as **Inigo Gets Out** and **Your Faithful Camel**. Amanda's clean, sweet style was just what I wanted, and she delivered a lovely set of images for the game. A few of my favorites are found in Figure 25.4.

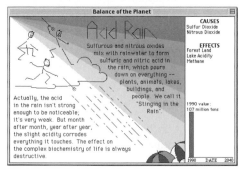

25.4 *A few of my favorite designs.*

As you can see, Amanda is an artist with strong vision and simplicity of line. In choosing her, I made a conscious decision that I wanted an artist, not an illustrator. I encouraged her to put her soul into the work, and she responded brilliantly. Hiring Amanda to create the artwork was one of the best decisions I made for the project. Most games these days seem to be illustrated by talented illustrators or artists who are not given any freedom. These people know their job; present them with your design goals and let them apply their creativity!

Schedule Hassles

The project was bedeviled by a series of scheduling problems. Halfway into the project, Epyx was forced to pull out due to financial problems of their own. As I had expected, Joe Miller handled the breakup with efficiency and honor. I decided to continue the project on my own, and to that end, I repaid the advances I had received from Epyx. Joe was instrumental in getting all the legal documents taken care of so that I could proceed with publication of the game without a legal cloud hanging over it. I continued working on the project, knowing that I had just six months to finish the program, prepare the manual, and arrange for porting it to the PC, manufacturing, and distribution. It was risky to self-publish, but I believed in the game and I didn't want to see it die.

The rush this imposed upon me did not seriously hurt the game; I had already solved all the serious design problems. The only detriment I suffered because of the new rush was a slight reduction in the total number of variables used in the simulation. I still had plenty of time to test and polish the equation system.

Nevertheless, the rushed schedule was stressful. I managed to find a developer willing to carry out the port on such a tight schedule, and with the help of my wife, Kathy, I was able to make all the other arrangements. We shipped the product in time for it to reach store shelves on the week of Earth Day 1990.

83 LESSON

Decide whether to hire an artist or an illustrator.

Results

Balance of the Planet was a commercial and critical near-failure. We sold about 12,000 units in total. Because of a combination of errors on the part of our distributor, we ended up losing about $20,000 on extra copies of the game that we need not have manufactured. This was counterbalanced by an unexpected offer for licensing rights in Japan. What saved the game was the unexpected sales to educational institutions; Marylyn Rosenbloom orchestrated this effort for us. For several years, we continued to sell copies into schools and colleges all over the country. All in all, we made a small profit on the game, probably not enough to justify our time expenditure, but enough to repudiate any sense of failure.

The critical response to the game was two-pronged. Basically, gamesters and computer people hated it, and educators and environmentalists loved it. One magazine reviewer lambasted it because, in his words, it "just isn't fun." I suppose this is understandable in a games magazine, but it still bothered me that a serious environmental game was being measured by the standards of shoot-em-ups. Another magazine gave it a negative review riddled with factual errors—the reviewer had evidently spent only a few minutes with the game.

On the other hand, the educators and environmentalists were pleased with the game. It was far and away the most thorough and accurate simulation of environmental problems available. It surpassed a number of purely academic simulations. The reviews from these people were uniformly positive.

I look back on the design with pride. Were I to do it all over today, I would make few fundamental changes. I'd add more variables to the simulation, and I'd certainly jazz up the cosmetics. I'd also like to augment the information presenting the overall state of the world to the user, and perhaps add links to websites with more information. But none of these possible improvements alter the design's core architecture.

patton
strikes back

It was my interest in wargames that brought me into the computer games universe. My first two wargames, **Tanktics** and **Legionnaire**, were groundbreaking in their time, but improved computer hardware had long since left them behind. **Patton Versus Rommel** was a good design, but again, the march of technology made it look pathetic. In the summer of 1990, after completing **Balance of the Planet**, I was ready to try my hand at something new. I very much wanted to tackle the problem of interactive storytelling, but I knew that would be a financially risky effort. It was safer to do something tried and true, and I sensed a market opportunity in the wargames field.

Wargames had continued to develop during the 1980s, but they had become increasingly specialized. In the early 1980s, board wargames were still the dominant form, and computer wargames were compared against the board games, never faring too well. As the decade of the 80s progressed, however, computer wargames grew richer and more complex, so that by 1990, they rivaled the board wargames. Everybody could see that board wargames were dinosaurs on their way to extinction. Curiously, as part of this process, computer wargames tried to mimic board wargames as closely as possible. Most companies used hexgrids because that's what the boardgames used. One company even presented its units as on-screen cardboard counters, just like the boardgames!

All this bothered me; I didn't like to see the hardcore gamers take over the industry. I felt that a healthy industry would have a wider array of games, including games for beginners, but all the games on the shelves were huge, complicated affairs that only the aficionados could appreciate. That deficiency, I decided, would set my goal. I would build "a wargame for the rest of us," an alteration of Steve Jobs' marketing slogan for the Macintosh.

This led me to three fundamental design principles that guided my work.

Simple Rules

Wargames by that time were putting on a lot of weight; complexity seemed to delight players. I did not want to bury my player in tons of rules, so I was determined to have a clean and transparent set of rules. The basic system constituted no more than the following.

Movement speed was based on terrain impediments: You moved faster down a road than through a forest. Each unit could be in one of three modes of deployment: movement, attack, and defensive. Each mode had its own benefits for movement, attack, and defense. Some amount of time was required to change modes. Units could face in one of the four cardinal directions; attacks and movement could be carried out only in the direction of facing. Attacking a unit on its flanks or rear was advantageous. Combat results followed a smooth simple curve; the bigger a unit was, the better its combat performance. I used the same disruption system I had used in my previous wargames. Units had zones of control (ZoC) that impeded but did not stop motion, and ZoCs blocked lines of supply. One innovation was that ZoCs had variable density; a big unit cast a bigger and more impeding ZoC.

Another innovation was the assignment of control to various towns and road junctions. At the beginning of the game, the Americans controlled all these "landmarks," but the Germans would capture them during the course of the game. The player's score was based on the possession of such landmarks. Moreover, supply lines could not be traced through an enemy landmark.

Clean User Interface and Strong Visual Presentation

The game had to be easy to play. The players would have no patience for complicated and obscure displays that required understanding some complex symbol code. Also, it was imperative that players be able to see everything about the game in a single view. Thus, the map clearly showed the terrain in each square, and units were shown with icons plainly indicating the mode. The player had available a wide variety of special displays showing particular aspects of the game. For example, the player could elect to show the game using icons that indicated the strength of each unit. Strong units were big on the map, and weak units were small on the map. With a display showing American or German flags on each of the landmarks, the player could also see who owned each landmark. The best of these displays was the supply display. This showed the supply lines for one side with small red dots moving along the roads toward the front to indicate where supplies were flowing.

Since the game was played in real time, orders entry presented me with the same problems I had with **Legionnaire**. The problems were even worse in **Patton Strikes Back**, because I elected to present the orders by putting the unit through a little dance showing its intended sequence of moves. When the player selected a friendly unit, that unit would dance out its current orders. The player could then enter orders using the keyboard, or simply click and drag to designate an objective. The problems arose from the many ways in which the player could enter orders during the dance. The player could add orders or delete orders midway through the dance; how was such a situation to be handled? I eventually got it straight, but the number of unanticipated logical possibilities was frustrating.

Explain the History

Since this was a "wargame for the rest of us," I had to assume that many of its players would be non-wargamers who probably weren't familiar with the details of the Battle of the Bulge. I wanted to take the opportunity to teach these people about the realities of the battle, and I wanted to cover every aspect of it: the technical factors, the strategy and tactics, and the human side as well. I came up with a system using some 50 different topics. Each topic had two aspects: a story from the battle and a discussion of some aspect of military matters highlighted by the story. Most of the stories were taken straight from the history books; some were fictionalized versions of real events that had taken place elsewhere during World War II. My system was geared to both time and location; at appropriate times, the game would halt and a particular topic story would appear on the screen, illustrated by a photograph. The player could return to the game after reading the story, or he could press a button that would bring up additional background information explaining some interesting point illustrated by the story. The stories covered a wide variety of topics: People such as Generals Patton and Bradley, Weapons such as Tiger tanks and bazookas, Tactics such as fighter bombers, and so on. The system was also available on demand via a menu.

I take pride in this system. I wanted to show war without the glamour that most wargames depict. No brilliant strategies, bold generalship, or glorious victories for me; I wanted my player to get a clear sense of the dirty mechanics of war. The technical discussions explained the logic of warfare, showing why and how certain techniques or weapons were used. The stories presented the war at the personal level, showing what ordinary people—civilians and soldiers alike—experienced during the battle. There were stories of luck, courage, tragedy, stupidity, and intense and widespread suffering. I believe that, in the moral sense, **Patton Strikes Back** remains one of the most realistic wargames ever created.

Color Hassles

The design was bedeviled by a nasty problem with color. In those days, color displays had penetrated only a portion of the installed computer systems; black-and-white displays were still common. It was therefore necessary to write software to support both groups. This was especially difficult, because color systems were not as simple as they are now. Back then, there were three common color systems: 1-bit, 4-bit, and 8-bit. Each system had to be handled differently. Moreover, most of the color systems had larger displays than the black-and-white systems; this meant that, to properly utilize the color displays, I had to present the graphics in two different scales. I eventually settled on four different displays based on two Boolean variables: presence of color and big screen. Every single display action had to be programmed with a double nested if-then statement, covering each of the four possible displays. The resulting code was a bloody mess. Toward the end of the project, I was giving some of my local variables names like "HateColor", "KillColor", "MurderColor", and so forth.

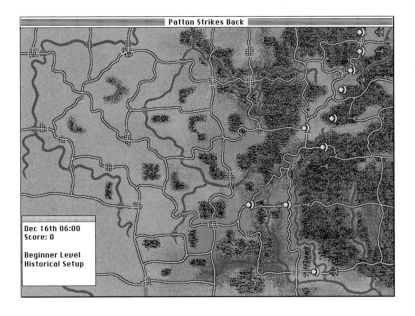

26.1 *Patton Strikes Back.*

Anti-Piracy

I have never been overly concerned with piracy of my games; it happens, and it does hurt financially, but my hunch is that the cost of preventing piracy is higher than the gains. However, I was irritated by the whining of games developers that the pirates were unstoppable, that no anti-piracy technology could withstand their assaults. "Everything is crackable" was the gleeful claim of the pirates, and the developers seemed to have glumly accepted their boasts. I thought it was time to put paid to that myth.

The Code Talkers

Time for a story. Armies face a similar problem: How do various military units communicate without the enemy intercepting their communications? This problem was so important that it quickly generated its own field of study: cryptography. Mathematicians devoted vast intellectual resources to this problem on which hung the lives of thousands. By World War II, cryptography was a major field of study, and cryptographic systems were perched on the sharp edge between security and failure. The Allies were able to crack the Japanese code in short order. The German codes were tougher, but they too succumbed to the assault. But how were the Allies to keep their own communications secure? It seemed at the time that no code system could be devised that was both practical and secure.

The US Marines hit upon a brilliant solution to the problem: the *Code Talkers*. They recruited Navajo Indians to act as communicators. Commander A gives his orders to Navajo Code Talker A, who speaks on the radio in a code based on Navajo with Navajo Code Talker B, who translates the orders for Commander B. The scheme was a smashing success. Marine communications remained secure throughout the war; Navy and Air Corps codes were successfully cracked by the Japanese.

The scheme even survived the capture of a native Navajo speaker in Bataan. Despite strong inducements to decode their communications, the POW was unable to figure out what the Code Talkers were saying, because he did not know the simple secondary code that the Code Talkers were using.

The brilliance of this scheme lay in its inversion of the normal process of code creation. Most code designers concentrate on the code itself; the Code Talkers scheme was based on an assessment of the people attempting to crack the code. Rather than "What can I build that's strong and uncrackable?" the starting question was "What will be impossible for the Japanese to crack?" The result was the most successful code in World War II.

Technology Versus Psychology

The lesson here is that the designers of anti-piracy schemes were taking the wrong tack. They saw the problem as a technological one, and so attempted to come up with technological solutions. Their opponents, the pirates, also saw the problem as a technological one, and greatly enjoyed the solution to the problem. In effect, the two sides were playing a silly game: The developers were trying to out-techie-macho the pirates, who in turn saw the anti-piracy schemes as a test of their technological manhood and therefore plunged into the cracking problem with relish.

The correct tack was to approach the problem as a psychological one rather than a technological one. The goal is not to challenge the pirate to a contest of skill; the goal is to discourage the pirate from completing the task.

The designer's biggest problem in creating copy protection is that everything he does is out in the open where the pirate can see it. The designer cannot guarantee the security of anything he does, because the cracker can observe any computation while it is being done. In short, our problem is to process information in full view of the cracker, yet not allow him to see it.

The trick here is misdirection. We cannot lock the information up; it's out in the open where he can see it. Our task is to camouflage the information, to make it look like something else. That way, the cracker can look right at it and never notice it. We want to give him so much stuff to look at, so many key look-alikes that, due to fatigue and frustration, he won't notice it when the real key comes into his field of view.

Remember that this is not an absolute solution. We cannot lock up the key behind a wall of steel. It will be out in the open. But we can create so many false keys, so many deceptive images of keys, that the cracker will probably not find the real key. We want to fatigue him and to demoralize him. We want to give him apparent successes and then yank those away. That is our fundamental strategy.

Basic Structure

The basic approach of any copy protection system is simple and requires three steps:

1. Present the user with a challenge, a question that can be answered only by using information from an uncopyable source, such as a code wheel or a word from the manual.

2. Compare the user's response with the correct response.

3. If the response is incorrect, disable the game.

There are many ways that such a system can be defeated. The one way that I will not address is for the pirate to copy the uncopyable external source of information. Some of the most common strategies available to the cracker are:

1. Find the internal file of challenge/password combinations and publish it.

2. Skip over the challenge so that it never happens.

3. Patch the challenge so that it always thinks that the correct password has been entered.

4. Patch the challenge so that its attempt to disable the game fails.

Hiding the Password File

Our first task is to retrieve the challenge and the password, presumably from a file on the hard disk. This is the most easily cracked process, and we must take special precautions.

First, we must disguise the contents of the file. The cracker could play the game once, find a single challenge/password, and then perform a simple file search for that text. This would reveal the critical file for his publication. The first step, then, is to encode the text of the file. We cannot use a standard encoding scheme; the cracker will surely try all the standard methods. Instead we must make up a simple but unique encoding system. A great variety of such systems are possible: moving-key arrangements, averaging systems, differential schemes, or whatever. The only requirement for such a system is that it render the data in the file immune to simple textual examination and that it be different for each product.

Now that our text is encoded, we must hide it. We can't just have a file called "Password File." And if we have a file just laying around with no obvious purpose, it's sure to attract attention. We want to hide that file somewhere inside another file, preferably in a way that allows the cracker to examine it without realizing that it's not quite right. I once hid my password file inside the sound file of an explosion. The cracker can look at the file, play it with a sound editor, and never realize that funny scratching sound in the middle of the explosion is really my password file. We could hide the password file by interleaving it through some other file; if every hundredth byte of a big sound effect is part of the password file, the user will never hear the difference. We could use a watermark system for an image file, or even a special texture. Lord knows that games these days have so many megabytes of files that a cracker could never find a few kilobytes of data tucked inside one of those files.

Reading the Password File

Now we have to get the password file into the computer so that we can select a password. This shouldn't be difficult; there will be megabytes of data in RAM. The important trick, though, is to load the data during game initialization, not immediately before the challenge—that's a dead giveaway.

Now we select our challenge/password pair from the full set of challenge/password pairs. But we don't decode it! If we decode it, it'll be sitting around in RAM just waiting to be found by a simple text string search. Instead, we leave it encoded; later, when we collect the user's input, we encode the input and compare the encoded strings. That's slightly more secure than decoding the password and comparing it directly with the user input.

How do we pass the encoded challenge/password data to the challenge routine? If you're a good little programmer, you probably want to declare it as data of the "Anti-Piracy" object. This is all wrong! You don't want to be writing clean, easily understood code: You want this code to be a bloody mess! Passing the data as a parameter is just as stupid, and making it a global variable is even worse. That data can't be sitting in any obvious location. It has to sneak into your routine through a back door.

At this point, consider a reverie to the impenetrable obscurities of the stack. Any idiot can scan through flat RAM searching for key data; digging up pointers to the data is only a tad more obscure. But stacks are without doubt the most godawful pains in the butt when debugging time comes. Nowadays, stack structures are kept behind many layers of operating system code to insulate the poor little wimp-programmer from their ferocious tendency to blow sky-high. That's why we cracker-bashers love them so much. Of course, we must remember that we are juggling with the programming equivalent of nitro-glycerin; we had better not drop any balls here!

My favorite solution is to store the data on the local variable stack frame. Remember what happens when a high-level language such as C or Pascal calls a routine? First it sets up a stack frame on the stack to reserve RAM space for the local variables. But these variables are not initialized; they initially contain whatever garbage was already present in the RAM. The trick is to make sure that the "garbage" just happens to contain the data we want to pass.

The stack accounting for this process can be tricky. The easiest way to accomplish it is to have one outer-level routine that calls both routines (the one that puts the data onto the stack and the other that uses it). Then you need merely ensure that the local variable declarations of the two routines are byte-harmonized. My approach was even simpler than that: I combined the local variable declarations for the two routines into one master local variable declaration which I then used for both routines. This has the bonus of making the cracker's stack-snooping that much more tedious.

A code example might help. Here's how the scheme might be implemented in C++. First, we have to place the data onto the stack. For purposes of simplicity, let's declare that the critical data consists of a 32-character string. Our first routine places that data onto the stack:

```
Void PutTheDataOntoTheStack()
{
        Short   j, k;
        Long    a, b;
        Char    SecretData[32];
// Let's assume that this particular C compiler
// reserves data on the stack in the order in which it
// is declared. Thus, the top two bytes are for the
// short variable j; the next two bytes for k, and so
// forth. Our character string will thus take the 13th
// through 44th bytes on the stack.
// First we do some officious-looking stuff to distract
// the cracker
```

```
      { blah, blah, blah }
// Now we get to the real task: this loop pulls data
// out of its secret hiding place and places it onto
// the local stack  frame.
      For (j = 0; (j < 32); ++j)
      {
              SecretData[j] = MysteriousLocation* + j;
      }
// now we do some more officious-looking stuff to
// distract the cracker.
      { blah, blah, blah }

Void GetTheDataOffTheStack()
{
      Short  n, m;
      Long   c, d;
      Char   NothingImportant[32];
      { blah, blah, blah}
}
```

So now we have our real challenge/password combination sitting in the garbage of our uninitialized variables, all ready to be used. But we must cover our tracks, lest the alert cracker ask where that data came from. We must now go through the motions of loading in a fake set of challenge/passwords. So we ostentatiously load a file called "Password File." This file must, of course, contain plausible challenge/password combinations. The trick is to make the first dozen password combinations legitimate copies of the real password file. That way, the careful cracker who double-checks the file will of course verify that its first entries are indeed genuine ones.

Now at this point we take advantage of one of the most common programming errors in the business. How many times have you set up some messy loop and screwed up the terminating conditions by just one step? In other words, does your loop go all the way to the very last value, or does it stop short by one, or does it do one loop too many? We all make that mistake—so let's use it as a means of messing with that punk cracker's mind. Let's deliberately screw up the terminating condition such that the very last entry in the list of challenge/passwords is not read in. That's where we arrange the real password to sit. Thus, we start with an uninitialized array of challenge/passwords, except that the very last entry is the honest-to-God challenge password left on the stack previously, then we load in all the false challenge/passwords, but due to a "bug" in our code, we fail to overwrite the honest-to-God one.

Now we have to select the genuine challenge/password. We have to be careful here; since we are inside the challenge routine, we know that the cracker is watching closely. Our problem is very similar to that of a card shark who wants to pick a particular card out of the deck without the audience understanding how he did it. I call the algorithm that I used for this "The Hand Is Quicker Than the Eye." We want to make sure that we always pick the last entry from the challenge/password table—without the watching cracker catching on.

At this point I take advantage of another bit of cracker psychology. Crackers are not well-rounded people. They're twisted personalities, obsessed with the computer and technical trivia. This means that while they know lots of petty crap about computers, they know very little else. In particular, crackers tend to regard arithmetic the same way that vampires view crucifixes. So a nice, complicated arithmetic calculation is sure to send them skipping to safer areas of code. So let's just wrap our critical work in some protective layers of arithmetic.

The algorithm I devised to solve my problem looks very much like a card-shuffling routine. It uses a complicated procedure to repeatedly exchange pairs of table entries, using an arithmetic formula to determine which pairs are shuffled. The formula is recursive, so that the cracker who wishes to penetrate it must follow it through all 300+

steps—and if he makes one mistake along the way, he's lost it. Suffice it
to say that the formula is rigged to ensure that after it has gone through
a certain number of steps (more than 300), our honest-to-God password
is sitting at the top of the table. We now pick the card from the top of
the pile. Lo and behold, it's the honest-to-God entry! The hand is
quicker than the eye, especially at 600MHz.

So now we go through the normal motions with the player. We perform
an ostentatious comparison of the player's entry with our table entry,
and then set a global flag that will later be used to disable the game if
it is FALSE. Of course, you didn't believe for one moment that this flag
really does anything, did you? You didn't think that I would be that obvious, did you? Silly boy!

No, we do the same trick going out that we did coming in. We put the
player's response to the challenge into a local variable where—guess
what?—it remains on the stack. A few million cycles later, we come back
to the stack location from a safe routine buried deep inside boring
housekeeping stuff. That routine retrieves the player's response as well
as the honest-to-God password, encodes the player's response, and
compares the encoded results. If they match, all is well. If not...

Bombs Away!

Our next task is to disable the game. Now, we must be circumspect here.
Initiating an immediate crash or lockup or putting up a dialog box that
terminates the game are all incorrect solutions, as they are dead give-
aways to the cracker. We should have taken care of the confused or
ignorant but otherwise innocent player in the original password dialog
box. We now need a scheme to deal with the cracker who has somehow
cracked the outer layer of protection.

There are two requirements for our disabling system: default failure and
delayed response. Default failure means that the program begins life
with a fatal but hard-to-find bug in it. The copy protection system repairs

the bug only if the player meets the password challenge. That way, the simple-minded strategy of patching out the password challenge will fail. Delayed response means that the disabling does not take place immediately. Instead, it takes place much later, so that when the crash happens, the cracker will have a whole lot of backtracking to do to get to its source.

In **Patton Strikes Back**, I took one of the military units and fudged its initializing data to a false value that, while initially harmless enough, was certain to cause a program crash just before the end of the game. The copy protection code sets the value back to the correct value. This has the advantage that the code looks for all the world like a typical unit-manipulation routine.

Guard Routines

But this is only the second layer of protection. The next layer uses *guard routines*. These are routines that checksum other routines, thereby ensuring that patches are detected at runtime. Guard routines should be executed rarely, because every time you call one, there's a chance that the cracker will be looking in on you at that moment. Besides, you only need to catch him once. Since guard routines are short and fast, it's a good idea to sprinkle them liberally throughout your code. Have them guard different things: different portions of the challenge routine or maybe the two routines that precede and follow the challenge routine.

Guard routines have a flaw: Since they use pointers into the code itself, they can be found with a carefully contrived automated code search, and when found, they will point to the routine they are guarding. Thus, guard routines can be "turned" and made to spill their guts about the other routines in the program. The best defense against this is to use many slight variations in your guard routine code, most especially in the line that directly accesses the client code. If just one guard routine uses a code sequence that slips past the automated code search, you've created a gigantic headache for the cracker, the more so because he will assume that his automated code search revealed all guard routines.

Harken to the wisdom of the lowly virus here. It does not seek to conquer the body's immune system. It just keeps making minor changes in its protein sheath, hoping to stay one jump ahead of the immune system's recognition subsystem. You should do the same.

Above all, have guard routines that guard other guard routines. The idea here is to create such an interlocking web of guard routines that the cracker will go nuts just trying to seek them out and neutralize them.

Do not have the guard routines generate the same bomb. Instead, have them do different things. My most fiendish trick was a guard routine that restores its client code to its original state. I can just see the cracker mumbling to himself, "I thought I disabled that thing half an hour ago...."

Recursion

Just as the stack is one of the safest places to hide data, recursion (the processing-equivalent of the stack) is one of the safest places to hide processing. It is easy to write a recursive routine whose function can only be determined by walking through every god-damned level of recursion. If you know where you're going with the routine, it takes a few minutes to write, but it can cost the cracker hours and hours to figure out.

Here's an example. Start with a long binary string:

1001110101011110010

Now create a Pascal triangle of recursive routines, each one looking rather like this:

```
Void RecurseNumber27(long tInput)
{
        short j, Sum;
        for (j = 0; (j < 27); ++j)
```

```
        {
                Sum += (tInput shifted right j times) & 1
        }
        if (Sum & 1)
                RecurseNumber22(tInput);
        Else
                RecurseNumber07(tInput);
}
```

Theoretically, this code could expand out to 2^{32} different recursive routines. The cracker knows this, but doesn't know that you have rigged the values to ensure that there are only, say, 23 routines. The only way the poor cracker can figure out what's going on is to track his way through every single routine. You, of course, can spike the set of recursive routines with a few never-called dummies that carry out the most bodacious computations. Let 'em wade through that mess!

Somewhere at the end of this shifting-walled rat's maze is a routine that actually does the useful work. You know that this is the only routine that will work—but your victim doesn't.

The Lord Giveth, and the Lord Taketh Away

One of the greatest differences between the experienced programmer and the neophyte is the former's debugging instincts. The neophyte blunders his way through a jungle of code and becomes hopelessly lost. The old pro creeps through the same jungle, sniffing, pausing to listen, and examining the ground for tracks. Working by a combination of instincts and well-honed hunches, he inevitably closes in on his quarry for the kill. Any cracker will rely heavily on those instincts to hunt down your secrets. Therefore, you must turn his instincts against him. Offer him hints that trigger his instincts; let him track down the quarry you offer, and then lead him into a dead end. Sprinkle short cryptic hard strings through your code, strings like "psswrd", "crypto", "crack", and "decrypt". They shouldn't do anything; just stick 'em in the middle of otherwise irrelevant routines. Let him go nuts trying to figure out why those strings are in there. Add a few extra, meaningless parameters to pass around through your routines. Write irrational code that carries out detailed calculations that don't do anything. Deliberately seed a few common programming errors into safe places in your code. Declare arrays to be bigger than you need, and use only the portion that you need. If your array is 10 elements longer than required, skip the first 10 elements rather than the last 10 elements.

Remember that the cracker is counting on you to write clean, rational code, so go wild! Be idiotic, insane; take everything you know about good programming practice and turn it upside down! Become a programming barbarian, lawless and uncouth! Have fun!

Back to Reality

There is one small catch with all this muddy fun: Your code must also work. Debugging deliberately psychotic code is almost as hard for you as it is for the cracker. Moreover, since the average game ships infested with a sewerful of bugs, you don't want to get carried away. My advice is to add the anti-piracy code after you have reached late beta; you don't want to burden your debugging efforts with egregious bugginess until the last moment.

And how did **Patton Strikes Back** fare against the crackers? I hired a cracker to beat the Mac system, and had him keep notes on his thinking as he worked. I could pay him for only twenty hours of work, but from his notes, it is obvious that, even after twenty hours, he had not come close to cracking the first layer of protection. I have never found a single cracked version of the game. There are plenty of versions posted on pirate sites, but they are all failed cracks; the crackers were so lazy that they never bothered to play the game to the end. If they had, they would have encountered the bomb that makes it impossible to complete the game. This, ultimately, is the best form of psychological protection. Let them think that they have won the battle of skills; let them hold their trophy aloft for all to see. So long as they can't actually play the game to completion, they have not taken anything of value from you. Everybody wins: They win their cracking techie-macho game, and you don't lose sales from people who actually want to play the game. Isn't that the best solution for all concerned?

Results

Patton Strikes Back was a market failure. A minor reason for this arose from the publisher's laggard publishing of the game. Our mutual understanding was that, so long as I delivered the golden master on their deadline, they'd get it out for Christmas. We met our deadline, but they failed to make theirs. That hurt.

The primary reason for the failure lay in the game itself. **Patton Strikes Back** was unquestionably an excellent "wargame for the rest of us"; the problem was that there was no "rest of us." By the time we published, the hard core wargamers had taken over the marketplace. As you might imagine, they derisively dismissed **Patton Strikes Back** as a beginner's game lacking the kind of challenging complexity they expected. Their badmouthing of the game spread through the overall community and killed its sales. The people who might have been interested in a "wargame for the rest of us" had already given up looking for wargames. I was too late to save wargaming from the aficionados.

84

LESSON

Defeat crackers with psychology, not technology.

themes and lessons

Over the course of my career as a game designer, a number of ongoing themes have played out. In this chapter, I shall summarize those themes and present some of the fundamental lessons I have learned.

People, Not Things!

This realization dawned upon me while at Atari Research. The narrowness of the range of games exercised me; it didn't take much deep thinking to comprehend that the underlying problem was the absence of human factors. That realization has informed all of my subsequent game designs. Its role is obvious in such designs as **Siboot**, but it played a role in every game I designed. For example, I believe that the real emotional kick in **Balance of Power** came from the feeling during the crisis that you were confronting a real person with a puzzling but consistent psychology. You were sure that, if only you could get underneath his skin, you'd have the upper hand and win every game. Yes, all those economic and military factors played a role, but when the moment of truth came, it was your hunch about your opponent that won or lost the game.

My wargames showed the same element at work. When you made a mistake, you'd see the angry face of your commanding officer chewing you out.

Faces

27.1 *Gossip* (1983).

27.2 *Siboot* (1987).

27.3 *Guns & Butter* (1990).

27.4 *Le Morte D'Arthur* (1989).

27.5 *Erasmatron Version 1* (1993).

If you want to have people in your games, you gotta have faces. Early on, I decided that faces were crucial to the emotional feel of any game. The work of Susan Brennan in the graphical representation of faces convinced me that face displays were feasible in games. My first attempt in this direction was the faces in **Gossip**; also important was the fact that these faces were emotionally manipulable, showing different expressions. The display of a Merlin face in **Excalibur** was another early example. The original **Balance of Power** lacked faces, but this was largely because I was sweating memory consumption; with the second edition of the game, I included faces of the advisors. In **Siboot** I went even further, using a generic face system that permitted expression of a variety of emotions. With **Guns & Butter**, I took the idea even further, using a variation of Susan Brennan's face-display technology to present a variety of faces. In the unfinished game **Le Morte D'Arthur**, I went much further, showing a great variety of faces with a great variety of emotions. Last, in the first version of **Erasmatron**, I took the concept its furthest. Figures 27.1 through 27.5 shows the progression of faces that I have used over the years.

As you can see, the faces grew bigger, more expressive, and more elaborate.

Gameplay Help

One of the downsides of designing so many original games is that the players don't know how to play them. Most games are variations on previous designs, so the players have a pretty good idea of how to play before they even fire up the game. Not so with my unconventional designs; players are often at a loss to figure out what's going on and what they should be doing. Therefore, since **Patton Versus Rommel**, all of my games have sported some sort of intelligent help facility. In most cases, I simply supplied some of the AI routines to the player. For example, the geometric AI for **Patton Versus Rommel** traced and measured the robustness of the front line; this measurement could be fed back to the player as a warning that the front line was growing ragged. In **Siboot**, I built special routines that measured the effectiveness of conversation in altering NPC's attitudes toward the player. If the player was making little progress, I presented a warning that the conversation was dull and needed some livening up.

For the second edition of **Balance of Power**, I extended the concept. Four advisors presented opinions to the player on crucial issues, and each advisor had a known bias. The player had to assess all the opinions of all the advisors to make a considered judgment.

Lastly, with **Patton Strikes Back**, I took the system even further. I built extensive analysis routines that examined a wide variety of issues: supply lines, robustness of the player's front lines, proper use of terrain, and so forth. These routines were not part of the AI system. I built them solely to provide the player with hints on how to play. If the player asked for advice, the help system invariably offered pertinent and intelligent advice.

Language

Balance of Power first brought up the problem of language. The headline generator started me thinking in terms of sentence structure as a means of representing the game state. At first, I missed the mark: I thought of sentence structure as merely a clever means of expressing the state of the game rather than the events taking place in the game. Conventionally, game states are represented with little bar graphs or icons. In **Doom**, for example, the state of health of the player is depicted with a small iconic face showing varying degrees of health. The player on the brink of death is shown with head hanging and blood dripping from the nose. I myself have used such methods in many of my games. So I was quite pleased with myself for dreaming up this idea of using language to communicate the same idea. What I missed, at first, was the idea that I could also use language to report events. That realization came to me serendipitously—and opened the door to a cornucopia of possibilities.

I further developed the use of language in game design with **Siboot**. The headline generator for that game elaborated the initial concepts used on **Balance of Power**. Much more important was the inverse parser I developed for input. Using language structures for both input and output changed everything.

Older readers may object that there's nothing revolutionary in this use of language; after all, text adventures have been using language for both input and output since the 1970s. But the parsers used in such text adventures are crippled by an internal contradiction. On the one hand, they seem to offer the player the prospect of communicating in natural language; on the other, they never come close to delivering on that offer. No matter how big you build your parser, no matter how large its vocabulary, the user will always struggle to find the right words to express his desires—or, more likely, like the man in the badly tailored suit, learn to live with a crippled vocabulary. The best evidence of the sterility of the parser concept is the fact that parsers have been the great software dinosaurs of the last twenty years. DOS, a parser-driven operating system, has already gone extinct, and text adventures are now the preserve of a small and dedicated band of retro-gamers.

The inverse parser system, however, still has lots of punch left in it. I attribute its rarity to ignorance, not conscious rejection. Nobody knows enough about inverse parsers to dismiss them based on noun. I myself see plenty of design potential.

Once I stopped thinking in terms of "user interface" and started thinking in terms of linguistics, my view of game design, interactivity, and software in general began to reorganize into a clearer system with a solid foundation. My studies in linguistics continue to illuminate my thinking on game design, while providing me with crucially useful nuggets of truth such as this one: The words "Kathy" and "castrate" come from the same Indo-European root. The reader may wish to consult some of the references to linguistics books listed in Chapter 9, "The Education of a Game Designer."

Art Over Money

I've never been much of a businessman; that doesn't make me an artist, but the choices I have made over the years certainly indicate as much. My failure to make sequels to my games (with the exception of **Balance of Power**, which I did as penance for **Siboot**, which bombed and cost the publisher, Mindscape, a pretty penny). Time and again, I have chosen the noble artistic road, forsaking the path of wealth. I'm sure that, had I been more receptive to my publishers' importations, I could have made more money than I actually did. In the nearly two decades that I have been a freelance computer game designer, I have earned about as much as I would have earned as a schoolteacher. In the process, I have explored more game design concepts and made more mistakes than any other game designer. All that creative effort, I suppose, uniquely qualifies me to write this book. So go buy some extra copies.

85
LESSON

A more
artistic
strategy
does not
obviate
commercial
success.

This does not mean that my artistic approach has made me a commercial failure. On the contrary, my commercial track record easily beats the industry average. I have published 13 computer games in my career; of these, two (**Eastern Front (1941)** and **Balance of Power**) were hits; two (**Trust & Betrayal** and **Guns & Butter**) lost money. The other nine were middling; they made some money and so were worthwhile projects, but no more. That's a hit rate of about 15% and a failure rate of about 15%. Industry average during the same period was about 1% hits and 30% failures. In other words, I did MUCH better than the industry as a whole. Another way to evaluate my overall commercial success is to look at my bottom line: Did I make money? If we confine the discussion to the period of my work on computer games, spanning 1979 to 1992, my earnings during that time average out to what any senior professional technical worker would have earned. In other words, I didn't get wealthy, but I made a comfortable living. If we define success to be the ability to earn a living while doing what you think is important, then my career path has been a great success.

There are, of course, other designers who have been even more successful. Their success surely deserves our admiration, and I heartily endorse any personal approach that emulates their strategy. My method worked for me; their methods worked for them; you must learn from all of these examples to decide your own strategy.

The Harsh Realities of Business

I must counterbalance my enthusiasm for the artistic strategy with a warning about the ugliness of business practices in the games industry. It's a brutal, ugly business, and in your business dealings, you must keep one rule above all others (Lesson 86).

In the games biz, trust no one.

There have been, and still remain, some truly honest people who conduct themselves with honor and good will. A few of these people have even risen to positions of power in the industry. Over the years, however, I have seen a steady decline in the number of such people; they are slowly being replaced by people who place little value on long-term relationships or personal integrity. I won't go so far as to say that the industry is full of crooks (although there are plenty of game designers who will enthusiastically endorse that notion). Instead, I suggest that, in your dealings with people in the games biz, that you assume that they will not hesitate to screw you if they find it in their own interests to do so. If they figure out a ploy that will cost you ten thousand dollars and make them an extra two thousand, they'll use it. If you protest, they'll shrug their shoulders and say, "Hey, it's just business."

If you are lucky enough to establish a relationship with one of those rare birds with a reputation for integrity and good will, cling to that relationship like a life raft in a stormy sea. Sure, the deal you get probably won't look as good as the deal offered by some shyster, but that is to be expected: An honest person will offer reality, which never looks as good as a gilded swindle.

Do not underestimate the degree to which most businesspeople engage in deception. They have developed a litany of euphemisms to anaesthetize their underdeveloped consciences. They deliberately misrepresent the truth and then call it "putting my best foot forward"; "emphasizing the positive"; and "painting the picture in the brightest colors." This, of course, means that they'll put their worst foot where you can't see it, they won't mention the negative, and the picture they paint won't include any of the darker colors that are really there. This is intrinsic to American business culture. As they say, "Everybody does it." You'll fit in just fine if you do it, too. But if your standards of integrity do not draw a line between active lying and passive deception, then you'd better watch out!

old fort stories

Having been in the business since the earliest days, I have accumulated a motley lot of tales, some of which I have already regaled you with. For those whose patience is not completely exhausted from such tales, I present here a selection of some of the finer items from my collection.

Early Sound and Music

This goes way back: In the 1960s, long before many readers of this book were born, there were no personal computers (horrors!). Instead, we had mainframe computers, great big monsters taking up entire rooms, with a clutch of incantation-chanting priests hovering about, serving their every need. Humble users would submit "jobs" on decks of punched cards, which the priests would feed into card readers. The computer would execute the job and print out results, which would be placed in a little mailbox for the user to pick up later. Sometimes the turnaround time for these jobs was rather long; I remember one professor at UC Davis complaining that the campus computer center was so slow that it would be faster for him to drive to UC Berkeley, 60 miles away, submit the job, wait for its return, and drive home.

Anyway, these computers didn't have any video output—it was just printers and card punchers in those early days. But the printers were unlike anything in use these days. They were rather like typewriters in that there were solid characters that were pressed onto an inked ribbon just over the paper. To achieve higher speeds, these printers used entire banks of such printing wheels, so that each column had its own dedicated printing wheel. This allowed an entire line to be printed in one step.

As these printers printed a page, they emitted a rough tone whose frequency depended on the number of hammers hitting the page on that line. A few hammers led to a high note; many hammers produced a low note. It did not take long for some bright young fellow to figure out how to formalize this process. And so, late at night, when the responsible adults were not around, you could hear the gravelly voice of the printer banging out great hits like "Swanee River."

An Early Multiplayer Game

I was lucky enough to experience one of the earliest multiplayer games. This was carried out at the University of California at Davis in 1972. A young sociology professor wanting to study group behavior set up a huge strategy wargame. He recruited several dozen wargamers, divided us into teams of six players, and gave each team a country to run. Each country had an economy, a foreign policy, military capabilities, and so forth. The economies were built around oil. There were about a dozen countries in the game world, which was represented on a huge hexgrid map. Every Sunday night, we would play one turn. The referees gathered at a secret location on campus containing a large map and telephoned each team at its designated home location. Then followed an hour-by-hour movement, with military units marching forward step by step. During the week, we would conduct negotiations with other countries.

My team played a small mountainous country bordering a powerful industrial nation short of oil. Our own oil resources were too meager to attract the attentions of our mighty neighbor, but we were nevertheless vulnerable. In effect, we were "Switzerland" to their "Germany." Being physics students, we ran computer simulations of the world economy and quickly discovered an impending oil crisis, which would almost certainly force "Germany" to attack "Poland," rich in oil and weak in armies. We therefore set out on a truly bold course of action: We planned, solely on the basis of our simulation, to invade "Germany" just as its armies were deeply enmeshed in a war with "Poland." To cover our sinister intentions, we offered to assist "Germany" in its upcoming invasion. The "Germans" were deeply suspicious of our foreknowledge of their plans, but willingly agreed to the help we offered. We marched into their land and, at the critical moment, seized one-third of their territory.

Their outrage at our betrayal towered over all other considerations. They made peace with the alliance arrayed against them and turned their armies on us. We feigned terror at the upcoming onslaught, begged for peace, promised reparations, if only they would deign to permit us to survive. The enemy, eager to wreak vengeance, accepted our proposal of immediate withdrawal and planned to double-cross us by slaughtering our retreating divisions. At the beginning of the next turn, their advance guards charged over the cease-fire line—to be mown down by our entrenched and waiting forces. We had no intention of retreating.

Triple-crossed, mighty "Germany" could think of only one course: vengeance on the perfidious "Swiss." But our calculations proved perfect; caught in a severe oil shortage, the "German" armies ground to a halt, their economy collapsed, and we were left holding one-third of their territory.

Throughout all this, we continued to carry on extensive discussions with the other teams. They were unsympathetic to our bold actions; even though "Germany" was their worst enemy, they had no interest in tiny "Switzerland," thinking discussions with us pointless. Nevertheless, we continued to play the role of pathetic weaklings, garnering reams of diplomatic intelligence, which we in turn bartered for even more intelligence. Our coup against "Germany" convinced the world that we were the espionage capital of the world.

None of this was done with computers. It was all carried out with telephones, maps, and teams of people. The various teams expended huge amounts of time negotiating deals; some of the discussions were carried out over the telephone, but most were done face to face. It was one of the most enjoyable games I have ever played.

Getting a Job

In the summer of 1979, my teaching job ran out and I was looking for something new. My wife had just gotten a job in Silicon Valley, and I was back at our house (some hundred miles away), tidying everything up for the move. Every week or so, I would drive down to Silicon Valley for a day to look for work.

Silicon Valley back then was not at all what it is now. It had fewer people, less traffic, and more orchards. The big difference was in the people culture. The denizens of Silicon Valley were engineers who loved to build wonderful toys. The very streets crackled with excitement over the myriad of possibilities opened up by fast-moving integrated circuit technology. There were many more opportunities opening up than could possibly be developed—the industry suffered from a desperate shortage of technical talent of all kinds. Although I had no specific experience in electronics and software, my master's degree in physics, my strong programming background, and my familiarity with digital electronics were solid qualifications; I was confident of securing a good job.

I answered a few ads, but the most interesting jobs required specific experience that I didn't have. There was one job at Lawrence Livermore Labs that caught my attention: writing targeting software for nuclear missiles. It was actually a very "sweet" task, meaning one full of interesting challenges. I wrestled with my conscience and decided against it. Who knows? Perhaps, if I had taken that job, I would now be some half-alive, faceless techie-bureaucrat in the military-technology business, rather than the lively, fascinating chap I have become!

87

To my surprise, I had little luck chasing after science-heavy technical jobs. But I remember interviewing with one chap at a big high-tech place. After half an hour, we both agreed that I wasn't right for the job opening. But then the fellow picked up the telephone and called a friend at another company. "Bill," he said, "I've got a young fellow over here who sounds just right for your group. Got any openings?" Well, Bill did indeed have some openings, and he could see me immediately, so five minutes later I was equipped with a name and directions. As I shook the interviewer's hand, I thanked him and asked why he had gone out of his way like that for me. "Silicon Valley is one big community," he said. "Our community is bigger than any single company." I was stunned. Later experience proved him right; most people in the Valley during the early 80s saw themselves as participants in a revolution first, and employees second. Money was low on everybody's priorities. It's a tragedy that the high-tech biz no longer cherishes these values.

> In the long run, the ethical choice is usually the most advantageous choice.

Bill's job opening was at Lockheed; I had been warned that Lockheed was known around the Valley as "The Lazy L." Bill received me warmly and proved to be quite personable. He took me up to his department on the second floor. We walked through a huge open room with engineers sitting at desks placed in neat rows and columns. They were busily drawing flowcharts and writing up code with pencil on form sheets. There wasn't a single monitor to be seen; everybody was working on sheets of paper. In his office, Bill the manager outlined the department's responsibilities. This huge department consisting of at least 50 engineers and had the sole responsibility of maintaining a custom programming language used internally at

Lockheed. Bill never once asked me about my qualifications; apparently my resume was good enough for him. Most of the interview was devoted to Bill telling me how wonderful life was at Lockheed. "We realize that you'll need time to come up to speed," he assured me, "so we won't be giving you any deadlines for six months. And we get three weeks off at Christmas!" I liked Bill and the job paid well, but somehow the corporate culture didn't seem right for me.

One evening, back at home, my wife called me from Silicon Valley. "I just found an interesting job in the classifieds," she told me. Then she read me the ad. "Programmers!" it read, "Program your own computer games!" I was flabbergasted. Somebody was actually paying people to write computer games? This was fantastic! It was right up my alley! And I, unlike almost anybody else, had impressive qualifications in the two games that I had already built and self-published. I was a shoo-in for a dream job. The very next day I called the headhunter who placed the ad and made an appointment for the following day.

I showed up at his office giggling with excitement. The interview started off well; the interviewer was impressed with my master's degree and my previous games. But one thing bothered him. "Your experience in programming seems thorough but you don't mention employment as a programmer. How many years of experience do you have working as a programmer?" I explained that I had never been employed specifically to do programming, but that I had done lots of scientific programming, worked in assembly language, and even taught several courses in programming. He wasn't impressed. "You mean that you have never actually worked in a real programming job?" I was beginning to feel cornered. "But I've actually done it—I've designed, programmed, and sold computer games!" He stood up and offered me his hand. "This job requires a minimum of three years of programming experience. Thank you very much, Mr. Crawford. We'll get back to you." Crushed, I slunk out of the office and drove home in tears.

That night, I poured out my sorrows to my wife. "It was the dream job!" I wailed. "And now it's gone!" My ever-supportive wife tried to console me. "There have to be other games companies; here, let me look in the phone book." She grabbed the yellow pages and ripped through the pages, searching. Sure enough, under "Games," she found two listings. The first was something called "Atari"; neither of us had ever heard of it. She called their personnel office the next morning. The lady there told her to come in and fill out an application form. Kathy explained that I was in Davis, the small college town where our home was. "Davis?" the personnel lady asked. "Are you guys Aggies?" She was referring to graduates of the UC Davis campus. "Yes, we are! '72 Physics and '73 Biochem!" It turned out that the personnel lady was an Aggie. She immediately scheduled an interview for me with the programming department, and I got the job.

Five weeks later, another programmer joined our team: Carla Meninsky. While chatting one day, Carla confided that she had to go through a really obnoxious headhunter to get this job. Something about her description rang a bell. "Was this guy in an office on Middlefield Road near Shoreline?" I asked. Sure enough, it turned out to be the same guy who had turned me down. His obnoxiousness had cost him a finder's fee.

E. T.

When Steven Spielberg's movie *E.T.* appeared in May of 1982, it was an instant hit. Ray Kassar, the CEO of Atari, decided that Atari must have an **E.T.** game for the Christmas 1982 season. He therefore flew to New York,

> The nasty choice is usually the least advantageous choice.

camped out in Spielberg's outer office, and eventually got the video-game rights for the appallingly high figure of $20 million. He immediately called the programming department of the VCS division, instructing them to get to work on an **E.T.** game for Christmas sale.

The VCS people were aghast at this. In order to have a game cartridge ready for Christmas, the game program had to be completely finished by September 1. This was because the process of manufacturing the ROMs was slow and required long lead times. Kassar had called them at the beginning of July: They had eight weeks to design, develop, test, and debug a major game. Typical development cycles in those days took nine to fifteen months. Kassar's demand bordered on the physically impossible.

Nevertheless, Howard Warshaw, one of Atari's best programmers, endowed with a better-than-average dollop of self-confidence, volunteered to tackle the impossible task. His plan, fully supported by management, was to modify a previous design in such a way as to get an **E.T.** game. He reworked the gameplay slightly, replaced all the graphics, and jammed **E.T.** into the game. The result was execrable, but it was without doubt the very best that could be done in the ridiculous amount of time available. After all, Ray Kassar had noted, people would buy the game for the brand name, not for the gameplay.

Like any licensed product, this game had to be approved by the licensor, in this case Steven Spielberg himself. Due to the tight timing, it was impractical to take the game to him; he would have to come to the lab in Sunnyvale and witness the game being played on the special development system there. And so one day in late summer, a caravan of limousines paraded down the broad streets of the industrial park where Atari lay scattered, and drew up in front of the programming labs for the VCS group. A crowd of bigwigs emerged and oozed into the lab, where Howard awaited them. After the introductions, Howard began his presentation by declaring, "This is the game that will make the movie famous."

Despite this inauspicious beginning, Spielberg approved the game and off it went to the ROM factory. Certain that it would be a huge hit, Kassar had millions of cartridges built. Lo and behold, everything worked perfectly and the game appeared on store shelves in time for the Christmas rush. Unfortunately, consumers proved to be less stupid than Kassar had thought. Word quickly got out that the **E.T.** game was a turkey, and sales drooped, then plummeted. Kassar was a man ahead of his times; like any good Enron or WorldCom executive, he dumped his stock in the company before word of the disaster got out. When the news was released, and people realized that Kassar had dumped stock, the stock price fell even further. The **E.T.** game did not, after all, make the movie famous, but it did manage to seal Atari's doom.

Alan Kay

One of the best things that CEO Ray Kassar did for Atari was to talk the great computer scientist Alan Kay into joining Atari to set up a research division. The first thing he did upon arriving was ask around to see if there were any bright young Turks hanging around who might be at risk of leaving the company. Apparently a great many fingers pointed him in my direction, so one day I got a call from his assistant asking me to meet him. My ignorance of the real world was too great to permit me to have any inkling who this man was; as far as I was concerned, this was just another technical orientation session for some clueless big shot executive. So I showed up at Alan's doorstep feeling slightly put out at being taken away from my real responsibilities just to hold the hand of somebody who was paid too much and knew too little.

The man who met me was not at all what I had expected. In the first place, he didn't wear fancy clothes, nor did he act like a big shot; he leaned back in his chair while we talked and put his tennis shoes on the desk. I rather liked that. Still, I was in a crotchety mood that day and managed to communicate an angry young Turk image to Alan. Despite

89

If you don't
fail at least
90 percent
of the time,
you're not
aiming high
enough.

my surly attitude, Alan saw promise in me and hired me
into the new Atari Research division. I was his first hire,
and he didn't hire anybody else for some months, which
meant that I had Alan Kay all to myself for the entire time.
This was the computer scientist's analogue of being
marooned on a desert island with Marilyn Monroe—except
that I was the computer scientist's analogue of a eunuch.
Nevertheless, I quickly realized that Alan was no ordinary
executive. Indeed, Alan Kay is one of just two or three
people whom I have met who strike me as out-and-out
geniuses. I find most people to be slow-thinking dullards
who must be handled with diplomatic gentleness, lest the
rush and thrust of my thinking overwhelm them and engen-
der resentful rejection. But with Alan Kay, the shoe was on
the other foot. I found myself struggling to keep up with his
stream of thought. The ideas came pouring out in a mighty
torrent that swept me along; only by dint of intense mental
effort could I keep my head above water. My conversations
with Alan were heady experiences; afterwards I would walk
into my office, close the door, and stare at the wall for an
hour digesting the experience.

I conclude this tale with one of Alan's favorite admonish-
ments (Lesson 89).

Lost in the Shuffle

During Atari's heyday in 1982, one of its brightest engineering talents was determined to move to New York City.
Not wishing to lose the fellow's skills, Atari agreed to set
him up with his own lab and employees right there in
Manhattan. The arrangement worked well: The hotshot

continued his prolific contributions to Atari and everybody was happy. But then, as Atari started to collapse, executive was replaced by executive who in turn was replaced by somebody else.

In one particularly brutal layoff, most of the engineering staff was let go—including everybody who knew of the existence of the Manhattan lab. The payroll computer didn't forget, of course, and so the paychecks kept going out punctually. In Manhattan, the elite engineering team realized that their time would come, so they patiently awaited the phone call that would mean the end of their time at Atari. But nobody back at Atari headquarters in California knew of their existence.

After some months, somebody finally took the time to go through the payroll carefully. I am told that the Manhattan people got a call from Sunnyvale asking who they were. Upon hearing the answer, the voice at the other end of the line told them they were all terminated.

International Sales

I self-published **Balance of the Planet** in April of 1990. You will recall that Saddam Hussein invaded Kuwait in July of 1990. In August of 1990, I received an unusual warranty card from a customer: The return address was in Kuwait, but it had been scratched out and a new return address in Virginia had been substituted. Obviously, when you're clearing out of town just ahead of the Iraqi army, you want to make sure to bring the most important stuff—like your **Balance of the Planet** warranty card.

The Locked File Cabinet

In July of 1984, the remaining shreds of Atari were purchased by Jack "Business is war" Trameil, who had destroyed Atari with his price wars using the Commodore 64.

This gentleman sported one of the more abrasive personalities in the business and was not well loved. But he did know how to cut costs ruthlessly. The first thing Jack did upon moving in was to hold a huge

Look
before you
liquidate.

auction of all the furnishings in the now-unpopulated buildings. Tables, chairs, filing cabinets—everything went in an effort to gather up a little cash. Around 2:00 on the day of the sale, I got a phone call from a reporter at the *San Jose Mercury News*. He told me that a local small businesswoman had purchased, for $125, a locked filing cabinet whose keys were lost. After getting it open, she discovered 84 files marked with the titles of many of Atari's games. Inside these files were thick computer printouts, big 8" floppy disks, and big electronic chips on small printed circuit boards. Could I tell him what those files were?

It took me a moment to stop laughing, and then I explained to him that the lucky purchaser was now the owner of the Atari engineering archive, the complete collection of the original masters of all the VCS games. The legal embarrassment that this could cause Atari would be worth hundreds of thousands or even millions of dollars to the sufficiently ruthless owner. Fortunately for Atari, the purchaser did not share Jack Trameil's attitude toward business. Indeed, it took numerous phone calls to convince the Atari people that they should come and collect their software. Late that afternoon, three Atari employees arrived to pick up the masters.

Bill Carris

Bill Carris was a sly chap. He had no college degree, but he was smart, personable, and immensely hard working; he lived and breathed his job. He started at Atari in Customer Service and was quickly promoted to run the ever-expanding group. He was often included in executive meetings so that he could offer his opinions on problems as perceived by customers. Bill's common sense, willingness

91
LESSON

to speak his mind, and good humor quickly earned him a place at the ear of the CEO, Ray Kassar. Ray trusted Bill's advice and relied on him for a number of special tasks. Besides, Bill had a wicked sense of humor and a penchant for practical jokes.

When Atari collapsed, Bill lost his job. Most Atari people landed on their feet, but Bill struck out everywhere he turned. He searched for a new job for months, but without a college degree, he had no credibility. This man, who had served for all intents and purposes as an executive at Atari, could not get a job even at the lowest levels of technical companies. One day, he put a gun to his head and pulled the trigger.

Business is indeed war in the sense that the casualties are real.

Marketing Wisdom

One day I was chatting with a marketing executive at a major games publisher. He was emphasizing to me how important the box was to the success of a game. In his enthusiasm for his subject, he went a little too far. "I could sell *dog shit* in the right box!" he proudly declared. Well, I couldn't let that one get by me unriposted. "And you do!" I chimed in.

92
LESSON

The Dragon Speech

The finest speech I gave in my entire life was The Dragon Speech, presented at one of the early Computer Game Developers' Conferences. In it, I used "The Dragon" as a metaphor for the unattainable goal of artistic expression through computer game design.

Hyperbole invites hi-larity.

The finale of the speech really blew their socks off. I confronted an imaginary dragon that I purported to see in the air at the back of the lecture hall. "After all these years, I can finally see you!" I declared. "And you're beautiful, but, you're also ugly beyond description. Yes, yes, I'm afraid of you—YOU HURT ME! I've felt your claws ripping through my soul!" These last lines were delivered with genuine anguish of an intensity that disturbed and frightened many in the audience. I continued, "But I've got to learn to face you, eyeball to eyeball, and I can't put it off any longer. I've got to do it NOW! HERE! Come, Dragon, I will fight you!" I turned to my right and hissed, "Sancho Panza, my sword!" and then grabbed a sword from its hiding place on the lectern. I brandished the sword and with the most deadly seriousness, intoned, "For Truth! For Beauty! For Art! CHARGE!" I galloped down the central aisle of the lecture room, shouting "CHARGE!" right out into the corridor. I never came back.

The audience, shocked, sat quietly for several moments. Only after it was obvious that I wasn't coming back did they disperse.

The Great Pratfall

I was once invited to deliver a lecture to several thousand people in Tokyo. I prepared the speech carefully, toning down the English, and eliminating all colloquialisms to make it easier for my audience to understand me. But as I gave the lecture, it was obvious that I wasn't getting through to my audience. I rely heavily on establishing a rapport with my listeners, but I just couldn't seem to break down the cultural barrier between myself and my audience. They would not laugh at even the most blatant jokes.

But then, halfway into the speech, I failed to take into account Japanese cleanliness as I pounced like a cat during a demonstration. The floor was waxed perfectly smooth and my feet whisked out from underneath me. My butt hit the floor with a heavy thud and I sat there stunned, flat on my butt in front of three thousand horrified Japanese.

After recovering from the initial shock of the impact, I remember thinking, "What do I do now?" I couldn't help myself—a smile crept across my face and widened into a grin. After all, it was a genuinely funny predicament. Seeing my grin, the audience burst into uproarious laughter and applause.

A More Serious Pratfall

There are *some* cultural universals, and falling on your butt is one of them.

My fame at Atari attracted a great deal of press attention, and my candor only enhanced my reputation with the press. I thought I had learned how to handle the press: Tell them the truth and don't ever try to manipulate them. I also learned that sometimes, the truth doesn't make much sense without knowing some of the underlying forces at work, forces that can't be published. In such cases, you tell the reporter, "This is background information and it is off the record," at which point the reporter switches off the tape recorder and you speak freely, secure in the knowledge that such information will go no further.

That's how it's supposed to work, but there are unscrupulous reporters out there, and I had the bad luck to run into one. In a long telephone interview, I was attempting to describe Atari's policy on some matter, and to do so I had to explain some of the internal politics. I asked the reporter if we could go off the record, he agreed, and I proceeded to unload the details, dirt and all. Two months later I saw the interview in a magazine, complete with the "off the record" material quoted word for word.

I was shattered. Some of my comments were not flattering to Atari, and they therefore made my boss, Alan Kay, look bad. By that time I had developed an intense respect for this man, who was virtuous as well as brilliant. I had inadvertently betrayed him, and I simply couldn't live with that. I typed up my resignation, walked into his office, and presented him with the magazine and the resignation letter. I apologized for my stupidity and turned to leave.

"Hold on!" he said. "Let's just look this over." He read the magazine article while I writhed in agony at each chuckle and sigh. "Yep" he announced, "this was pretty stupid, but I can see how you were ambushed. It's a good thing you brought this to me first. I'll talk to Ray Kassar and straighten it out."

I didn't know how to respond. "But..." I stammered, "this is plainly wrong. Ray Kassar had personally warned me about shooting my mouth off...I don't want you to suffer political damage because of my stupidity." Alan assured me that he could handle it. He then gave me a quick lecture about handling the press, and made me promise that I would never trust reporters again. I fell all over myself promising to never again be a bad boy. Then I retired to my office to brood over my mistake.

Problems of Decentralization

I once attended a presentation on military wargaming. The lecturer presented a tale that deserves repeating here. It seems that the military had built a huge networked system that allowed simulation of large combined arms operations. Officers at different bases all over the country, representing different services, could participate in a large simulated operation. The processing of each unit's actions was carried out locally, and then distributed to the other units across the country via the network. The simulation presented beautiful 3D camera views of any location on the battlefield. Our lecturer was presenting videotapes of some of those camera views.

Decentralized computing has many advantages to recommend it, but it also suffers from some difficulties. In this case, the operation being simulated was a beach landing on hostile territory, with Navy units providing the transport, Air Force units suppressing ground fire, and Marine units being ferried from Navy ships to the beach in big helicopters. Scores of virtual ships, planes, and helicopters, and thousands of virtual soldiers, all functioned smoothly together in an impressive demonstration—until a Marine helicopter came in to land on a Navy ship. Just as it touched down and powered down its engines, the computer controlling the Navy ship suffered a glitch and dropped off line. The simulation, no longer aware of any Navy ship, presented the helicopter floating 50 feet above the surface of the water, with no power. It promptly dropped into the drink, losing all aboard.

A similar story arises from the pioneering Genie multiplayer air combat game **Air Warrior**. As the game evolved, Genie added more aircraft, including bombers that could be manned by large crews of players. However, a problem soon emerged: If the player piloting the bomber dropped offline, the bomber would slowly spiral into the ground, taking its frantic crew with it.

The Unrevenged Review

Shortly after I released my educational game, **Balance of the Planet**, an important magazine reviewed it. The review was written by the senior editor himself, and it was most unflattering. It was obvious from the details he provided that the chap had given the program the most cursory of reviews. He thought it was a HyperCard stack when it was a standalone program; he complained about a lack of documentation when in fact the example he provided was handled in complete detail in the most obvious place in the manual; and so on. I was understandably upset with this grossly unfair review and wrote a letter to him decisively refuting his every complaint. He called me up to discuss the letter, and seemed apologetic. "Look," he said, "if you can boil this letter down to less than 100 words, I'll print it in the letters column. Just keep it civil." I thanked him for his consideration and promised that my letter would meet his requirements. Now, writing a good

94

Integrity
is an
unexpected
virtue.

letter in 100 words or less is a tall order, but I managed to craft something that was short, diplomatic, and to the point. Unfortunately, the editor broke his word: He never published the letter.

Just four months later, the same editor wrote a letter to the Computer Game Developers' Conference requesting a special arrangement in support of an event he wanted to set up. He had no idea of my position as Chairman of the Board. I discussed the matter with the Board, and they were amenable to working something out. So I called him and offered our services. He was confused; why was I so cooperative after that bad review? I explained that I was wearing my CGDC hat, not my Chris Crawford hat. He didn't get it. Taken aback at his inability to comprehend a simple concept, I explained that my role as CGDC Chairman required me to act in the best interests of the CGDC, not my own best interests. He still didn't quite believe it; my attitude was most unusual to him.

Failed Humor

I once sat on a panel discussion at a conference for non-games people attempting to learn more about entertainment software. These were big-media people, people with lots of money to throw around, and they were deadly serious. The moderator had asked me how I wished to be introduced, and I replied that he could present me as "Zee Greatest Game Designer in Zee Universe." He smilingly agreed to indulge me. But when the time came to introduce me, he mistakenly used "The Greatest Game Designer in The Universe." Worse, nobody laughed; the room was full of the sound of scribbling from people dutifully noting my official title.

Attempting to salvage the joke, I leaned forward to the microphone and corrected him, "That's 'Zee Greatest Game Designer in Zee Universe.'" The mighty roar of hundreds of erasers rubbing out hundreds of The's echoed through the hall. The moderator and I exchanged worried glances, and I instantly resolved to expunge all attempts at humor from my presentation.

The Sins of Youth

I have never taken any courses in computer programming; I am completely self-taught. This is not so impressive; a great many good programmers are self-taught. However, I taught myself back in the 1960s, when programming languages were more primitive. I learned FORTRAN, a clumsy language designed for scientific programming. If you use variable names like "I," "J," and "K" for index variables for loops, you are using one legacy of FORTRAN: It defined all variables beginning with the letters I through N to be integers, while everything else was a floating point variable.

Now, learning to program using FORTRAN was rather like learning to drive in a demolition derby, and I seem to have learned all the wrong lessons. My youthful exuberance could not tolerate dull variable names like I or J; I wanted something with a little panache! I therefore created a set of variables with colorful names like KKRAP, and so on. It wasn't a very utilitarian naming system; it was hard to remember what the variables meant. But it seemed right to me, and I was so intensely involved in my code that I could keep all the variables straight in my head. However, this did cause me some problems when I ran into difficulty and needed help. The university computer center provided consulting programmers to help out users, and when I took my problems there, as often as not, the consulting programmer was a woman. In such cases, she would become flustered asking clarifying questions such as, "So, what function does NFUCK perform here?"

Corporate Politics

For about a year, I ran the Software Development Support Group at Atari; it was about eight people whose job it was to provide technical support to programmers, both inside and outside Atari, who were writing software for the Atari Home Computers. I traveled all over the country giving technical seminars to programmers, and my seminars were very popular. Atari International caught wind of these seminars and asked me to do one in London and another in Hamburg; these were also great successes, so they asked me to do it again in Hong Kong and Singapore. Once again they were pleased with my performance and asked me to do it again in Kuwait.

At this point, I decided that it was time to share the perks of the job. My subordinate Jim Dunion had handled my responsibilities while I was gone on these long trips, and he had learned the ropes well. I therefore assigned him to the Kuwait trip, and, after assuring Atari International that Jim could do the job just as well as I could, secured their approval.

All the preparations went smoothly until about a week before Jim's departure, when my superior, John Powers, mentioned to the Vice President of Software Development, Bruce Irvine, that Jim would be going to Kuwait. Bruce was furious and called both John and me into a meeting. "Why wasn't this cleared with me in advance?" he demanded to know. John explained that he considered it unnecessary because there was no budgetary impact of the trip: Atari International was paying all of Jim's costs. I backed him up with the information that there was a lull in our schedule during this time, so Jim's absence would not be felt.

"Nevertheless," the VP declared, "you should have informed me of his trip. Cancel it!" I was flabbergasted.

"But all the preparations have been made! We can't cancel it now! This will seriously hurt Atari International, and Jim has been looking forward to the trip eagerly!"

Bruce was unmoved. "You have to learn to go through the proper channels, and the only way to teach you is to punish you for your mistakes."

It seems that Atari was very concerned about going through proper channels. Here's a similar tale: One of the first things I did in my new position at Atari Research was to set up a weekly seminar on game design issues for all the designers in the company. My plan was to begin each seminar with a quick five-minute introduction to some interesting idea or problem, and then turn the discussion loose. The idea seemed perfect; there were three separate divisions of game designers at Atari (Coin-Op, VCS, and Home Computers) who seldom spoke with each other. After putting all the pieces together, I sent out invitations to everybody I could think of. A few days later I received a call from a manager at Coin-Op. He was displeased that I had sent the invitation to his designers, rather than solely to him; he asserted that such invitations had to go through the proper channels. He had therefore forbidden any of the Coin-Op people to attend my seminars.

Blinded by Your Own Equipment

I was once asked to help save a floundering project. This game was in serious trouble: It was behind schedule, over budget, and not fun. I played the early alpha version and was appalled; it was an agony to play, and the reason was obvious: It was too damned slow. This was in the early days of single-speed CD-ROM drives, and the designers were eager to take advantage of the vast opportunities made available by this new technology, so they stuffed the game chock full of glorious graphics at every opportunity. Since RAM in those days was rather paltry, they didn't buffer anything; all the graphics had to be loaded off the CD every time they were displayed. The result was a triumph of tedium; every time you clicked the mouse or pressed a key, the game would run off to the CD for five seconds before redrawing the screen. After two hours of this torture, I shut the damn thing off in fury.

95

Your game
must be fun
on typical
machines,
not top-of-
the-line
machines.

When I arrived at the studio, I did not immediately confront the developers with this blunder; I first wanted to feel them out. It took less than five minutes to discern the problem. Their development systems placed the CD-ROM images on hard drives, permitting lightning-fast response times. They had no inkling of just how much the slow response times ruined the game; on their machines, it flowed along nicely. When I tried to explain the problem to them, they were dismissive; it couldn't be that bad, they were sure. I had to insist that they sit down and play their own game off the CD-ROM before they appreciated the magnitude of the problem.

This tale provides the most egregious example of a common problem. Game developers use the very best equipment, and they often fail to appreciate just how far ahead of the population curve they are. This leads them to produce games demanding the very best equipment, which is confined to the most dedicated aficionados. The result: an ever-more insular and isolated gaming community.

Thinking Big

In 1983, I was asked to attend a meeting in Southern California to discuss a standard for CD-I, a scheme to build a CD player that would include interactive elements. The standard was being put together by Sony and Philips. The meeting consisted of about 20 people: engineers from Philips, a few Hollywood people, and some Atari Research people, including Alan Kay and myself. Like any huge committee meeting, this was a ghastly bore and a great waste of time, as the engineers picked over lots of tiny details that would only be significant much later in the standards-setting process.

I had looked over the technical specifications and was disturbed by the limited processing power that the standard included: They were contemplating an 8-bit, 1MHz processor with a few KB of RAM. After several hours, there was a lull in the discussion and I saw my opportunity. I plunged in with my concern about the limited processing power, noting that interactivity relies heavily on processing power. I dismissed the 8-bit processor as too weak to take proper advantage of the data capabilities of the CD. And then I staked my claim: CD-I needed to have nothing less than the latest, most powerful processor available: a 16-bit 68000 running at 8MHz, equipped with at least 64K of RAM.

Having blurted out my little speech, I looked around the room nervously to gauge the reaction. It was one of stunned silence. I could see the Philips engineers staring at me with looks of utter incredulity on their faces; they obviously thought that I had lost all touch with economic realities. It was Alan Kay who broke the long silence. "Is that *all*?" he asked. "This machine is going to need a lot more horsepower than that!"

The CGDC

I founded the Computer Game Developers' Conference; the first one was held in my home. Realizing that a volunteer organization runs more efficiently when the workers have a say in its operation, I agreed to turn over ownership of the Conference to the volunteers who agreed to run the conference, with each of us owning equal shares. I retained the position of Chairman of the Board. We all preferred to incorporate as a non-profit, because we were unanimous in perceiving the CGDC as a service organization. But our treasurer convinced us to incorporate as a for-profit corporation, because the paperwork would be less onerous that way. After all, we could always refuse to make a profit—that wouldn't be hard.

96

Money can
ruin a noble
cause.

The conference was a huge success, enjoying exponential growth. In an effort to keep the growth manageable, we kept raising fees to chase people away and providing better services to get rid of all the money the fees generated. But the attendee list just kept growing, the money kept pouring in, and we couldn't keep ahead of it. Despite our best efforts, we were reaping huge profits.

Then disaster struck. Perhaps it was the overweening ambition of one board member, the fiery temper of another, the ugly vindictiveness of a third, or the hurt pride of a fourth, that contributed to the confrontation. Surely my own brusque style of running meetings antagonized the others. And there's no question that greed played a large role in subsequent events. Whatever the details, the final result was that the other board members kicked me out of the CGDC, confiscated my stock, and sold the conference for $3 million, divvying up the proceeds and all previous profits among themselves. I contested their actions, but settled for a small fraction of what each of them got.

glossary

Arcade game   A custom-built game placed in a public setting such as an arcade. For years, arcade games had the best hardware and therefore the best games, but during the 80s this advantage slowly evaporated and arcade games are now rarer than during their heyday in the late 70s and early 80s. Also known as *quarter-grabbers* for their success in extracting "just one more quarter" out of hopelessly addicted players.

Combat flight sim   The player flies a warplane and engages in aerial combat.

Computer game   A game played on a personal computer.

Dungeon crawl   A term of derision for a role-playing game in which the player must clear out a huge dungeon, battling hordes of monsters with no seeming end.

Fantasy   A context for games involving dragons, magic, trolls, and so forth. Thus we have "fantasy role-playing games," known as FRPGs, "fantasy strategy games," and so on.

First-person   The player sees the world through the eyes of his character. Requires a 3D graphics engine.

Flight sim   The player flies an airplane.

God game   The player acts as a god who seeks to influence or control myriad little human characters who act out their lives on the screen.

Graphic adventure   Same as a text adventure, but now there are pretty pictures to assist less imaginative players. The pretty pictures often have clues cleverly tucked in.

MMOG   "Massively multiplayer online game." A huge online game featuring a large world and thousands of players wandering about. The primary themes are fantasy role-playing and first-person shooter.

MUD   "Multi-user dungeon." A game put together, most often by college students, sporting a dungeon through which players move. A major phenomenon in the early 1990s, MUDs have now been pushed aside by the big, well-funded professional games.

Platform game   The screen shows from the side what is in effect a building with four or five floors. The player enters the screen at one corner and must get across the screen by moving between floors. Numerous obstacles block his progress. Sometimes called *running, jumping, climbing* game. Later versions of this genre are sometimes called *side scrollers* because the levels in the game extend across many horizontal screen lengths.

PW "Persistent world." The term applies to online games in which the game state created by the player(s) remains even while they are not playing.

Real-time Not turn-sequenced. The action keeps going even if the player does nothing. This puts time pressure on the player.

Real-time strategy A strategy game played in real time. The player must make strategic decisions rapidly.

Resource management A style of gameplay in which the player must juggle a large number of complexly inter-related resources, such as fuel, ammunition, aircraft, etc.

Role-playing The player assumes the identity of a character who engages in a quest requiring him to slay lots of nasty enemies. Along the way the character becomes stronger, acquires better weapons, and accumulates wealth. These acquisitions enable the player to take on even more powerful foes.

Sci-fi Another context for games, leading to SFRPGs, sci-fi strategy games, etc.

Second-person The player sees the world from just behind and above his character, or from some other vantage point that follows his character closely.

Shooter A game in which the player spends most of his time shooting at others.

Sim Short for *simulation*. A game that simulates some real-world process, usually with some variations for making it more fun. A nuclear reactor sim, for example, wouldn't be any fun without plenty of meltdowns.

Skill and action   An old term referring to any game requiring fast motor skills of the player. Also known as a *hand-eye coordination* game.

Strategy   A game requiring careful, deliberate—and therefore time-consuming—planning. Strategy games are usually slow in pace.

Text adventure   Using a pure text interface, the player must navigate through verbally described mazes, getting past obstacles by solving complicated and often arbitrary puzzles.

Third person   The player sees the world as a fixed map, and his character is a little figure that moves through that world.

Turn-sequenced   Players take turns in alternation. A player has plenty of time to make his move during his turn.

Wargame   Used by gamers to refer to a game requiring careful military strategy. Used by the general public to refer to any violent game.

index

H

I